SUPER ABOUNDING GRACE

A Study in the Book of Romans

on the Life Changing Effect of the Doctrine of Grace

M. J. Tiry

SUPER BOUNDING GRACE
Copyright © 2023 **M.J. Tiry.**

Authorunit
17130 Van Buren Blvd., Ste. 238,
Riverside, CA 92504
877-826-5888
www.authorunit.com

Because of the dynamic nature of the Internet, any web addresses or links contained in this book may have changed since publication and may no longer be valid. The views expressed in the work are solely those of the author and do not necessarily reflect the views of the publisher, and the publisher hereby disclaims any responsibility for them.

Any people depicted in stock imagery provided by Getty images are models, and such images are being used for illustrative purposes only.

ISBN 978-1-958895-83-2 (Paperback)
ISBN 78-1-958895-84-9 (Ebook)

Printed in the United States of America

CONTENTS

PREFACE

This book in its original printing was entitled "More than Conquerors." It is here re-titled "Super Abounding Grace." This new title is taken from the passage in Romans 5:19-21 "For as by one man's disobedience many were made sinners, so by the obedience of one shall many be made righteous. Moreover the law entered, that the offence might abound. But where sin abounded, grace did much more abound: That as sin hath reigned unto death, even so might grace reign through righteousness unto eternal life by Jesus Christ our Lord." Where sin abounded, grace literally (according to this verse) did super-abound. The greatest problem that has plagued humanity through all of history has been sin. The message of Romans is that there is only one thing that can defeat sin in humanity either in an individual life or corporately in a society – that being the grace of God. The ability of the grace of God to gain victory over sin is laid out in its full power and glory in the Book of Romans. Paul tells the Romans: "But God be thanked, that ye were the servants of sin, but ye have obeyed from the heart that form of doctrine which was delivered you." (Romans 6: 17) What delivers people from slavery to sin is a form of doctrine. That special form of doctrine is revealed by our Savior to the world though Paul, the apostle of the Gentiles in Romans. This study is a tour through the Book of Romans to present an in depth look at the life changing effect of the gospel of grace when it is understood and applied by the Bible believer.

Paul the apostle of the Gentiles writes to believers "... if by one man's offence death reigned by one; much more they which receive abundance of grace and of the gift of righteousness shall reign in life by one, Jesus Christ." (Romans 5:17) The Book of Romans contains the foundational doctrine of deliverance from sin's penalty. It also teaches the believer how to use the spiritual resources that God gives to deliver the child of God from sin's power. Further, whereas before soul salvation, death reigned in that life, now the believer can truly reign in life. It is the grace that is ours in the person and work of Jesus Christ that gives the believer His life.

The gift that the believer receives is imputed righteousness. It is the very righteousness the Savior Himself imputed to the believer's spiritual account. Eternal life automatically comes with that gift of righteousness. In the pages that follow we will look at the joy of knowing that the believer is reckoned by God as being fit for heaven - as fit as the Lord Jesus Christ is Himself. In Romans, we enter into the adventure of the Christian life in which we can truly reign in this life while we wait in eager anticipation of eternal life yet to come.

This study is in three parts as the book of Romans is clearly in three sections. The first section (Chapters 1 through 8) presents the total absolute victory that the believer has by standing in the grace that is ours in Christ. Believers are truly "more than conquerors through him that loved us." The second section (Chapters 9 through 11) answers the question "Why have not the promises that God made to Israel come to pass for His favored nation?" The third section (Chapters 12 through 16) then presents seven spheres of Christian service to answer the question "What should the Christian life look like?"

"Nay, in all these things we are more than conquerors through him that loved us. For I am persuaded, that neither death, nor life, nor angels, nor principalities, nor powers, nor things present, nor things to come, Nor height, nor depth, nor any other creature, shall be able to separate us from the love of God, which is in Christ Jesus our Lord." (Romans 8:37-39)

AN INTRODUCTION TO THE BOOK OF ROMANS

The book of Romans is the first of the Pauline epistles in the New Testament scriptures. Therefore, the book of Romans is the foundational book for the Pauline revelation. This epistle then is the place where we ought to take people when they first come to our Lord Jesus Christ to receive the gift of eternal life. In fact, Romans 3 is often called the "Romans Road to Salvation" because it clearly and concisely presents the information that results in the salvation of the soul once it is believed.

The Bible is a very structured and carefully organized book. The New Testament scriptures are particularly so. It is laid out in the order in which its doctrine is presented to man as God's plan for man unfolds. In the four Gospel accounts, we find our Lord presented as Israel's Messiah. It concerns Israel and a kingdom that will one day be set up on earth through that nation. In the book of Acts, we see the actual offer of that kingdom to Israel in chapters 1–6 and the nation's official rejection of that offer with the stoning of Stephen in chapter 7, where the nation committed the unpardonable sin of blaspheming the Holy Spirit by rejecting His witness through the twelve apostles at Pentecost (Matthew 12:31). The book of Acts then presents to us the temporary interruption of God's dealing with that nation, the salvation of Saul of Tarsus, and the testimony to that nation that "the salvation of God is gone to the Gentiles and they will hear it" (Acts 28:28).

What follows then (the Pauline epistles) comprises the preaching of Jesus Christ according to the revelation of the mystery concerning the church, the body of Christ, and information concerning the present dispensation of the grace of God. We refer you, the reader, to Appendix 1, a graphic presentation of the books of the New Testament, which shows where they fit into the overall New Testament. One day the dispensation of grace will end with the catching away of the church, the body of Christ (1 Thessalonians 4:17). Then the fulfillment of God's plan and the program for the nation of Israel is presented in Hebrews through Revelation. This last section of the Bible culminates with fulfillment of prophecy, with Jesus Christ returning to Israel to finally establish that long-promised kingdom. The reader is encouraged to take a look at the divine balance of history and prophecy as it is presented in Appendix 2.

Some background about the book of Romans is helpful. The apostle Paul (Romans 1:1), of course, wrote the epistle to the saints in Rome (Romans 1:7). According to Romans 16:23, Paul was staying with Gaius, who (according to 1 Corinthians 1:14) lived in Corinth. Paul also sent greetings from Crispus (Romans 16: 23), who (according to 1 Corinthians 1:14) was also living in Corinth. Romans 15:25–26 makes it apparent that this epistle was written when Paul was making plans to go to Jerusalem to take the Gentile churches' collection "for the poor saints which are at Jerusalem" to them at Jerusalem. First Corinthians 16:3–5 indicates that the journey would take Paul through Corinth. The epistle was apparently written during Paul's three-month stay in Greece while en route to Macedonia, as documented in Acts 20:3, in about the year AD 56.

Paul's first epistle in the canon of scripture is addressed to believing Gentiles in the capital city of the Gentile world political system. Under the gospel of the kingdom, all these Gentile powers were to be destroyed and replaced by Messiah's kingdom. But here we find these Gentiles "beloved of God" and "called to be saints" in spite of Israel remaining in unbelief. Such is the marvel of the dispensation of the grace of God. Getting a handle on the doctrine of this important book of the Bible will equip you to better minister the gospel of the grace of God to saved and lost people alike.

We trust that you will enjoy the study in this great epistle to the Romans. This study in Romans is presented in three parts since the book of Romans is naturally divided into three well-defined sections. The first part covers the first eight chapters of the book of Romans. These eight chapters present the basic and fundamental principles that enable believers in the dispensation of grace to live the Christian life. The study draws on the reader's understanding and his or her ability to use the important key of Bible study—that of rightly dividing the Word of truth. If you aren't familiar with this important key, we trust it will unfold for you as you follow this study. The illustration (Appendix 1) is presented as a summary of the layout of the New Testament based on the principle of right division.

Simply put, there are two programs God administers in the New Testament scriptures. There is the program the Bible calls "prophecy," which involves the nation of Israel, and a kingdom God will one day establish on this earth with Jesus Christ as the king (the Messiah) of Israel. There is another program in the New Testament scriptures the Bible calls "the preaching of Jesus Christ according to the revelation of the mystery." (Romans 16:25) This second program is a Gentile program that involves God calling out from the lost masses of today's humanity a body of believers called "the church which is Christ's body." This is a body of believers with Jesus Christ as Savior and head. The program called "prophecy" involves twelve apostles, who will one day sit on twelve thrones and judge the twelve tribes of Israel (Matthew 19:28). However, the program called the "mystery" involves one apostle called "the apostle of the Gentiles" (Romans 11:13). It is in the epistles written by Paul, the apostle of the Gentiles, that we find all the doctrine concerning how God has designed us as members of the church, Christ's body, to live and operate today in the dispensation of the grace of God.

This study in the epistle of Romans is not only an expose of this great epistle but also a look at (literally a course of instruction in) the entire Bible as seen from the vantage point of the foundational epistle of the Pauline revelation. The Bible wasn't complete until the revelation of the mystery our Lord revealed to us through Paul, the apostle of the Gentiles (Romans 11:13), was added to it. It was when his epistles were added to the Bible that, according to Colossians 1:25, the Word of God was fully filled.

There is key information presented in this epistle that is found nowhere else; it focuses on the ultimate work of Jesus Christ as Creator and Redeemer. Romans 3, for example, views God at the time of the crucifixion as having reached back through time to bring the sins of Old Testament saints forward through time to Calvary. Then He imputed them to His Son to show how He could be just in remitting sins that are past (in other words, in past dispensations). Romans 3 also views God as reaching into the future to where we are and bringing us back through time to impute our sins to the Savior and show how He can be just and the justifier of those who believe in Jesus today. Indeed, Romans goes further to show how it is that God joined us into an eternal spiritual union with Jesus Christ to provide total victory over sin and death for us.

A word is in order here on how to study the Bible and approach it. Some basic principles are the following:

1. All scripture came from the mouth of God, and it fully equips the man of God to do anything God would have him do. "All scripture is given by inspiration of God, and is profitable for doctrine, for reproof, for correction, for instruction in righteousness: That the man of God may be perfect, throughly furnished unto all good works" (2 Timothy 3:16–17). It can be said that the Holy Spirit never works apart from the Bible and that the Bible never works apart from the Holy Spirit.

2. The term "inspiration of God" in 2 Timothy 3:16 means scripture was breath out of God's mouth. It is truly as the Lord tells the devil in Matthew 4:4: "It is written, Man shall not live by bread alone, but by every word that proceedeth out of the mouth of God." And that is the origin of every word of scripture— from the mouth of God.

3. Scripture must be studied in its context to make sense. There are two contexts: the immediate context in which the passage is set and the remote context that looks at the Bible as a whole. Billy Sunday (the great evangelist of the early part of the twentieth century) said, "A text without a context is a pretext." That concept is what Peter was communicating when he said in 2 Peter 1:20–21, "Knowing this first, that no prophecy of the scripture is of any private interpretation. For the prophecy came not in old time by the will of man: but holy men of God spake as they were moved by the Holy Ghost." No passage of scripture is intended to stand by itself, but rather each passage actually relates to every other passage of scripture. One of the greatest tools of Bible study is a good cross-reference (e.g., The Treasury of Scripture Knowledge). By comparing scripture with scripture, the Bible teaches itself. The Bible itself is its greatest and best teacher.

4. While all scripture is written for our learning, not every passage of scripture is specifically addressed to us. The word of truth then must be "rightly divided." Paul tells us this in 2 Timothy 2:15, "Study to shew thyself approved unto God, a workman that needeth not to be ashamed, rightly dividing the word of truth." We again direct your attention to Appendix 1.

5. Another key to understanding the Bible is simply to let it mean what it clearly says. It's a major mistake to spiritualize scripture. The Bible is written to be taken literally. There are times when the Bible uses figures of speech (figurative language), but when it does so, it is apparent that such is the case. Basically, we must remember the adage "If the literal sense makes perfect sense, seek no other sense."

6. God has taken great care to give us His inspired Word and gave it without error. He has also pledged to preserve it so. Psalm 12:6–7 says, "The words of the LORD are pure words: as silver tried in a furnace of earth, purified seven times. Thou shalt keep them, O Lord, thou shalt preserve them from this generation forever." The conviction of this author is that there exists today a preserved text of the inspired and inerrant Word of God. This preserved text is not found in the original manuscripts, since they have been lost through time, but this preservation of scripture exists in the multiplicity of copies. It was God's desire and design that the Bible get into the hands of the people. If there is a doctrine of preservation, then that preservation is found in the preservation of the scripture in the multiplicity of copies. This author holds the conviction that the preserved text line is the Received Text (Majority Text) of the New Testament and the Masoretic Text of the Hebrew Old Testament. Since there is only one translation in print in English today from these, all scripture quotations in this study are taken from the King James Version of the Bible.

7. There is yet another key to an effective study of the Word of God. That is the heart attitude of the Bereans, described in Acts 17:11. They received the Word with open minds, but they didn't take any man's word for truth or error until they searched it out in the scripture. That approach gave them protection from error, for they made the Word of God their final authority and examined what everyone said based on the Word of truth, the Bible.

8. One final key regarding the Bible having the impact in our lives God intended is to simply believe it. Paul told the Thessalonians that when they received the Word of God, they "received it not as the word of men but as it is in truth the word of God", which "effectually worketh in you that believe." It's not just understanding the Bible that makes it effective, but applying it by faith to one's life makes it effective to give spiritual strength and vitality.

What a wonderful epistle the epistle to the Romans is. May the Lord richly bless you, dear reader, as you enjoy this study of God's infallible Word - the Bible as we view it from the vantage point of the Book of Romans.

SUPER ABOUNDING GRACE,
Part 1
A Study of the Book of Romans, Chapters 1-8

"Nay, in all these things we are more than conquerors through him that loved us. For I am persuaded, that neither death, nor life, nor angels, nor principalities, nor powers, nor things present, nor things to come, Nor height, nor depth, nor any other creature, shall be able to separate us from the love of God, which is in Christ Jesus our Lord." (Romans 8:37-39)

How to Use These Study Notes

These study notes were originally written as annotation from a structural analysis of the text of the book of Romans from a King James Bible. The structural analysis is eliminated and replaced with the text of Romans. The notes are lettered. The letters correspond to letters in the text preceding the corresponding notes. The text has numbers for the verses and letters for the annotations. The letters appearing in the smaller text size, in superscript (for example, [d]) in the Bible text, correspond to the lettered notations presented here. The notations themselves are lettered with the corresponding Letter (for example, [d]). So too the verse numbers in the Bible text are written in superscript (for example, 4 for verse 4) We trust that you will enjoy this study of the Word of God.

Please note that all Bible references and quotes are from the King James Version.

M. J. Tiry

CHAPTER 1

THE POWER OF GOD UNTO SALVATION

¹ Paul[a], a servant of Jesus Christ, called[b] to be an apostle, separated[c] unto the gospel of God, ² (Which he had promised[d] afore by his prophets in the holy scriptures,) ³ Concerning his Son Jesus Christ our Lord, which was made of the seed[e] of David according to the flesh; ⁴ And declared to be the Son of God with power, according to the spirit of holiness, by the resurrection[f] from the dead: ⁵ By whom we[g] have received grace and apostleship, for obedience to the faith among all nations, for his name: ⁶ Among whom are ye also the called of Jesus Christ: ⁷ To all that be in Rome, beloved of God, called to be saints: Grace to you and peace from God our Father, and the Lord Jesus Christ. (Romans 1:1–7)

[a] Paul, the apostle of the Gentiles (Romans 11:13), is the writer of this epistle. Paul calls himself a servant of Jesus Christ in 2 Timothy 1:3. Paul says he served God from his forefathers "with a pure conscience," yet he refers to himself as having been a "blasphemer and a persecutor and injurious" (1 Timothy 1:13). But then he goes on to say, "But I obtained mercy because I did it ignorantly in unbelief." We would conclude that his conscience was pure because he was operating on the basis of ignorance. This is the condition of the people our Lord spoke of in John 16:2. "They shall put you out of the synagogues: yea, the time cometh, that whosoever killeth you will think that he doeth God service." Saul of Tarsus thought he was doing service to God in persecuting the believers in Jerusalem. A study of our Lord's parable in Matthew 21:33–38* makes it clear that this wasn't the condition of some of the leaders of Israel. They knew Jesus was the Christ but weren't willing to let Him have what was rightfully His. Had that been Paul's case, he would not have obtained mercy.

* Acts 4:13–30 indicates that those same leaders of Israel took knowledge of the disciples after our Lord's resurrection that they had been with the resurrected Lord.

[b] Paul is called to be an apostle. He is a special apostle, being uniquely "the apostle of the Gentiles" (Romans 11:13). As such, he was given the apostleship of the uncircumcision, while Peter and the Twelve were given the apostleship of the circumcision (Galatians 2:6–8). Paul's apostleship involved making known the work Jesus Christ did as the "one mediator between God and men, the man Christ Jesus; Who gave himself a ransom for all, to be testified in due time. Whereunto I am ordained a preacher, and an apostle, (I speak the truth in Christ, and lie not;) a teacher of the Gentiles in faith and verity" (1 Timothy 2:5–7). There are twelve apostles who are one day going to sit on the twelve thrones in the kingdom of heaven, judging the twelve tribes of Israel (Matthew 19:28). Matthias was selected to fill the place among the apostles that had been (Acts1:16–26), vacated by Judas.

[c] Paul says in verse 1 that he was "separated unto the gospel of God, (which he had promised afore by his

prophets in the Holy Scriptures)." This is the first verse of Romans. As we compare this (the first verses in the book of Romans) with the closing verses, there appears to be a contradiction. Let's note those closing verses: "Now to him that is of power to stablish you according to my gospel, and the preaching of Jesus Christ, according to the revelation of the mystery, which was kept secret since the world began, But now is made manifest, and by the scriptures of the prophets, according to the commandment of the everlasting God, made known to all nations for the obedience of faith" (Romans 16:25–26).

In Romans 16:25. the apostle speaks of the revelation of the mystery, which was kept secret since the world began; but in 1:1–2 he talks about being separated unto the gospel of God, which he had promised afore by his prophets in the holy scriptures. Realizing that there are no contradictions in the Bible, we look for the solution to this dilemma, whereby Paul says he was "separated onto the gospel of God which [God] had promised afore by his prophets" in 1:1 and tells us about the mystery, which was "kept secret" and "in other ages not made known."

The solution is to recognize that Paul is talking about two different things in Romans 16:25. When he speaks of "my gospel" and "the preaching of Jesus Christ according to the revelation of the mystery," he is talking about two different concepts our Lord revealed to and through Paul. What Paul called "my gospel" in 16:25 is what he called "the gospel of God" in Romans 1:1. This is the gospel God spoke in Genesis 3:15 regarding the "seed of the woman," which would one day crush Satan's head. The means by which the seed of the woman would do that wasn't (indeed couldn't be) revealed until after it was accomplished. It was the work of the Lord Jesus Christ on the cross that totally defeated Satan. This fact was first made known through Paul as "the mystery of the gospel" (Ephesians 6:19). Paul therefore calls it "the gospel of Christ" (Romans 1:16) and "my gospel" (Romans 2:16).

What our Savior accomplished on the cross had to be kept a secret, or it wouldn't have been accomplished (1 Corinthians 2:6–10). The full meaning of what was accomplished on the cross is actually presented for the first time in the Bible in Romans 3:21–28. First Corinthians 15:3–4 simply states that "Christ died for our sins according to the scriptures; And that he was buried, and that he rose again the third day according to the scriptures." What Paul calls "the mystery" in Romans 16:25 involves God calling out a body of believers from the Gentiles (fallen Israel included [Romans 11:32]) called "the church which is his body" (Colossians 1:24). No Old Testament prophet spoke anything about this mystery, because it was "hid in God" (Ephesians 3:9) from the beginning of the world until it was revealed through Paul.

Paul is the only Bible writer who talks about this mystery. In Ephesians 3:2–6, he says, "If ye have heard of the dispensation of the grace of God which is given me to you-ward: How that by revelation he made known unto me the mystery; (as I wrote afore in few words, Whereby, when ye read, ye may understand my knowledge in the mystery of Christ) Which in other ages was not made known unto the sons of men, as it is now revealed unto his holy apostles and prophets by the Spirit; That the Gentiles should be fellowheirs, and of the same body, and partakers of his promise in Christ by the gospel." He goes on in Ephesians 3 to describe the content of this message Jesus Christ revealed to the world through him. There we find the following:

- The subject of the mystery is the one body (Ephesians 3:6).

- The ministry of the mystery is given to Paul (Ephesians 3:7–8).

- The operation of the mystery is fellowship (Ephesians 3:9).

- The divine purpose for it is to show the wisdom of God (Ephesians 3:10).

The mystery our Lord revealed to and through the apostle Paul is different and distinct from the mysteries of the kingdom of heaven our Lord speaks of in Matthew 13:11. The mystery Paul speaks of wasn't revealed until the Lord revealed it to him. This was after the death, burial, and resurrection of Christ and actually after His ascension back to heaven. The mysteries of the kingdom of heaven have to do with the fact that the gospel of the kingdom (the good news of the establishment of an earthly kingdom through redeemed Israel) will be preached without the king being present. The mysteries of the kingdom of heaven in Matthew's Gospel are intended to prepare the Twelve for their ministry in the early period of the book of Acts and eventually to prepare the Jewish remnant for their ministries in the coming tribulation period.

[d] It is a most interesting fact that the gospel the prophets "promised" wasn't made known to the prophets. Isaiah 64:4 says, "For since the beginning of the world men have not heard, nor perceived by the ear, neither hath the eye seen, O God, beside thee, what he hath prepared for him that waiteth for him." Paul quotes this verse in 1 Corinthians 2:6–10 but adds, "But God hath revealed them unto us by his Spirit: for the Spirit searcheth all things, yea, the deep things of God" (1 Corinthians 2:10). What "eye had not seen nor ear heard nor entered into the heart of men" in Isaiah 64:4 is now made known to us in Paul's epistles (1 Corinthians 2:6–10). If you asked Paul, "What is the gospel?", he would have given you 1 Corinthians 15:3–4. But during our Lord's earthy ministry and at Pentecost, the Twelve couldn't tell anyone that because they didn't know it yet.

The Twelve preached what is called "the gospel" (Luke 9:6). When the Lord sent the Twelve out, it is said, "And they departed, and went through the towns, preaching the gospel, and healing every where" (Luke 9:6, emphasis added). Yet in Luke 9:44–45, we find something very interesting. Jesus told them, "Let these sayings sink down into your ears: for the Son of man shall be delivered into the hands of men" (Luke 9:44–45). The next verse says, "But they understood not this saying, and it was hid from them, that they perceived it not: and they feared to ask him of that saying."

In Luke 18, the point is driven home to us even more plainly. There the Lord starts to prepare them for what was coming. "Then he took unto him the twelve, and said unto them, Behold, we go up to Jerusalem, and all things that are written by the prophets concerning the Son of man shall be accomplished. For he shall be delivered unto the Gentiles, and shall be mocked, and spitefully entreated, and spitted on: And they shall scourge him, and put him to death: and the third day he shall rise again." Yet note the very next verse, which says, "And they understood none of these things: and this saying was hid from them, neither knew they the things which were spoken" (Luke 18:31–34).

We may think, Surely by the time we get to Pentecost at the beginning of the book of Acts, they would have known what was really accomplished on the cross. Yet we don't find in Peter's message to Israel at Pentecost any reference to the fact that Jesus Christ died on the cross for their sins. What we do find is that Peter warns Israel that the one they crucified was truly their Messiah and that Jesus was going to sit at the Father's right hand until it was time to make His enemies His footstool. Carefully note Peter's words: "This Jesus hath God raised up, whereof we all are witnesses. Therefore being by the right hand of God exalted, and having received of the Father the promise of the Holy Ghost, he hath shed forth this, which ye now see and hear. For David is not ascended into the heavens: but he saith himself, The LORD said unto my Lord, Sit thou on my right hand, Until I make thy foes thy footstool. Therefore let all the house of Israel know assuredly, that God hath made that same Jesus, whom ye have crucified, both Lord and Christ" (Acts 2:32–36).

When Peter's audience (which included only "Jews and proselytes" [Acts 2:10]) was convicted of the fact that they had put their Messiah to death, they asked, "Men and brethren what shall we do?" What would Peter's answer then be? Would Peter tell them what Paul had said in 1 Corinthians 15:3–4, "that Christ died for their sins"? Had they known that, they would certainly have made that known to their audience. Rather, Peter tells them to "repent, and be baptized every one of you in the name of Jesus Christ for the remission of sins, and ye shall receive the gift of the Holy Ghost." Clearly their message of Pentecost didn't include the message of what was accomplished on the cross (Acts 2:38).

(Which he had promised afore by his prophets in the holy scriptures,) Concerning his Son Jesus Christ our Lord, which was made[e] of the seed of David according to the flesh; And declared[f] to be the Son of God with power, according to the spirit of holiness, by the resurrection from the dead·[g] (Romans 1:2–4)

[e] Verse 3 says Jesus Christ, our Lord, was made of the seed of David according to the flesh. The phrase "according to the flesh" refers to His earthly ministry to Israel under the gospel of the kingdom, which the Twelve preached. The gospel of the kingdom included the following:

A king—Jeremiah 23:5 says, "Behold, the days come, saith the LORD, that I will raise unto David a righteous Branch, and a King shall reign and prosper, and shall execute judgment and justice in the earth."

A kingdom—Daniel 2:44 says, "And in the days of these kings shall the God of heaven set up a kingdom." Our Lord ministered this gospel to Israel.

* Matthew 4:23 says, "And Jesus went about all Galilee teaching ... in their synagogues and preaching the gospel of the kingdom" This will again be the message in the coming tribulation.

* Matthew 24:14 says, "And this gospel of the kingdom shall be preached in all the world for a witness unto all nations." This promise will ultimately be fulfilled.

* Revelation 11:15 says, "The seventh angel sounded ... The kingdoms of this world are become the kingdoms of our Lord and of his Christ."

Verse 4 goes on to add, "And declared to be the son of God with Power ... by the resurrection from the dead." While the Lord's earthly ministry was "to the lost sheep of the house of Israel" (Matthew 15:24), His resurrection ministry was much broader (as we shall see).

Christ is presented as man—the seed of David and as God—the Son of God with power. He was "made" the seed of David, but He was "declared" to be the Son of God with power.

He always was the "the Word" (John 1:1–14) from eternity past, but He began to be referred to as the Son of God when He became man. He was the Son of God by birth but only needed to be "declared to be the Son of God with Power" by the resurrection. The words "according to the flesh" described His human nature, while the words "according to the Spirit" described His divine nature.

[f] Though our Lord did many miracles and demonstrated His power during His ministry here on earth, His resurrection from the dead fully demonstrated his power. Ephesians 1:19–23 says, "And what is the exceeding greatness of his power to us-ward who believe, according to the working of his mighty power, Which he wrought in Christ, when he raised him from the dead, and set him at his own right hand in the heavenly places, Far above all principality, and power, and might, and dominion, and every name that is named, not only in this world, but also in that which is to come: And hath put all things under his feet, and gave him to be the head over all things to the church Which is his body, the fullness of him that filleth all in all."

Hebrews 5:5–6 refers to the day of our Lord's resurrection as the day He was begotten as the Son (Psalm 2:7; Acts 13:33; Hebrews 1:5). Though He was begotten of God when He was conceived in Mary's womb (Luke 1:35), He is declared the son of God with power by His resurrection. As a result, He will be preeminent from eternity past to eternity future (Ephesians 1:10; 2 Timothy 1:9) and from things under the earth to things far above all heavens (Philippians 2:10). As a result of His resurrection, "all power is given unto me in heaven and in earth" (Matthew 28:18).

> By whom we[g] have received grace and apostleship, for obedience[h] to the faith among all nations, for his name: Among whom are ye[g] also the called of Jesus Christ: To all that be in Rome, beloved of God, called to be saints: Grace to you and peace from God our Father, and the Lord Jesus Christ." (Romans 1:5–7)

[g] Who are the "we" of verse 5 and the "ye" of verse 6? Verse 5 speaks of Paul and his companions, Timothy, Luke, Jason, and Sosipater (Romans 16:21) as well as Tertius, the gramateus (16:22). The apostleship, which is spoken of, is that of Paul and Timothy (Paul's yokefellow). The "ye" of verse 6 speaks to the saints of Rome. who received salvation and were called to be saints because of their "obedience of faith."

[h] The phrase "for the obedience of faith among all nations" is significant here because our Lord's earthly ministry was only to the "lost sheep of the house of Israel" (Matthew 10:6; 15:24; Romans 15:8). However, the resurrected Christ now had a ministry to the Gentiles through Paul, the apostle of the Gentiles. That ministry is actually a result of Israel's rejection of Him as their resurrected Messiah.

> 7 To all that be in Rome[i], beloved of God, called to be saints: Grace[j] to you and peace from God our Father, and the Lord Jesus Christ. 8 First, I thank[k] my God through Jesus Christ for you all, that your faith is spoken[l] of throughout the whole world. 9 For God is my witness, whom I serve with[m] my spirit in the gospel[n] of his Son, that without ceasing I make mention of you always in my prayers; 10 Making request, if by any means now at length I might have a prosperous journey by the will of God to come unto you. (Romans 1:7–10)

[i] Paul's first epistle in the canon of scripture is addressed to believing Gentiles in the capital city of the Gentile world political system. Under the gospel of the kingdom, all these political systems were to be destroyed and replaced by Messiah's kingdom. But here we find these Gentiles "beloved of God" and "called to be saints" in spite of Israel remaining in unbelief.

[j] Each of Paul's epistles starts with the greeting "grace and peace from God our Father and the Lord Jesus Christ." This is significant because what was due prophetically when Saul got saved was actually the tribulation period in which Jesus Christ would come to "judge and make war" (Revelation 19:11).

[k] Paul, as in all of his epistles, gives thanks to God for fellowship and upholds his fellows before God in prayer. Paul's prayers to God are in the name of Jesus Christ. His thanks to God for fellow believers are through Jesus Christ.

[l] Paul's thankfulness concerning the Roman saints is that their faith is spoken of through the whole world. Faith is rooted in understanding a thing that is known to be true and therefore trustworthy (Philippians 1:27; 1 Thessalonians 2:13). It is the result of teaching (Romans 10:14–17). Faith can be subjective (our faith) or objective (Christ's faith). Our faith must have an object—in other words, a trustworthy basis. The object of saving faith for us today is the Lord Jesus Christ and His work on Calvary. Faith must have a basis. The basis of our faith is the infallible, inerrant Word of God. Saving faith here is referred to as obedience in the sense that it is implemented in one's life. The obedience of faith is heart belief as opposed to simple head knowledge (Romans 10:10). Obedience to the faith is a conformance of one's life to the Word of God (1:5). These Roman saints were basically Gentiles. This is the first place in the scripture where the Word of God addresses Gentiles independently of Israel.

[m] Paul served the gospel of Christ with his spirit. Our human spirit is the part of our makeup that enables us to relate to God and communicate with Him to provide a means whereby God communicates with us.

[n] "The gospel" is the focus of this epistle as is evident by its repetitive use of the following:
- The gospel of God (v. 1)
- The gospel of His Son (v. 9)
- The gospel of Christ (v. 16)
- My gospel (2:16)

The expression "of God" is also found often in this epistle. Note the following:
- "The gospel of God" (v. 1)
- "The Son of God" (v. 4)
- "The will of God" (v. 10)
- "The power of God" (v. 16)
- "The righteousness of God" (v. 17)
- "The wrath of God" (v. 18)

> For I long to see you, that I may impart[o] unto you some spiritual gift, to the end ye may be established; That is, that I may be comforted together with you by the mutual faith both of you and me. Now I would not have you ignorant, brethren, that oftentimes I purposed to come unto you, (but was let hitherto,) that I might have some fruit among you also, even as among other Gentiles. I am debtor[p] both to the Greeks, and to the Barbarians; both to the wise, and to the unwise. (Romans 1:11–14)

[o] Paul's desire to serve the saints of Rome was so he could impart unto them some spiritual gift. The end result of imparting that spiritual gift would be the following:
1. The saints would be established, and
2. Paul would be comforted together with them by their mutual faith.

What would be the nature of that gift Paul wanted to give (to impart) to them? There are several possibilities we might consider.

It could be any of the various "gifts of the Spirit" that were in operation during the period the Acts of the Apostles covered. There are four lists of such gifts:

First Corinthians 12:8–10—These are sign gifts and include the following:

1. The word of wisdom
2. The word of knowledge
3. Faith
4. Gift of healings
5. The working of miracles
6. Prophecy
7. Discerning of spirits
8. Diverse kinds of tongues
9. The interpretation of tongues

Romans 12:6–8 lists what is called "service gifts." They include the following:

1. Prophecy
2. Ministry
3. Teaching
4. Exhorting
5. Giving
6. Ruling
7. Showing mercy

Ephesians 4:11–12 presents what are called "ministry gifts." These include the following:

1. Apostles
2. Prophets
3. Evangelists
4. Pastors and teachers

First Corinthians 13:13 presents the abiding gifts, which will never pass away:

1. Faith
2. Hope
3. Charity (the greatest of all gifts)

The Holy Spirit gave the sign gifts during the Acts period, "dividing to every man severally as he will" (1 Corinthians 12:11). The Holy Ghost gave these as He (the Holy Ghost) decided. Paul wouldn't be imparting one of these gifts, for they were not his to impart.

It could be that Paul might have been thinking of the ministry gifts, because they were given "for the edifying of the body of Christ." They would be given "till we all come to the unity of the faith, and of the knowledge of the son of God, unto a perfect [fully mature] man" (Ephesians 4:13). This full knowledge Paul talks about in Ephesians 4:13 came when the Pauline revelation was completed. These ministry gifts in Ephesians 4 were gifts whereby God, the Holy Spirit, ministered to the body of Christ through men who were supernaturally enabled to do so. This work of the Holy Spirit was necessary because the full revelation of the mystery hadn't come yet during the time frame of the book of Acts. The church was in its infancy and needed the special attention (1 Corinthians 13:11) of these ministry gifts. Additionally, without the full revelation of the Word of God, the church saw only a fuzzy, wavy image of God's program for man (like looking at one's image in a mirror versus looking face-to-face [1 Corinthians 13:12]). The full revelation of the mystery would change all that. The church then (with the full revelation of the mystery) would have reached manhood (1 Corinthians 13:11) and would put away the childish things of the Acts period. The church could then, in the completed revelation, see a clear image of God's plan for man as though man were looking face-to-face (1 Corinthians 13:12). We today have perfect (in the sense of being complete) knowledge and prophecy (1 Corinthians 13:9–10) in the completed Word of God. Having the completed Word of God, we can all come to the unity of the faith (Ephesians 4:13) as laid out in the Word of God (Ephesians 4:3–6), and therefore, "henceforth be no more children, tossed to and fro, and carried about with every wind of doctrine, by the sleight of men, and cunning craftiness, whereby they lie in wait to deceive." (Ephesians 4:14).

More likely the gift Paul hoped to impart would be another installation in the progressive revelation of the mystery as it was in progress at the time. Paul received the mystery concerning the body of Christ directly from the Lord Jesus Christ (Ephesians 3:1–6). However, Christ didn't reveal it to Paul all at once. Paul spoke of visions and revelations of the Lord (2 Corinthians 12:1; Acts 26:16). Paul told the Romans that, when he came, he was sure he would come "in the fullness of the blessing of the gospel of Christ" (Romans 15:29). That is to say, he was sure he would have the complete revelation by the time he came to them.

[p] Paul views himself as the debtor, but grace by definition doesn't incur a debt (Romans 4:4 –5). Salvation is a free gift of God's grace and doesn't depend on any pledge to perform. How then was Paul a debtor? Paul was a debtor to the Greeks and the barbarians—in other words, to the educated and uneducated (the wise and unwise respectively). That is to say, Paul owed something to both the Greeks and the barbarians. What could that thing be? We've got a glimpse of what that is in reading Romans 15:8–16, where we see the blessing that would have come to the Gentiles under Israel's program. Paul, however, before he was saved led Israel in the rejection of Jesus Christ as the Messiah. The blessings that were to flow to the Gentiles were to go to the Gentiles through Christ through Israel. Israel was to be God's channel of blessings to the Gentiles (Genesis 18:18; 22:18; 26:4). However, the children of Israel must first be filled (Mark 7:27). "It was unto [Israel] first. God, having raised up his Son Jesus sent him to bless you in turning away every one of you from his iniquities" (Acts 3:26). In persecuting the "little flock," Paul stopped that channel of blessings to the Gentiles. After Paul was saved and learned that God had temporarily set Israel aside, he realized that the only way the Gentiles could get saved now was through the message the Lord gave him. He therefore was indebted to the Gentiles to get that message out.

The Righteousness of God and the Wrath of God revealed

¹⁵ So, as much as in me is, I am ready to preach[q] the gospel to you that are at Rome also. ¹⁶ For I am not ashamed of the gospel[r] of Christ: for it[s] is the power of God unto salvation[t] to every one

that believeth[u]; to the Jew first[v], and also to the Greek. ¹⁷ For therein is the righteousness of God revealed[w] from faith[x] to faith: as it is written[y], The just shall live by faith. ¹⁸ For the wrath of God is revealed from heaven[z] against all ungodliness and unrighteousness[aa] of men, who hold the truth in unrighteousness. (Romans 1:15–18)

[q] In verse 15, Paul speaks of preaching the gospel "to you that are of Rome also." If he addressed this to the saints of Rome (as he apparently did), then he addressed this statement to believers who were already "sealed with the Holy Spirit of promise" (Ephesians 1:13). What gospel would be preached to believers? Obviously the gospel Paul had in mind encompasses more than the good news of Christ's payment for the believer's sin debt. The gospel Paul has in mind is the complete gospel that includes deliverance from the penalty of sin, its power, and finally its very presence.

[r] Paul would and did take the good news of Christ everywhere without hesitation, because he knew it would always accomplish its purpose of salvation whenever and wherever it was believed.

[s] The gospel is the power of God to save. Paul used the term salvation in a fuller sense than we usually think of salvation. The fullness of salvation is understood as being in three tenses. The past tense of salvation is salvation from the penalty from sin. The present tense is salvation from sin's power. The future tense is salvation from its very presence. Paul lays out all three tenses of salvation in 1 Corinthians 15:1–4.

- Past tense: In 1 Corinthians 15:1, we see salvation from sin's penalty. "Moreover, brethren, I declare unto you the gospel which I preached unto you, which also ye have received, and wherein ye stand." We will see this in Romans 3:21–26.

- Present tense: In 1 Corinthians 15: 2, we see salvation from sin's power. "By which also ye are saved, if ye keep in memory what I preached unto you, unless ye have believed in vain" (emphasis added). The words "ye are saved" are in the present tense, passive voice. This is salvation from the power of sin, as presented in Romans 6. This salvation depends on the believer keeping "in memory what [Paul] has preached."

- Future tense: In the rest of 1 Corinthians 15, we see salvation from sin's presence with the rapture of the church. The resurrection will be in an incorruptible body, into which the ultimate victory over sin is in the resurrection (1 Corinthians 15:56–57).

[t] God's power to work in people's lives is today confined to the gospel of Christ. God saves people today solely on the basis of faith, but "faith cometh by hearing, and hearing by the word of God" (Romans 10:17).

[u] The gospel of Christ is the power of God unto salvation only to those who believe it. It is the power of God to everyone, but it is unto salvation to those who believe it.

[v] The gospel of Christ was the power of God unto salvation to the Jew first (v. 16). This is the gospel of Christ as the Messiah of Israel under the preaching of the gospel of the kingdom in Matthew, Mark, Luke, and John. In Acts 13:46, Paul and Barnabas state the case of Israel's rejection of the gospel with the words "It was necessary that the word of God should first have been spoken to you: but seeing ye put it from you, and judge yourselves unworthy of everlasting life, lo, we turn to the Gentiles." The gospel of the kingdom (the gospel the Lord preached as being "at hand" during His earthly ministry) was to go to the Gentiles but only after Israel was

saved (Romans 15:8–12). However, Paul, "the apostle of the Gentiles" (Romans 11:13), ministered the gospel of God to the Gentiles (Romans 15:16) today in spite of Israel not preaching it. Today "the gospel of Christ" is the power of God unto salvation to the Gentiles in the form of the "gospel of the grace of God" (Acts 20:24). It is also called "the gospel of the uncircumcision" (Galatians 2:7).

[w] The gospel of Christ answers the question Job raised: "How can a man be just with God?" (Job 9:2). Paul presents the gospel of Christ as the righteousness of God revealed being available to those who merit the wrath of God (Romans 1:17–18). Paul presented this righteousness of God as now being available to all men "without the law" by "the faith of Jesus Christ" (Roman 3:21).

[x] The phrase "from faith to faith" means the righteousness of God, which every person needs to have eternal life, is available to all on the faith principle. It is available "from faith"—that is, because of the faithfulness of Jesus Christ. It is His faithfulness (trustworthiness, veracity, reliability, and so forth) that makes the righteousness of God available to every person to be received by faith. The righteousness of God is therefore secured for us by Jesus Christ through His faithfulness and is now offered as a gift of God to every man, to be received only by faith. Going back to verse 16, we see and note that it is "the power of God unto salvation to everyone that believeth" (emphasis added).

[y] "The just shall live by faith." This expression can be understood three ways—each being true. The expression is found in three contexts in the Bible, each time with a slightly different emphasis.

1. In Habakkuk 2:4, the emphasis is on the just person under law. The just person shall live by faith.
2. In Romans 1:17, the emphasis is on being justified by faith, as is the case in Galatians 3:11. The idea is that the person who was justified by faith shall live.
3. In Hebrews 10:38, the emphasis is on faith. The just person should live on the faith principle.

[z] For the wrath of God is revealed from heaven against all ungodliness and unrighteousness of men who hold the truth and unrighteousness.

Question: Against what is this wrath revealed?

Answer: Against all ungodliness and unrighteousness of men who hold the truth and unrighteousness

Ungodliness literally means "no worship."

Unrighteousness literally means "no righteousness."

To hold the truth in unrighteousness means to intentionally suppress the truth. The issue here is the truth. God can only use the truth. Jesus Christ is "the way, the truth, and the life" (John 14:6). A refusal to give God the worship (the reverence and awe He should rightfully have as Creator and Lord) is to suppress the truth in unrighteousness.

Question: Where do we find the wrath revealed?

Answer: God's wrath is revealed all through scripture.

- He revealed the wrath against His people Israel if they didn't live up to the covenant (Deuteronomy 29:23–25; Joshua 22:20; 2 Kings 22:13; 2 Chronicles 19:10; and so forth). John the Baptist warned Israel of wrath to come when God would "thoroughly purge his floor" (Matthew 3:7–12). The Lord speaks of this wrath from God in Luke 21:23. This wrath would fall on everyone in Israel who didn't "believe on the Son" (John 3:36).

- Most importantly, however, this wrath was revealed in the cross, where the wrath of God the Father against sin in the human race was poured out on His only begotten Son when "he was made to be sin for us who knew no sin that we might he made the righteousness of God" (2 Corinthians 5:21). God's wrath is against ungodliness (the attitude of refusing to give God glory) and unrighteousness (the actions of living for self without regard for God).

- One of the clearest statements regarding this wrath is found in Psalm 2, where we find Israel and the Gentiles taking council together "against the Lord, and against his anointed." God's response would be to speak to them in His wrath and vex them in His sore displeasure. In Revelation 6:15–16, John foresaw this wrath ready to be poured out as the kings of the earth said to the mountains, "Fall on us and hide us from the face of him that sitteth on the throne, and from the wrath of the Lamb." That will be when the wrath of God is poured out without mixture (Revelation 14:10 cf. 19:15).

Note that verse 18 says the wrath of God "is" revealed (i.e., in the present tense). This is therefore not future wrath but wrath that is now revealed. This wrath is revealed in a number of ways:

- It is revealed in the fact that God had to vent His wrath against sin on His only begotten Son to save souls.
- It is revealed in His Word in regard to the coming judgment of God on the unsaved.
- It is revealed in that men still die as a result of the sin of Adam.

There have been times when God delayed and withheld His wrath and when He vented His wrath against sin. God's wrath and anger against sin were first demonstrated to the angels when He created the lake of fire to eventually be the abode of the angels who had sinned (Matthew 25:41). But the fallen angels are not there yet. The Gentile nations turned against God at Babel in Genesis 10–11, but God's wrath wasn't fully vented against them. Paul talks about that in Acts 17:30–31. "And the times of this ignorance God winked at; but now commandeth all men every where to repent: Because he hath appointed a day, in the which he will judge the world in righteousness by that man whom he hath ordained; whereof he hath given assurance unto all men, in that he hath raised him from the dead."

The wrath of God is also revealed in the Law of Moses. Paul said. "Because the law worketh wrath: for where no law is, there is no transgression" (Romans 4:15). The law principle is stated in Galatians 3:10. "For as many as are of the works of the law are under the curse: for it is written, Cursed is every one that continueth not in all things which are written in the book of the law to do them" (cf. Galatians 3:19).

The promised wrath of God will come on all unbelievers, those who haven't come to God in "the obedience of faith." Ephesians 5:1–6 and Colossians 3:6 speak of sins for which God's wrath will be vented. However, believers will be saved from wrath (Romans 5:9; 1 Thessalonians 5:9) because God poured out His wrath against the sins of the believer on His Son.

God's wrath against the nation of Israel is revealed in 1 Thessalonians 2:16, in that the nation is concluded in unbelief (Romans 11:32) with the Gentiles so her program whereby that nation would be a blessing to the Gentiles was interrupted. God's wrath against individuals, though, has been delayed until the great white throne of Revelation 20:11. In the meantime, men are "treasuring up unto themselves wrath against the day of wrath and revelation of a righteous judgment of God" (Romans 2:5). The only way to escape that wrath is to trust Jesus Christ as Savior.

[aa] Ungodliness and unrighteousness (v. 18) are characteristics of "the sin nature" every human being who had a human father was born with. Ungodliness literally means "no worship." The natural man, because of his fallen nature, won't freely give to God the worship due Him. To be ungodly is to fail to recognize God as the all-powerful, all-knowing, all-present, eternal, loving, holy, just, and perfect Creator. Ungodliness is described in Ephesians 2:1–3, whereby the natural man is a child destined for wrath. The natural man can maintain his outward form of godliness, but he doesn't know the power of true godliness (true worship) whereby one recognizes the glory of God (Titus 3:1–5). While ungodliness refers to the heart attitude of failure to worship God, unrighteousness refers to conduct that expresses that attitude. Unrighteousness is defined by acts such as those listed in verse 29–31 of Romans.

An ungodly person is one in whose life God has no welcome part. Suppressing the truth in unrighteousness is to promote the "fun" of ungodliness and unrighteousness while deliberately covering up the final results of unrighteousness.

On the matter of righteousness, there was a works righteousness under the law as identified in Ezekiel 18. When Israel's judges were instructed, "Thou shalt justify the righteousness, and condemn the wicked" (Deuteronomy 20 5:1), they were to do so according to the righteousness of the law. On the other hand, Proverbs 17:15 declares, "He that justifieth the wicked, and he that condemneth the just, even they both are abomination to the Lord." This righteousness of the law is the righteousness that man can know. Job asked, "But how should man be just with God?" (Job 9:2 cf. 8:20). There is a paradox here, though. God Himself found a way to justify the ungodly (Romans 4:5) and to be just in doing so. We will see more on how this could be later.

We will study much about the righteousness of God in this epistle of Romans. Under the law, we find God "showing mercy unto thousands of them that love Me and keep my commandments" (Exodus 20:6). Under grace, we find God showing mercy and love to "the children of disobedience" and "the children of wrath" (Ephesians 2: 2–7). How can a righteous God do this? Because the cross settled the account between God and men by means of the death of the one who is both God and man in one person. Christ there became the guilty party, and people become identified with Him by faith. He was there made to be sin for us (2 Corinthians 5:21). He gave Himself a ransom for all as "the one mediator between God and men" (1 Timothy 2:5–6). The good news of Christ is therefore "the power of God onto salvation to all who believe." Therefore, Paul was proud of (gloried in) the gospel. Believers ought to remind themselves daily that the gospel isn't something to be ashamed of, but it is something to glory in. "But God forbid that I should glory, save in the cross of our Lord Jesus Christ, by whom the world is crucified unto me, and I unto the world" (Galatians 6:14). Paul's reasoning then is summarized thus:

Question: Why is Paul not ashamed of the gospel?

Answer: Because it is the power of God unto salvation.

Question: Why is the gospel the power of God unto salvation?

Answer: Because therein is the righteousness of God relieved.

Question: How is the righteousness of God revealed in the gospel?

Answer: From faith to faith. Because of the faithfulness of Christ on the cross, believers can come to the absolute confidence of having the very righteousness of Jesus Christ (i.e., the righteousness of God) credited to their spiritual bank account.

A Special Note to the Reader

In Romans 1:19 through chapter 3, we find what appears to be a trial scene being played out. It is, in fact, a trial that takes place in what we might call the courtroom of divine justice. We can call it "the world on trial." All the parts of a trial are here. As you read the study notes in the next few pages, take note to see whether you can identify each part. There is a judge presented, who will judge all men. There are three different defendants, who represent all humanity. There are three witnesses called to testify against the accused. There is one who acts as the prosecuting attorney in these chapters. There is a verdict rendered, a sentence set, and an execution carried out. However, this trial has a wonderful ending. We will pick up on this again at the end of chapter 3. See if you can identify each of the players.

Creation—A Witness to the Heathen

> [19] Because that which[ab] may be known of God is manifest in them; for God hath shewed it unto them. [20] For the invisible[ac] things of him from the creation of the world are clearly seen, being understood by the things that are made, even his eternal power and Godhead; so that they are without excuse: [21] Because that, when they knew[ad] God, they glorified him not as God, neither were thankful; but became vain in their imaginations, and their foolish heart was darkened. [22] Professing themselves to be wise, they became fools, [23] And changed[ae] the glory of the uncorruptible God into an image made like to corruptible man, and to birds, and fourfooted beasts, and creeping things. (Romans 1:19–23)

[ab] The first defendant brought into the courtroom of divine justice is the heathen. The phrase "that which may be known of God" literally means "the knowledge of God." The "natural man" cannot receive the things of God (1 Corinthians 2:14). Unsaved (unregenerate) man cannot know the "deep things of God" (1 Corinthians 2:10). However, he can and should know that there is a God he must give account to simply by looking at the beautiful creation around him. The knowledge of God is stated in this verse as "his eternal power and Godhead." This is stated in Psalm 19:1–6. "The heavens declare the glory of God; and the firmament sheweth his handywork. Day unto day uttereth speech, and night unto night sheweth knowledge. There is no speech nor language, where their voice is not heard. Their line is gone out through all the earth, and their words to the end of the world. In them hath he set a tabernacle for the sun."

> Lift up your eyes on high, and behold who hath created these things, that bringeth out their host by number: he calleth them all by names by the greatness of his might. (Isaiah 40:26)

> But the LORD is the true God, he is the living God, and an everlasting king: at his wrath the earth shall tremble, and the nations shall not be able to abide his indignation. (Jeremiah 10:10)

Even when the Gentiles were in a given up state, God still gave them a testimony of His eternal power and Godhead. Acts 14:16–17 says, "Who in times past suffered all nations to walk in their own ways. Nevertheless he left not himself without witness, in that he did good, and gave us rain from heaven, and fruitful seasons, filling our hearts with food and gladness." Paul told the Athenians on Mars Hill,

I perceive that in all things ye are too superstitious. For as I passed by, and beheld your devotions, I found an altar with this inscription, TO THE UNKNOWN GOD. Whom therefore ye ignorantly worship, him declare I unto you. God that made the world and all things therein, seeing that he is Lord of heaven and earth, dwelleth not in temples made with hands; Neither is worshipped with men's hands, as though he needed any thing, seeing he giveth to all life, and breath, and all things; And hath made of one blood all nations of men for to dwell on all the face of the earth, and hath determined the times before appointed, and the bounds of their habitation; That they should seek the Lord, if haply they might feel after him, and find him, though he be not far from every one of us: For in him we live, and move, and have our being; as certain also of your own poets have said, For we are also his offspring. (Acts 17:22–28)

[ac] Verse 19 says God has showed it unto them. What was it that God showed unto them? The knowledge of God that He showed people was the invisible things of God (i.e., "his eternal power and Godhead"). The "invisible things" of God are "clearly seen" from a study of the creation of the world. These "invisible things" are "understood by the things that are made."

[ad] In verses 21–23, we see a seven-step downward path the Gentiles took. Historically this seven-step process of spiritual degradation took place between the time Noah came off the ark and the time of the confusion of tongues of Babel in Geneses 11:1–9. When Noah got off the ark, the entire human race knew God. However, man as a race began to slide into degeneracy, as shown in verses 21–23.

1. They knew God (Genesis 9:1–17, especially verse 7).
2. They glorified Him not as God.
3. They were not thankful.
4. They became vain in their imaginations.
5. Their foolish heart was darkened.
6. While professing themselves to be wise, they became fools.
7. They changed the glory of the incorruptible God into an image made like the following:
   - Corruptible man (bringing God down to man's level)
   - Birds (something to be captured for food)
   - Four-footed beasts (something man can control)
   - Creeping things (something underfoot man can step on)

God then rejected the nations and scattered them. He then set aside one nation as His unique nation (Genesis 12). Personally (i.e., on a personal level), this degeneration repeats itself as people depart from the faith; as a result, successive generations depart from the truth. Exodus 20:5 states this principle with the words "For I the Lord thy God am a jealous God, visiting the iniquity of the fathers [i.e., who departed from faith] upon the children [i.e., as a result of the fathers turning from truth] unto the third and fourth generation of that that hate me." But the blessed result of repentance and recovery is stated in the next verse: "And showing mercy unto thousands of them that love me, and keep my commandments."

[ae] Note the devolution from the incorruptible God to corruptible man.

- Then from corruptible man to birds

- Then from birds to four-footed beasts
- Then from four-footed beast to creeping things

Once God was rejected, there was no stopping the degeneration process until the bottom was reached. It may not be in one or two generations, but the degenerative process will continue in successive generations until and unless someone in the line returns to the truth and comes to God in faith. These degenerative processes affect whole cultures. The cultural deterioration can be seen in all aspects of society—in its art, music, ethics, morale, literature, and entertainment.

The degenerative process involves changes man made:

1. Man changed the glory of God into an image (v, 23).
2. Man changed the truth of God into a lie (v. 25).
3. Man changed the natural use unto what was against nature. (v. 26).

The Heathen Given Up

> ²⁴ Wherefore God also gave them up[af] to uncleanness through the lusts of their own hearts, to dishonour their own bodies between themselves: ²⁵ Who changed the truth of God into a lie, and worshipped and served the creature more than the Creator, who is blessed for ever. Amen. ²⁶ For this cause God gave them up unto vile affections: for even their women did change the natural use into that which is against nature: ²⁷ And likewise also the men, leaving the natural use of the woman, burned in their lust one toward another; men with men working that which is unseemly, and receiving in themselves that recompence of their error which was meet. ²⁸ And even as they did not like to retain God in their knowledge, God gave them over to a reprobate mind, to do those things which are not convenient. (Romans 1:24–28)

[af] God's response to this threefold change on the part of man is God's threefold giving up of man.

1. God gave them up to uncleanness (v. 24). This involved the degeneration of the body, since it states "to dishonor their own bodies between themselves."

2. God gave them up to vile affections (v. 26). This involves the degeneration of the soul, the seat of our affections.

3. God gave them over to a reprobate mind (v. 28). This involves the degeneration of the spirit, the seat of the rational thinking part of man.

   > ²⁹ Being filled[ag] with all unrighteousness, fornication, wickedness, covetousness, maliciousness; full of envy, murder, debate, deceit, malignity; whisperers, ³⁰ Backbiters, haters of God, despiteful, proud, boasters, inventors of evil things, disobedient to parents, ³¹ Without understanding, covenantbreakers, without natural affection, implacable, unmerciful: ³² Who knowing the judgment of God, that they which commit such things are worthy of death, not only do the same, but have pleasure in them that do them. (Romans 1:29–32)

[ag] As stated in the note on verse 18, ungodliness is the mental attitude of rebellion against God. Unrighteousness is the conduct that grows out of that attitude. Here in verses 29–32, different manifestations of unrighteousness are listed. But rather than being filled with all unrighteousness, man can now be filled with the Spirit by the

process of regeneration (Ephesians 5:18). The unrighteousness of man can be replaced with the righteousness of God (Romans 3:21). The whole spirit, soul, and body can be preserved blameless (1 Thessalonians 5:23).

Study Questions on Chapter 1

1. Who wrote this epistle and to whom did he write it?

2. About what year A.D. was this Book written?

3. At what point in the Book of Acts was it written?

4. Who was the "Called apostle" and to what was he separated?

5. Paul talks about a gospel of God that God had promised afore. What was that gospel? At what point in history was the "aforetime"?

6. Verse 2 speaks of prophets. Who were these prophets?

7. If this gospel was prophesied, how in light of Romans 16:25 was Paul then separated unto it?

8. What is the purpose for this message now revealed?

9. To whom was Paul a Debtor? Why do you suppose that was? Are you a debtor?

10. Is the Gospel of Christ in verse 16 the same as the Gospel of God in verse 1?

11. To whom is the gospel of Christ the power of God unto salvation?

12. What is revealed in the gospel according to verse 17? Explain

13. Did God provide a testimony of Himself to man before the Bible was written?

14. What beside the righteousness of God is revealed from heaven?

15. Man professed to be wise but what did they become in the process?

16. What did man change the glory of God into?

17. What did God do as a result?

18. When in human history do you see the event of verses 24 through 28 taking place?

19. What effect did mankind being given up by God have on man?

20. Has man's moral character improved in modern time from what it was at Babel

Chapter 2

THE WITNESS OF CONSCIENCE

¹ Therefore thou art inexcusable, O man, whosoever thou art that judgest[a]: for wherein thou judgest another, thou condemnest[b] thyself; for thou that judgest doest the same things. ² But we are sure that the judgment[c] of God is according to truth against them which commit such things. ³ And thinkest thou this, O man, that judgest[d] them which do such things, and doest the same, that thou shalt escape the judgment of God? (Romans. 2:1–3)

[a] Here in chapter 2, Paul brings the second defendant into the courtroom of God's justice. The phrase "whosoever thou art that judgest" refers to the Gentile moralizer who judges the totally degraded Gentile of chapter 1. The concluding verse of chapter 1 indicates that degraded people are in that state not because they are the unfortunate victims of happenstance but rather because they like it that way. They exist in a degenerated state in spite of the knowledge that there is the holy God who will judge them for it. But the sophisticated moralizing philosophers who look down on the degenerated Gentile and stand in judgment also stand condemned before God because they do the same thing. They cover up their actions better and have perhaps succeeded in euphemizing the sin to make it appear moral and just. For example, taking money by force from someone who earned it for the express purpose of giving it to someone who didn't would be judged by the moralists as wrong. But the moralists would do the same thing through a system of taxation and give themselves a pat on the back for doing so. Another example is the case of abortion. The moralists pass laws and legislation to protect children from harm. Yet they also pass a law that would have allowed the same child to be killed in the most inhumane fashion just hours earlier.

[b] The moralizers condemn themselves by their act of judging because their judging of others demonstrates that they have the capacity to know right from wrong. This capacity to know the difference between good and evil is what we understand to be conscience. Conscience entered the human race with the first sin of mankind in Genesis 3:5–7 when they ate of the tree of the knowledge of good and evil. That tree gave people the knowledge that what they were doing wasn't acceptable to God. Adam and Eve knew they were naked after they ate of that tree because the sense of innocence was gone, and likely they lost an aura or innocence that covered them instead of clothing. It should be noted that the tree isn't the tree of the knowledge of righteousness and wickedness but the tree of the knowledge of good and evil. They acquired a conscience when they ate of that tree.

[c] The judgment of God referred to in verse 2 is a righteous judgment of God stated in verses 6–8. Everyone knows in his or her heart of hearts that there is a God and that everyone will stand before that God in judgment one day. God put that knowledge within every man as innate knowledge. It is only the unrighteousness of man that prompts him to concoct a system of belief (or more properly, disbelief) that enables him to get around seeing that truth. Psalm 14:1 states, "The fool hath said in his heart, there is no God." But he has to tell himself

this in his heart because in his spirit (in his mind) he knows it isn't true. He knows, as Romans 1:20 states, that "the invisible things of him from the creation of the world are clearly seen being understood by the things that are made, even his eternal power and Godhead."

[d] A desire to appear "good" in their actions of judging others motivates the moralizers. Yet the apostle brings moralizers to the sobering reality that they do the same thing and will therefore fall into the same judgment of God. Every human must come to reality as King David did. "O lord, thou hast searched me, and known me. Thou knowest my downsitting and mine uprising, thou understandest my thought afar off" (Psalm 139:1–2). All people must realize this if they are to deal with the reality of their indwelling sin nature. We don't need to argue the existence of God with anyone in the process of evangelizing the lost. All we need to do is turn the Word of God loose. "For the word of God is quick and powerful and sharper than any two edge sword, piercing even in to the dividing asunder of soul and spirit, and of the joints and marrow, and is a discerner of the thoughts and intents of the heart" (Hebrews 4:12–13).

God's Standard of Perfection

> [4] Or despisest[e] thou the riches of his goodness and forbearance and longsuffering; not knowing that the goodness of God leadeth thee to repentance? [5] But after thy hardness[f] and impenitent heart treasurest up unto thyself wrath against the day of wrath and revelation of the righteous judgment[g] of God; [6] Who will render[h] to every man according to his deeds: [7] To them who by patient continuance in well doing seek[i] for glory and honour and immortality, eternal life: [8] But unto them that are contentious, and do not obey the truth, but obey unrighteousness, indignation and wrath, [9] Tribulation and anguish, upon every soul of man that doeth evil, of the Jew first[k], and also of the Gentile; [10] But glory, honour, and peace, to every man that worketh good, to the Jew first, and also to the Gentile: [11] For there is no respect[l] of persons with God. (Romans 2:4–11)

[e] Verse 4 says it's the goodness of God that leads to repentance. It's in that influence of God at work through His Word that anyone is protected from active participation in gross and open sin. But the moralizer "despiseth … the riches, [God's riches] of his goodness and forbearance and longsuffering" because he or she doesn't know that the goodness of God is designed by God not only to keep him or her from further degeneration but also to lead him or her to repentance—i.e., to lead him or her to turn to God in faith.

[f] Moralists preach virtue but practice the vice they condemn. The hardened and impenitent heart here is the heart that refuses to recognize it was God's goodness and forbearance and long-suffering that kept him or her from the same degraded condition of the reprobate of chapter 1. Rather than repenting, he or she persists in refusing to acknowledge his or her guilt and therefore treasures up wrath against the day of wrath and revelation of the righteous judgment of God.

[g] The righteous judgment of God is here stated for the purpose of showing God will (must) reward the just but must punish the wicked. Later, we will see that "there is none righteous," but let's study the righteous judgment of God here first: God will render

> "[7] To them who by patient continuance in well doing seek for glory and honour and immortality, eternal life: [8] But unto them that are contentious, and do not obey the truth, but obey unrighteousness, indignation and wrath, [9] Tribulation and anguish, upon every soul of man that doeth evil, of the Jew first, and also of

the Gentile; [10] But glory, honour, and peace, to every man that worketh good, to the Jew first, and also to the Gentile" (Romans 2:7–10).

The phrase "patient continuance in well doing" in verse 7 means "perfect" (without a single failure) continuance in well doing. God would give such a person eternal life because that person earned it. However, we will see that no man ever does attain to that high standard.

[h] The righteous judgment of God is that He "will render to every man according to his deeds." This is the judgment of the great white throne in Revelation 20:12. "And I saw the dead, small and great, stand before God; and the books were opened: and another book was opened, which is the book of life: and the dead were judged out of those things which were written in the books, according to their works" (emphasis added). However, the believers of this present dispensation are judged not according to their works but rather according to grace. Paul tells us it's "not by works of righteousness which we have done, but according to his mercy he saved us, by the washing of regeneration, and renewing of the Holy Ghost" (Titus 3:5). He tells us further, "But to him that worketh not, but believeth on him that justifieth the ungodly, his faith is counted for righteousness" (Romans 4:5).

[i] Theoretically and potentially (according to v. 7), eternal life could be earned by patient continuance in well doing. The point of Romans 1:17–3:20 is that no one can do this. To even attempt it would indicate that the person genuinely seeks glory, honor, and immorality; but the Lord says, "I am the Lord: that is my name: and my glory will I not give to another, neither my praise to graven images" (Isaiah 42:8 cf 43:11). Under God's grace, all the glory goes to God. Believers live "to the praise of the glory of his grace, wherein he hath made us accepted in the beloved" (Ephesians 1:6) "that we should be to the praise of his glory" (v. 12). God gets the glory when He justifies people by grace.

[j] The phrase "indignation and a wrath" refers to God's mental attitude toward the contentious attitudes of men. Unrighteousness is the action that results from man's contentious attitude. Tribulation and anguish are the outworking of God's judgment on man's unrighteous actions of disobedience to the faith. Man's rebellion leads him into an attitude of ungodliness with the resulting action being unrighteousness. God's judgment results in an attitude on God's part of indignation and wrath, with the resulting action on God's part of tribulation and anguish on every soul of man who does evil.

[k] "To the Jew first and also to the Gentile" is an expression to show uniformity and state the chronological order of the application of God's salvation. It is used here in 2:9–10 and in 1:16. In 1:16, the gospel of Christ was the power of God unto salvation to the Jew in the prophetic program, and now it is that same power to the Greeks (Gentiles) in the mystery program (i.e., in the dispensation of grace committed to Paul). The universal principle of justice in 2:5–10 applied both to Israel in their program and to the Gentiles today.

[l] "There is no respect of persons with God." Paul here states the universal condition of man and a universal application of the divine principle of justice stated in verses 5–10. There is no respect of persons with God. "Those who have sinned without law, shall also perish without law: and as many as have sinned in the law shall be judged by the law." (Romans 2:12)

God's Standard of Justice

God is no respecter of persons when executing this universal principle of justice, even though He respects persons in regard to those who are His elect. When God worked with Israel as "His people," He said, "The people shall dwell alone, and shall not be reckoned among the nations" (Numbers 23:9). During our Lord's ministry on earth, He repeatedly pressed the fact, saying, "I am not sent but unto the lost sheep of the house of Israel" (Matthew 15:24). The woman with the spirit of infirmity in Luke 13:11–15 was healed because she was "a daughter of Abraham." In Matthew 10:5–6, our Lord instructs His disciples, "Go not into the way of the Gentiles, and into any city of the Samaritans enter ye not: but go rather to the lost sheep of the house of Israel." Peter, on the day of Pentecost in Acts 2:22–39, says, "Ye men of Israel, hear these words ... the promise is to you and to your children and to all [Israelites] that are afar off." Therefore, there is a sense in which God is a respecter of persons regarding His elect, but He is not a respecter of persons in regard to divine justice. This seeming paradox is seen and explained in Deuteronomy 10:13–17.

> "To keep the commandments of the Lord, and his statutes, which I command thee this day for thy good? Behold, the heaven and the heaven of heavens is the Lord's thy God, the earth also, with all that therein is. Only the Lord had a delight in thy fathers to love them, and he chose their seed after them, even you above all people, as it is this day. Circumcise therefore the foreskin of your heart, and be no more stiffnecked. For the Lord your God is God of gods, and Lord of lords, a great God, a mighty, and a terrible, which regardeth not persons, nor taketh reward."

God instructs His people in Deuteronomy 16:19–20, "Thou shalt not wrest judgment; thou shalt not respect persons, neither take a gift: for a gift doth blind the eyes of the wise, and pervert the words of the righteous. That which is altogether just shalt thou follow."

- With respect to communicating the gospel of the uncircumcision, Paul states, "Whosoever they were, it maketh no matter to me: God accepteth the no man's person" (Galatians 2:6).

- With respect to the manner of sowing and reaping, Paul states, "Whatsoever a man [any man] soweth that, that also shall ye reap." In Ephesians 6:9, masters are admonished to treat servants well because "there is no respect of persons with [God]."

- In Colossians 3:25, Paul states, "But he that doeth wrong shall receive for the wrong which he hath done and there is no respect of persons." This is in respect to "the reward of the inheritance."

- In 1 Peter 1:17, Peter states, "The Father, who without respect of persons judgeth according to every man's work." Peter is speaking in regard to leadership, but in Acts 10:34, Peter speaks of a dispensational lesson God was teaching him when he said, "Of truth I perceive that God is no respecter of persons: but in every nation he that feareth him, and worketh righteousness, is accepted of him."

- The Pharisees and Herodians at least gave lip service to the impartiality of God's judgment. "We know that thou art true and teacheth the way of God in truth, neither carest thou for any man for thou regardest not the person of men" (Matthew 22:16).

Conscience Does for the Gentiles What the Law Does for Israel—It Convicts of Sin

[12] For as many as have sinned without law shall also perish without law: and as many as have sinned in the law shall be judged[m] by the law; [13] (For not the hearers[n] of the law are just before God, but the doers[o]

of the law shall be justified. [14] For when the Gentiles, which have no[p] the law, do by nature the things contained in the law, these, having not the law, are a law unto themselves: [15] Which shew[q] the work of the law written in their hearts, their conscience also bearing[r] witness, and their thoughts the mean while accusing or else excusing one another;) [16] In the day when God shall judge the secrets of men by Jesus Christ according to my gospel. (Romans 2:12–16)

[m] In verse 12, the principle of God having no respect of persons is applied to the Law of Moses. Just having the Law of Moses didn't give an advantage in reckoning one righteous, but rather the doing of the law by faith did. By the law is the knowledge of sin (Romans 3:20), but sin will be judged, whether the knowledge of it comes from the law or from the conscience.

[n] God's purpose in giving Israel the law was that she should obey it.

> Now therefore hearken, O Israel, unto the statutes and unto the judgments, which I teach you, for to do them, that ye may live, and go in and possess the land which the LORD God of your fathers giveth you. (Deuteronomy 4:1)

> Hear, O Israel, the statutes and judgments which I speak in your ears this day, that ye may learn them, and keep, and do them. (Deuteronomy 5:1)

> Hear therefore, O Israel, and observe to do it; that it may be well with thee. (Deuteronomy 6:3)

> But the word is very nigh unto thee, in thy mouth, and in thy heart, that thou mayest do it. See, I have set before thee this day life and good, and death and evil; In that I command thee this day to love the LORD thy God, to walk in his ways, and to keep his commandments and his statutes and his judgments. (Deuteronomy 30:14–16)

> And I gave them my statutes, and shewed them my judgments, which if a man do, he shall even live in them. (Ezekiel 20:11)

However, Israel didn't keep the law (Ezekiel 33:30–32). Our Lord identified His true brethren as those who hear the words of God and do them (Luke 8:21). He laid out the requirements of entering the kingdom of heaven as doing the will of His Father (Matthew 7:21–21).

[o] There was a way to be justified under law (Luke 18:14). However, it took more than giving just a halfhearted effort of keeping the law (Luke 10:25–37). But even this justification wasn't complete. In Acts 13:39, Paul states regarding Christ, "Through him everyone who believes is justified from everything you could not be justified from by the Law of Moses." Paul expands on that in Galatians.

> Knowing that a man is not justified by the works of the law, but by faith in Jesus Christ, even we, too, have believed in Jesus Christ that we may be justified by the faith of Christ, and not by the works of the law, for by the works of the law shall no flesh be justified. (Galatians 2:16)

> But that no man is justified by the law in the sight of God, it is evident: for, The just shall live by faith. And the law is not of faith: but, The man that doeth them shall live in them. (Galatians 3:11–12)

[p] Verse 14 talks about the Gentiles not having the law. The law wasn't given to the Gentiles. The Gentiles were

"given up" by God at Babel (Romans 2:24, 26, 28). "That at that time ye [Gentiles] were without Christ, being aliens from the commonwealth of Israel, and strangers from the covenants of promise, having no hope, and without God in the world" (Ephesians 2:12). It is as Paul states, that God "in times past suffered all nations to walk in their own ways" (Acts 14:16). "And the times of this ignorance God winked at; but now commandeth all men every where to repent: Because he hath appointed a day, in which he will judge the world in righteousness by that man whom he hath ordained" (Acts 17:30–31).

[q] To understand verse 15, one must remember the lawful use of the law, as Paul states in 1 Timothy 1:9. "Knowing this, that the law is not made for a righteous man, but for the lawless and disobedient, for the ungodly and for sinners, for unholy and profane, for murderers of fathers and murderers of mothers, for manslayers, For whoremongers, for them that defile themselves with mankind, for menstealers, for liars, for perjured persons, and if there be any other thing that is contrary to sound doctrine." "The work of the law" is to bring to light the knowledge of sin (Romans 3:20). If the Gentiles could by nature live a righteous life as the law demanded, they would "be a law unto themselves." But because they don't by nature live a righteous life, they instead show the work of the law (i.e., conviction) written in their hearts (conscience).

[r] The Gentiles, being convicted by conscience, even though they don't have the law, will do one of two things: First, they will be accused of their lost state. Or second, they will make excuses for themselves.

Enter the Jew, the Religionist

> [17] Behold, thou art called[s] a Jew, and restest[t] in the law, and makest[u] thy boast of God, [18] And knowest[v] his will, and approvest the things that are[w] more excellent, being instructed[x] out of the law; [19] And art[y] confident that thou thyself art[z] a guide of the blind, a light of them which are in darkness, [20] An instructor of the foolish, a teacher of babes, which hast the form of knowledge and of the truth in the law. 21 Thou therefore which teachest another, teachest thou not thyself? thou that preachest a man should not steal, dost[ab] thou steal? [22] Thou that sayest a man should not commit adultery, dost thou commit adultery? thou that abhorrest idols, dost thou commit sacrilege? [23] Thou that makest[ac] thy boast of the law, through breaking the law dishonourest thou God? 24 For the name of God is blasphemed among the Gentiles through you, as it is written. (Romans 2:17–24)

[s] Here in verse 17 the third defendant enters the courtroom. "Jew" is a term that once, after the apostasy of the ten northern tribes, referred to the two southern tribes of Judah and Benjamin. However, after the Assyrian captivity of the ten tribes and the return of captivity of the two southern tribes from Babylon, the term again applied to all tribes (Acts 2:5, 22, 36; 26:7; Romans 3:1–2). The terms are Hebrew, referring to the race—Israelites in reference to the nation and Jews in reference to the religion.

[t] Israel rested in the law, trusting that they had salvation in that. In reality, all it did for them was accuse them. "Do not think that I will accuse you to the Father: there is one that accuseth you, even Moses, in whom ye trust. For had ye believed Moses, ye would have believed me; for he wrote of me. But if ye believe not his writings, how shall ye believe my words?" (John 5:45–48).

[u] Israel could boast of God.

> For the LORD hath chosen Jacob unto himself, and Israel for his peculiar treasure. (Psalm 135:4)

Jews by nature, and not sinners. (Galatians 2:15)

Blessed is the nation whose God is the LORD; and the people whom he hath chosen for his own inheritance. (Psalm 33:12)

Surely, shall one say, in the LORD have I righteousness and strength: even to him shall men come; and all that are incensed against him shall be ashamed. In the LORD shall all the seed of Israel be justified, and shall glory. (Isaiah 45:24–25)

[v] Israel knew God's will because of the law. "For what nation is there so great, who hath God so nigh unto them, as the LORD our God is in all things that we call upon him for? And what nation is there so great, that hath statutes and judgments so righteous as all this law, which I set before you this day? Also take heed to thyself, and keep thy soul diligently" (Deuteronomy 4:7–9). See also Nehemiah 9:13–15. Psalm 147:19–20 says, "He sheweth his word unto Jacob, his statutes and his judgments unto Israel. He hath not dealt so with any nation: and as for his judgments, they have not known them. Praise ye the LORD."

[w] "Things that are more excellent" (emphasis added) in verse 18 uses the same term used in Philippians 1:10. To approve things that are more excellent is to discern what God would have us do in each and every opportunity and to recognize God's will as being vastly superior to the deeds done by those who do not know God. We who are under grace are to do that today.

[x] The only way anyone can approve the things that are more excellent is to be instructed of God (2 Timothy 3:16–17). For Israel, that instruction comes from the law. For us, it comes from Paul's epistles (1 Corinthians 14:37; Philippians 3:17–21; 1 Timothy 1:16; and so forth).

[y] The expression "and art confident that thou art" should be cause for concern. Being self-confident and seeing oneself as wise in one's own eyes are dangerous for a person with revelation from God if that person doesn't see himself or herself as being in need of the truth first.

Woe unto them that are wise in their own eyes, and prudent in their own sight! (Isaiah 5:21)

Seest thou a man wise in his own conceit? there is more hope of a fool than of him. (Proverbs 26:12)

[z]. It is true that, until Paul was sent as the apostle of the Gentiles, it could be said, as our Lord stated in John 4:22, "Salvation is of the Jews." As the channel of salvation, Israel was to be the following:

"A guide to the blind," but our Lord refers to them as "blind leaders of the blind. And if the blind lead the blind, both shall fall into the ditch" (Matthew 15:14). With respect to spiritual vision, our Lord stated, "For judgment I am come into this world, that they which see not might see; and that they which see might be made blind" (John 9:39–41).

"A light to them which are in darkness." Isaiah prophesied that "the Gentiles shall come to thy light, and kings to the brightness of thy rising" (Isaiah 60:3). Isaiah 60:2 tells us when that will be. "Behold, the darkness shall cover the earth, and gross darkness the people: but the LORD shall arise upon thee, and his glory shall be seen upon thee."

In Isaiah 49:3–6, the Lord says, "Thou art my servant, O Israel, in whom I will be glorified. Then I said, I have laboured in vain, I have spent my strength for nought, and in vain: yet surely my judgment is with the LORD, and my work with my God. And now, saith the LORD that formed me from the womb to be his servant, to bring Jacob again to him, Though Israel be not gathered, yet shall I be glorious in the eyes of the LORD, and my God shall be my strength. And he said, It is a light thing that thou shouldest be my servant to raise up the tribes of Jacob, and to restore the preserved of Israel: I will also give thee for a light to the Gentiles, that thou mayest be my salvation unto the end of the earth." "Go forth to them that are in darkness" (v. 9).

Israel was to be "the light of the world" (Matthew 4:16). Christ is the light that shines through that nation (Matthew 4:16). But when gross darkness covered Israel (Isaiah 60:2 quoted above), then God sent Paul, the apostle, to the Gentiles. "To open their eyes, and to turn them from darkness to light, and from the power of Satan unto God, that they may receive forgiveness of sins, and inheritance among them which are sanctified by faith that is in me" (Acts 26:18). Now there are the members of the body of Christ who are to "shine as lights in the world" (Philippians 2:15).

"An instructor of the foolish, a teacher of babes" because they had the form of knowledge and the truth in the law. Israel had the very form of the only true knowledge from God that was available to man, and they were to teach it to the nations (who didn't have it). But Paul says of them, "They profess that they know God; but in works they deny him, being abominable, and disobedient, and unto every good work reprobate" (Titus 1:16).

[aa] Psalm 50:16–21 speaks volumes on Israel's inability to live up to the standards of the law they were not only to live but also to proclaim to others. God says to Israel, "What hast thou to do to declare my statutes, or that thou shouldest take my covenant in thy mouth? Seeing thou hatest instruction, and casteth my words behind thee. When thou sawest a thief, then thou consentedst with him, and hast been partaker with adulterers. Thou givest thy mouth to evil, and thy tongue frameth deceit. Thou sittest and speakest against thy brother; thou slanderest thine own mother's son." Of the leaders of Israel, our Lord states, "They say, and do not" (Matthew 23:3).

Paul says of the Judaizers in Galatians 6:12–13, "As many as desire to make a fair shew in the flesh, they constrain you to be circumcised; only lest they should suffer persecution for the cross of Christ. For neither they themselves who are circumcised keep the law; but desire to have you circumcised, that they may glory in your flesh."

[ab] Israel's history is filled with the failure of keeping the law.

"Dost thou steal?"

- "They are greedy dogs which can never have enough, and they are shepherds that cannot understand: they all look to their own way, every one for his gain" (Isaiah 56:11).

- Speaking to Jerusalem, God says through Ezekiel, "In thee have they taken gifts to shed blood; thou hast taken usury and increase, and thou hast greedily gained of thy neighbours by extortion" (Ezekiel 22:12).

- "The people of the land have used oppression, and exercised robbery, and have vexed the poor and needy: yea, they have oppressed the stranger wrongfully" (Ezekiel 22:29).

- Our Lord, speaking of the money changers at the temple, says, "It is written, My house shall be called the house of prayer; but ye have made it a den of thieves" (Matthew 24:13).

- He says of the leaders of the nation, "Ye devour widows' houses" (Matthew 23:14).

"Dost thou commit adultery?"

- "They then committed adultery, and assembled themselves by troops in the harlots' houses" (Jeremiah 5:7).

- "And one hath committed abomination with his neighbour's wife; and another hath lewdly defiled his daughter in law; and another in thee hath humbled his sister, his father's daughter" (Ezekiel 22:11).

- Our Lord referred to Israel as "a wicked and adulterous generation" (Matthew 12:39; 16:4).

"Dost thou commit sacrilege?"

- "And if ye offer the blind for sacrifice, is it not evil? and if ye offer the lame and sick, is it not evil? offer it now unto thy governor; will he be pleased with thee, or accept thy person?" (Malachi 1:8).

- "But cursed be the deceiver, which hath in his flock a male, and voweth, and sacrificeth unto the LORD a corrupt thing" (Malachi 1:14).

- "Will a man rob God? Yet ye have robbed me. But ye say, Wherein have we robbed thee? In tithes and offerings" (Malachi 3:8).

[ac] Israel boasted in the Law. Jeremiah 8:8–9 says, "How do ye say, We are wise, and the law of the LORD is with us? Lo, certainly in vain made he it; the pen of the scribes is in vain. The wise men are ashamed, they are dismayed and taken: lo, they have rejected the word of the LORD; and what wisdom is in them?"

> 25 For circumcision verily profiteth, if thou keep[ad] the law: but if thou be a breaker of the law, thy circumcision is made uncircumcision. 26 Therefore if the uncircumcision keep the righteousness of the law, shall not his uncircumcision be counted for circumcision? 27 And shall not uncircumcision which is by nature, if it fulfil the law, judge thee, who by the letter and circumcision dost[ae] transgress the law? 28 For he is not a Jew, which is one outwardly; neither is that circumcision, which is outward in the flesh: 29 But he is a Jew, which is one inwardly; and circumcision is that of the heart, in the spirit, and not in the letter; whose praise is not of men, but of God. (Romans 2:25–29)

[ad] The only way circumcision is profitable is if the one circumcised keeps the law. If someone breaks the law, he or she is regarded as no different from an uncircumcised person. The only way Israel will ever be able to truly do that is when the new covenant takes effect for Israel. Deuteronomy 30:6 says, "And the LORD thy God will circumcise thine heart, and the heart of thy seed, to love the LORD thy God with all thine heart, and with all thy soul, that thou mayest live." Until then, Israel is admonished to "circumcise yourselves to the LORD, and take away the foreskins of your heart, ye men of Judah and inhabitants of Jerusalem."

When Paul comes on the scene with the new revelation of the mystery, he says, "For I testify again to every man that is circumcised, that he is a debtor to do the whole law. Christ is become of no effect unto you, whosoever of you are justified by the law; ye are fallen from grace. For in Jesus Christ neither circumcision availeth any thing, nor uncircumcision; but faith which worketh by love" (Galatians 5:3–6). "For in Christ Jesus neither circumcision availeth any thing, nor uncircumcision, but a new creature" (Galatians 6:15). That new creature is found in Ephesians 2:11–15 (i.e., the one new man consisting of believing Jews and believing Gentiles being joint members of "the body of Christ," the church of this present dispensation of grace).

[ae] If those who are circumcised break the law, their circumcision is regarded as uncircumcision. Stephen pressed this point with the leaders of Israel when he said, "Ye stiffnecked and uncircumcised in heart and ears, ye do always resist the Holy Ghost: as your fathers did, so do ye" (Acts 7:51).

Study Questions on Chapter 2

1. According to verse 2, on what basis will God judge?

2. According to verse 4, what is it that leads men to repentance? How do men often react to the goodness of God?

3. According to verse 5, what are men treasuring up for themselves?

4. According to verse 6, God will render to every man what?

5. Taking verses 6 & 7 together, to whom will God give receive eternal life? Does verse 7 teach salvation by works?

6. What (in verse 12) will be the end of those who have sinned without the law? Is it any different from those who have sinned with the law?

7. Verse 8 lists two words that describes God's attitude toward those who obey unrighteousness. What are they?

8. Verse 9 lists two words that describe the result of God's attitude toward disobedience. What are they?

9. In verse 14 did the Gentiles have the Law? What is the work of the Law in verse 15 in the Gentiles who did not have the Law?

10. Romans 1 spoke of God judging men for their outward conduct. Verse 16 of this Chapter tells us that there is something else that God will judge. What is it?

11. List some advantages th**Study Questions on Chapter 2**at the Jew had as listed in verses 17 thru 20.

12. Did the advantages that the Jew have help him with regard to his relationship to God?

13. How could circumcision according to verse 25 help the Jew?

14. According to verse 27, could an uncircumcised person judge the Jew? How?

15. What is the circumcision of the heart that verse 29 talks about?

CHAPTER 3

WHAT ADVANTAGE HAD THE JEW?

¹ What advantage then hath[a] the Jew? or what profit is there of circumcision? ² Much every way: chiefly, because that unto them were committed[b] the oracles of God." (Romans 3:1–2)

[a] "What advantage then hath the Jew?" Paul is still dealing with the Jews here. The fact that God gave up on the Gentile nations is stated in Romans 1:17. Historically, this giving up of the Gentile nations occurred in Genesis 11:1–9, when God scattered the nations after the judgment of tongues at Babel. This event occurred in approximately the year 2247 (give or take a few decades) BC. Now, in Romans 3, we see the Jews being placed on the same level as the Gentiles as far as justification is concerned. Here we will see that both Jews and Gentiles stand before God equally condemned. As the Gentile nations became enemies of God (Romans 1:21–23), they began a downward spiral into degeneration and progressively deeper immorality, corruption, and spiritual blindness (Romans 1:24–31). God separated from the Gentile masses one man (Abram) to maintain a testimony of the truth through him (Romans 1:18) and to ensure the continuance of the line of the woman's seed, as promised in Genesis 3:15. When God found Abram, he was an idolater when he was called, but "Abraham believed God and It was counted to him for righteousness" (Genesis 17:4–8, 15–19; cf Romans 4:17–22). Abraham then became justified by faith and became the progenitor of the seed line.

[b] The phrase "the oracles of God" is the entire volume of revelation and the temple service authorized in the written Word of God. It was through Israel that God established a sanctuary on earth, through which people could approach God. At that time (i.e., in the Old Testament), salvation was of the Jews (John 4:22). The worship and service of God belonged to Israel (Romans 9:4). Today, however, the worship and service of God are within the body of Christ.

³ For what if some did not believe? shall their unbelief make[c] the faith of God without effect? ⁴ God forbid: yea, let God be true, but every man a liar; as it is[d] written, That thou mightest be justified in thy sayings, and mightest overcome when thou art judged. (Romans 3:3–4)

[c] The phrase "the faith of God" here refers to the trustworthiness of God. God is always faithful, but not all men have faith in His faithfulness. The fact that some men possessed the law without profiting from it (because they possessed it in mere formality) doesn't alter the faithfulness of God one bit. God's trustworthiness and veracity are not affected by man's lack of a response of faith to Him and His faithfulness.

[d] This verse (v. 4) is quoted from Psalm 51:4. This statement says in effect, "Let God be found to be ever truthful, though every man is a liar to the end that he may be acknowledged to be righteous in his words and prevail whenever and wherever and by whoever he might ever be put to the test." God can be judged and, when judged, will always prove to be righteous. He can be tested and will always prove that His Word can be relied on.

⁵ But if our unrighteousness commend the righteousness of God, what shall we say? Is God unrighteous who

taketh vengeance? (I speak[e] as a man) [6] God forbid: for then how shall God judge the world? [7] For if the truth of God hath more abounded through my lie unto his glory; why yet am I also judged as a sinner? [8] And not rather, (as we be slanderously reported, and as some affirm that we say,) Let us do evil, that good may come? whose damnation is just. (Romans 3:5–8)

[e] Verses 5–8 can be understood only by remembering that we are looking at "the righteousness of God" through the eyes of unrighteous man (i.e., "I speak as a man"). George Williams in his Student Commentary explains, "Man's words and ways demonstrate the truth of this Divine statement [i.e., "Let God be true, but every man a liar"]." Therefore, the more untruthful and unholy men are, the more they demonstrate the truthfulness and holiness of God. Two objections are consequently proposed.

- First, is it not unrighteous for God to punish people for proving the righteousness of God (v. 5)? The answer is conclusive. It is that God shall judge the world (v. 6).

- Second, if man's falsehood makes God's truth abound (v. 7), then man brings the greatest glory to God by continuously committing the greatest sins. Consequently, it would not be just that God should judge him or her as a sinner (v. 7). To this second objection, the answer is simply that all who reason and act thus shall suffer a just judgment (v. 8).

Though the depravity of man exalts the glory of God by comparison, God is still righteous and still hates sin and judges sin. God wouldn't have us do evil so He might be glorified by comparison, as some slanderously accused Paul of saying.

The Prosecutor's Evidence

[8] And not rather, (as we be slanderously reported, and as some affirm that we say,) Let us do evil, that good may come? whose damnation is just. [9] What then? Are[f] we better than they? No, in no wise: for we have before proved both Jews and Gentiles, that they are all under sin; [10] As it is[g] written, There is none righteous, no, not one: [11] There is none that understandeth, there is none that seeketh after God.

[12] They are all gone out of the way, they are together become unprofitable; there is none that doeth good, no, not one. [13] Their throat is an open sepulchre; with their tongues they have used deceit; the poison of asps is under their lips: [14] Whose mouth is full of cursing and bitterness: [15] Their feet are swift to shed blood:16 Destruction and misery are in their ways: [17] And the way of peace have they not known:" [18] There is no fear of God before their eyes. (Romans 3:8–18)

[f] The "we" of verse 9 describes the Jews Paul has been addressing since Romans 2:17, while "they" refers to the Gentiles. Paul includes himself as a Jew who was no better than the Gentiles.

[g] Verses 10 through 18 have a number of quotations from the Old Testament scriptures, which list fourteen statements that prove that even the best representatives of humanity (i.e., God's chosen people Israel) come short of the standards. The list moves from general statements in verses 10–12, which prove the universality of sin, to particular statements in verses 13–18, which prove that every one comes in guilty in that every man comes in convicted by this list of particular sins. Together, this list comprises the prosecutor's evidence with Paul the apostle serving as the prosecutor in this courtroom of divine justice.

The Law as a Witness

> [h]
> ¹⁹ Now we know that what things soever the law saith, it saith to them who are under the law: that every mouth may be stopped, and all the world may become guilty before God. ²⁰ Therefore by the deeds of the law there shall no flesh be [i] justified in his sight: for by the law is the knowledge of sin. (Romans 3:19–20)

[h] Verse 19 points out the fact that the law speaks to those who are under law (i.e., the Jew). In verses 10–18, the apostle was using the Jews' own scripture to show them they were no better than the Gentiles. He showed them that the law isn't just a guide as to how to live righteously; rather, it is an accuser to show those who are under it that they don't live righteously (v. 20). The Gentiles have already been proven guilty before this court of God's justice in Romans 1:21–2:16. It wasn't difficult to prove the Gentiles' guilt. The Jew, however, might boast in being different as in an elite group because he or she was given the law. Therefore, the apostle appeals to the law to testify against the Jew and to the Jews' own scripture to convince of guilt. Now, therefore, with Israel being shown guilty, all the world may become guilty before God in two ways:

1. Israel is now proved guilty along with the Gentiles, as stated above.

2. Israel, as a kingdom of priests (Exodus 19:5–6), was to represent the Gentiles before God. But if the representatives prove to be guilty, the Gentiles are guilty as well.

[i] There is a lesson that God's giving of the law to Israel was intended to teach. That lesson is that by the deeds the law prescribes, no flesh will be justified in God's sight because all the law can do is convict those under it of sin. When Israel was under law, the only hope of salvation for any Jew was the blood-sprinkled mercy seat covering the ark of the covenant. The vast majority of people today still haven't learned this lesson. Rather, they suppose the law was given as some general guide as to how to be righteous and acceptable to God by human merit. When the law came on the scene after about twenty-five hundred years of human history had passed, it added its testimony to that of the conscience (Romans 5:20; 7–13).

Now the Righteousness of God without the Law Is Manifest

> ²¹ But now the righteousness of God without the law is [j] manifested, being witnessed by the law and the prophets; ²² Even the righteousness [k] of God which is by [l] faith of Jesus Christ unto [m] all and upon all them that believe: for there is [n] no difference. (Romans 3:21–22)

[j] The statement in verse 21 that the righteousness of God without the law is "witnessed by the law and the prophets" needs some careful consideration. In what sense could the law and the prophets witness the righteousness of God, apart from law keeping? Verse 20 explains that. The law cannot produce the righteousness it demands. In fact, all the moral law could do was condemn people for failing to keep it. However, the ceremonial law involved the mercy seat, on which the blood of the innocent animals was applied. That blood covered sin until the real sacrifice that took sin away was made. If people were to have the righteousness of God, they would need to have it by a means outside the law.

[k] In the passages from 3:19 through 3:28, Paul clearly states the gospel. Here we see something that had never been done before, nor will ever be done again, at a trial scene. The Judge (who is actually the Creator)

steps down from the bench and takes the penalty for the broken law. God judicially declares righteous the one who admits to guilt and trusts in Jesus Christ and His work of redemption on the cross. This is an imputed righteousness. Note the summary of the sequence of events:

- Verse 19 declares all men guilty.

- Verse 20 declares that it's impossible by religious effort, moral culture, or priestly ceremonies to obtain a righteousness God will accept.

- Verse 21 reveals that now, with the advent of the dispensation of grace, the righteousness of God, by which every man, woman. and child needs to stand accepted of God, is available without personal merit.

- Verse 22 states that the righteousness of God everyone needs to have eternal life is available to everyone by means of the work Jesus Christ performed on the cross in the sacrifice of Himself. Such righteousness is applied to ever one who believes (cf. 2 Corinthians 5:21).

- Verses 23–24 state that there is no difference (between the Jews and Greeks of v. 9) in two ways.

  1. For all (Jews and Gentiles) have sinned and come short of the glory of God.

  2. All can be justified freely (1) by His grace and (2) through the redemption in Christ Jesus.

Verse 25 is the pivotal verse of the whole Bible. It points to the blood our Savior shed on the cross as the propitiation (i.e., the fully satisfying payment) through faith on the part of those who are justified. It declares further how God could be righteous in remitting sins that were committed by people living in the past dispensations but were covered by the blood of bulls and goats (cf. Hebrews 10:4).

Verse 26 is God's declaration that today (i.e., at this time) God, because of Christ's work of redemption, can be a just God and at the same time justify the one who trusts in Jesus.

[l] The righteousness of God in verses 21–22 is the righteousness of God stated in Romans 1:16–17 as the righteousness of God revealed in the gospel of Christ.

[m] The righteousness of God is made available to all by "the faith of Jesus Christ." This is faith that belongs to Jesus Christ. It is His faithfulness on the cross to endure the just punishment for our sins that makes the righteousness of God available without law keeping. We are justified by faith, but our faith has to have an object. The object of our faith is the faithfulness of Christ. Thus, the apostle states that "therein is the righteousness of God revealed from faith to faith (Romans 1:17) and that "a man is not justified by the works of the law, but by the faith of Jesus Christ, even we have believed in Jesus Christ" (Galatians 2:16). "But the scripture hath concluded all under sin, that the promise by faith of Jesus Christ might be given to them that believe" (Galatians 3:22). Paul's desire is that he might "be found in him, not having mine own righteousness, which is of the law, but that which is through the faith of Christ, the righteousness which is of God by faith" (Philippians 3:9).

[n] The righteousness of God without the law is here (v. 22) said to be "unto all and upon all that believe." "Unto all" speaks of the unlimited provision of that righteousness of God without the law. The "upon all that believe" speaks to the limited application of that righteousness of God. Every person on earth today can come to the righteousness of God and can have it credited to his or her spiritual bank account by faith. Though it is available

to everyone, the only ones who are justified (i.e., declared righteous) are those who believe Christ's shed blood is the fully satisfying payment for his or her sins.

[o] The statement "there is no differences" in verse 22 raises a question. No difference between whom? To answer that question, we go back to verse 9, where Paul asks a rhetorical question. "Are we [Jews] better than they [Gentiles]?" There is no difference between Jews and Gentiles today in two respects:

1. All (Jews and Gentiles) have sinned and come short of the glory of God. No one qualifies for eternal life on the basis of Romans 2:5–7, the "righteous judgment of God; Who will render to every man according to his deeds: To them who by patient continuance in well doing seek for glory and honour and immortality, eternal life."

2. All (Jews or Gentile) can be "justified freely by his grace through the redemption that is in Christ Jesus."

The Verdict, the Sentence, and the Conclusion

23 For all have sinned, and come short of the glory of God; 24 Being justified[p] freely by[q] his grace through the redemption[r] that is in Christ Jesus: 25 Whom God hath set[t] forth to be a propitiation through faith in his blood, to declare[v] his righteousness for the remission of sins that are past, through the forbearance of God; 26 To declare, I say, at this time his righteousness: that he might be just, and the justifier of him which believeth in Jesus. 27 Where is boasting then? It is excluded. By what law? of works? Nay: but by the law of faith. 28 Therefore we conclude that a man is justified by faith[u] without the deeds of the law. 29 Is he the God of the Jews only? is he not also of the Gentiles? Yes, of the Gentiles also: 30 Seeing it is one God, which shall justify the circumcision by faith, and uncircumcision through faith. 31 Do we then make void the law through faith? God forbid: yea, we establish the law. (Romans 3:23–31)

[p] The believer today is "justified freely." The word translated "freely" here has the idea of "without a cause" and is translated so in John 15:25, where we read of Christ, "They hated me without a cause." There was no just cause for anyone to hate our Lord, but they did hate Him unjustly. God had no cause to justify believers, but He does so by grace.

[q] Being justified by grace means it is only by the unmerited favor of God that anyone is justified today. The word grace has the idea of "delight." God delights in saving sinners.

[r] Justification today is through the redemption in Christ Jesus. The word for "redemption" here carries the idea of setting one free from bondage by the payment of a price.

[s] The summary of justification today then is as follows:

- The manner of justification is freely by God's grace.
- "By grace" speaks of the basis of justification.
- Through the redemption that is in Christ Jesus is the means of justification.

[t] God set Christ forth to be the propitiation through faith in His blood. The word translated "propitiation" is translated "mercy seat" in Hebrews 9:5. It has the idea of a fully satisfying payment. The blood applied to the

mercy seat in the Old Testament enabled God to remit sins of the Old Testament saints because the Father had faith in the coming shed blood of His Son. It is the blood of Jesus Christ that really gets the job done.

[u] The believer's faith is found here in verse 28, while our Savior's faith (faithfulness) is found in verse 22. The believer's faith must have an object. The object of the believer's faith is Christ's blood.

[v] God declared two things when He set Christ forth as the fully satisfying payment for sin. First, He declared His righteousness for the remission of sins that are passed through the forbearance of God. Second, He declared His righteousness that He would be both just and also the justifier of sinners. The sins that "are past" here are those committed in Old Testament times before the truth of what the cross accomplished was revealed. This includes sins committed under the old covenant "that by means of death, for the redemption of the transgressions that were under the first testament, they which are called might receive the promise of eternal inheritance" (Hebrews 9:15). "It is not possible that the blood of bulls and of goats should take away sins" (Hebrews 10:4). Therefore, God's justice demanded that the blood of the redeemer be shed to truly take away the sin. God couldn't overlook sin; His justice demanded that the account be settled.

It should be noted that every Old Testament saint could identify a blood sacrifice that remitted his or her sins. For Adam and Eve, it was the blood shed by the animals that provided the clothing to cover their nakedness. For Abel it was the sacrifice he brought. God remitted their sins on the basis of the Father's faith in the coming shed blood of Jesus Christ, the Son.

The World on Trial

In the special note to the reader on page 18, we drew attention to the fact that there is what appears to be a trial going on in chapters 1–3. Indeed there is. The apostle Paul, as the apostle of the Gentiles through whom our Lord revealed the truth for the dispensation of grace, is there presenting the gospel of Christ so as to see lost people become saved and rejoice to have their sins forgiven. But before people can become saved, they must first come to the point in life where they see their lost condition. Therefore, the apostle seeks to bring all people to the point of conviction for their sins and their need of the Savior.

By now we trust that you were able to identify the players in this scene. Let's start with the prosecuting attorney, who turns out to be Paul, the apostle of the Gentiles, who wrote this epistle. However, before he could be the apostle of the Gentiles, he had to become the guilty party himself. He refers to himself as the chief of sinners in 1 Timothy 1:12–17. He says he was before a blasphemer. He had actually committed what our Lord designated as an unpardonable sin in Matthew 12:32, in that he blasphemed the Holy Ghost by rejecting the witness of the Holy Ghost through the Twelve at Pentecost. Yet he was forgiven.

How could one who had committed an unforgivable sin be forgiven? Our Lord did forgive Paul and saved him by introducing a new dispensation, in which there was no unpardonable sin. Not only was Paul forgiven, but the Lord chose him to be the revealer of the dispensation of grace (Eph. 3:2) and the apostle of the Gentiles (Romans 11:25). It is as the apostle of the Gentiles that Paul sought to bring the whole world in guilty before God so God could have mercy on all by granting eternal life to everyone who believes.

The apostle brings an indictment against three different defendants who represent all humanity.

- The first defendant is found in Romans 1:13–32. We can call him "the man of the world." He represents the bulk of the Gentiles masses, in whose life God has no welcome place. He is often referred to as the "heathen." That makes us think of the infamous pygmy in Africa. That term heathen comes short of describing him. He might be better described as "the man of the world." He is sometimes referred to as "Joe six-pack." He is just a member of the amorphous masses of humanity, who see no real purpose to life than to simply live it and enjoy it for what it is without giving serious thought to there being a purposeful Creator. He is the product of the world system, in which God has no welcome place.

- The second defendant is described in Romans 2:1–16. We will call him the "moralist." He is more educated and sophisticated than the man of the world. He looks on the man of the world and judges him as "uncouth." He has a well-developed system of values and ethics, which are moral and give him purpose in life. However, his system of values doesn't originate in the Bible but rather comes from the philosophies and traditions of men.

- The third defendant brought into the courtroom of divine justice is the Jew in Romans 2:18–23, who represents the "religionist" of our day. He claims to have superior scruples because of his observance of his religious convictions. The religionist has a tradition he holds to and hopes will give him eternal life.

The charges brought against the defendants are that (1) man's character is sinful by nature and by choice (10–12) and that (2) man's conduct is sinful in thought, word, and deed (3:12–18).

The apostle seeks to bring conviction on each of these representative citizens of planet earth by calling four different witnesses. Each of these witnesses speaks to address one or more of the defendants.

- The first witness called is creation (Romans 1:20). This witness is primarily against the man of the world, who rejects the witness of creation that there is a God, to whom he must be accountable.

- The second witness is conscience (Romans 2:14 –15). Conscience does to the moralist what the law does to the Jew (the religionist of our day). In other words, it convicts of sin.

- The third witness called is the Law of Moses, which witnesses against the Jew (who represents the religionist). He rests on his ability to make himself righteous enough to save himself by adhering to his tradition and creed.

- There is one more witness we might add, that being the gospel (Romans 2:16). This witness says God will one day judge the secrets of men by Jesus Christ according to what Paul calls "my gospel."

The judge in this trial is our Lord Jesus Christ, who will one day judge the world according to Paul's gospel. He is the only one who is fit to judge because He is not only the Creator God (John 1:1–4) but also a man (the only man) who lived a perfect, sinless life (John 5:22). He alone has power to judge righteously. He alone has power to carry out the sentence (Romans 3:4–6).

The verdict issued from the bench here is that all are guilty (Romans 3:19–20) on a fourteen-count indictment (Romans 3:10–18). There is none righteous. There are none qualified in their own right to be in God's eternal kingdom.

The sentence: There is glory and honor that will be given to those who are vindicated and a sentence meted out to those who fail to pass the muster at this trial. That is given in Romans 2:7–10. "To them who by patient continuance in well doing seek for glory and honour and immortality, eternal life: But unto them that are contentious, and do not obey the truth, but obey unrighteousness, indignation and wrath, Tribulation and anguish, upon every soul of man that doeth evil, of the Jew first, and also of the Gentile; But glory, honour, and peace, to every man that worketh good, to the Jew first, and also to the Gentile." Indignation and wrath describe God's attitude toward sin, while tribulation and anguish describe the results of His attitude toward sin.

Now we go back to the judge. He is the judge because He is the Creator, and He is both God and man in one person. He lived a perfect human life for thirty-three years on this earth and was tempted in all points as we are, but He never sinned. Then at the age of thirty-three He surrendered the only perfect life ever lived. He did that to be the propitiation for the sins of all people. The judge steps down from the bench to take the sentence for every one of the defendants who will acknowledge his or her guilt. Romans 3:21–25 is the most blessed and exciting passage in all the Word of God. The righteousness of God everyone needs to enter the presence of God, but which no one has in his or her own right, is now available to everyone as a gift of God's grace. There is an unlimited provision of that righteousness in that it is unto all. However, there is a limited application of it. It is upon only them who believe.

Study Questions on Chapter 3

1. God is obviously still addressing the Jew in verse 1. At what point in history did God give up on the Gentiles?

2. What did God do following His giving up on the Gentile nations?

3. What is the faith of God in verse 3?

4. What Old Testament passage is quoted in verse 4? Could anyone judge God?

5. Write the truth of verses 5 through 8 in your own words.

6. Is who better than who in verse 9?

7. Verses 10 through 18 are quotes from the O T to bring conviction to the Jew. List the O T verses.

8. Who was under Law in verse 19? How then can Paul say that "every mouth might be stopped and all the world guilty before God"?

9. What great lesson (vs. 20) should man have learned from Israel having been under Law?

10. Verse 21 says that now the righteousness of God without the law is manifest. How is it manifest?

11. How is the righteousness of God without the law being witnessed by the law?

12. In what sense is the righteousness of God available to us by the faith of Jesus Christ in vs. 23?

13. The righteousness of God by the faith of Jesus Christ is available to how many in verse 22? This speaks of unlimited _____. Though that righteousness of God is available to all (i.e. unto all) it is only

upon who? This speaks of a limited _____.

14. How many have sinned and come short of the glory of God?

15. To be justified is to be reckoned righteous. How according to verse 24 are people justified today?

16. What is a propitiation? Who is that propitiation in verse 25 that God set forth? Whose sins are those sins that are past? What does the forbearance of God mean in verse 25?

17. Whose sins are in view in verse 26? When is the time denoted by the term "at this time"?

18. How is it that God can now be just and at the same time the justifier of him who believes in Jesus?

19. Why is there no room for boasting in verse 27?

20. What is the conclusion of Paul's argument in the first three chapters?

CHAPTER 4

IMPUTED RIGHTEOUSNESS

1 What shall we say[a] then that Abraham[b] our father, as pertaining to the flesh, hath found? 2 For if Abraham were justified[c] by works, he hath whereof to glory; but not before God. (Romans 4:1–2)

[a] Here is an overview of the chapter: Paul made the most astounding statement of scripture in Romans 3:21 (i.e., that now the righteousness of God without the law is manifested and that this principle is witnessed by the law and the prophets). Paul begins to illustrate this truth using two Old Testament examples: Abraham (4:1–5), the father of the Jewish people; and David (4:4–8), the progenitor of the lineage of kings leading to Israel's Messiah. Both men were ungodly by nature. Both had righteousness reckoned to them in spite of the fact that they didn't deserve it. Therefore, they are outstanding examples of the truth of Romans 4:5. "But to him that worketh not, but believeth on him that justifieth the ungodly, his faith is counted for righteousness." Both men believed God and made Him their salvation.

[b] "Abraham our father" has to be understood in light of the words that follow "as pertaining to the flesh." Here the reference is apparently to Abraham as the father of the Jewish people. Elsewhere in Paul's epistles (e.g., v. 11 of this chapter and Galatians 3:7–29), Abraham is the father of all believers, whether Jews or Gentiles. The point Paul makes is that the father of the Hebrew people was justified by faith apart from works.

[c] If Abraham had been justified by works, he would have had something to boast about (i.e., he would have boasted about the works he did that justified himself). Abraham had nothing to boast about before God because all Abraham did was trust God. "Abraham believed God and it [his act of believing] was counted to him for righteousness."

3 For what saith the scripture? Abraham believed God, and it[d] was counted[e] unto him for righteousness. 4 Now to him that worketh is the reward not reckoned[f] of grace, but of debt. 5 But to him that worketh[g] not, but believeth on him that justifieth[h] the ungodly, his faith is counted for righteousness. 6 Even as David also describeth the blessedness of the man, unto whom God imputeth righteousness without works, 7 Saying, Blessed are they whose iniquities are forgiven, and whose sins are covered. 8 Blessed is the man to whom the Lord will not impute sin. (Romans 4:3–8)

[d] What was "it" that was counted unto Abraham for righteousness? Abraham's act of believing the promise of Genesis 15:4–6 was what enabled God to reach and save him. The thrust of this passage is that when God sees faith in what He said, He imputes righteousness to the one who believes.

[e] Romans 4:2–5 appears to contradict James 2:20–24, where we read, "But wilt thou know, O vain man, that faith without works is dead? Was not Abraham our father justified by works, when he had offered Isaac his son upon the altar? Seest thou how faith wrought with his works, and by works was faith made perfect? And the

scripture was fulfilled which saith, Abraham believed God, and it was imputed unto him for righteousness: and he was called the Friend of God. Ye see then how that by works a man is justified, and not by faith only."

Here, as in so many other places where there appears to some to be contradictions in scripture, the solution to the perplexing contrast is found in 2 Timothy 2:15, "rightly dividing the word of truth." Before looking at the differences, we must first note the similarities. In both passages, Abraham was justified by God through his faith, through his act of believing. Works, in and of themselves, never did or could save anyone. In any dispensation, people were reckoned righteous by believing what God had said to them and acting accordingly. Faith always approaches God in God's way and on His terms. The case of Cain and Abel illustrates this truth. Humanly speaking, Cain brought a more attractive sacrifice. However, it wasn't the sacrifice God had asked for (Genesis 4:5).

When God Said	**Faith Responded By**
Bring a blood sacrifice.	Bringing a blood sacrifice (Abel)
Build an ark.	Building an ark (Noah)
Obey the Law of Moses.	Seeking to keep it
Repent and be baptized for the remission of sins (Luke 7:30).	Repenting and being baptized
But now the righteousness of God without the law is manifested."	Simply believing and accepting righteousness of God, which is in Jesus Christ by faith apart from works.

And

| "To him that worketh not but believed on him that justifieth the ungodly, his faith is counted for him for righteousness." | Simply believing it |

Now let's look at the differences between these few verses.

Romans 4:3–5	**James 2:21–24**
The writer is Paul.	The writer is James.
Paul addresses the Gentiles after the fall of Israel (Romans 11:11).	James addresses believing Jews who were looking toward the tribulation (James 1:1)
Paul deals with Abram before he was circumcised.	James deals with Abraham after he was circumcised.
Paul quotes from Genesis 15:5. Paul cites belief of a promise	James cites Genesis 22:1–8. James cites a severe test

(Genesis 15:4–6).   (Genesis 22:16–18).

We note here that in Israel's program works were required as a manifestation of faith. Under grace, it's faith alone without works that justifies.

[f] The reward for the one who works for salvation is reckoned out of debt. God wouldn't be beholding to someone who works so God owed him or her eternal life. Under Israel's program, salvation was given in response to faith, but it was (and will be again during the tribulation period) a faith demonstrated by works. In and of themselves, works under the law never did or could save a person, but they were required as a manifestation of faith.

[g] If one is justified without working for it but by simply believing God, the reward isn't reckoned of debt but rather of grace. Today in the dispensation of the grace of God, we are justified by pure grace through faith alone apart from any works when we trust what our Savior accomplished for us by His sacrificial death, burial, and resurrection. Under Israel's program, righteousness was imputed in response to faith, but it was a faith that was asked to work, and therefore that faith did work (cf. James 2:22–25). Today the faith that saves is one that doesn't work but rather simply believes. Works in the dispensation of grace are an expression of appreciation for the righteousness imputed to the believer's account (Ephesians 2:10). Today works follow justification. In Israel's program, works were a factor in justification.

[h] What is the faith that saves today? It believes God will justify the ungodly if the ungodly will just recognize his or her lost state and realize that "Christ died for the ungodly" (Romans 5:6). An ungodly person is one who has no reverence or place for God is his or her life. The only qualification for being a candidate for salvation is to be an ungodly person. A person can be religious and lost, as every religious person is if he or she has never trusted the Savior. However, before that religious person can get saved, he or she must recognize that he or she is in fact an ungodly person and place himself or herself at the mercy of God's grace for salvation.

[i] Here Paul quotes Psalm 32:1–2, where we find David, after confessing his sin with Bathsheba and the murder of Uriah, rejoicing in having been forgiven for the iniquity of his "sin" in Psalm 32:5.

> Blessed is he whose transgression is forgiven, whose sin is covered. Blessed is the man unto whom the LORD imputeth not iniquity, and in whose spirit there is no guile. When I kept silence, my bones waxed old through my roaring all the day long. For day and night thy hand was heavy upon me: my moisture is turned into the drought of summer. Selah. I acknowledge my sin unto thee, and mine iniquity have I not hid. I said, I will confess my transgressions unto the LORD; and thou forgavest the iniquity of my sin. Selah. (Psalm 32:1–5)

The account of David's repentance is documented in 2 Samuel 12:1–14. Nathan the prophet confronted and charged David, "Thou hast killed Uriah the Hittite with the sword, and hast taken his wife to be thy wife, and hast slain him with the sword of the children of Ammon." This account should be read in its entirety to understand the conviction that came on David. Then in Psalm 51 we see David's repentant heart. "For I acknowledge my transgressions: and my sin is ever before me. Against thee, thee only, have I sinned, and done this evil in thy sight: that thou mightest be justified when thou speakest, and be clear when thou judgest" (Psalm 51:3–4). While in

Psalm 32, David rejoiced to know his iniquity was forgiven; in Psalm 51 we see that David was concerned about his eternal destiny as a result of sin. "Cast me not away from thy presence; and take not thy Holy Spirit from me. Restore unto me the joy of thy salvation; and uphold me with thy free spirit … Deliver me from bloodguiltiness, O God, thou God of my salvation: and my tongue shall sing aloud of thy righteousness" (Psalm 51:11–12, 14). The repentant heart God desires is seen is Psalm 51:17. "The sacrifices of God are a broken spirit: a broken and a contrite heart, O God, thou wilt not despise."

Paul's point here is that even under law (as David was), God could impute righteousness to a repentant heart in spite of the grossest of sin. The imputed righteousness David enjoyed is described in Ezekiel 18:20–28, where we see God dealing with the covenant people of Israel. Being born under the covenant God gave Israel, David was reckoned righteous until he committed this gross immorality and wickedness. Had David not repented, he would have been "cut off" from God's people. But David's repentance brought him back into a state of being forgiven and righteous (Ezekiel 18:21–22). But that was what life was like under the law. Though David found forgiveness, he didn't know security as we know it today under grace.

> [9] Cometh this blessedness[j] then upon the circumcision only, or upon the uncircumcision also? for we say that faith was reckoned to Abraham for righteousness. (Romans 4:9)

[j] The blessedness verse 9 speaks of is the blessedness of the man to whom the Lord imputes righteousness without works and to whom the Lord won't impute sin. This verse speaks of security. David, being a man under law and under the conditions of Ezekiel 18, had a conditional security. He was secure as long as he abode under the conditions of the covenant God gave Israel. We today enjoy the blessedness of not having our transgressions imputed to us. However, unlike David, we have unconditional security because our justification isn't according to a conditional covenant but according to an eternal purpose God made in Himself (Ephesians 1:9) that He promised before the world began (Titus 1:2). Abraham was reckoned righteous by faith before he was circumcised so he could be the father of all who believe though they be not circumcised (Galatians 3:6–10).

> [10] How was it then reckoned? when he was[k] in circumcision, or in uncircumcision? Not in circumcision, but in uncircumcision. [11] And he received the sign of circumcision, a seal of the righteousness of the faith which he had yet being uncircumcised: that he might be[l] the father of all them that believe, though they be not circumcised; that righteousness might be imputed unto them also: [12] And the father of circumcision to them who are not of the circumcision only, but who also walk in the steps of that faith of our father Abraham, which he had being yet uncircumcised. (Romans 4:10–12)

[k] Abraham was reckoned righteous before he was circumcised. Therefore, righteousness isn't something imputed only to a circumcised person. Circumcision, according to this verse, was given to Abraham as a sign of the righteousness he acquired by faith before he was circumcised. Here in Romans is the first place where righteousness is said to be imputed to a person by faith apart from works, since Abraham was reckoned righteous by faith in Genesis 12.

[l] Abraham is the father of all who believe in spite of the fact that they weren't circumcised. The fatherhood of Abraham is centered in his faith. It was his faith that enabled God to reckon him righteous when God had given up on the Gentile nations in Genesis 11, as recorded in Romans 1:24, 26, and 28. Because of his faith, Abraham became the progenitor of the seed line promised in Genesis 3:15. That seed line led to our Lord Jesus Christ.

It is in Christ that anyone will have eternal life. In that sense, as the physical father of our Lord Jesus Christ, Abraham is the father of all who believe. He is the father of those who believe and are reckoned righteous being uncircumcised. Everyone who is justified before God is justified in Christ (Romans 3:23–26; see Galatians 3:6–9). Verse 12 makes it clear that just being a physical descendent of Abraham and being circumcised weren't enough to render a Jew a child of Abraham. They each must have the faith Abraham had. See Romans 2:28 and Philippians 3:3.

13 For the promise, that he should be[m] the heir of the world, was not to Abraham, or to his seed, through the law, but through the righteousness of faith. (Romans 4:13)

[m] Abraham became the heir of the world through the righteousness of faith. It is significant that God gave up the Gentiles (Romans 1:24, 26, 28; Genesis 11) before Abraham was called. By faith Abraham was reckoned righteous and given the promise of the land of Palestine and eternal life along with the promise that in his seed would all nations be blessed. By faith Abraham in effect inherited the earth. See Galatians 3:18 and note [u] (below).

¹⁴ For if they which are of the law be heirs, faith is[n] made void, and the promise made of none effect: ¹⁵ Because the law worketh[o] wrath: for where no law is, there is[p] no transgression. (Romans 4:14–15)

[n] Who are "they which are of the law"? These are those who are trusting in their ability to be righteous by law keeping. Though God did have Israel under law, the works of the law weren't per se what justified them but rather their faith. The faith that saved those who under law was faith in the blood sacrifice, which covered their sin. By faith they then followed the law as best they could. The Jews under the law also have as an object of their faith the promise given to his father, Abraham. When God had a covenant in place for a people, that covenant was the object of saving faith. Israel was under both the covenant with Abraham and the Mosaic covenant.

[o] The law in and of itself couldn't save anyone. All it could do was condemn the one who broke it. In that sense it worked wrath from God against sin. It was only the blood-sprinkled mercy seat that abated the wrath of God against sin for those under the law (see note [v]).

[p] There is no transgression when there is no law to transgress. But the law was given for a purpose. The purpose wasn't to provide a means of righteousness by works. Rather, it was given to point sin out as sin. As the means of pointing out sin, it eventually worked (produced) wrath against sin. The law thus condemns the sinner.

- "It was added because of transgressions" (Galatians 3:19).
- "That every mouth may be stopped, and all the world may become guilty before God" (Romans 3:19).
- "The law entered, that the offence might abound" (Romans 5:20).
- "That sin by the commandment might become exceeding sinful" (Romans 7:13).
- The law is said to be "against us" and "contrary to us" (Colossians 2:14).
- "As many as are of the works of the law are under the curse" (Galatians 3:10).
- The law is "the ministration of condemnation" (2 Corinthians 3:9),
- "the ministration of death" (2 Corinthians 3:7).
- The sting of death is sin, but the strength of sin is the law (1 Corinthians 15:56).

Therefore, It Is by Faith That It Might Be by Grace

> [16] Therefore it is of faith, that it might be by[q] grace; to the end the promise[r] might be sure[s] to all[t] the seed; not to that only which is of the law, but to that also which is of the faith[u] of Abraham; who is the father[v] of us all, [17] (As it is written, I have made thee a father of many nations,) before him whom he believed, even God, who quickeneth the dead, and calleth those things which be not as though they were. [18] Who against hope believed in hope, that he might become the father of many nations, according to that which was spoken, So shall thy seed be. [19]And being not weak[w] in faith, he considered not his own body now dead, when he was about an hundred years old, neither yet the deadness of Sara's womb: [20] He staggered not at the promise of God through unbelief; but was strong in faith, giving glory[y] to God; [21] And being fully persuaded that, what he had promised, he was able also to perform. [22] And therefore it was imputed to him for righteousness. [23] Now it was not written[x] for his sake alone, that it was imputed to him; [24] But for us also, to whom it shall be imputed, if we believe on him that raised up Jesus our Lord from the dead; [25] Who was delivered for our offences, and was raised again for our justification. (Romans 4:16–25)

[q] Because the law couldn't impart righteousness but rather could only condemn, righteousness has to be of faith (on the faith principle) by means of grace.

[r] What is the promise? The promise is righteousness, the subject of Paul's treatise, beginning in verse 2.

[s] The only way the promise could be sure to anyone is if the promise is bestowed by grace. If we would have to do so much as lift our hands, we would not know whether we did it right. "Therefore, it is of faith, that it might be by grace."

[t] Who are the seed? The seed are people of every dispensation who come to God in faith. It includes the circumcision believers and those who believe God's Word to them though they aren't circumcised (vv. 11–12).

[u] What is the faith of Abraham in verse 16? In Genesis 12:1–5, Abraham was given the promise of the following:

1. A land ("unto a land that I will shew thee")
2. A nation ("And I will make of thee a great nation")
3. A blessing ("and I will bless thee")
4. A great name ("and make thy name great")
5. He would be a blessing ("and thou shalt be a blessing").
6. He would be protected or avenged ("And I will bless them that bless thee, and curse him that curseth thee").
7. All families of the earth would be blessed in him ("And in thee shall all families of the earth be blessed").

None of this was promised contingent on Abraham's performance. Rather, it was promised on the basis of grace. God promised it on the grace principle. In Genesis 15:1–6, Abraham had grown old and was still childless. God told him he would have a seed "out of thine own bowels." God also told him his seed would be as innumerable as the stars of heaven. Abraham then believed God, "and he counted it to him for righteousness." Abraham produced no works for that righteousness. All he did was believe that God would do what to the natural man would seem impossible.

[v] Abraham's faith (v. 16) is the same faith all believers have, whether they are of the circumcision or of the uncircumcision. Therefore, he is the father of all who approach God in faith. In Galatians 4:26–27, we find that Sarah represents Jerusalem, which is above and free. If Abraham represents faith, Sarah represents grace. Grace is what gives life. A mother gives life. Therefore, grace is presented here figuratively in Galatians 4:26 as a mother.

Abraham's faith is the faith of the circumcision believers who aren't just physical descendants of Abraham but also come to God in faith. The circumcision believer knows it's not the physical ritual of circumcision that saves but the faith of Christ. When the circumcision believer is under the law, he or she does the law out of faith, knowing it is not his or her works per se that justifies, but rather it is the faith of the believer. For the uncircumcision of this present dispensation, it is again the faith of the believer that justifies … without works.

[w] In verses 19–21, Paul details the faith of Abraham. We can understand the faith of Abraham by going back to Genesis, where we see the barren Sarah and the promise of God that Abraham would have a son. We find that Abraham believed God could quicken the dead and call things that be not as though they were. We need to go back to Genesis to see that faith of Abraham in action.

In Genesis 15:4–6, God promised Abraham a seed out of his own bowels.

In Genesis 16:1–4, Abraham and Sarah decided they needed to help God keep His promise. Sarah gave Abraham her maid, the Egyptian slave girl, Hagar. Hagar conceived and bare Ishmael to Abraham. Ishmael was born as a result of Abraham's fleshly strength. God rejected what they could do in the flesh (Galatians 4:30). The son of the slave girl was a slave, but the son of the free woman was free (Galatians 4:22–31).

In Genesis 17:15, Abraham was promised a son through Sarah when he was ninety-nine and Sarah was eighty-nine. Abraham fell on his face and laughed for joy (v. 17). Isaac was named before birth (v. 21).

In Genesis 18:10, God told Abraham that Sarah would conceive. She was ninety years of age. Sarah laughed in unbelief (vv. 12, 15).

In Genesis 21: 1–7, the promised son, Isaac, was born. Abraham named the child "Isaac," meaning "laughter." They both laughed for joy (vv. 6–7).

[x] The account of the faith of Abraham (v. 24) and the birth of Isaac weren't written for Abraham but for us when we believe God would give life to our dead spirits when we trust in Christ's work of redemption on the cross. We were as spiritually dead when we were saved as Sarah's womb was when she conceived. The same faith Abraham had, being fully persuaded that what God promised He would perform, is the faith a believer has when he or she believes the promise that Christ was delivered for our offences and rose again for our justification. His death was the payment for our sins; his resurrection was the receipt that says in effect "Paid in full"

[y] "It is no glory to me if I believe God: rather my faith glorifies him. The hand receives food and the body is strengthened—by the food, not by the hand," said C. R. Stam. (a popular Christian author of the twentieth century).

Study Questions on Chapter 4

1. Paul talks about Abraham our father in verse 1. Whose father was he? Was he your father?

2. Was Abraham justified by works?

3. Paul and James both talk about Abraham being justified. Paul says that he was justified by faith without works. James says that he was justified by faith that was demonstrated by works. Does Romans 4:3 contradict James 2:21 & 22? Explain.

4. What was it about Abraham that enabled God to reckon him righteous?

5. Does Roans 4:5 contradict James 2: 21 and 22? Explain.

6. If one does not work but is rewarded, is the reward of works or grace?

7. According to verse 5, what kind of people does God justify? How can He do that?

8. How was David different from Abraham in regard to justification?

9. Was Abraham circumcised or uncircumcised at the time in Genesis 12 when God reckoned him righteous? Why is that significant regarding Paul's point in Romans regarding justification?

10. According to verse 11, what was Abraham's circumcision a sign of?

11. According to verse 11, how can Abraham be the father of all who believe?

12. According to verse 13, how can Abraham be the heir of the world?

13. What does the law work?

14. Why according to verse 16 is salvation by faith and not by works?

15. What does the statement in verse 17 that God "quickeneth the dead" have to do with Abraham and his salvation?

16. Verse 18 speaks of Abraham being the father of many nations. Can you name some of them?

17. What does it mean in verse 18 that Abraham "against hope believed in hope..."?

18. In what sense were Abraham's and Sarah's bodies dead?

19. According to verse 21, what was God able to perform? Can you claim such a promise today?

20. Abraham being reckoned righteous by faith was for whose sake according to verse 24?

Chapter 5

RESULTS OF BEING JUSTIFIED BY FAITH

¹ Therefore[a] being justified[b] by [c] faith, we have[d] peace with God through our Lord Jesus Christ: ² By whom also we have access[e] by faith into this grace[f] wherein we stand, and rejoice[g] in hope of the glory[h] of God. ³ And not only so, but we glory[i] in tribulations also: knowing that tribulation worketh[j] patience; ⁴ And patience[k], experience[l]; and experience, hope: ⁵ And hope maketh[m] not ashamed; because the love of God is shed[n] abroad in our hearts by[o] the Holy Ghost which is given unto us. (Romans 5:1–5)

[a] The "therefore" of verse 1 takes us back to the closing verse of chapter 4. "But for us also, to whom it [righteousness] shall be imputed, if we believe on him that raised up Jesus our Lord from the dead; Who was delivered for our offenses, and was raised again for our justification."

[b] In the first eleven verses of chapter 5, Paul lists seven results of being justified by faith. They are the following:

1. We have peace with God through our Lord Jesus Christ.
2. We have access by faith into this grace wherein we stand.
3. We rejoice in the hope of the glory of God.
4. We glory in tribulations.
5. The love of God is shed abroad in our hearts by the Holy Ghost.
6. We shall be saved from wrath through Christ.
7. We have now received the atonement.

These seven results involve two basic benefits:

1. The joy of having peace with God
2. The joy of being disciplined by the trials of life as the Holy Ghost works in our lives to produce the love of God in our hearts

[c] The believer has been justified upon believing. Believers today in the dispensation of grace have salvation from the debt penalty of sin the moment they trust Jesus Christ's work of redemption on their behalf. This process of being justified involves God imputing the "righteousness of God" (Romans 1:17) to "all them that believe" (Romans 3:22). This all hinges on "the faith of Jesus Christ" (Romans 3:22). Paul alone among the apostles makes the conclusion of Romans 3:28. "Therefore we conclude that a man is justified by faith without the deeds of the law." Israelites under law were justified according to the terms of Ezekiel 18:20–24 (i.e., they were reckoned righteous only as they adhered to and embraced the covenant God had made with their fathers).

Ezekiel described the justification the law could provide. The law required faith that would perform and endure, but Paul describes a different process for justification. "Be it known unto you therefore, men and brethren, that through this man is preached unto you the forgiveness of sins: And by him all that believe are justified from all things, from which ye could not be justified by the law of Moses" (Acts 13:38–39). Paul described this righteousness in Philippians 3:9–10. "Not having mine own righteousness, which is of the law, but that which is through the faith of Christ, the righteousness which is of God by faith."

[d] Peace with God is the first and primary result of having been justified by faith. Paul starts his epistle to the Romans by saying, "To all that be in Rome, beloved of God, called to be saints: Grace to you and peace from God our Father, and the Lord Jesus Christ" (1:7). Here is divine peace, extended to the capital city of the Gentile world system that stood against God and His prophetic program to establish a kingdom upon the earth. Peace (along with righteousness and joy) is a characteristic of the kingdom of God (Romans 14:17). God would have believers "filled with joy and peace" (15:13, 33). The very premise of the gospel is peace (14:17). It was so when it was preached to Israel as the gospel of the kingdom (Acts 10:36). It is particularly so today as "all things are of God, who hath reconciled us to himself by Jesus Christ, and hath given to us the ministry of reconciliation; To wit, that God was in Christ, reconciling the world unto himself, not imputing their trespasses unto them; and hath committed unto us the word of reconciliation" (2 Corinthians 5:18). Peace is an integral part of God's plan to reconcile all things to Himself. "And you, that were sometime alienated and enemies in your mind by wicked works, yet now hath he reconciled In the body of his flesh through death, to present you holy and unblameable and unreproveable in his sight" (Colossians 1:20–22). God would have peace be the heart attitude of believers with each other as well: "Let the peace of God rule in your hearts, to the which also ye are called in one body; and be ye thankful" (Colossians 3:15). "God is love" (1 John 4:8), and as such He is "the very God of peace" (1 Thessalonians 5:23).

[e] Both believing Jews and believing Gentiles have access to God the Father through Jesus Christ by the Holy Spirit (Ephesians 2:18). It is in Christ Jesus, our Lord, that we have "access with confidence by the faith of him" (Ephesians 3:12). Here in Romans 5:2 we see that we have this access by faith into this grace. In Ephesians 3:12, we have access with confidence by the faith of Him (i.e., by Christ's faithfulness). We can have faith because He is faithful. We can have confidence in access to God because Christ will ever grant us that access.

[f] We have access into this grace wherein we stand. In Corinthians 15:1. Paul speaks of "the gospel … wherein ye stand." The verb stand is in the perfect tense, meaning we took a stand in the past and have a present standing in it. The concept here is that of having taken a stand in the grace of God, and therefore we have access to God in that stand. This is a once-for-all standing in grace the believer has. There is also a standing the believer takes against the evil of our day. That standing is described in Ephesians 6:13. "Wherefore take unto you the whole armour of God, that ye may be able to withstand in the evil day, and having done all, to stand." But the once-for-all standing that gives the believer access is described in Romans 8:30–39. That is a standing of absolute security (Romans 5:2).

[g] The third result of being justified by faith is that we rejoice in the hope of the glory of God. We have, no matter what the circumstances of our life might be, the absolute assurance (that's what hope is) of an eternal home in glory. Hope has been often defined as the "confident expectation of a future blessing." Romans 8:22–24 describes that hope: "For we know that the whole creation groaneth and travaileth in pain together until now.

And not only they, but ourselves also, which have the firstfruits of the Spirit, even we ourselves groan within ourselves, waiting for the adoption, to wit, the redemption of our body. For we are saved by hope: but hope that is seen is not hope: for what a man seeth, why doth he yet hope for? But if we hope for that we see not, then do we with patience wait for it." Paul speaks of this hope in Romans 12:12 ("Rejoicing in hope") and again in Romans 15:13 ("Now the God of hope fill you with all joy and peace in believing").

[h] The future blessing we believers in the atoning work of our Savior look forward to is "the glory of God." Moses desired to see God's glory in Exodus 33:18–23. However, God told him that "there shall no man see me, and live." Mortal, sinful man cannot be in the presence of a holy and perfect God and live. Yet we who have trusted the Savior will one day stand in His presence with eternal life. This is possible because of imputed righteousness, the righteousness of God imputed to the believer. Apart from faith in the atoning work of our Savior, we might "seek for glory and honour and immortality" (Romans 2:7), but we find that we "all have sinned and come short of the glory of God" (Romans 3:23, emphasis added). Now, as believers, instead of coming short of the glory of God, we rejoice in the hope of the glory of God. Paul says in Romans 8:18, "For I reckon that the sufferings of this present time are not worthy to be compared with the glory which shall be revealed in us." What a wonderful future that is for the believer. We who once were dead in trespasses and sins now look forward to God revealing His glory in us.

[i] The fourth result of being justified by faith is that we can now look at tribulation in a different light. We know that neither tribulation nor anything else can separate us from the love of God (Romans 8:35–37). Tribulation for the believer is an honor; the saints in Acts 5:41 went "rejoicing that they were counted worthy to suffer shame for his name." Paul endured tribulation as much as any (2 Corinthians 11:23–30) and yet said, "If I must needs glory, I will glory of the things which concern mine infirmities." Paul had learned the lesson our Lord taught him, and God said, "My grace is sufficient for thee: for my strength is made perfect in weakness" (2 Corinthians 12:9–10). Paul understood that the tribulation that had come upon him was necessary if the gospel was to be communicated to others. The adversaries of the gospel will bring tribulation to bear on those who proclaim it. Such tribulation, though, "is to them an evident token of perdition, but to you of salvation, and that of God. For unto you it is given in the behalf of Christ, not only to believe on him, but also to suffer for his sake" (Philippians 28–29). Paul could say wholeheartedly, "If I be offered upon the sacrifice and service of your faith, I joy, and rejoice with you all" (Philippians 2:17).

[j] We can glory in tribulations because they do a positive work in us. The primary work the tribulation produces is the development of patience within the believer. This is the patience to wait on God for deliverance through the tribulation. God would have us to understand some things about tribulation:

2 Corinthians 4:17

"It is light."

It is but for a moment.

It works a far more exceeding eternal weight of glory.

It teaches us to focus on the things that cannot be seen.

2 Corinthians 4:8–12

Though we are troubled on every side, we need not be distressed

Though we are distressed, we need not be in despair.

Though we might be persecuted, we are not forsaken.

Though we might be cast down, we are not destroyed.

We bear with us the dying (the mortality) of the Lord Jesus so that the life (Galatians 2:20) of Jesus might be manifest in our bodies.

1 Corinthians 10:13

If any temptation comes into your life as a believer, you will be able to bear and will be able to go through it. Paul experienced such deliverances as the Lord strengthened him so he wouldn't cave in on the message committed to him (2 Timothy 4:16–18). That same deliverance is available to every believer. Patience provides experience and success in Christian living.

[k] Patience is a virtue produced by the Word of God that works in the heart of a yielded believer (Romans 15:4). "For whatsoever things were written aforetime were written for our learning, that we through patience and comfort of the scriptures might have hope." Note too that Romans 15:5 refers to God as "the God of patience and consolation." Patience is rooted in hope, the confident expectation of the glory of being one day with God in His heaven. "But if we hope for that we see not, then do we with patience wait for it" (Romans 8:25). Having such hope, any tribulation that we might endure now would be light and short. These tribulations we endure today, while things are "hidden" because of "darkness," will one day bring "praise of God" (1 Corinthians 4:5). Until then we look for God to strengthen us so we might remain faithful through the tribulation (2 Timothy 4:16–18). Patience and hope are vital parts of our Christian testimony: "Rejoicing in hope; patient in tribulation; continuing instant in prayer" (Romans 12:12).

[l] Experience of successfully living the Christian life produces hope, the confident expectation of deliverance through the tribulations. David learned this lesson when he grew through the experiences of dealing with a lion and a bear to the point that he took on Goliath, the Philistine giant who "defied the armies of the living God" (1 Samuel 17:34–37). From these experiences, he knew God would give him the needed victory. David states this principle in Psalm 27:1–3. "The LORD is my light and my salvation; whom shall I fear? The LORD is the strength of my life; of whom shall I be afraid? When the wicked, even mine enemies and my foes, came upon me to eat up my flesh, they stumbled and fell. Though an host should encamp against me, my heart shall not fear: though war should rise against me, in this will I be confident." It is interesting to note, though, that even David had to remind himself of this lesson often (Psalm 42:5). His heart desire, even in old age, was to communicate his lesson to younger generations (Psalm 71:14–24, especially v. 18).

[m] "Hope maketh not ashamed" (i.e., it does not disappoint). Israel, instead of walking by the Word of God, took refuge in the strength of their own arms and that of their old ways. As a result, Israel was indeed ashamed because their strength was directed against God (Isaiah 28:15–18). Any action taken that is contrary to the Word of God is action that will lead to shame. Often believers find themselves in a culture where they could avoid tribulation by taking a course of action contrary to the revealed will of God as it is revealed in the Word of God. But when such action is taken, an opportunity for growth is missed, and the believer is ashamed. "But Israel shall be saved in the LORD with an everlasting salvation: ye shall not be ashamed nor confounded world without end" (Isaiah 45:17–18). But those who wait on the Lord have assurance that they won't be ashamed. "And kings

shall be thy nursing fathers, and their queens thy nursing mothers: they shall bow down to thee with their face toward the earth, and lick up the dust of thy feet; and thou shalt know that I am the LORD: for they shall not be ashamed that wait for me" (Isaiah 49:23). Jeremiah 17:5–8 says,

> "Thus saith the LORD; Cursed be the man that trusteth in man, and maketh flesh his arm, and whose heart departeth from the LORD. For he shall be like the heath in the desert, and shall not see when good cometh; but shall inhabit the parched places in the wilderness, in a salt land and not inhabited. Blessed is the man that trusteth in the LORD, and whose hope the LORD is. For he shall be as a tree planted by the waters, and that spreadeth out her roots by the river, and shall not see when heat cometh, but her leaf shall be green; and shall not be careful in the year of drought, neither shall cease from yielding fruit."

Paul, when facing possible execution for his testimony, prayed, "That in nothing I shall be ashamed, but that with all boldness, as always, so now also Christ shall be magnified in my body, whether it be by life, or by death" (Philippians 1:20). Paul stated what he had learned about enduring tribulation in 2 Timothy 1:12. "For the which cause I also suffer these things: nevertheless I am not ashamed: for I know whom I have believed, and am persuaded that he is able to keep that which I have committed unto him against that day." He told the Thessalonians, "Now our Lord Jesus Christ himself, and God, even our Father, which hath loved us, and hath given us everlasting consolation and good hope through grace, Comfort your hearts, and stablish you in every good word and work" (2 Thessalonians 2:16–17).

[n] "The love of God" (v. 5) is the love a father would have for his children. That love is reciprocated in the lives of believers. "For as many as are led by the Spirit of God, they are the sons of God. For ye have not received the spirit of bondage again to fear; but ye have received the Spirit of adoption, whereby we cry, Abba, Father. The Spirit itself beareth witness with our spirit, that we are the children of God: And if children, then heirs; heirs of God, and joint-heirs with Christ; if so be that we suffer with him, that we may be also glorified together. For I reckon that the sufferings of this present time are not worthy to be compared with the glory which shall be revealed in us" (Romans 8:14–18). That love is passed on through the believer. "If any man love God, the same [i.e., the edification of others in v. 1] is known of him [i.e., that believers are known for loving edification of other people]" (1 Corinthians 8:1–3).

[o] This reference to the Holy Ghost in verse 5 is the first mention of the Holy Ghost (Holy Spirit) in Paul's epistles. We find, as we study the Pauline epistles on the subject of the ministry of the Holy Spirit, that He works differently today during the dispensation of the grace of God than He did with Israel. For Israel, the Lord Jesus Christ baptized the believers of Israel with the Holy Ghost (Matthew 3:11). Today it is "by one Spirit are we all baptized into one body, whether we be Jews or Gentiles" (1 Corinthians 12:13, emphasis added). The ministry of the Holy Spirit in Israel under the coming "new covenant" will be to supernaturally take control of believers, whereby God says, "I will put my Spirit within you, and cause you to walk in my statutes, and ye shall keep my judgments, and do them" (Ezekiel 36:25–27).

The ministry of the Holy Spirit today is different from what it will be with Israel under her new covenant. Today the Holy Spirit leads believers through the Word (Romans 8:14–17), indwells believers (Romans 8:9–11), regenerates (Titus 3:5), circumcises with a circumcision make without hands (Colossians 2:10–12), and seals (Ephesians 1:13; 4:30; 1 Corinthians 1:22), but He does not take supernatural control. Today, it is the work of the Holy Spirit to transform believers into the image of the glory of Christ (2 Corinthians 3:18) as He uses the gospel of Christ to work in the lives of yielded believers (2 Corinthians 4:1–7). The Holy Spirit does this work in believers by giving believers the "Abba Father" heart attitude of a genuine son in the family of God (Galatians 4:6; Romans 8:15), The fruit of the Spirit is then the manifestation of the love that is shed abroad by that working of the Spirit of God in the family of God (Galatians 5:22).

> [6] For when we were[p] yet without[q] strength, in due time[r] Christ died[s] for the ungodly. [7] For scarcely for a righteous[t] man will one die: yet peradventure for a good man some would even dare to die. [8] But God commendeth his love toward us, in that, while we were yet sinners, Christ died for us. [9] Much more then, being now justified[u] by his blood, we shall be saved from wrath through him. (Romans 5:6–9)

[p] There is a significant shift in the theme of Romans, beginning in 5:6. Thus far (up to v. 12), Romans has dealt with justification (Christ's work for the believer). In 5:12, we will see that the focus shifts to sanctification (Christ's work in the believer).

> 5:6—"When we were yet without strength" (emphasis added), in due time Christ died for the ungodly.

> 5:8—"While we were yet sinners" (emphasis added), Christ died for us.

> 5:10—"When we were enemies" (emphasis added), we were reconciled to God by the death of His Son.

[q] The concept of being "without strength" is portrayed well in Lamentations 1:6. "Her princes are become like harts that find no pasture, and they are gone without strength before the pursuer."

[r] "In due time Christ died for the ungodly" (v. 6). There was a time God set up that would be the pivotal point in all time. That was to be that point in time when Christ would enter His creation to accomplish redemption for the redeemed of mankind. Paul uses similar language in Galatians 4:3–5. "Even so we, when we were children, were in bondage under the elements of the world: But when the fullness of the time was come, God sent forth his Son, made of a woman, made under the law, To redeem them that were under the law, that we might receive the adoption of sons" (emphasis added).

[s] "Christ died for the ungodly" so that once believers "turned to God from idols to serve the living and true God" (1 Thessalonians 1:9), God would, by means of His grace, teach them to deny ungodliness and worldly lusts (Titus 2:12).

[t] The righteous man here in verse 7 is a man who essentially always does what is right. Paul says "scarcely" for such a man will one die. The good man is a man who does good things for people. David would be an example of a "good man," for whom one would even dare to die (2 Samuel 18:3; 23:14–17). "But God commendeth [the word means "to show forth"] his love for us in that, while we were yet sinners, Christ died for us" (1 Corinthians 15:3–4; Philippians 2:8).

> All we like sheep have gone astray; we have turned every one to his own way; and the LORD hath laid on him the iniquity of us all. (Isaiah 53:6)

> For Christ also hath once suffered for sins, the just for the unjust, that he might bring us to God, being put to death in the flesh, but quickened by the Spirit. (1 Peter 3:18)

[u] In verse 9, the phrase "being now justified" is in the passive participle, as is the phrase "being reconciled"

in verse 10. This recognizes that we are justified and reconciled because of a once-for-all act by God on the believer's behalf.

> [10] For if, when we were enemies, we were reconciled[v] to God by the death of his Son, much[w] more, being reconciled, we shall be saved[x] by his life. [11] And not only so, but we also joy[y] in God through our Lord Jesus Christ, by whom we have now received[z] the atonement. [12] Wherefore, as by one man sin entered into the world, and death by sin; and so death passed upon all men, for that all have sinned. (Romans 5:10–12)

[v] Verse 10 speaks of being reconciled to God. Now the question arises. Is this reconciliation to God speaking historically of the human race or of the individual believer? There are four different reconciliations in Paul's epistles, two of which might be applicable here. The four are the following:

1. The reconciling of the world to God (2 Corinthians 5:19) made the whole world savable.

2. The reconciling of Jews and Gentiles to God in one body (Ephesians 2:16) made the forming of the church, which is Christ's body, possible.

3. The reconciling of all things to God (Colossians 1:20) enables Christ to be preeminent in all things (Colossians 1:18), whether they be things in heaven or in earth.

4. The reconciling of individuals to God (Colossians 1:21; 2 Corinthians 5:20) made personal soul salvation possible.

Both the first and the last could be applicable here. However, because the language of verse 1, it is apparent that Paul is talking about individual reconciliation (i.e., the ones who are "justified by faith"). Christ didn't die for us when we were justified. Rather, He died for us when were "yet without strength" and "ungodly." This was the state of the Gentiles en masse before the revelation of the mystery, and it was the state of individuals (whether Jews or Gentiles) before they each came to personal faith in the work of Jesus Christ on the cross. Individually, we each (now justified people) once "walked according to the course of this world, according to the prince of the power of the air, the spirit that now worketh in the children of disobedience." (Ephesians 2:2) At that time we walked "in the lusts of our flesh, fulfilling the desires of the flesh and of the mind; and were by nature [as lost Gentiles before the dispensation of the grace of God] the children of wrath, even as others" (Ephesians 2:2–3). We were (as Gentiles) then "dead in [our] sins and the uncircumcision of [our] flesh" (Colossians 2:13). Paul reminds us in Titus 3:3 that we "were sometimes foolish, disobedient, deceived, serving diverse lusts and pleasures, living in malice and envy, hateful, and hating one another."

[w] The words "much more" in verses 9 and 10 speak of "to a greater extent." To an even greater extent than to the degree that we have been justified by Christ's shed blood, we shall be saved from the wrath through Him. So, too, to an even greater extent than to the degree that we have been reconciled to God when we were enemies, yet will we be saved by His life. In light of what we know God has already done for us in justifying us through Christ's blood and in reconciling us through His death, we can with all the more confidence affirm that we shall be saved from wrath in the future and saved by His life. Because of Christ's past work on our behalf, we are confident of future safety. Paul writes to the Thessalonians of the deliverance "from the wrath to come." There is wrath coming in the form of "the great day of his wrath" (Revelation 6:16) in the tribulation and in the

lake of fire (Revelation 19:20; 20:14). But believers have been saved from that wrath.

[x] The life of Christ in verse 10 is the resurrection life of Christ as presented in Galatians 2:20. "I am crucified with Christ: nevertheless I live; yet not I, but Christ liveth in me: and the life which I now live in the flesh I live by the faith of the Son of God, who loved me, and gave himself for me." This verse introduces the theme of sanctification, which begins in Romans 5:12. Up to 5:6, Romans addresses the theme of justification. From Romans 5:6 through Romans 8, Paul addresses the theme of how the believer can live a holy life under grace and because of grace.

[y] The word for "joy" in verse 11 is the same as "rejoicing" in verse 2 and "glory" in verse 3. It has the idea of being excited about a blessing we have as believers.

[z] The word atonement is from Old English for at-one-ment. In the Greek it is from the noun form of the verb rendered "reconciled." We today have received the atonement individually (i.e., personal reconciliation) when we believed the gospel. The nation of Israel still looks forward to their "day of atonement." Note Peter's words in Acts 3:19. "Repent ye therefore, and be converted, that your sins may be blotted out, when the times of refreshing shall come from the presence of the Lord." Peter (and all the circumcision believers) still looks forward to receiving as a nation what each believer in the dispensation of grace receives at the moment of salvation. Remember that Israel is a covenant nation. God deals with that nation on the basis of covenants. God deals with us today on the basis of the mystery revealed through Paul (Ephesians 3:1–3).

[aa] Verse 12 warrants special study in that it contains four key doctrines. Let's start with a structural analysis of the verse: "Wherefore as by one man sin entered into the world and death by sin; ... and so death passed upon all men, ... for all have sinned."

> **First,** "by one man sin entered into the world." This statement goes back to Adam at the fall, documented in Genesis 2:17; 3:6. "But of the tree of the knowledge of good and evil, thou shalt not eat of it: for in the day that thou eatest thereof thou shalt surely die" (2:17).
>
> It was Eve who initiated the act, but it is Adam who is here held responsible for it. To understand why, we turn first to 1 Corinthians 11:3, where we see "that ... the head of the woman is the man." We also consider 1 Timothy 2:14, where we find that "Adam was not deceived, but the woman being deceived was in the transgression." To understand this further, we turn to Genesis 2:16, where we find that the Lord God commanded the man (i.e., Adam), saying, "Of every tree of the garden thou mayest freely eat: But of the tree of the knowledge of good and evil, thou shalt not eat of it: for in the day that thou eatest thereof thou shalt surely die" (Genesis 2:16–17). He told Adam that before He created either the animals or the woman (Genesis 2:20–22). As a result of their mutual sin, both bore the consequences. These consequences include the following:

To the woman (3:16):

- Multiplied sorrow
- Multiplied conception
- Loving service to the husband
- Rulership of the husband

To the man (3:17):

- Hard labor to get the ground to yield a living to him

- Thorns and thistles (and ticks and mosquitoes) added to an otherwise beautiful and pleasant creation.

- Sweat of face to work for his existence

- The ground from which his body was formed shall claim his body in death, but the greatest consequence of all was "death."

Second, death came by means of sin. In Genesis 2:17, God said that "in the day that thou eatest thereof thou shalt surely die" (emphasis added). The thou is singular.

Note that it was "in the day" (i.e., in the very day) that Adam ate of that tree that he would die. But he didn't die physically that day. Therefore, the death he died that day wasn't a physical death but a spiritual one. Note the suddenness of their realization of their nakedness in 3:7. "And the eyes of them both were opened, and they knew that they were naked; and they sewed fig leaves together, and made themselves aprons." It is apparent from the Genesis account that man is both a spiritual being ("God created man in his own image" [Genesis 1:27]) and a physical being ("God formed man of the dust of the ground, and breathed into his nostrils the breath of life; and man became a living soul" [Genesis 2:7]). Adam's physical life could have gone on forever if he would have taken of the tree of life (Genesis 3:22: "lest he put forth his hand, and take also of the tree of life, and eat, and live for ever") in a fallen (spiritually dead) state. Therefore, God "sent him forth from the garden of Eden, to till the ground from whence he was taken" and set cherubim to guard the tree of life. As a result, "the creature was made subject to vanity, not willingly, but by reason of him who hath subjected the same in hope, Because the creature itself also shall be delivered from the bondage of corruption into the glorious liberty of the children of God" (Romans 8:20–22).

Third, we observe that death passed unto all men through Adam. This death is both spiritual and physical. Just as Adam died spiritually the moment he ate of the fruit and then at a later time died physically, so too the members of the race that descended from him were born with the fallen nature of Adam and therefore die physically. However, as soon as death (particularly spiritual death) entered the human race, God gave the promise of spiritual life in the promise of Genesis 3:15.

Fourth, we observe that death passed on to all men, "for all have sinned." But we note that innocent children die when they haven't personally sinned. Therefore, we understand that all sinned in Adam. We inherit the results of Adam's sin as his descendants. Adam's disobedience made us sinners (Romans 5:19). We inherit physical death (mortality) along with a sin nature. Our sin nature leads us to sin (i.e., we sin because we are sinners). Sin brings spiritual death to each of us. Death and sin go together and are essentially inseparable. Romans 8:3 calls it "the law of sin and death." Ephesians 2:3 describes our sin nature: "Among whom also we all had our conversation in times past in the lusts of our flesh, fulfilling the desires of the flesh and of the mind; and were by nature the children of wrath, even as others." The whole human race was in Adam when Adam sinned, and therefore they were party to it by inheritance. The sin nature Adam passed unto his children is one he apparently received from the devil. There is therefore some type of father-child relationship between lost men and the devil. In John 8:44, our Lord referred to some religious leaders of the time as being "of your father the devil." He referred to the tares in Matthew 13:38 as being "the children of the wicked one." Christ referred to Cain as being "of that wicked one" (John 3:11). We will see more about this in upcoming chapters.

Sin and Death Entered by Adam, Law Entered by Moses, but Grace Entered by Jesus

¹²Wherefore, as by[ab] one man sin entered into the world, and death by sin; and so death passed upon all men, for that all have sinned: ¹³ (For until the law sin was in the world: but sin is not imputed when there is no law. ¹⁴ Nevertheless death reigned[ac] from Adam to Moses, even over them that had not sinned after the similitude of Adam's transgression, who is[ad] the figure of him that was to come. ¹⁵ But not[ae] as the offence, so also is the free gift. For if through the offence of one many be dead, much more the grace of God, and the gift by grace, which is by one man, Jesus Christ, hath abounded unto many. ¹⁶ And not as it was by one that sinned, so is the gift: for the judgment was by one to condemnation, but the free gift is of many[af] offences unto justification. ¹⁷ For if by one man's offence death reigned by one; much more they which receive abundance of grace and of the gift of righteousness shall reign in life by one, Jesus Christ.). (Romans 5:12–17)

[ab] Romans 5:12–21 compares and contrasts two men: Adam and Christ. While Adam brings the law of sin and death into the human race, Christ brings righteousness and life into the race. Verses 13–17 are a parenthesis. The flow of thought can best be obtained by reading verses 12 and 18 together and then reading 13–17 for clarification. One man's disobedience assigns sin to all. One man's obedience ensures life for all who will receive it. "Wherefore, as by one man sin entered into the world, and death by sin; and so death passed unto all men, for that all have sinned … Therefore as by the offence of one judgment came upon all men to condemnation; even so by the righteousness of one the free gift came upon all men unto justification of life."

[ac] Verses 13–14 speak of death reigning from Adam to Moses, in that Adam sinned against a direct command of God as did those under Moses. Those who sinned from Adam to Moses sinned but not against a law. Therefore, a penalty of death wouldn't be exacted for these sins, because there was no broken law as a direct command from God as was the case with Adam. The fact that death nonetheless reigned during this time, however, proves that physical death was a result of Adam's sin.

[ad] Verse 14 says Adam is a figure of Christ. In what sense was Adam a figure (type) of Christ? Adam brought ruin to the entire race by one act of disobedience, but Christ brought life to the race by one act of obedience.

[ae] The language of verse 15 conveys the thought that, though Adam and Christ are similar in one way (i.e., they both brought dramatic results from one single act), they are also very different in that the results are opposite. Adam's one act brought death, but Christ's one act brought life.

[af] How many are "many"? Through Adam's offence, the entire human race died, but not all the human race is now dead (speaking spiritually now). Some have life in Christ (Ephesians 2:3). The grace of God and the gift by grace (i.e., righteousness) have abounded unto "many"—that being the entire human race. This means the redemption Christ accomplished is unlimited and has the potential to save all sinners.

Verse 15—"Through the offence of one many be dead" (emphasis added). All were dead (Ephesians 2:3

cf. v. 18). "The grace of God hath abounded unto many" (Romans 3:22, emphasis added). God's grace is "unto all."

Verse 16—The free gift of many offences unto justification. Righteousness is upon all who believe (Romans 3:22).

Verse 18—"By the offence of one, judgment cometh upon all men" (emphasis added) "By the righteousness of one, the free gift come upon all men unto justification" (emphasis added).

Verse 19—"By one man's disobedience many were made sinners." "By the obedience of one shall many be made righteous" (emphasis added). Every believer is reckoned righteous, though all men were born sinners (Romans 5:3).

By One's Disobedience Condemnation on All or by Another's Obedience—Justification of Life

¹⁸ Therefore as by the offence of one judgment came upon all men to condemnation; even so by the righteousness of one the free gift came upon all men unto justification of life. ¹⁹ For as by one man's disobedience many were made sinners, so by the obedience of one shall many be made righteous. ²⁰ Moreover the law entered, that the offence might[ag] abound. But where sin[ah] abounded, grace did much more abound: ²¹ That as sin[ai] hath reigned unto death, even so might grace[ai] reign through righteousness unto eternal life by Jesus Christ our Lord. (Romans 5:18–21)

[ag] According to verse 20, the law entered for the purpose of causing the offense to abound. This takes us back to verse 13, where we see that sin (i.e., both the sin nature and the acts of sin) was in the world from Adam to Moses but that sin wasn't imputed when there was no law. Sin in this context isn't imputed in the sense of not bringing physical death. Physical death came to the entire race because of the sin of Adam. Spiritual death came from personal acts of sin. Personal acts of sin came from the sin nature. The sin nature was inherited from our human fathers (note that the only person born into the human race who didn't have a sin nature [Christ] has a human mother but didn't have a human father). The sin nature produced acts of sin from Adam to Moses. With Moses, the Law was added as a means of conviction to show Israel that, though their nation was set aside from other nations, they were also in need of spiritual salvation because they were violating direct commands of God. Therefore, with the law, sin was made to abound. Actually, two things (two negatives) were made to abound as a result of the giving of the law: the offence and "sin."

[ah] Where sin abounded (i.e., in the human race as the sin nature produced acts of sin), grace did "much more abound." Grace abounds even more than sin. Grace is the undeserved favor of God in the lives of believers. Grace defeats sin and goes beyond that; it produces practical righteousness in the lives of believers.

[ai] It must be noted that, from Romans 5:21 until the end of chapter 8, "sin" is used as a reference to the sin nature and not sin as acts of sin. In fact, both sin and grace are used in this verse as a figure of speech (i.e., personification). In the past (speaking dispensationally) the Adamic sin nature ruled in the human race to produce death (spiritual death). Now, under the dispensation of grace, grace can (note the word might) reign in the lives of believers. This reigning of grace is through the means of imputed righteousness. The end result of the reign of grace is "eternal life." This eternal life is available "by Jesus Christ our Lord."

Study Questions on Chapter 5

1. Peace with God is based on what? By whom do we have access to God? Into what is the access of 5:2?

2. What is shed abroad in our hearts?

3. What does it mean to glory in tribulation? What is it that enables us to glory in tribulation?

4. Verses 6, 8, and 10 describe man's condition and then presents God's means of addressing it. List those conditions and God's provision to meet it.

5. Verses 7 and 8 describe different kinds of men and the likeliness of someone dying for each. Who (according to verse 8) did Christ die for?

6. What is the difference between a righteous man and a good man?

7. What are we justified by in verse 1 and verse 9?

8. What are we saved from in verse 9? Explain why.

9. What does it mean to be saved by His life in verse10?

10. What did the believer receive in verse 11?. When will Israel receive the atonement (Acts 3:19)?

11. Compare and show the contrast between the two men in verses 12 through 21.

12. What entered the world through the first man? What was the result?

13. Verse 12 says "all have sinned" as was stated previously in Romans 3:23. Is this just repetition or is there a difference in the perspective on each?

14. What time period is referred to in verse 13 when it says "until the Law"? Name the men whose lives set the boundary of this time period.

15. What was "the similitude of Adam's transgression" in verse 14? In what sense was Adam's sin different from that of the men who followed after?

16. How is Adam's offence contrasted with Christ's Righteousness in verse 15 through 17?

17. Who is affected by Adam's sin? Contrast that with who is affected by Christ's righteousness.

18. What penalty did Adam's sin lead to? What blessing did Christ's righteousness lead to?

19. What reigned in verse 14? What reigned in verse 21

20. Who is it that shall reign in life in verse 17?

21. Verses 18 and 19 summarize verses 12 through 17. State that summary in your own words.

22. The word "many" is used twice in verse 19. Who are the many in each case?

23. Why (according to verse 20) did the Law enter?

24. Where and in what sense did sin abound in verse 20 and where and in what sense did grace super abound?

CHAPTER 6

THE WALK AFTER THE SPIRIT

The first fourteen verses of chapter 6 lay out for believers how grace works in them to enable believers to live lives separated from sin unto God. These verses comprise the simple and basic doctrine that enables the believer to live a life free from the dominion and tyranny of the sin nature. That freedom comes by faith in the operation of God in baptizing believers into Christ's death, burial, and resurrection. The Holy Spirit performs that baptism in believers at the moment lost sinners trust Christ. He joins believers to Jesus Christ and indeed places them in an eternal, living relationship with Him. In that baptism, believers are so joined to Christ that they are members of His body, His flesh, and His bones much like how a man and a woman are joined in marriage (Ephesians 5:30).

The point to note, though, is that when He receives us as members of His body, He receives our sin so it (our sin) actually becomes His, in that what was ours becomes His. He then, having acquired our sin and guilt by virtue of this baptism, could then pay the debt of our sin. This He did on the cross of Calvary. This baptism is referenced in Colossians 2:12, where we see that this baptism is "the operation of God." In 1 Corinthians 12:13, we see that the Holy Spirit performs this baptism. But here in Romans 6 we see that this baptism has results that go beyond simply transferring our sin and guilt to the Savior so He could pay its debt. As a result of this baptism, our old man (i.e., our souls under the rule of our sin nature) has been crucified with Christ so we can now lead a different life. The end result is that we "are dead to sin" (v. 2). Paul therefore asks (and answers) the rhetorical question of verse 1.

Shall We Continue in Sin That Grace May Abound?

[1] What shall we say then? Shall we continue[a] in sin[b], that grace may abound? [2] God forbid. How shall we, that are dead to sin, live any longer therein? [3] Know ye not, that so many of us as were baptized[c] into Jesus Christ were baptized into his death? [4] Therefore we are buried[d] with him by baptism into death: that like as Christ was raised[e] up from the dead by the glory of the Father, even so we also should walk in newness of life. (Romans 6:1–4)

[a] The question raised in verse 1 ("Shall we continue in sin, that grace may abound?") addresses a common objection thrown up to the gospel when that objection is verbalized. If salvation is by grace through faith apart from works, then people could do anything they want and still be saved. Because soul salvation (i.e., having eternal life) is a gift of God (v. 23), truly people can do whatever they want and still be saved (in the sense of being saved from sin's debt penalty in the lake of fire). However, grace doesn't save people to sin but rather saves them from sin. Apparently people were accusing Paul of making the argument that where sin abounded, grace superabounded; then the more one sinned, the more grace there was (according to this argument), and the more God was glorified. Paul's answer to that false accusation that we should continue in sin that grace may

abound was an emphatic statement: "God forbid." Nothing could be further from the truth.

[b] In this chapter Paul often uses the figure of speech of personification. Personification is the imparting of personality to an inanimate thing for discussion purposes. The names given to the two natures in this passage are very informative. Here in verse 1 "sin" is the old sin nature. Mr. Sin used to run our lives and used to (before we were justified by faith) actually own our physical bodies. We will see more on this issue later.

Names for the old man:
- "Sin" (vv. 1, 2, 6–7, 10–12, 14, 16–18, 20, 23)
- "Our old man" (v. 6)
- "Uncleanness" (v. 19)
- "Iniquity" (v. 19)
- "Death" (v. 9)

Names for the new man:
- "Obedience" (v. 16)

Names for the inner man (Ephesians 3:16):
- "Righteousness" (vv. 18–20)
- The inward man (2 Corinthians 4:16)

[c] The believer was baptized into Jesus Christ by the Holy Spirit at the very instant he or she trusted in Jesus Christ as Savior (1 Corinthians 12:3; Colossians 2:12). This baptism has nothing to do with water or speaking in tongues. This baptism isn't Pentecostal baptism, where Christ baptized the believers of Israel with "the Holy Spirit" (Matthew 3:4). This baptism is done by the Holy Spirit into Christ. This baptism of Romans 6:3 is done by the Holy Spirit in response to our faith. "For ye are all the children of God by faith in Christ Jesus. For as many of you as have been baptized into Christ have put on Christ" (Galatians 3:26–27). The common misconception among professing believers today is that baptism refers to either a water rite or speaking in tongues, but there are many other baptisms in the New Testament.

- Our Lord's death is referred to as a baptism (Matthew 20:22–23).
- There was a baptism unto Moses (1 Corinthians 10:2).
- John the Baptist talked about a baptism with fire (Matthew 3:11).

This baptism of Romans 6:1–4 is a baptism into Christ. Note that it's not a baptism into water, a baptism by water, or a baptism with the Holy Spirit, as was the case in Matthew 3:11. It's a baptism the Holy Spirit performs. In Israel's program, there was a water rite required for salvation. "He that believeth and is baptized shall be saved; but he that believeth not shall be damned" (Mark 16:16, emphasis added). Nowhere in Paul's epistles, however, do we find a reference to water baptism as a requirement for salvation. In quite the opposite terms, Paul says. "Christ sent me not to baptize but to preach the gospel" (1 Corinthians 1:17). The only baptism Paul preached was the baptism the Holy Spirit performed in the process of forming the church, which is Christ's body (1 Corinthians 12:13, 27; Ephesians 1:22–23; Colossians 1:18). Based on his statement regarding "one baptism" in Ephesians 4:4–5, we would conclude that the water rite is not only not necessary but inappropriate for practice today under the dispensation of the grace of God. Note that Paul's commission to be the apostle of the Gentiles didn't include water baptism (1 Corinthians 1:17), while the commission given to the Twelve did. In the early part of his ministry as the apostle of the Gentiles, he baptized some with water (1 Corinthians 1:14–16). In the same epistle of 1 Corinthians, he also proclaimed a baptism whereby the Holy Spirit joined individual believers to Jesus Christ at the moment of conversion to make that person eternally a member of the body of Christ (1 Corinthians 12:13).

[d] Verses 4–5 speak of our identification with Christ in both His death and resurrection from the dead. This identification of us with Him in His death, burial, and resurrection guarantees for us our resurrection. But our resurrection is presented here as a two-fold resurrection. We have a spiritual resurrection now as believers (i.e., "that we also should walk in newness of life") and a physical resurrection later (i.e., "we shall be also in the likeness of his resurrection").

[e] According to 1 Corinthians 15:3–4, the gospel is defined as "Christ died for our sins according to the scriptures; and that he was buried, and that he rose again the third day according to the scriptures." The burial of our Lord was necessary to prove He was indeed dead. For us, His burial (and our burial with Him) presents a demarcation between the life we had before salvation and the life we now have as believers. As a result of that baptism into His death, burial, and resurrection, we can now walk a new walk because we now have and live a new life.

The Old Man Crucified, the Body of Sin Destroyed?

⁵ For if we have been planted together in the likeness of his death, we shall be also in the likeness of his resurrection: ⁶ Knowing this, that our old man[f] is crucified with him, that the body of sin[g] might be destroyed, that henceforth we should not serve[h] sin. (Romans 6:5–6)

[f] Here the apostle again uses a figure of speech to refer to the person we were before conversion as "our old man." Verse 6 tells us that that person was crucified. He or she was crucified with Christ. It was the baptism of verse 3 that resulted in our old man being crucified along with Christ. So let's ask two important questions here:

1. Who is our "old man"?
2. What is the significance of him being crucified?

The answer to each is profound:

1. Our old man is the person we were before conversion when the old Adamic sin nature reigned in our lives and in fact owned our bodies.

2. The significance of him being crucified (as indeed he was for the believer) is that the old man no longer exists. We will see in chapter 7 that the old sin nature still resides in our physical bodies, but the person we were under his rulership no longer exists.

[g] The term "the body of sin" is also a figure of speech. We ask ourselves two questions regarding this body of sin:

1. What is the body of sin?
2. In what sense was it destroyed when we trusted Jesus Christ?

Here, too, the answers to these questions teach profound truth on the life-changing work of grace:

1. The term "the body of sin" is in the genitive case, indicating in this case possession. The body of sin in this case is the body every believer has now as a saved person but refers to its state before conversion to Christ when the old sin nature still owned it.

2. When we were baptized into His death, burial, and resurrection, our old man was thereby crucified. The ownership of our body by the sin nature ceased, and in that sense it was "destroyed" as "the body of sin." (i.e., it is no longer the body Mr. Sin owns). As believers, our bodies are now under new ownership, that being of Christ (1 Corinthians 6:15–17).

[h] God's purpose in baptizing us into Christ's death is that we henceforth don't have to serve sin. Paul was using the figure of speech of personification, in which he was treating the sin nature that still dwells in our physical bodies as if it were a person trying to control us. As I teach this chapter of scripture, I put a title on sin for illustration purposes. I call him "Mr. Sin" to convey the concept that the sin nature once controlled us, lost that control, and is trying to gain it back. To get the impact of this, read Romans 5–7, and whenever "sin" is used as a noun, put the title "Mr." in front of it to convey the impact of the doctrine the apostle taught regarding how we have victory over him through Christ. It is truly the working of God's grace that results in our being set free from the dominion of "Mr. Sin."

Dead unto Sin; Alive unto God

> [7] For he that is dead is freed[l] from sin. [8] Now if we be dead with Christ, we believe that we shall also live[j] with him: [9] Knowing that Christ being raised from the dead dieth no more; death hath no more dominion over him. [10] For in that he died, he died[k] unto sin once: but in that he liveth, he liveth unto God. [11] Likewise reckon[l] ye also yourselves to be dead indeed unto sin, but alive unto God through Jesus Christ our Lord. [12] Let not sin therefore reign[m] in your mortal body, that ye should obey it in the lusts thereof. [13] Neither yield[o] ye your members as instruments of unrighteousness unto sin: but yield yourselves unto God, as those that are alive from the dead, and your members as instruments of righteousness unto God. [14] For sin shall not have dominion[n] over you: for ye are not[o] under the law, but under grace. (Romans 6:7–14)

[i] "He that is dead is freed from sin" (v. 7). Not only is my old man (the person I was) crucified, but I am also dead to sin (dead to Mr. Sin). Death is separation from someone or something. Physical death is separation of the soul and spirit from the physical body (Genesis 35:18). So also "the world is crucified unto me, and I unto the world" (Galatians 6:14). Also, I was once a child of the devil (Ephesians 2:2; Matthew 13:38; John 8:8), but I am now a child of God by that baptism of verse 3.

[j] The doctrine of deliverance from the power, reign, and dominion of sin (the old Adamic nature) is given in Romans 6:1–6. The means by which it is appropriated is in verses 7–14. There are three actions needed to appropriate the victory of that deliverance:

1. Believe that our baptism into Christ's death delivers us from both the penalty and power of sin and made us alive unto God. (vv. 8–10).

2. Reckon it to be a fact that we are indeed dead unto sin but alive unto God through Christ. (vv. 11–12).

3. Refuse to yield the use of our members to the old sin nature (i.e., to old Mr. Sin) but rather yield ourselves

unto God as those who are alive from the dead to yield our members as instruments of righteousness unto God (vv. 13–14).

[k] The Lord Jesus Christ died unto sin once (v.10). You can pay the death penalty only once. The significance for the believer is that there was one life surrendered—that of the old man. So there is now one life to live—that of the life of Christ. The life that Jesus lives now He is living unto God, and we share that life with Him (cf. Galatians 2:20). In other words, we are living that life with Him.

[l] Verse 11 talks about us reckoning ourselves to be dead indeed to sin and also reckoning ourselves to be alive unto God. To "reckon" means to make a faith application of something we know to be true in our lives (i.e., to reckon is to come to a logical conclusion on a matter). That is, we need to see ourselves as God sees us. He sees us as fit for heaven as His Son is (2 Corinthians 5:21). We are called to live as adult children of God in His family and to engage ourselves in the soul-saving business with our heavenly Father.

[m] The verb rendered "let not reign" in verse 12 is in the present tense and imperative mode. This speaks of continuous action. The instruction is, "Do not allow Mr. Sin to reign in your mortal body." The fact that the reference is to the mortal body means this is instruction for the here and now. Do not allow him to run your life. So also the verb yield in verse 13 is in the present tense and imperative mode. Mr. Sin's power over you as a believer and your body was truly broken by the baptizing work of the Holy Spirit to baptize you into an eternal, living relationship with Jesus Christ. The sin nature cannot do anything in your life unless you allow him to use the members of your body to do so. His power over you has been broken. To have victory over him, one has to simply reckon it to be a fact that his power over the believer is broken.

[n] Here in verse 14, the apostle presents the reason for the injunction of verse 13. Believers should yield themselves unto God and their members as instruments of righteousness rather than yielding their members to the indwelling sin nature for him to use as instruments of unrighteousness. Believers are not under the dominion of the old sin nature; they are therefore free to choose between the two since they are not bound to follow the old man, who was crucified. While a man was yet an unbeliever, the only nature he had was the old sin nature, and it (the sin nature) therefore ran his life (i.e., sin had dominion over him).

[o] Due to the fact that the believer is under grace and not under law, he or she is free from sin. This is the theme of the rest of this chapter and all of chapter 7. For the believer, being put under law would give sin (the old sin nature) dominion over him or her. Chapter 7 will go on to explain why that would be so.

A Form of Doctrine That Delivers from Sin

¹⁵ What[p] then? Shall[q] we sin, because we are not under the law, but under grace? God forbid. ¹⁶ Know ye not, that to whom ye yield[r] yourselves servants to obey, his servants ye are to whom ye obey; whether of sin unto death, or of obedience unto righteousness? ¹⁷ But God be thanked, that ye were[s] the servants of sin, but ye have obeyed[t] from the heart that form of doctrine which was delivered you. ¹⁸ Being then made[u] free from sin, ye became the servants of righteousness. ¹⁹ I speak after the manner of men because of the infirmity of your flesh: for as ye have yielded your members servants to uncleanness and to iniquity unto iniquity; even so now yield your members servants to righteousness unto holiness. ²⁰ For when ye were the servants of sin, ye were free from righteousness. ²¹ What fruit had ye then in those things whereof ye are now ashamed? for the end of those things is death. ²² But now being made[u] free

from sin, and become[v] servants to God, ye have your fruit unto holiness, and the end everlasting life. [23] For the wages[w] of sin is death; but the gift of God is eternal life through Jesus Christ our Lord. (Romans 6:15–23)

[p] This rhetorical question (v. 15) is almost identical to that of verse 1. However, here in verse 15, "sin" is a verb and denotes the act of sinning, while in verse 1, "sin" is a noun and denotes the old sin nature. Paul answers the first question (v. 1) by pointing out that we are dead to sin by our baptism into Christ's death, burial, and resurrection. He answers the second by pointing out that serving sin brings to the believer functional death of his or her not experiencing victory in life, but serving righteousness, however, brings eternal reward.

[q] The structure of Paul's answers to the rhetorical questions of verses 1 and 15 is the same. He first gives the simple but emphatic answer: "God forbid." Then he gives the reason for his answer. Whereas the believer is dead to sin and no longer under the dominion of the sin nature, verses 15–23 state that the believer can still serve the sin nature. The believer has a choice the unbeliever doesn't have. The believer can either serve "sin" or "obedience," a synonym for the new nature. The "know ye not" is Paul's way of introducing a fundamental truth, as in verse 3. Here the fundamental truth is that believers have the choice of whom they will serve. They can either serve the sin nature, whose power has been broken (v. 6), or serve Christ, here referred to as "obedience."

[r] Service to "sin" (the old Adamic sin nature) results in death. This death is neither physical death nor the spiritual death Adam died when he sinned. Rather, this death is best understood as spiritual dormancy, as Romans 8:13 states. "For if ye live after the flesh, ye shall die: but if ye through the Spirit do mortify the deeds of the body, ye shall live." Rather than serving sin, the believer is here admonished to serve "obedience" (the new man who exhibited "the obedience of faith" in getting justified) with the end result being righteousness—righteousness in practice.

[s] "Ye were the servants of sin" (v. 17). This takes us back to the time before we came in faith to the Savior, back in our individual lives before we were baptized into Christ's death to render our old man "crucified" (Romans 6:6). At that time our bodies belonged to "sin" (the old man), and therefore we served sin.

[t] The phrase "ye have obeyed from the heart" is an expression for faith in "a form of doctrine." That "form of doctrine" is found back in Romans 3:21–28 and 6:1-4 regarding the cross and what was accomplished there. See Romans 1:5, especially 16:26, on how this term is used elsewhere.

[u] The believer was "made free from sin" (i.e., set at liberty from it) by believing the form of doctrine that resulted in him or her being justified. When my old man was crucified with Christ, the body of sin was no longer the body the sin nature owned, and I was set free from him.

[v] The physical body of the believer, as is his or her soul and spirit (1 Corinthians 6:19–20), is now owned by Jesus Christ to form the new creature of 2 Corinthians 5:17 ("Therefore if any man be in Christ, he is a new creature: old things are passed away; behold, all things are become new"). Now then, as one who has been delivered from the bondage to sin, the believer is now a servant to what is here called "righteousness." This term is yet another name for the new nature. Note in verse 22 that, when the believer became a servant to righteousness, he or she became a servant to God. Later in Romans, other names are added. The sin nature is called "the flesh" in Romans 8:1. The new man is called "the Spirit of Christ" in Romans 8:9. Each of the two

natures, the sin nature and the Spirit of Christ, will produce fruit. We don't gather grapes from a thorn (Matthew 7:16). The end result of the fruit the old sin nature produces is death. On the other hand, the fruit the new nature produces in the believer is holiness. This fruit will abide forever, and the believer will enjoy that fruit in the eternal life the believer has.

[w] Not surprisingly, Mr. Sin pays wages. The wages he pays is death. Romans 6:23 says wages are the recompense for work, while a gift is bestowed by grace. This takes us to the concept of the works of the flesh versus the fruit of the Spirit in Galatians 5:19–23. Sin (the old nature) pays wages, those being death. The death is spiritual death, resulting in the second death in the lake of fire in the unsaved man or death as far as one's Christian experience is concerned in the saved man. The gift of God, however, is eternal life. This life is the resurrection life given to every believer (both spiritual resurrection as in Philippians 3:11 and physical, bodily resurrection as in 1 Corinthians 15:51).

Grace and our Human Makeup

What we have learned so far from Romans 1–6 is that God's grace changes the believer from being a lost soul in Adam's race to being a saint in the family of God, destined for glory. Figure 1 is a presentation in graphical form that illustrates that change and how the Holy Spirit of God works to apply our Lord Jesus Christ's work of redemption to bring about that change. We will see as we go on into chapters 7–8 that God continues that work of grace to conform the believer into the image of His Son. Chapter 6 presents the walk after the Spirit, while chapter 7 talks about the walk after the flesh.

We consider our human makeup as a three-part creature. God is a trinity, and He created man in His image as a three-part creature that corresponds with His very image. "And God said, Let us make man in our image, after our likeness: and let them have dominion over the fish of the sea, and over the fowl of the air, and over the cattle, and over all the earth, and over every creeping thing that creepeth upon the earth. So God created man in his own image, in the image of God created he him; male and female created he them" (Genesis 1:26–27).

Though God is one in essence and being, He is three in person. We, as members of this human race as creatures of God, are each a unique person. That person is what the Bible calls the "soul." We each are a soul who has a body and who has a spirit. Each of these three parts of our makeup has a consciousness. Out physical bodies give us each a world consciousness—we function in a physical creation by means of our physical bodies. We each also have a consciousness of the existence of God, our Creator. People try to deny His existence, but they have to be taught to do so. How foolish—the atheist has to acknowledge God to deny Him. "The fool says in his heart there is no God" (Psalm 14:1), but in his mind he knows there is a God and that he will give account to Him. While our bodies give each of us a world consciousness, our spirits give us a God consciousness. The soul, however, is the real person. The soul is our very personality and gives us a self-consciousness, the unique identity of who we are.

While each part of us has a consciousness, each part also has a mentality. The spirit has a mentality the Bible refers to as the "mind." We do our thinking in our spirits, especially our thinking about spiritual realities and convictions. The soul is the part of us that makes decisions in life. It is where we form affections and desires. The Bible calls the mentality of the soul the "heart." We will see in Romans 10:10 that "with the heart man believeth unto righteousness" (Romans 10:9–10). In each of us, the physical body also has a mentality the Bible calls the "flesh." The flesh is that part of us that seeks to gratify itself.

Each part of our makeup is involved in the activities of life. We make decisions in our souls out of the affections of our hearts, but these are based on the thinking we do in our spirits based on the contents of our minds. We then carry out those decisions in this world in our physical bodies. First Corinthians 6:19–20 says, "What? know ye not that your body is the temple of the Holy Ghost which is in you, which ye have of God, and ye are not your own? For ye are bought with a price: therefore glorify God in your body, and in your spirit, which are God's." In this verse the subject is "you." You are a soul who has a body and also a spirit. You (the soul that is you) decide what you will do with your body and spirit. You form your mind by what you put into your spirit. When you fill your mind with the Word of God as a believer, you form the mind of Christ (1 Corinthians 2:16). As we study the Word of God, we should put our affections on the things of God and decide to live those things out in life; we engage in a walk after the Spirit.

A change takes place in the whole person when one gets saved (i.e., when one is justified by faith). That change affects the whole person. What brings about that great change is the baptism of Romans 6:1–4. Each part of our makeup is affected. Before soul salvation, the spirit was there but dead and dormant. It didn't function as God intended it to. It "received not the things of God" (1 Corinthians 2:14) because the things of God were foolishness to the man who was spiritually dead. Immediately upon the soul making a decision to trust Jesus Christ as Savior, the Holy Spirit baptizes the believer into an eternal spiritual union with Christ. The believer is joined to Him in His death for our sins, into His burial, and into His resurrection. It is as a result of this union with Christ that our previously dead spirits are regenerated (Titus 3:5). The spirit that was previously "dead in trespasses and sins" is now made alive or quickened (Ephesians 2:2).

The soul experiences a great transformation. Before salvation, the soul was in darkness (Ephesians 5:8), but now the light of Jesus Christ comes, and life enters the soul. The believer can now truly walk in newness of life (Romans 6:4). Along with the Holy Spirit baptizing the believer into Christ, He also circumcises the believer with a spiritual circumcision—a circumcision made without hands. This circumcision can be thought of as spiritual surgery that separates our outward man (our physical body) that perishes from our inward man (our redeemed soul and spirit) that is renewed day by day (2 Corinthians 4:16). While for the believer the soul and spirit are redeemed at the moment of salvation, the body still waits for its redemption. The redemption of the body will happen when the Lord returns to catch the church, His body, up to meet Him in the air (1 Thessalonians 4:15–17).

Our physical bodies, though not redeemed yet, nonetheless undergo a change too. Before salvation, our bodies were owned by the sin nature indwelling them. At salvation, the bodies underwent a change of ownership. Jesus Christ now owns the bodies of believers (1 Corinthians 6:20), and believers belong to Christ as members of the church, His body (1 Corinthians 12:12–13). The believer's body is destroyed as "the body of sin" (Romans 6:11) in that it is no longer under the ownership of the sin nature. Sin can no longer use the body to do its bidding unless the believer chooses to allow it to do so. Though the body isn't redeemed yet, it is nonetheless the only body we have, in which to live the Christian life in this world. Therefore, God can and does quicken this mortal body by His Spirit, which dwells within it (Romans 8:11). We will see more on this topic in chapters 7–8.

In 2 Corinthians 10:5, Paul talks about "casting down imaginations." Imaginations in 2 Corinthians 10:5 are presented as the activity of the soldier in the spiritual warfare of which Paul speaks in 2 Corinthians 10. The spiritual battle that rages is the battle for the mind of people. In Colossians 2:18, Paul warns about people who intrude in the unseen spiritual realm without the knowledge of Christ and end up being "vainly puffed up by his fleshly mind." Paul identifies a two-fold stronghold here:

1. The "every high thing that exalts itself against the knowledge of God" in 2 Corinthians 10:5 is the array of thrones, dominions, principalities, and powers in the unseen realm (Colossians 2), which comprises spiritual wickedness in high places (Ephesians 6:12). These spiritual forces of wickedness

- blind the minds of them who believe not (2 Corinthians 4:4);
- work in the children of disobedience (Ephesians 2:2); and
- take ignorant believers captive (2 Timothy 2:26).

2. The "imaginations of a fleshly mind" are the thoughts people come up with when they do their thinking out of their own creative, cognitive processes based on how they feel about things they experience. Such imagination will lead people astray unless they are brought captive to the obedience of Christ (i.e., to the Word of God). Making life decisions based on our emotions rather than on sound thinking based on the Word will lead people to make bad decisions. People develop what we call "issues" that come out of the heart set on the things of the flesh.

The imaginations of a fleshly mind will cause problems in the lives of those who are caught up with them. People develop what we call "personality disorders" when they respond to abusive treatment from others in a fleshly manner, especially when the abuse persists over a long period. What is happening in such cases is that the sin nature develops defense mechanisms to deal with such abuse. Victims of such abuse, whether verbal, emotional, or physical, will react to it in either a positive or a negative way. They can internalize it, in which they form various mental imaginations regarding themselves and the abuser. These eventually become part of the fabric of their personality, or they can understand the spiritual realities of what is happening to them and to the perpetrator of the abuse. If they internalize the abuse without a proper scriptural understanding of the sin nature in themselves and the other party, believers can develop behavior patterns that are destructive to a healthy lifestyle.

If one reacts to abuse (which unfortunately occurs all around us in varying amounts and degrees) by becoming angry and bitter, that abuse turns only to one's own detriment. However, the believer can go to the Word of God and understand why people do the things they do. With such spiritual understanding, the believer can draw on the spiritual resources God has given us by His grace to successfully deal with such mistreatment or at least to understand what is happening and why. This is the outworking of the grace of God Paul was talking about in 2 Corinthians 1.

Blessed be God, even the Father of our Lord Jesus Christ, the Father of mercies, and the God of all comfort; Who comforteth us in all our tribulation, that we may be able to comfort them which are in any trouble, by the comfort wherewith we ourselves are comforted of God. For as the sufferings of Christ abound in us, so our consolation also aboundeth by Christ. And whether we be afflicted, it is for your consolation and salvation, which is effectual in the enduring of the same sufferings which we also suffer: or whether we be comforted, it is for your consolation and salvation. (2 Corinthians 1:3–6)

Paul tells the Corinthians in 1 Corinthians 2:15–16, "But he that is spiritual judgeth all things, yet he himself is judged of no man. For who hath known the mind of the Lord, that he may instruct him? But we have the mind of Christ." If you understand why people do the things they do and why they treat you as they do, you don't need to get angry with them; rather, you can love them and seek to help them by the same consolation you receive from the Word. What needs to happen is that the believer needs to be filled with the Spirit by letting the Word of Christ dwell in him or her richly, speaking to himself or herself "in psalms and hymns and spiritual songs, and singing with grace in the heart to the Lord" (Ephesians 5:18 cf. Colossians 3:16).

At this point, we ought to make an observation regarding the Bible and secular psychology (and any psychology, for that matter). Psychology can identify psychological and personality disorders and can often tell people how they got to the point of having issues. What it cannot do is solve the problem. Jay Adams, who writes on the subject of Christian counseling, says that if you tell others they are sick, you effectively give them an excuse for their issues and remove hope of recovery. However, if you tell others the problem is sin, then you can point them in the direction whereby there is hope of recovery. There is a solution for the sin problem. The cross solves the sin issue if one will simply believe what the scriptures say about the cross and what our Lord Jesus Christ accomplished there.

Figure 1

Our Human Makeup of Spirit Soul and Body (1 Thessalonians 5:23)

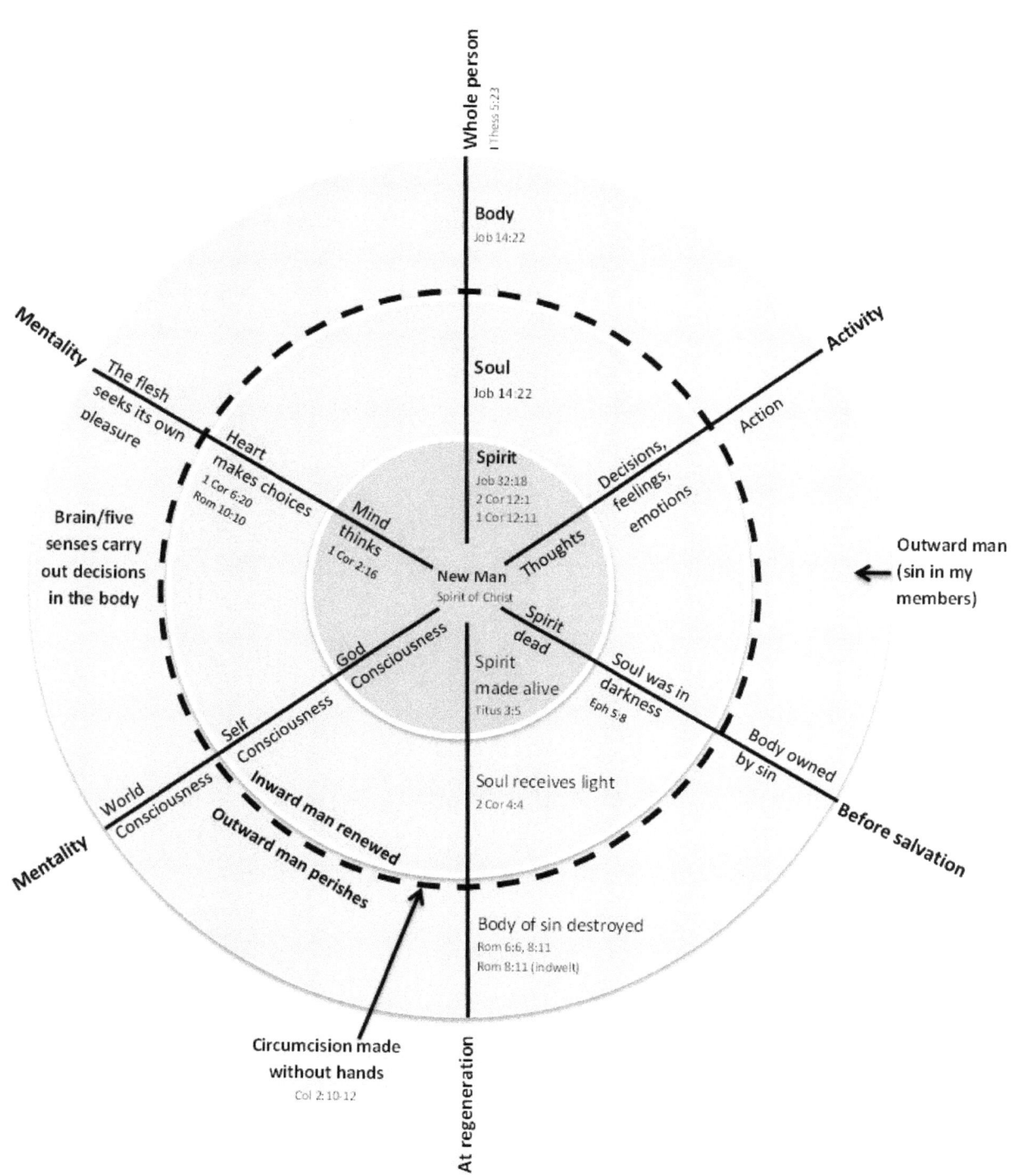

Study Questions on Chapter 6

1. Why would Paul even consider the suggestion of our continuing in sin that grace might abound?

2. What is it that actually makes grace abound?

3. Compare the term "dead to sin" in verse 2 with the term "dead in sin" in Eph. 2:1. What is the difference between being dead to sin and being dead in sin?

4. Verse 3 talks about being baptized into Christ and into His death. What kind of a baptism is this? How can a person be buried with Christ by baptism into death?

5. What does the term "planted together" in verse 5 mean? Is the resurrection of verse 5 talking about our future physical resurrection?

6. Below are four questions that need to be answered in order to understand verse 6. Write a clear answer to each.

      Who is our old man?

      In what sense was he crucified?

      What is the body of sin?

      In what sense was it destroyed?

7. How is it that one who is dead is "freed from sin"?

8. Verse 9 says that death no longer has dominion over Christ. Did death ever have dominion over Him? Did death have dominion over us?

9. According to verse 10, what was it that Christ died unto?

10. The term "Likewise reckon..." in verse 11 relates back to verse 10. What is the connection?

11. What is it in verse 12 that we are not to obey? Is Sin a person that it can cause us to obey it?

12. To what does the term "Members" in verse 13 refer? What does the term "Yield" imply?

13. Sin was reigning in 5:21 but 6:14 says that sin shall not have dominion over you. What made the difference? What brought about the change?

14. How does our not being under Law result in sin not having dominion over us?

15. Why would Paul even ask such as question as "Shall we sin because we are not under Law?"

16. What is the term "obedience" in verse 16 referring to? What does such obedience result in?

17. There is a change of masters described in verses 16 through 21. Who were/are the two masters referred to?

18. Verse 20 refers to the believer being free from righteousness. When was that?

19. Go through the chapter once more and list the words that are in contrast with each other.

20. What are the wages that sin pays? Is he ever late in paying his wages? What gift does God give?

CHAPTER 7

THE WALK AFTER THE FLESH

Chapters 5–7 of Romans deal with the believer's liberty from death, sin, and the law respectively. It is the believer's association with our Savior's death that earned all three for us.

In chapter 5, death reigned (5:12–17).

5:15—Sin came upon all to condemnation, but righteousness come upon all men unto life.

In chapter 6, sin was the master.

6:22—Sin was over a person and had domination over him or her. But now, being made free from sin, holiness and eternal life can reign.

In chapter 7, law was a husband.

7:6—Sin in a person rebels against the law and results in desperation. But now we are delivered from the law.

Death, sin, and the law triumphed over our Savior on the cross. But the dominion of all three ended when He died to them and rose again. The believer died there with Christ, and therefore the dominion of all three ended for the believer as well. The believer not only died with Christ but also rose with Him so the believer can be joined to the risen Lord as the new husband. The result of our union with the Lord in His death, burial, and resurrection is new life for the believer and liberty and sanctification in the power and energy of the indwelling Spirit. Chapter 7 addresses the Law in a way that has never before this point been seen in the scriptures. There is a figure of speech used in verses 4–6 that is deep and requires careful thought.

The Dominion of the Law Has Ended

[1] Know ye not, brethren, (for I speak[a] to them that know the law,) how that the law hath dominion over a man as long as he liveth? [2] For the woman which hath an husband is bound by the law to her husband so long as he liveth; but if the husband be dead, she is loosed from the law of her husband. [3] So then if, while her husband liveth, she be married to another man, she shall be called an adulteress: but if her husband be dead, she is free from that law; so that she is no adulteress, though she be married to another man. [4] Wherefore, my brethren, ye also are become[b] dead to the law by[c] the body of Christ; that ye should be married[d] to another, even to him who is raised[e] from the dead, that we should bring forth[f] fruit unto God. [5] For when we were[g] in the flesh, the motions[h] of sins, which were[i] by the law, did work in our members to bring forth fruit unto death. [6] But now we are delivered from the law, that being dead[j]

wherein we were held; that we should serve[k] in newness[l] of spirit, and not in the oldness of the letter. (Romans 7:1–6)

[a] In this passage Paul addresses those who know the principle of law. The law could be any law here, Jewish or Roman. The law of marriage of Genesis 2:24 could be in view here. The law of marriage is that the wife "is bound by the law to her husband so long as he liveth." The point the apostle is making is that only death can break the marriage contract in the proper sense. However, based on what we will see as we go on to chapter 7, it is apparent that he is speaking of the Law of Moses and the believer. Before being baptized into Christ's death, burial, and resurrection, a man had only one avenue of approach to God—he had to come through Israel's Law of Moses. In verses 1–3, the husband is the law. It is only if the husband (the law) is dead that the believer can be married to another.

[b] Here in verse 4, Paul switches from the husband being dead to the wife having died to the law. In making application of the illustration of verses 2–3, the husband is the law. It is the wife (the believer) who dies to the husband (Law of Moses). But the wife doesn't stay dead; she rises with Christ (Romans 6:4). Having died to the law in Christ and having been raised with Christ, the believer is now freed from the law and freed to be joined to the risen Savior forever. The result of this union with Christ is that we can now bring forth real fruit (i.e., the fruit of the Spirit of Galatians 5:22).

[c] The believer is dead to the law "by the body of Christ" (i.e., by means of our Savior's physical body that died in payment for our sins). In Colossians 1:22–23, the apostle says Christ reconciled us "in the body of his flesh through death to present you holy and unblamable and unreprovable in his sight." Peter says of Christ, "Who his own self bare our sins in his own body on the tree that we, being dead to sins, should live unto righteousness: by whose stripes we are healed" (1 Peter 2:24).

[d] The concept of being married (v. 4) is a reference to the spiritual union that forms the one new man of Ephesians 2:15. The apostle elaborates on this relationship in Ephesians 5:23–29. "For we are members of his body, of his flesh, and of his bones." This spiritual union is formed by the baptizing work of the Holy Spirit (1 Corinthians 12:13).

[e] With Jesus Christ, our Lord, the one who was raised from the dead is the same who died on our behalf. However, with the believer, the one who was raised from the dead (spiritually) is a different person from the one who died. The believer was baptized into Christ and His death (Romans 6:3–4) so "that our old man was crucified with him, that the body of sin might be destroyed, that henceforth we should not serve sin" (Romans 6:6, emphasis added). Here we see that union with Christ in His death enabled us to die to the law so we could be joined to the risen Lord, being now free from the law due to the fact that we had died to it. It is apparent from several passages (Ephesians 2:15; Colossians 2:14; 2 Corinthians 3:11; and so forth) that the law has been taken out of the way for the believer so grace can produce our real life (the life of Christ) in us. "For he is our peace, who hath made both one, and hath broken down the middle wall of partition between us; Having abolished in his flesh the enmity, even the law of commandments contained in ordinances; for to make in himself of twain one new man, so making peace" (Ephesians 2:14–15). The typology of the giving of the law is very appropriate. God gave the law to Israel and told them to put it in a coffin, which was fitted with a covering called the "mercy seat" (Exodus 25:10, 16–17, 21–22; Leviticus 16:14–15). The law worked death (v. 5) and was destined to die itself. The death of the law for the believer is the result of Christ's work on the cross, which was "blotting out

the handwriting of ordinances that was against us, which was contrary to us, and took it out of the way, nailing it to his cross" (Colossians 2:14).

[f] The purpose of our union with the risen Lord Jesus Christ is here given "that we should bring forth fruit unto God." This fruit is the fruit of the Spirit of Galatians 5:22. This fruit can be produced only by Christ living in and through the believer (Galatians 2:20). The believer can accomplish this by "reckoning the old man dead" and the new man "alive unto God." This reckoning of the old man dead describes "the law of the spirit of life in Christ Jesus" that we will see in Romans 8:1–4.

[g] The phrase "when we were in the flesh" (v. 5) refers back to the time before we were saved. At that time we weren't "in Christ" by baptism into His death (Romans 6:3–4). Rather, we were "in Adam." Here the apostle uses another figure of speech for being in Adam (i.e., being "in the flesh"). The "flesh" here refers to being physically descended from Adam.

[h] The word motions literally means "passions." The word gives us our modern English "emotions." These are the desires of our souls. But we need to look at the entire phrase, "the motions of sin." This is a reference to the actions (sins) that are the result of the outworking of the old sin nature.

[i] Here we find an interesting statement in scripture. The actions resulting from the outworking of the desires of the sin nature were "by the law." Now we must ask, "In what sense were those actions by the law?" The apostle answers that question in verses 7–8. We state simply here that the law incited the rebellious sin nature to act contrary to the law.

[j] The actions of the sin nature (i.e., the motions of sin) did work (i.e., were energized) in our members to produce death. When sin worked in our members, it produced fruit. But the fruit it produced was fruit that made us worthy of death. However, the fruit that results from the union of the believer with the risen Christ is fruit God produced, and it's fruit that will last for eternity.

[k] We are now delivered from bondage to the law. The "but now" signifies the change that occurred with regeneration. The deliverance is the result of something being dead. We ask, "What is it that died in order that we might be delivered?" There are two possibilities:

1. The believer's old man is crucified; the believer has become "dead to the law by the body of Christ" (v. 4).

2. Or the law is also dead to the believer (Colossians 2:14; 2 Corinthians 3:11; Ephesians 2:14–15).

We know from scripture and from our experience that sin isn't dead—it still lives in our flesh (Romans 7:18). Considering the context, however, it is apparent that the reference is to the first—the believer being "dead to the law." More specifically, it was the old man that put me in bondage to the law in that my old man rebelled against the law. The death of the old man takes us back to Romans 6:3–6, where we see the old man crucified with Christ.

[m] The purpose of the old man being crucified is that we can now serve God in a new way (i.e., new in respect to quality, not time). This new way is through a new Spirit within the believer. In Romans 8:9, that new spirit is said to be the Spirit of Christ. The old way was to serve God in the oldness of the letter (i.e., the letter of the law). The contrast is that of the living Spirit of Christ in the believer living the life of Christ out through the believer

(Galatians 2:20) in comparison to the cold, hard letter on the pages of the law demanding the flesh to perform up to its standards.

So Then Is the Law Sin?

> [7] What shall we say then? Is[m] the law sin? God forbid[n]. Nay, I had not known sin, but by the law: for I had not known lust, except the law had said, Thou shalt[o] not covet. [8] But sin, taking occasion by the commandment, wrought[p] in me all manner of concupiscence. For without the law sin was dead. [9] For I was[q] alive without the law once: but when the commandment came, sin revived, and I died. [10] And the commandment, which was ordained[r] to life, I found to be unto death. [11] For sin, taking occasion by the commandment, deceived[s] me, and by it slew me. [12] Wherefore the law is[t] holy, and the commandment holy, and just, and good. [13] Was then that which is good made[u] death unto me? God forbid. But sin, that it might appear sin, working death in me by that which is good; that sin by the commandment might become exceeding sinful. (Romans 7:7–13)

m Verse 7 presents the third of four significant rhetorical questions Paul asks to guide the flow of thought through chapters 6–7. The questions and answers are the following:

- Question: "Shall we continue in sin that grace may abound?" Answer: "God forbid. How shall we that are dead to sin, live any longer therein?" (6:1–2).

- Question: "Shall we sin, because we are not under law, but under grace?" Answer: "God forbid. Know ye not that to whom ye yield yourselves servants to obey, his servants ye are to whom ye obey; whether of sin unto death, or of obedience unto righteousness?" (6:15–16).

- Question: "Is the law sin?" Answer: "God forbid. Nay, I had not known sin, but by the law: for I had not known lust, except the law had said, Thou shalt not covet" (7:7).

- Question: "Was then that which is good made death unto me?" Answer: "God forbid. But sin, that it might appear sin, working death in me by that which is good; that sin by the commandment might become exceeding sinful" (7:13).

The first two of these questions address objections to the fact of deliverance from the mastership of sin. The last two address objections to the truth of liberation from the dominion of law. In verse 5, the objection is that the law must somehow be sin if the effect it has on man is to bring forth fruit unto death. This objection is answered by the fact that the law is holy, but the problem is with me. The objection in verse 13 is in even granting that the law is good and holy, yet in its use in that it produces the sin it forbids, the horribleness of Mr. Sin becomes exceedingly evil. The answer to this objection is that the moral effect of the law is beneficial in that it reveals the evil that lies within man. The law shows the sin nature to be exceedingly sinful and therefore makes it evident to man's own consciousness.

This question in verse 7 is the result of the truth of verse 5. "For when we were in the flesh, the motions of sin which were by the law, did work in our members to bring forth fruit undo death." If the result of the law working on man is to bring forth fruit unto death, then one ought well to ask whether the law was actually the sin nature.

[n] Paul's quick answer to the question "Is the Law sin?" is an emphatic "God forbid." A more detailed answer

follows in verses 7–12. Paul says we wouldn't know sin to be an affront to God except for the fact that the law of God says, "Thou shalt not covet." This takes us back to Romans 3:20: "by the law is the knowledge of sin."

[o] The law isn't sin, but the law incites sin to act. When the law said, "Thou shalt not covet," Paul knew that covetousness offended God, and then sin (the Adamic nature that is at enmity with God [Ephesians 2:2–3]) produced in Paul the covetousness the law forbade. It was not the law that produced "fruit unto death" but rather sin that did it. Sin, however, took occasion by the commandment to produce covetousness. It did so by doing what it does naturally; it rebels against God. Romans 8:7 says that "the carnal mind is enmity against God: for it is not subject to the law of God, neither indeed can be."

[p] Sin (the old nature) is "dead" without the law in the sense that, without a direct command from God, sin has nothing to rebel against, and therefore it has no incitement. This is not to say that sin doesn't do its work of bringing fruit unto death without the presence of the law, but rather it says sin is in a relatively dormant state when there is no law for it to rebel against.

[q] "I was alive without the law once" (v. 9). A number of questions come up relative to this statement:

1. When was Paul alive without the law?

2. And when did the commandment come to Paul? After all, he was born under the law.

Paul is here continuing the thought of sin being relatively dead without the law. Paul essentially says, "There was a time in my life before I understood what the law was really saying when I felt good about myself. Then after I understood what the law said (i.e., I understood the moral excellency it demanded), the sin nature in me rebelled against it, and I suddenly realized that what it forbade was what I was doing, and I was under the penalty of violating it."

Paul, when he was first justified by faith, became spiritually alive and he felt alive. Then he considered the moral dictates of the Law and tried to make his flesh perform up to its standard. At that point, he became conscious of the fact that his flesh could not live up to that standard. Instead, the sin nature within his flesh was activated by the Law. He then perceived himself as being spiritual dead and incapable of living up to what God expected of him. This then produced the frustration that we see in verses 14 through 25 and the self-condemnation of verse 24.

[r] The commandment was ordained unto life in the sense that, if a person would have perfectly kept it, it would have produced life. This takes us back to Leviticus 18:5. "Ye shall therefore keep my statutes, and my judgments: which if a man do, he shall live in them: I am the LORD" (cf. Ezekiel 20:11, 13, 21). Our Lord told the rich young ruler the same thing, saying in Luke 10:28, "'This do and thou shalt live.'" Though the commandment was ordained to life, it could produce only death. Paul therefore referred to it as "the ministration of death" in 2 Corinthians 3:7. The commandment that was ordained to life actually produced death in Paul as the sin nature rebelled against it.

[s] The old sin nature is extremely deceitful. "The heart is deceitful above all things, and desperately wicked: who can know it" (Jeremiah 17:9). Here we see that the sin nature in a man deceived him to think he could perform up to the expectations of the law, only to turn and rebel against the commandment. Sin took occasion by the commandment to slay the man. Sin actually uses the commandment as a weapon to slay whoever will put

himself or herself under it. The case of Adam illustrates this use of the law by the sin nature. Adam was innocent until he decided to yield to the temptation. He sinned in his heart before he sinned in actions. James states the case in James 1:14–15. "But every man is tempted, when he is drawn away of his own lust, and enticed. Then when lust hath conceived, it bringeth forth sin: and sin, when it is finished, bringeth forth death." Adam became a sinner when he believed the devil's lie that he could be as a god by eating of the forbidden fruit. As soon as Adam believed that lie, he acquired a sin nature, which used the only command he had from God to rebel against God; and thus the sin nature Adam acquired from the devil used that one commandment to slay Adam.

It is good to ask ourselves at this point what the origin of the sin nature really is. The Lord told the unregenerate scribes and Pharisees, "Ye are of your father the devil, and the lusts of our father we will do. He was a murderer from the beginning, and abode not in the truth, because there is not truth in him" (John 8:44). When Adam fell to the temptation of the devil in Eden, he acquired something from the devil. The word translated "murderer" in John 8:44 is literally in the Greek "manslayer." The devil wasn't a murderer from his beginning, but he was a murderer from man's beginning. As soon as there was a man to slay, the devil was there to slay him. There was some kind of genetic defect placed in Adam's paternal genetics as a result of this encounter with the devil that left him with a sin nature. Adam then passed the sin nature on to each of his children. Since then, every person born into the human race with a human father also has a sin nature. There was one person born into the human race, however, who didn't have a sin nature. He, the Lord Jesus Christ, had a human mother, but God was His Father. His paternal genetics came from God, who is His Father. One day, due to the event we call the "rapture," every believer will have a body fashioned after Christ's body (Philippians 3:21), and it won't have a sin nature.

[t] Here is the final answer to the question of verse 7 (i.e., the law [all three parts: the ceremonial, the moral, and the civil] is holy). Also, the commandment (i.e., the moral law) is holy, just, and good). While that describes the law, it doesn't describe us. The problem is not with the law but with us.

[u] The good thing referred to in verse 13 is the law. The objection raised here is that, granting that the law is holy and just and good, it becomes an evil thing, in that the effect it has on me is to produce sin and death. But God allows sin (the nature) to use what is good (the law) to work death in me so the true nature of sin (Mr. Sin) is pressed on my consciousness. Thus the real effect is benevolent to the believer in that it teaches him or her sin's true character (i.e., that sin has no regard for the welfare of the individual in whom it dwells).

Two Natures within the Believer

¹⁴ For we know that the law is[v] spiritual: but I am carnal, sold under sin. ¹⁵ For that which I do[w] I allow not: for what I would, that do[x] I not; but what I hate, that do I. ¹⁶ If then I do that which I would not, I consent unto the law that it is good. ¹⁷ Now then it is no more I that do[y] it, but sin that dwelleth in me. ¹⁸ For I know that in me (that is, in my flesh,) dwelleth no good thing: for to will is present with me; but how to perform that which is good I find not. ¹⁹ For the good that I would I do not: but the evil which I would not, that I do. ²⁰ Now if I do that I would not, it is no more I that do it, but sin that dwelleth in me. ²¹ I find[z] then a law, that, when I would do good, evil is present with me. ²² For I delight[aa] in the law of God after the inward man: ²³ But I see another law in my members, warring[ab] against the law of my mind, and bringing me into captivity to the law of sin which is in my members. ²⁴ O wretched man that I am! who shall deliver[ac] me from the body of this death? ²⁵ I thank[ad] God through Jesus Christ our Lord. So then with the mind I myself serve the law of God; but with the flesh the law of sin." (Romans 7:14–25)

[v] Paul comes to the same understanding here that every believer eventually comes to. The law is spiritual, but the problem rests with me. I am carnal (fleshly). I am sold under sin. I am the guilty party, not the law. In Galatians 5:18–21, we see what the flesh produces. Note we see this in the present tense: "I am carnal," even as a believer under grace. The phrase "sold under sin" is in the perfect tense, passive voice. That means he has been sold under sin to be a slave to sin by another, that being through Adam and ultimately through the devil. This takes us back to Roman 5:12–14, 19. Since it is in the perfect tense, we understand that the results of the action continue, that result being that we have a propensity to sin (Romans 7:24–25; 8:13). That means we still have to struggle with the sin nature.

[w] Here (in vv. 14–25) we see the two natures at work in the believer. That this experience is of a believer is evident from verse 22, where we see that this person delights in the law of God. An unsaved person couldn't do so (Ephesians 2:2). This shouldn't be the normal Christian experience, though. However, this will be the experience of the believer who puts himself or herself under law. The believer's new nature doesn't profit from the law because the new nature, which is the Spirit of Christ within the believer (Romans 8:9), cannot and will not sin. The old nature, however, needs only to have a law of God to rebel against, and it will rebel. Therefore, the believer who puts himself or herself under a performance-based acceptance system will experience the frustrations of Romans 7:15–23 and will experience the self-condemnation of Romans 7:24. We will see that this is the condemnation of which Romans 8:1 and 4 refer back to.

[x] "For that which I do I allow not: for what I would, that do I not; but what I hate, that do I" (v. 15). Wow! How do we sort this out? The real person of the believer is the new man of Ephesians 2:15, who is joined eternally to the Savior to form the new creature (2 Corinthians 5:17). The real person of the believer is the inward man of verse 22 (cf. Ephesians 3:16) and the mind of verses 23 and 25. It is the regenerated spirit (cf. Romans 8:10) within the believer.

[y] Paul's words "It is no more I that do it" sounds like some kind of a cop-out. What we are seeing here is that Mr. Sin (the sin nature) is distinct from the real Paul, but they both dwell in the same place. However, Paul dwells in his body Mr. Sin no longer owns, but sin dwells in his flesh (i.e., that part of the physical makeup in which the sin nature resides). Bodies are what we live in to live the life of Christ (Romans 8:11), but the flesh is something that dwells in our bodies.

[z] "I find" (v. 21) is in the present tense. The believer is constantly in the state of discovering that there is a law (a phenomenon so often repeated that it's a fixed principle) that, when the real man (the new man) would do good, evil is lurking in his flesh to hinder his progress. Up to this verse, every time Paul used the word law except for one use in 3:27, he referred to the Law of Moses. However, in 7:22–23, 25; 8:2, 4, 7, he used the term in reference to a principle or rule. This principle is that, when I want to do good, evil is present in me to stand opposed to what I desire to do. That conflict is present in every believer.

In verses 21–23, we see three different laws.

1. In verse 21, we see the law of sin and death. Here the term law refers to an operating principle. An operating principle is like the law of gravity. Every time it is applied, it works. The law of sin and death (Romans 8:1–4) is the operating principle of the indwelling sin nature producing spiritual death in the believer. This is the principle that "when I would do good, evil is present with me." In verse 24, it is the

"law in my members" that wars against the law of my mind.

2. The "law of God" in verse 22 is the righteous standard established by the Law of Moses.

3. The "law of my mind" in verse 23 is the understanding of the working of the Spirit of God under grace. This is the new man working in the believer to produce "fruit unto God" (v. 9). This is the inward man of verse 22. We will see all three of these laws again in Romans 8:1–4.

[aa] Paul delights in the law of God (as does every genuine believer). The law is a teacher. It teaches men and angels things about man and the wisdom of God. Consider the following:

The law was "ordained by angels" (Galatians 3:19). In Hebrews 2:2, we see that angels spoke it. One can picture a meeting at the mount of the congregation, where the angels meet with God (Isaiah 14:13) as in Job 1:6 and 2:1, when God asked angels how He might keep His nation Israel from going the way of the other nations God rejected at Babel. The angels offered a suggestion that God put them under a system of blessings for obedience and cursings for disobedience. God didn't need advice from the angels, but He is teaching angels something about His wisdom (Ephesians 3:10). The angels learned that law couldn't produce the obedience it demanded, but grace can. We will see in Romans 8:1–4 that grace can and will produce what the law demanded of us but couldn't produce in us.

The law teaches unsaved people that they need the redemption offered in Christ (Galatians 3:22–24). "The law was our schoolmaster to bring us unto Christ."

The law teaches the believer as God allows sin to use the law to slay (spiritually) the man who is under it (v. 13).

[ab] In verse 24 we see warfare within the believer in which "the law in my members" wars against "the law of my mind." We see this in Galatians 5:17. "For the flesh lusteth against the Spirit, and the Spirit against the flesh: and these are contrary the one to the other: so that ye cannot do the things that ye would." This is not to say that the believer is mastered by the flesh; Romans 6 teaches that believers are set free from the flesh. Galatians 5:17 says the flesh has a purpose (i.e., to keep the believer from doing what it would). Romans 7:20 says that if I do what I would not, it is obviously not I, the new creature in Christ, that is doing it but sin that dwells in me. Paul recognizes two forces at work in the world:

> First, God is at work in the world to save lost people (1 Timothy 1:15) and to work in believers to will and do of His good pleasure (Philippians 2:13).

> Second, Satan is at work in unbelievers to hide the gospel from them (2 Corinthians 4:4) and to set the course of this world in opposition to the cause of Christ (Ephesians 2:2). Though Satan apparently doesn't have access to the mind of believers anymore (Ephesians 2:1–6), his seed (Genesis 3:15), the flesh (old Mr. Sin), is still in the believer. These two forces are seen in Genesis 3:5 as "the seed of the woman" (Christ) and the "seed of the serpent" (the sin nature in man). Before regeneration, the real Paul was the seed of the serpent, sold under sin. After regeneration, the real Paul was the new man, Christ living out His life through Paul. The real Paul now willed to do what was right. However, he observed something being done in his members he didn't will to do. This he attributed to the sin nature living in his members.

[ac] Paul's cry in verse 24 is the cry of a frustrated and miserable person. Paul expressed this misery as a person

who had put himself under the law and had demanded that his flesh produce righteous conduct. The more he demanded righteousness of himself, the more the sin nature in him rebelled and produced the very thing the law forbade. This is the frustration Galatians 2:21 describes when it says, "I do not frustrate the grace of God: for if righteousness comes by the law, then Christ is dead in vain." The answer to Paul's question "Who shall deliver me from the body of this death?" is in verse 25. "I Thank God through Jesus Christ our Lord." Though the actual answer is in chapter 8, this prayer of thanks to God implies that God delivered him from this misery though the work Jesus Christ did.

[ad] Here is the conclusion Paul comes to as a result of his experience in chapter 7: "I myself serve the law of God but with the flesh [i.e., what I can do in my own strength] I serve the law of sin."

Study Questions on Chapter 7

1. We saw that chapter 6 was deliverance from Sin's mastery. What is the believer delivered from in chapter 7?

2. What concept is Paul drawing the reader's attention to in the parenthesis in verse 1?

3. According to the law principle, how can a woman be legitimately freed from her husband?

4. Is it appropriate for a woman to have two husbands? There is a principle that Paul is bringing to our attention here. What is it?

5. Verse 4 says that we believers became dead to the Law. How did that happen?

6. Verse 4 also says that we are in a new relationship to our Lord Jesus Christ. How does this new relationship compare with our Lord's earthly ministry to Israel?

7. What should this new relationship produce according to verse 4? What verse in chapter 6 does this contrast with?

8. What fruit did our lives bare before we were saved?

9. According to verse 6, our deliverance should result in our service to God being on a difference basis. What was the old basis and what is the new?

10. Paul asks in verse 7 "Is the Law sin?" Why would he ask such a question?

11. Taking verses 7 & 8 together, tell me what you think the Law was given for?

12. Paul says that he was alive without the Law once. But then the commandment came and he died. When was he without the Law and how did the command come and slay him?

13. In verse 9 sin revived and Paul died. How did the Law make sin revive?

14. In verse 10, the commandment was ordained to what? What did it really produce?

15. In verse 11, something slew Paul. What was it? What did it use to slay him?

16. Verse 12 lists three characteristics of the Law. Do these characteristics describe us?

17. In verse 13, what did the Law make sin to be in Paul's eyes?

18. According to verse 14 is the Law the problem or is the problem in me?

19. Put verses 15 and 16 in your own words. Should this be regarded as the normal Christian life?

20. In verse 17 and again in verse 20, who was really doing the bad things in Paul's life?

21. According to verse 18, where in me does the problem lie?

22. What principle is expressed in verse 21?

23. What was it within Paul that delighted in the law of God? What other law was in his members?

24. How did Paul feel about the conflict within himself?

25. What did Paul desire according to verse 24?

26. Did Paul find the deliverance that he was looking for? In whom did he find it?

27. Does verse 25 provide a satisfactory conclusion to the statements made in verses 4 through 6 or do you have the sense that there is more to come in chapter 8 on the subject?

Chapter 8

TOTAL VICTORY IN CHRIST

¹There is therefore now no[a] condemnation to them which are in[b] Christ Jesus, who walk[c] not after the flesh, but after the Spirit. ² For the law[d] of the Spirit of life[e] in Christ Jesus hath made me free from the law of sin and death.[f] ³ For what the law could[g] not do, in that it was weak through the flesh, God sending his own Son in the likeness of sinful flesh, and for sin, condemned sin in the flesh: ⁴ That the righteousness of the law might be fulfilled in us, who walk not after the flesh, but after the Spirit. (Romans 8:1–4)

[a] Upon whom is there "no condemnation"? The KJV says it is on those who are in Christ Jesus, "who walk not after the flesh but after the Spirit." Modern translations, based on the Siniaticus and Vaticanus manuscripts, leave off the last part of verse 1. The KJV is correct in that the "no condemnation" here refers to the self-condemnation we saw in the close of the last chapter. That self-condemnation was the result of a believer who had put himself or herself under law and thereby incited the sin nature that dwelt in his or her flesh to rebel against that law. The new man desired to keep the law because the law is good (Romans 7:12) and spiritual (Romans 7:14), but the sin nature stood against performing the law. The result is that the believer who has put himself or herself under law is a miserable creature and brings self-condemnation upon himself or herself. However, there is hope; there is an alternative. The believer can walk after the Spirit, not after the flesh.

[b] The first step in having no condemnation is to be "in Christ Jesus." For us living in the dispensation of the grace of God, we are "in Christ Jesus" by having trusted that He (Christ) is the propitiation for our sins (Romans 3:21) through His shed blood. At the moment one trusts Christ's work on the cross as payment in full for one's sins, the Holy Spirit baptizes the believer into Christ (Galatians 3:27) and makes him or her a member of the church, Christ's body (1 Corinthians 12:12–13).

[c] The walk after the flesh is the walk described in Romans 7:8–25. The walk after the flesh is a walk in which the believer endeavors to live a life according to the standard of the law in his or her own strength, trusting that such an effort will gain merit with God. The walk after the Spirit, on the other hand, is a walk according to the doctrine of Romans 6:6–13, in which the believer understands he or she needs not let sin reign in his or her mortal body and then reckons himself or herself dead to sin and alive unto God. Galatians 5:16–25 describes the enmity of the flesh versus the Spirit. These two principles are contrary the one toward the other. When the believer would walk after the flesh, the Spirit stands in opposition to him or her, but when the believer would walk after the Spirit, the flesh stands in opposition. Thankfully, though, the believer can reckon himself or herself to be dead indeed unto sin and alive unto God.

[d] There are three laws in Romans 8:2–3. These laws are the following:

1. The law of the Spirit. This is also the law "of life in Christ Jesus." This is the principle of the indwelling

Spirit of Christ in the believer, producing the life of Jesus Christ in him or her. The law is stated in Romans 6:4–6 and is put into effect in the believer by the work of the Holy Spirit of God, baptizing the believer into Christ. This law operates on the faith principle as the believer reckons himself or herself to be dead indeed unto sin and alive unto God. Thus the life of Christ (Galatians 2:20) is lived out in the believer. The Spirit of Christ in the believer is the seed of the woman of Genesis 3:15, because Christ Himself is the promised seed of the women.

2. The law of sin and death. This is the principle of the indwelling sin nature within the believer that is at enmity against God. The natural man (i.e., an unregenerate man) is dominated by that sin nature and therefore cannot understand the things of the Spirit of God (1 Corinthians 2:14). It is called the law of sin and death because the sin nature produced sin, resulting in death. Because my old man has been crucified with Christ when I believed the gospel of 1 Corinthians 15:3–4, I do not need to be in bondage to the sin nature anymore.

3. The law of verse 3 is the Law of Moses. The Law of Moses (i.e., moral law) couldn't produce in me the righteousness it demanded because it depended on the strength of my flesh to do it, and the truth remains that "in my flesh dwelleth no good thing" (Romans 7:18).

[e] In verse 2, it should be noted that the theme of this chapter is the sanctification of the believer. The theme of chapter 3 is justification; God reckons the sinner righteous. Here we see God working in the believer to make the believer holy as God applies the operating principles of grace. While chapter 3 deals with Christ's work for the sinner, this chapter deals with Christ's work in the believer. Chapter 8 can be analyzed in four parts.

1. The basis of sanctification (vv. 1–4)

2. The flesh and spirit in conflict (vv. 5–14)

3. The attitude of sonship (vv. 15–17)

4. The believer's hope and patience (vv. 18–28)

[f] It should be noted that the law of the Spirit produces life, but the law of sin produces death.

[g] The simple statement has its subject in the first part of verse 3 and its compliment in the last part of verse 4; all in between are subordinate clauses. The simple truth is, "what the law could not do … God … fulfilled in us who walk not after the flesh but after the Spirit." God did this by sending His own Son in the likeness of sinful flesh. Note that it was not "as sinful flesh" but "in the likeness of sinful flesh." God the Father "sent" His own Son, Jesus Christ, into our fallen human race to remove the cause for the fall (i.e., the sin nature, the seed of the serpent). Jesus Christ "was in all points [1 John 2:16 cf. Genesis 3:6] tempted like as we are, yet without sin" (Hebrews 4:15). God the Father sent His own Son "for sin" (i.e., as a sacrifice for sin). He did this to condemn sin (i.e., to pronounce a death sentence on the sin nature, the seed of the serpent of Genesis 3:15) in the flesh.

[h] We might ask, What is it that the law couldn't do? The answer is in verse 4. The law couldn't produce the righteous conduct it demanded. The weakness and impotency of the law weren't due to any inherent weakness in the law itself. Rather, they were due to the inability of the flesh of man to keep it. God does indeed desire righteousness put into practice in believers' lives. However, righteousness in practice is in reality the righteousness of God imputed to the believer, which is then lived out through the believer by faith. We can

no more live the Christian life in our own strength than we can enter the Christian life in our own strength. All salvation is of the Lord in its entirety, whether it be salvation from sin's penalty or power or ultimately being delivered from sin's presence with the rapture.

Are You in the Flesh or in the Spirit?

> [5]For they that are after the flesh[i] do mind[j] the things of the flesh; but they that are after the Spirit the things of the Spirit. [6] For to be[k] carnally minded is death; but to be spiritually minded[l] is life and peace. [7] Because the carnal mind is[m] enmity against God: for it is not subject to the law of God, neither indeed can be. [8] So then they that are[n] in the flesh cannot please God. [9] But ye are[o] not in the flesh, but in the Spirit, if so be that the Spirit of God dwell[p] in you. Now if any man have not the Spirit of Christ, he is none of his. (Romans 8:5–9)

[i] There are two wills set in contrast to each other here in verse 5. They are (1) the will of the carnal nature (they who are after the flesh) and (2) the will of God (they who are after the Spirit).

We need to ask some questions here. The first is, Who are they that are after the flesh in verses 1, 4, and 5? Another relative question is, Who are they who are "in the flesh" in verse 8?" To be "in the flesh" is to be an unbeliever who is still "in Adam" as a member of the fallen human race (Romans 5:12). All who are "in Adam" die, but all who are "in Christ" shall be made alive (1 Corinthians 15:22). To be "in Christ" is to be a believer who was baptized into one new man (Ephesians 2:15). This happens the moment one first came to faith in the work Jesus Christ did on the cross (1 Corinthians 12:13; Galatians 3:27; Romans 6:1–4). The believer isn't "in the flesh" (v. 9) but rather "in the Spirit." However, the believer can "walk after the flesh" because the flesh is still in the believer until either death or the rapture.

Those who are "in Christ" have a decision to make that unbelievers don't have. They can either "walk after the flesh" or "walk after the Spirit." To "walk after the flesh" is to "let sin reign in our mortal bodies" (Romans 6:12). The believer can be "after the flesh" by setting his or her affections on the things of the flesh and thus focusing his or her mind on the flesh. On the other hand, the believer can set his or her affections on the Spirit and focus on the will of God. This defines the difference between the carnal believer and the spiritual believer in 1 Corinthians 3:1. The believer, even though he or she isn't in the flesh, can still mind the things of the flesh and be just as carnal as an unbeliever. However, the believer must quench the indwelling Spirit to live a carnal life (1 Thessalonians 5:19).

[j] Those who live after the flesh set their minds on the things that can be seen, tasted, smelled, heard, and touched. All these things, however, are temporal (2 Corinthians 4:18) and will perish. However, those who live after the Spirit set their minds on things that aren't seen but are eternal. The unseen things of the Spirit are the things of Romans 3:21 through chapter 8. They include the following:

- Being justified freely by God's grace through the redemption in Christ Jesus (3:24)
- Having the blessedness of not having sins imputed to us (4:7)
- Having peace with God through our Lord Jesus Christ (5:1)
- Having access by faith in God's grace (5:2)
- Having the hope of glory (5:2)

- Being able to rejoice in tribulation (5:3)

- Having the love of God filling us to overflowing (5:5)

- Being saved from God's wrath (5:9)

- Having the indwelling Spirit of God, who guides us through the Word (5:5)

- Having the indwelling Christ to give us the spirit of adoption (5:10; 8:7)

- Having received the atonement (5:11)

- Having the old man crucified so we need not obey the sin nature (6:6)

- Having the opportunity to bear fruit unto God (6:22)

- Having received eternal life as a gift (6:23)

- Having been freed from the law (7:4)

- Being children of God, joint heirs with Christ (8:17)

The difference between walking after the flesh and walking after the Spirit comes down to a decision the believer makes. The walk after the Spirit is a mental attitude Paul describes in 6:11–13. "Reckon ye also yourselves to be dead indeed unto sin, but alive unto God through Jesus Christ our Lord. Let not sin therefore reign in your mortal body, that ye should obey it in the lusts thereof. Neither yield ye your members as instruments of unrighteousness unto sin: but yield yourselves unto God, as those that are alive from the dead."

[k] To be carnally minded (v. 6) is death. We ask, What kind of death is this? It's not spiritual death in the sense of being separated from God because, by the baptism by which the believer is joined to Christ, the believer shares in the life of Christ (Galatians 2:20; 3:17; Romans 6:4). Death can mean physical death (the separation of the soul from the body), as in Genesis 35:18, or spiritual separation from God for eternity, as with the second death (Revelation 2:11; 20:6, 14). It can also mean dormancy, as here and 1 Timothy 5:6 and so forth. The death here is death of one's Christian experience. It should be noted that the Bible describes several kinds of death:

- Physical death is the separation of the soul and spirit from the physical body (Genesis 35:18).

- Death of the soul is the death Adam and Eve died when they sinned in Eden (Genesis 2:17).

- There is a functional death, in which a regenerated spirit doesn't function for a lack of yielding of one's will to the revealed will of God as it is revealed in the Word of God. This is the death as far as the believer's Christian experience is concerned. This is the death Romans 8:6 is describing.

- There is what the Bible calls the second death (Revelation 2:11; 20:6, 14; 21:8). This is the eternal separation of the soul of the unbeliever from the life of God in Christ.

- There is also the death of the old man, which happened at conversion to Christ in Romans 6:6.

[l] To be spiritually minded is life and peace, because the mind focused on the real working of God, as described in Romans 6:3–4, taps into the very life of Christ. It is life because it's Christ who is the originator of life living His life out through the believer. It is peace because the believer is at peace with God by means of justification and is at peace with himself or herself, because he or she has reckoned the old man dead. The believer lives a life free from sin's power and a life of practical righteousness that is independent of the law. Such a believer sees

the fruit of the Spirit in his or her life being produced by the Spirit of Christ within him or her.

[m] The carnal mind is enmity against God, because it sets its affections on what it can do in its own strength. Whether it be the carnal mind in the believer or the carnal mind in the unbeliever, its nature is the same; it sets its affections on gratifying itself. Romans 1:28–32 describes the actions and attitudes of the carnal mind. This description pictures mankind when God gave up on the Gentiles in Genesis 11. The carnal mind is thus not in submission to the revealed will of God (i.e., the law of God), because that mind is promoting its own will.

[n] Those who are "in the flesh" are natural-born people who are still "in Adam" (i.e., unbelievers). Unbelievers (unconverted people) can do many good and noble deeds. In fact, unbelievers can and often appear outwardly more righteous than some believers. However, God can take no pleasure in the efforts of the flesh to make itself acceptable to God, because the flesh does so in rejection of the truth God declares regarding His holy character and the sinful nature of man. God rejected Cain's sacrifice because it was the work of his hands; it was his effort at righteousness while not acknowledging his sin. The flesh sets its righteousness up next to God's and says they are equal. Such a comparison cannot please God. Without the aid of a quickened spirit (Ephesians 2:1–2), the natural man has no capacity to see and comprehend the great gulf that exists between his sin-based, self-centered existence and the holy, righteous, and loving character of God. In short, the "natural man receiveth not the things of the Spirit of God for they are foolishness unto him neither can he know them because they are spiritually discerned" (1 Corinthians 2:14).

[o] Paul addresses these Roman believers as being in the Spirit if the Spirit of God dwells in them; therefore, they are not in the flesh. Here again it must be noted that there is a difference between being in the flesh and walking after the flesh. Every regenerated person is transferred from the realm of the flesh to that of the Spirit when God, the Holy Spirit, enters his or her life upon conversion.

[p] It's interesting to note that the Spirit of God in verse 9 is identical to the Spirit of Christ in verse 10. Though God, the Holy Spirit, is obviously a separate person (Acts 5:4; Ephesians 4:30) from either God the Father or Christ, the presence of the Holy Spirit brings with Him the presence of the Spirit of Christ. At the baptism of Christ, the Father spoke from heaven, and the Spirit descended (Matthew 3:16 cf. John 5:7). The Spirit of Christ within the believer is the new nature the believer has. Without this new nature, the believer wouldn't belong to Christ. This Spirit of Christ is as the nerve system to the church, which is Christ's body (1 Corinthians 12:27; Ephesians 5:23; Colossians 1:24). Without this Spirit of Christ, a person wouldn't belong to "the church which is [Christ's] body" (Ephesians 1:22). He or she wouldn't be a member of the "one new man" (Ephesians 2:15). It is a fact that this new nature within the believer is the Spirit of Christ Galatians 2:20 talks about: "the life that I now live in the flesh I live by the faith of the Son of God." Christ is the only one who can live the Christian life in a manner pleasing to God. As the believer walks after the Spirit, it's Christ who lives His life out, in, and through the believer.

This is not the Spirit of bondage but the Spirit of adoption:

10 And if Christ be[q] in you, the body is dead because of sin; but the Spirit is life because of righteousness. 11 But if the Spirit of him that raised[r] up Jesus from the dead dwell in you, he that raised up Christ from the dead shall also quicken[s] your mortal bodies by his Spirit that dwelleth in you. 12 Therefore, brethren, we are[t] debtors, not to the flesh, to live after the flesh. 13 For if ye live[u] after the flesh, ye shall die: but

if ye through the Spirit do mortify[v] the deeds of the body, ye shall live. ¹⁴ For as many as are led[w] by the Spirit of God, they are[x] the sons[y] of God. ¹⁵ For ye have not received[z] the spirit of bondage again to fear; but ye have received the Spirit of adoption[y], whereby we cry, Abba, Father. ¹⁶ The Spirit itself[aa] beareth witness with our spirit, that we are the children[y] of God: ¹⁷ And if children, then heirs; heirs[y] of God, and joint-heirs[ab] with Christ; if so be that we suffer[ac] with him, that we may be also glorified together. (Romans 8:10–17)

[q] If Christ be in you (i.e., if you are a believer), your body is still mortal because the old sin nature is still resident in it. However, the Spirit (i.e., the indwelling Spirit of Christ, the new nature) is immortal because it is righteous and sinless.

[r] There is a significant change in the point of reference in verse 11 from "Jesus" being raised from the dead to "Christ" being raised (literally, "out from among") the dead. The reference to Jesus is a reference to our Lord being personally raised back to physical life after His death payment for our sins. However, the reference to "Christ" being raised from among the dead is a reference to Christ corporately. That is Christ personally together with the church, His body. This takes us to Ephesians 2:5, where we see that "even when we were dead in sins, hath quickened us together with Christ (by grace ye are saved;) And hath raised us up together, and made us sit together in heavenly places in Christ Jesus."

[s] It is the same Spirit (i.e., the Holy Spirit) who raised Jesus Christ personally from the dead, raised the believer spiritually from the dead, and will quicken the mortal bodies of the believers. This quickening of our mortal bodies isn't a reference to the bodily resurrection the believer will one day have. Our bodily resurrection is seen in verse 23. Rather, this quickening of our mortal bodies in verse 11 is a reference to the bodies we have right now. Though the body is dead and mortal because sin dwells in it, it also has the presence of the Holy Spirit within it and, associated with Him, the Spirit of Christ, the new nature. The Holy Spirit then gives life to these mortal bodies to enable us to live the Christian life right now in this mortal body.

[t] We are debtors, but we aren't debtors to the flesh. We don't owe the flesh anything because it hasn't done a thing for us as far as our relationship with God is concerned.

[u] The statement "if ye live after the flesh" (v. 13) implies that it's possible for a believer to live after the flesh. If a believer would live after the flesh, he or she would die as far as his or her Christian experience is concerned (cf. v. 6). This is like the Christian woman in 1 Timothy 5:6. "She that liveth in pleasure is dead while she yet liveth."

[v] Real life for believers comes from mortifying (making to die) the deeds of the body (v. 13). Believers cannot kill the indwelling sin nature. They can, however, mortify (cause to die) the activity of sin in their bodies by walking after the Spirit. This message takes us back to Romans 7:5. "When we were in the flesh, the motions of sin, which were by the law, did work in our members to bring forth the fruit undo death." The motions are the actions the sin nature does and carries out in our bodies. Though that sin nature is still resident in us, we won't be able to be rid of it until either physical death or the rapture; we can stop its actions in our bodies by not yielding the members of our bodies to it (Romans 6:13). Romans 8 can be divided into sections as follows: verses 1–13, sanctification; verses 14–17, sonship; and verses 18–28, sympathy.

[w] The verb "are led" in verse 14 is significant to Paul's defining the mode of obedience of believers to God. Paul as the apostle of the Gentiles, ministering the dispensation of the grace of God to members of the body

of Christ, cites God's control over believers as a leading of the Holy Spirit. This form of divine control of the lives of believers is unique to the present dispensation. Prior to the revelation of the mystery (except for a brief foretaste of life in the kingdom at Pentecost), God exercised control over believers by various works or performance-based means of acceptance. Under the Law of Moses, God commanded obedience and blessed His people when they obeyed but cursed them when they didn't (Deuteronomy 30:16–19). When God dealt with Israel, the means by which any Gentiles would be accepted of God was to bless Israel (Genesis 12:2; Numbers 24:9). Under the new covenant God will make with Israel, God is going to cause His people to keep His statutes and judgments by putting His Spirit within them, taking the "stoney heart" out of their flesh, writing His law in their hearts, and giving them supernatural knowledge of Him (Jeremiah 31:31–33; Ezekiel 36:27; Hebrews 10:10).

Today, in the dispensation of grace, God doesn't put his law within the believer or take the stony heart (the old nature) out of the flesh of believers. He does, however, crucify the old man. Also, God today doesn't give supernatural knowledge of His will though He does give His completed and perfect Word, which enables the believer to know His will. The believer, thus having that anti-God old man crucified, the Holy Spirit of God dwelling within the believer and the external testimony of the will of God in the written Word of God, is led by the Spirit of God into the will of God. (See Appendix A of chapter 8 for a discussion of the leading of the Spirit.)

[x] Verses 13–15 are actually items of further expansion of verse 12. The believer isn't a debtor to the flesh for the following reasons:

1. We can have a vital Christian life only by mortifying the deeds of the body (v. 13).

2. We are sons of God and are thus led by the Spirit of God.

3. God has given us the Spirit of adoption whereby the Holy Spirit testifies to our human spirit that we are born into the family of God.

[y] In verses 14–17, we find four terms referring to the father-child relationship of God and the believer. In verse 14, we find the declaration by the Holy Spirit of God that believers today in the dispensation of grace are sons of God. This is a reference to believers being adult sons in God's family. As adult sons in the family, we are "led by the Spirit" as opposed to being "under tutors and governors" (Galatians 4:2). This relationship is possible because of the work God does in each believer at the moment of conversion. Being joined to Jesus Christ is to be "members of his body, of his flesh, and of his bones" (Ephesians 5:30). More than that, we are "one spirit" with Christ (1 Corinthians 6:17). The same Spirit that prompted our Lord to cry, "Abba Father" is resident in each believer as well (Romans 8:15; Galatians 4:6). Only with us, it isn't the spirit of an only-begotten Son, as was in Christ, but the spirit of adoption that gives us the assurance of having been brought into God's family. The word adoption refers to the placement of children who were born into a family as adults in the family. It makes the child an heir to the family fortune. The word children refers to someone born into the family. Our English language doesn't have a direct counterpart or equivalent except to say "born ones." Believers today are indeed born into God's family by regeneration (Titus 3:5). Regeneration literally means "new beginning."

[z] Two spirits are set in contrast to each other here in verse 15. They are the following:

The spirit of bondage. This is the law system grace replaced. This is the system whereby God said, "If ye will obey my voice indeed, and keep my covenant, then ye shall be a peculiar treasure unto me above all people: for all the earth is mine" (Exodus 19:5, emphasis added). This law system made people "all their lifetime subject to bondage" (Hebrews 2:15). Peter, by comparing the grace of this present dispensation with the law he was under, said, "Now therefore why tempt ye God, to put a yoke upon the neck of the disciples, which neither our fathers nor we were able to bear" (Acts 15:10).

The spirit of adoption, whereby we cry "Abba Father." This is the Spirit of Christ within the believer. Jesus Christ is personally the only begotten Son of God (John 1:18; 3:18; 1 John 4:9). The presence of the Spirit of Christ in us gives us an internal witness to the fact that we believers are children of God by virtue of the fact that we were born into His family. This is by means of the redeeming work of Jesus Christ (Ephesians 1:5–7) and the work of the Holy Spirit in joining us to Jesus Christ to make us members of His body (Galatians 3:27; 1 Corinthians 12:13; Ephesians 5:30) (i.e., the church, His body) (1 Corinthians 12:27; Ephesians 1:22; Colossians 1:18). This birth into the family of God is by the process of regeneration (Titus 3:5). Regeneration means "new beginning." Having been born into the family of God, God adopts us as full-grown sons in His family (Ephesians 1:4–5).

[aa] What spirit is it that witnesses with our spirit that we are the children (born ones) of God? Note, it's not the Spirit "himself" with reference to the Holy Spirit but the spirit "itself." This spirit is the spirit of adoption of verse 15. It is the spirit of Christ within the believer that gives him or her the attitude of a son in the father's family and a partner of the family business.

[ab] The "spirit of adoption" of verse 15 is the spirit of a son in the family in business with the father. This goes back to a custom of the Romans at the time of the writing of the book of Romans. At a time determined by the father, a son who was born into the family (and thus a child of the father) was officially adopted into the family. At the time of adoption, the child was reckoned as a "son," became a full heir with the father, and was reckoned as one with the father in the sense of being an heir of both property and civil status. The son was then heir to both the burdens and the rights of the adopter. Being born into God's family by faith in the redeeming work of Christ, the believer then becomes an heir of God because he or she is a joint heir with Christ. Being joined to Christ by the baptizing work of the Holy Spirit, the believer not only has His righteousness imputed to him or her but also becomes a joint heir with Christ into what He is heir to.

[ac] Believers are joint heirs with Christ, according to verse 17. But the verse also appears to add this condition: "if so be that we suffer with him, that we may also be glorified together." To study this passage, we need to compare it to 2 Timothy 2:11–13. "It is a faithful saying: For if we be dead with him, we shall also live with him: If we suffer, we shall also reign with him: if we deny him, he also will deny us: If we believe not, yet he abideth faithful: he cannot deny himself." The passage here in Romans 8:17 says, "Joint-heirs with Christ; if so be that we suffer with him, that we may be also glorified together." Both passages appear to say the same thing, but there is a difference. Before considering the differences, let's first look at the similarities:

- Both passages talk about eternal glory.
- Both passages talk about suffering.
- Both passages talk about a union with Christ.

Now we consider the differences. While 2 Timothy 2:12 views the suffering believer as a joint reigner with Christ,

Romans 8:17 views the suffering believer as a joint sharer in the glory of Christ. Also, the suffering of 2 Timothy 2:12 is for one's testimony, while here in Romans 8 it is the suffering of this present time (i.e., the suffering associated to living in a sin-cursed world).

Lest we miss the point, let's note that the suffering with Christ in Romans 8:17 is the result of living in this world, which "groaneth and travaileth in pain together until now." Such suffering will bring joint heirship with Christ. The sufferings of 2 Timothy 2:11–13 come from standing for the truth, and that will bring joint reigning with Christ.

Our Earnest Expectation of Adoption—the Redemption of Our Bodies

[18] For I reckon that the sufferings[ad] of this present time are not worthy to be compared with the glory which shall be revealed in us. [19] For the earnest expectation of the creature waiteth for the manifestation[ae] of the sons of God. [20] For the creature[af] was made subject to vanity, not willingly, but by reason of him who hath subjected the same in hope, [21] Because the creature itself also shall be delivered from the bondage of corruption into the glorious liberty of the children of God. [22] For we know that the whole creation groaneth[ag] and travaileth in pain together until now. [23] And not only they, but ourselves also, which have the firstfruits of the Spirit, even we ourselves groan[ah] within ourselves, waiting for the adoption, to wit, the redemption of our body. [24] For we are saved by hope: but hope that is seen is not hope: for what a man seeth, why doth he yet hope for? [25] But if we hope for that we see not, then do we with patience wait[ai] for it. (Romans 8:18–25)

[ad] "The sufferings of the present time" are defined in verse 20. They are the suffering of "this present evil world." These are sufferings that come with living in a creation that "was made subject to vanity" (8:20) when God put a curse on it for the sin of man. Going back to Genesis 3:17, we see that the ground was cursed "for thy sake" (speaking of Adam). These sufferings of verses 17 and 20 are those incurred as a result of living in an environment that "groaneth and travaileth in pain together until now" (Romans 8:22). Our Lord Jesus Christ lived and labored in the same sin-cursed creation we do. These sufferings are common to all, whether believers or unbelievers. These sufferings won't be present during the kingdom reign of Christ on earth (Isaiah 35:1; 11:6–12; and so forth), nor will they be present in heaven. In this passage, the believer is seen as a joint sufferer and a joint sharer in glory with Christ. But there is another passage (2 Timothy 2:12) that speaks of the believer being a joint reigner with Christ because of sharing in His sufferings, while Romans 8:17 speaks of suffering being common to all believers.

Second Timothy 2:12 speaks of sufferings that come only to those believers who will take a stand for the truth. There, in 2 Timothy 2:12, it is only those believers who are willing to suffer for their testimony who will reign with Christ. The reigning for members of the body will, of course, be in heaven because that is where the believer's resurrection body will be (2 Corinthians 5:1). The concept of the believer having obtained an inheritance is related to this issue. The inheritance is eternal life. The believer has already inherited it (Ephesians 1:11). The presence of the Holy Spirit within the believer is the guarantee of it (Ephesians 1:3–14). Every believer has been cleansed so as to be qualified to receive the inheritance (Ephesians 5:5; Colossians 11:20). However, there is a reward of the inheritance that goes only to the faithful believers (Colossians 3:24; 1 Corinthians 3:8–16; 2 Timothy 2:10–15).

It is noteworthy that the Greek word translated "suffer" in Romans 8:17 is a different word than the word translated "suffer" in 2 Timothy 2:12. The word translated "suffer" in 2 Timothy 2:12 is the same word translated "endure" in 2 Timothy 2:10. The suffering in 2 Timothy 2:12 is what one endures for standing for the truth of the word rightly divided (as 2 Timothy 2:15 exhorts believers to do). Those who will reign with Christ in the heavens are those who have come to maturity by studying the word rightly divided and then, by taking a stand for it, hold forth that word to the world around them today. Just learning sound doctrine doesn't produce godliness. It's the faith application of the doctrine that produces maturity.

[ae] The term "sons of God" in verse 19 is an interesting term. It's used in the Bible of persons God directly created. In the genealogy of Luke 3, only Adam is called "the son of God" because Adam had no other father, but God had created him. Angels are called "sons of God" (Genesis 6:2; Job 1:6; and so forth) because they are created directly from the hand of God. Here believers are called "sons of God" because each believer is a new creature (2 Corinthians 5:17), in that each is regenerated at the moment of conversion to Christ. The manifestation of the sons of God refers to a future time when God will set His workmanship (Ephesians 2:10) on display in the dispensation of the fullness of times (Ephesians 1:10). Then He will "gather together in one all things in Christ, both which are in heaven, and which are on earth; even in him." That will take place and coincide with "the adoption, to wit, the redemption of our body" (Romans 8:23). At that time, each believer will have a resurrection body fashioned after Christ's resurrection body (Philippians 3:21).

[af] The "creature" here in verses 19 –20 is God's creation. This takes us back to Genesis in the first three chapters. Apparently God designed the creation we see in Genesis 1:1–31 so it could have lasted forever. Had man not sinned, it would have. However, with the entrance of sin into God's innocent creation, the creation had to be made "subjected to vanity." God's statement in Genesis 3:17–19 ("Cursed is the ground for thy sake; in sorrow shalt thou eat of it all the days of thy life; Thorns also and thistles shall it bring forth to thee. In the sweat of thy face shalt thou eat bread, till thou return to the ground") introduced the decay principle into God's creation. This decay principle is what is known as the second law of thermodynamics or the entropy principle. Briefly stated, this principle says that the universe is winding down and running out of gas. Things in creation are gradually and steadily going from a given state of order to a state of less order and more randomness.

In terms of energy, the sum total energy in God's universe remains constant for now. However, the availability of that energy to do useful work diminishes with time. In every energy transformation process, some amount of the energy goes into its waste form of heat. If the universe were to go on indefinitely in this state, the universe would die a heat death, in which all available energy would have gone into its waste form (i.e., heat). At that point, any further motion would be impossible because energy has to be at two different levels to produce motion. This also gives us empirical verification that the universe hasn't existed from eternity past (based on what we see in its present state); otherwise motion would be impossible. Also, the fact that matter and energy can be neither created nor destroyed (i.e., the first law of thermodynamics) means that the universe must have had a point of miraculous and supernatural beginning (i.e., it had to have been created by someone outside of itself). Also, in addition to the introduction of the second law of thermodynamics, the curse of Genesis 3:17–19 added many unpleasant things to God's creation. We could probably put mosquitoes and wood ticks in with the thorns and thistles as well as viruses, pathogenic bacteria, and so forth.

The creature is a reference to all God's creation, both animate and inanimate. All God's creation was made subject to the curse of Genesis 3:17–19. As stated earlier, this subjection was for man's sake. God's creation would rather be free of the curse, but it can't be until God has accomplished His work of reconciling all His creation back to Himself (Colossians 1:20). The groaning creation has a story to tell (Job 12:6–12). The sin of man stains the environment where man lives (Isaiah 24:2–6; Jeremiah 12:4, 11; 14:5). That is why the heavens and earth as they are now will have to be done away with (i.e., because they are stained by sin [Isaiah 51:6; Revelation 21:1]). The present physical heaven and earth, just because they are stained with sin, will flee from the presence of God one day (Revelation 20:14). There are many Old Testament prophecies about the deliverance of creation from the bondage of corruption (Isaiah; 11:6–12; 35:1–9; 40:31).

[ag Verse 22 speaks of the creation groaning. God's creation will groan under the curse of Genesis 3:18–19 until God creates the universe new again as He stated He will do in Isaiah 65:17. "For, behold, I create new heavens and a new earth: and the former shall not be remembered, nor come into mind." Revelation 21:1 states a future reality of that promise.

[ah] We find in verse 23 a sympathy believers have with creation (i.e., with the environment in which they live). Believers, as regenerated creatures of God, become children of God at the time of conversion, regeneration. They thus have the indwelling Spirit of God, who testifies to their human spirit through the Word of God that they are sons of God. Yet the body in which they live and the environment in which they function is still under the bondage of corruption. Believers, and only believers, can relate to the groaning creation, which was made subject to vanity because of the sin of man but will one day be released from that bondage. This will occur on that future day when all believers will be manifest in glory in a resurrection body, which will be incorruptible (1 Corinthians 15:42). Believers share with Christ this experience of living in a creation that was made subject to vanity with Christ, our Savior. Our Lord left heaven to enter this sin-cursed creation to be "in all points tempted like as we are, yet without sin" (Hebrews 4:15) and to be "made under the law, to redeem them that were under the law, that we might receive the adoption of sons" (Galatians 14:5).

Williams in the Student Commentary makes a statement in respect to this sympathy that is hard to improve on.

> The link which unites the believer with the suffering creation is his body. Because of sin, it is subject to pain, decay, and death. This connection with the creation brings into conscious suffering the heart that is indwelt by the love of Christ. It is the suffering of sympathy. The sense of the pain and evil that encompass the Christian oppresses him; and the more conscious he is of the indwelling warmth and liberty and power of the divine nature, which is love, the more is he sensible of the weight of the misery introduced into the creation by sin. Thus the believer is united to the creation by the body and to heaven by the Spirit; and the sympathy which he feels for the suffering creation is a divine sympathy. (Williams Student Commentary, p. 865)

The bondage of corruption of verse 21 is mortality. The glorious liberty of the children of God is immortality. The word firstfruits of verse 23 is significant. The believer has the Holy Spirit (or, perhaps better, the Holy Spirit has the believer) as a pledge that the redemption of the body will follow (Ephesians 1:13–14; 2 Corinthians 5:2–4).

[ai] "Hope" (v. 24) is one of the enduring gifts of the Spirit (1 Corinthians 13:13). It is the absolute assurance of a future blessing. In verse 20, we see God has hope of one day removing the curse He had to impose on His creation as a result of sin. Here in verse 25 we see the believer can have the same confidence God has that the

bondage of corruption is only temporary.

All Things Are Being Worked Together for Good to the Believer

²⁶ Likewise the Spirit also helpeth[aj] our infirmities: for we know not what we should pray for as we ought: but the Spirit itself maketh[ak] intercession for us with groanings which cannot be uttered. ²⁷ And he that searcheth the hearts knoweth what is the mind of the Spirit, because he maketh[al] intercession for the saints according to the will of God. ²⁸ And we know that all things work[am] together for good to them that love God, to them who are the called according to his purpose. ²⁹ For whom he did foreknow, he also did predestinate[an] to be conformed to the image of his Son, that he might be the firstborn among many brethren. ³⁰ Moreover whom he did predestinate, them he also called: and whom he called, them he also justified: and whom he justified, them he also glorified. (Romans 8:26–30)

[aj] The word likewise in verse 26 takes us back to the previous verse. While we patiently wait for glory, the Spirit helps us by interceding for us. Note that the Spirit "helps" our infirmities. He doesn't deliver us from the bondage of corruption in this life on earth but He helps us go through it. See also 1 Corinthians 10:13 where we see the same help available for the believer. The Spirit "helpeth" our infirmities, which are listed in verses 22–23. Let's look at these infirmities.

1. The environment in which we live "groaneth and travaileth in pain together."

2. In ourselves also, who have the firstfruits of the Spirit, even we ourselves groan within ourselves, waiting for the adoption, the redemption of our bodies. These infirmities take us back to Genesis 3:17, where the creation and man were cursed for man's sake.

3. But there is yet another infirmity, that of 2 Corinthians 5:2–7. For in this we groan, earnestly desiring to be clothed upon with our house which is from heaven: If so be that being clothed we shall not be found naked. For we that are in this tabernacle do groan, being burdened: not for that we would be unclothed, but clothed upon, that mortality might be swallowed up of life. Now he that hath wrought us for the selfsame thing is God, who also hath given unto us the earnest of the Spirit. Therefore we are always confident, knowing that, whilst we are at home in the body, we are absent from the Lord: (For we walk by faith, not by sight:).

   The third infirmary we would list then is that we walk by faith.

   But it is the very act of successfully living the Christian life in spite of these infirmities that allows us to be a testimony to "the principalities and powers in heavenly places" (Ephesians 3:10). We live and function under such infirmities by God's design. The mature saint, once he or she comes to realize this, says with Paul, "Most gladly therefore will I rather glory in my infirmities, that the power of Christ may rest upon me. Therefore I take pleasure in infirmities, in reproaches, in necessities, in persecutions, in distresses for Christ's sake: for when I am weak, then am I strong" (2 Corinthians 12:9–10).

4. Another infirmity is that we each carry sin (the old man) around with us in our flesh (Romans 7:16–17). We must therefore be ever vigilant that we don't let sin reign in our mortal bodies (Romans 6:11).

5. Yet another infirmity is the hostile spiritual environment in which the believer lives. The believer

wrestles not with or against human weakness but against "spiritual wickedness in high [heavenly] places" (Ephesians 6:11; cf 1 Timothy 3:7; and 2 Timothy 2:26). We wrestle with spiritual creatures who have had six thousand years of experience fighting against the likes of us. How we need the armor of God in this fight.

The word helpeth in verse 26 is very significant here. It means the Holy Spirit doesn't do the job for us, but He helps. It also means we aren't in this situation alone because He helps by taking our ignorant prayers and making wise intercessions for us.

Verse 26 speaks of something we don't know, while verse 22 speaks of something we do know. We do know that we believers groan under the curse of sin along with all creation. Also in verse 28, we know that all things work together for the good of those who love the Lord, to those who are called according to His purpose. What we don't know is just what we should pray for in any particular circumstance. We don't know what to pray for because we are spiritual creatures living in dying bodies in a sin-cursed creation, which is under the control of persons who are in rebellion against God and are stronger than we are. Paul called this time "this present evil world" (Galatians 1:4) and said Satan is the god of this world (2 Corinthians 4:2–4). The primary reason for our ignorance, though, is in the fact that the new covenant hasn't taken effect yet. When the new covenant is in effect, those believers living under it will know what to pray for because God will "put [His] law in their inward parts, and write it in their hearts … And they shall no more teach every man his neighbor, and every man his brother, saying know the LORD: for they shall all know [God] from the least of them to the greatest of them" (Jeremiah 31:33–34). Because they will supernaturally know God and His will, they will make wise prayers and will therefore receive what they ask for in that they will know what to ask for (Matthew 21:22; John 14:13; 16:23; John 3:22; 5:14).

[ak] In verse 23, we saw that we (believers) groan within ourselves. Here in verse 26, we see the spirit itself "making intercession for us with groanings which cannot be uttered" (emphasis added). The neuter gender indicates that this is our regenerated spirit groaning as we labor in the sin-cursed environment around us. This is the inward man who delights in the law of God (Romans 7:22) and which is being renewed day by day (2 Corinthians 4:16), reaching out to God with affections that cannot be articulated.

[al] In verse 27, we find the Holy Spirit's work of intercession. The Holy Spirit is the one who searches our hearts and knows what the mind of our human spirit is. Our "minds" are the mentality of our human spirit. We form our minds by what we put into them. God would have us form the mind of Christ by taking the Word of God into our minds. The Holy Spirit then makes intercessions to the Father for the saints according to the will of God.

The will of God here in verse 27 is the purpose of God in verse 28. This is the "eternal purpose of God" Paul speaks of in Ephesians 3:11. God's will is that saints be "transformed by the renewing of [their] mind" (Romans 12:2). God's will is also that believers live holy, separated lives (1 Thessalonians 4:3) of gratitude to God (1 Thessalonians 5:18). In all the circumstances of life in which the groaning believer reaches out to God in prayer, the Holy Spirit intercedes to accomplish His will in believers' lives.

[am] Though we don't know what to pray for as we ought, we do know that "all things work together for the good to them that love God, to them who are the called according to his purpose" (8:28). Now we need to ask, What are the "all things" that work together for good, because there are bad things that happen to believers.

Do the all things really include all things in an absolute sense? Yes, this verse is to be taken in the absolute sense. However, the all things are being worked together for the good of the inner man. "For which cause we faint not; but though our outward man perish, yet the inward man is renewed day by day ... While we look not at the things which are seen, but at the things which are not seen: for the things which are seen are temporal; but the things which are not seen are eternal" (2 Corinthians 4:16, 18).

God can and does allow bad things to happen to the outward man for the good of the inward man (cf 1 Corinthians 5:5). The believer's hope is to be delivered from the bondage of corruption that affects our outward man (Romans 8:21). Our hope is not a reviving of this body but a new body, as 2 Corinthians 5:1–5 describes. "For we that are in this tabernacle do groan, being burdened: not for that we would be unclothed, but clothed upon, that mortality might be swallowed up of life" (2 Corinthians 5:4).

[an] The word for of verse 29 is the particle of further explanation. In verses 29–30, Paul expanded on the common knowledge that "all things work together for good to them that love God, to them who are the called according to his purpose." As we study these verses, we see that the focus is on redemption truths laid out in a five-step process of redemption. It starts with foreknowledge and ends with glorification. The process may be laid out like this:

1. Doubtless God foreknew before the world began who would, of their own free will, trust in the redeeming blood God provided. God didn't force, coerce, trick, or impose irresistible grace on some people to get them to trust in His redeeming work on their behalf. However, He did have foreknowledge of those who would, of their own free will, trust Jesus Christ as Savior. We mortals are locked in the space, matter, and time continuum and can see only the present. But God sees the end even before the beginning and therefore has foreknowledge of all events in history. However, the foreknowledge here has reference to the fact that the church, the body of Christ, existed in the mind of God before He created anything. The one whom God did foreknow wasn't so much the individual as it was the one new man of Ephesians 2:15. It is the one new man God predestinated to be conformed to the image of His Son. It is all who freely of their own free will trust Christ as Savior who are predestinated to be conformed to the image of His Son. Any reference to predestination in Paul's epistles is to a corporate predestination—that of the entire body of Christ.

2. "Remember the former things of old: for I am God, and there is none else; I am God, and there is none like me, Declaring the end from the beginning, and from ancient times the things that are not yet done, saying, My counsel shall stand, and I will do all my pleasure" (Isaiah 46:9–10).

3. To predestinate simply means to preset someone's destiny. Those who have trusted Jesus Christ as Savior have a preset destiny—preset by God. That destiny is to be conformed to the image of His Son (Jesus Christ, our Lord). Jesus Christ as the eternal Word (cf. John 1:1–4) entered our fallen human race as the only begotten of the Father to die under the curse of sin, to personally be the atonement for our sin, and to pay the death penalty for sin. He rose from the grave in resurrection life not only as the first of a new human species but also as the firstborn among God's family of sons (Colossians 1:18).

4. God called those whom God predestinated to be conformed to the image of His Son (the Lord Jesus Christ). The word called can have several meanings:

- To call to one's presence (Matthew 2:7)

- To summon (Matthew 2:15; 25:14)

- To invite (Matthew 22:9)

- To call to a task (Matthew 9:13; Hebrew 11:8)

- To call to an office (Matthew 9:13)

- To name or characterize (Matthew 1:2; 5:9; 9:19)

But here in Romans 8:30 is to call to participation in the privilege of the gospel, as it is in Romans 9:24; 1 Corinthians 1:9; 7:18. Those God in His foreknowledge predestined to be conformed to the image of Christ were then called by Him to occupy positions in glory whereby "glory" will be revealed "in us" (Romans 8:18).

5. God justified those He called. The process of justification in Paul's epistles is involved with the ministry of the Holy Spirit to baptize believers into Jesus Christ and into His death so our Savior receives each of us believers to Himself, and He gets (actually acquires as though they were His) our sin and guilt as well. Having thus, by the work of the Holy Spirit, acquired sin and guilt, Christ could then pay sin's penalty for every believer, and the believer is reckoned by God as righteous as Christ Himself. "For he hath made him to be sin for us, who knew no sin; that we might be made the righteousness of God in him" (2 Corinthians 5:21).

6. God glorified those He justified. The word glorified denotes a past-tense action. The believer has been glorified, but we are not in glory yet. However, we understand from verse 18 that glory will be revealed in the believer. Actually, glory is in each believer now because Christ is in each believer. So glory is in the believer, even though the believer isn't in glory yet. But our appearing in glory is so sure to be accomplished that God puts it in the past tense for us.

If God Be for Us, Who Can Be against Us (and win)?

> ³¹ What shall we then say to these things? If God be[ao] for us, who can be against us? ³² He that spared not his own Son, but delivered him up for us all, how shall he not with him also freely give us all things? ³³ Who shall lay any[ap] thing to the charge of God's elect? It is God that justifieth. ³⁴ Who is he that condemneth? It is Christ that died, yea rather, that is risen again, who is even at the right hand of God, who also maketh intercession for us. ³⁵ Who shall separate us from the love of Christ? shall tribulation, or distress, or persecution, or famine, or nakedness, or peril, or sword? ³⁶ As it is[aq] written, For thy sake we are killed all the day long; we are accounted as sheep for the slaughter. ³⁷ Nay, in all these things we are more than conquerors through him that loved us. ³⁸ For I am persuaded, that neither death, nor life, nor angels, nor principalities, nor powers, nor things present, nor things to come, ³⁹ Nor height, nor depth, nor any other creature, shall be able to separate us from the love of God, which is in Christ Jesus our Lord. (Romans 8:31–39)

[ao] This is one of the most comforting passages in the Bible for the believer. If God be for us, then who could ever be against us and prevail against us? We know that

- Satan is against us (1 Peter 5:8; Ephesians 6:12);

- unregenerate men opposes us (1 Timothy 5:14);
- the world is against us (Matthew 4:19; Luke 16:8; John 8:23, 12:25, 31; Galatians 1:4); and
- the flesh within us is against us (Romans 7:17–18).

But none of these can ultimately prevail against us. We can be

- troubled on every side but not distressed (2 Corinthians 4:8-11);
- perplexed on every side but not in despair;
- persecuted on every side but not forsaken; and
- cast down on every side but not destroyed.

We can bear about in our bodies the dying of the Lord Jesus, but the life of Jesus can also be manifest in our bodies. If God delivered His Son up for us, He will surely with Him freely give us all things. Along with giving us His own Son, God will freely (without charge) give us all things (i.e., all the things of glory).

[ap] If God Himself reckoned the believer righteous, who will ever lay anything to the charge of the elect (i.e., the called, v. 30)? Obviously no one can.

- Satan means adversary. Devil means slanderer. The devil is the accuser of the brethren (Revelation 12:10). Satan would accuse believers before God, but it is God, the judge, who has already justified the believer.

- To condemn is to place a sentence on one, but Christ Himself, the one who would pronounce judgment, is the very one who has personally paid the sentence of death for the believer. More than that, He rose again from the dead as proof that the penalty was paid. Yet even more than that, He is personally at the right had of the Father in heaven, making intercessions for the believer. Here in verse 32, we see Christ, the Son, making intercessions for the believer, while in verse 26 we see the Holy Spirit making intercession for us.

- God's love for the believer isn't measured in terms of material things or physical blessings. Rather, God's love for us is manifest in redemption and is measurable only in redemption terms. Seven weapons used to try to convince believers that God doesn't love them are listed in verse 35.

  1. Tribulation: To have the resources necessary for your livelihood turn against you

  2. Distress: To be pressed and stressed with no apparent way to turn

  3. Persecution: To be ill treated for your testimony

  4. Famine: To be starving

  5. Nakedness: To have inadequate clothing

  6. Peril: To be in imminent danger or physical harm

  7. Sword: To be in danger of losing your life

[aq] In all seven weapons, listed in verse 35, used against the believer, the believer comes out as more than a conqueror. To be a conqueror is to simply win the conflict against these weapons. We are more than conquerors in that we have an inheritance our Savior won for us when He "spoiled principalities and powers" (Colossians 12:15) and gave us what He won as an inheritance (Ephesians 1:10–13). Jesus Christ, our Savior, has won the ground for the believer. All the believer has to do is stand the ground (Galatians 5:1–2). These weapons are

used against the believer to get him or her to give up the ground. The victory God won for Jehoshaphat in 2 Chronicles 20:14–27 is a parallel application to our spiritual victory today. Note 2 Chronicles 20:15. "The battle is not yours but God's."

[ar] Verse 36 is a quote from Psalm 44:22. This is a statement that explains why the seven weapons of verse 35 are hurled at the believer. It is for God's sake that the weapons are used against the believer. As Paul states in 1 Corinthians 15:30, "We stand in jeopardy every hour." In the statement "we are accounted as sheep for the slaughter," several observations about sheep destined for the slaughter need to be made to understand the parallel:

1. These sheep don't know what is coming. So, too, the believer knows not what to pray for.

2. These sheep wouldn't be able to do anything about their situation even if they did know. So also believers can do nothing about this present evil world we live in except to walk circumspectly.

3. These sheep go to their death while trusting that someone is in control, someone who has their best interest at heart. So also believers could go to their deaths, trusting they still remain the object of God's love and will throughout eternity.

We can have such an outlook because we "look not at the things which are seen, but at the things which are not seen: for the things that are seen are temporal; but the things which are not seen are eternal" (2 Corinthians 4:18).

[as] There is an interesting comparison between Romans 8 and some of the closing verses of the Gospel of John relating to the activity of the Holy Spirit. In Romans 8, we see that the Holy Spirit

- sanctifies (v. 4);
- quickens (v. 8);
- witnesses (v. 16);
- sympathizes (v. 23);
- animates (v. 24);
- teaches (v. 26);
- intercedes (v. 27); and
- conforms (v. 29 cf 2 Corinthians 3:18; Philippians 3:21).

These correspond with verses in John's Gospel, where we see that the Holy Spirit

- comforts, sympathizes, and quickens (14:16–17);

    "And I will pray the Father, and he shall give you another Comforter, that he may abide with you for ever; Even the Spirit of truth; whom the world cannot receive, because it seeth him not, neither knoweth him: but ye know him; for he dwelleth with you, and shall be in you."

- teaches (14:26);

    "Comforter, which is the Holy Ghost, whom the Father will send in my name, he shall teach you all things, and bring all things to your remembrance, whatsoever I have said unto you."

- witnesses (15:26);

  "He shall testify of me."

- convicts (16:8);

  "He will reprove the world of sin, and of righteousness, and of judgment."

- teaches (16:13); and

  "He will guide you into all truth: for he shall not speak of himself; but whatsoever he shall hear, that shall he speak: and he will shew you things to come."

- conforms and quickens (16:14).

  "He shall glorify me: for he shall receive of mine, and shall shew it unto you."

Appendix A

The Leading of the Holy Spirit

The material in Appendix A of chapter 8 is a summary of a study on decision-making gleaned from _Decision Making and the Will of God by Garry Friesen_ (Portland, OR: Multnomah, 1980).

Romans 8:14 says, "For as many as are led by the Spirit of God, they are the sons of God."

Romans 8 speaks of the fact that as many who are led by the Spirit of God are the children of God. Does this statement teach that the Spirit teaches by inner promptings?

- Let's make some observations:
- The word led means or implies guidance.
- The Holy Spirit is the agent of guidance.
- There is no indication in the context that the guiding or the leading is to direct believers into the individual will of God.
- Neither this verse nor its context indicates that the means of the leading is by "inward impressions." There are a number of reasons to reject "inner impressions" as direction from God.
- The scripture says nothing about the Holy Spirit leading believers through inner impressions.
- We can't be certain of the source of inner impressions.
- We can't be certain of the message inner impressions would communicate if they ever were given to convey a message.
- There would have to be outside sources to verify the genuineness of these inner impressions.
- Inner impressions lack authority to compel obedience.

- The apostle Paul discusses in this passage righteousness living by believers, not the individual, mundane decisions of daily living. The entire passage of Romans 8:1–17 addresses the deliverance from the law as discussed in Romans 7:7–25. The passage sets mutually exclusive things in contrast with each other.

Consider the contrasts of the following:

- Good versus evil (7:19)
- The law of sin and death versus the law of the spirit of life in Christ (8:2)
- Being hostile to God versus being pleasing to God (8:7–8)
- Being in the flesh versus being in the Spirit (8–9)
- Being indwelt by the Spirit versus not having the Spirit of Christ (8:9)
- Living after the flesh versus mortifying the deeds of the flesh (8:13)

Considering the above, it is apparent that the passage is looking at the revealed moral will of God, not an individual will God would supposedly have for one's life.

Conclusions Drawn from These Observations

It is the life-changing presence and empowering of the Holy Spirit (8:6, 13) that enables the believer to be so led. The leading is by the Spirit of God working through the Word of God (Ephesians 5:17–18 cf. Colossians 3:16). The Spirit of God thus leads the believer through the Word of God into the moral will of God as expressed in the Word of God (Romans 7:12, 14, 22; 8:3–4).

The above question on the leading of the Spirit of God revolves around a more fundamental question: Does God have three wills? Let's consider two wills of God that are evident in the scripture.

1. God has a sovereign will. This is to say that God has a purpose for His creation, and He will do what He intends to do with it. This is the will of God, as expressed in verse 27. This sovereign will deals with dispensational issues. It deals with God's purpose for Israel (Isaiah 14:26) and the earth. It also deals with the body of Christ and His purpose for the heavens (Ephesians 1:9–10) and mankind in general (Hebrews 2:5–10).

2. God has a moral will revealed in scripture. This will is the sum total of what He expects as conduct from His creature, man. This will is fully revealed in the Word of God. Under the Law, His will was contained in the Law of Moses. Under grace, they are the commands of Christ given through Paul for Christian living (1 Corinthians 7:9; 14:37; 1 Thessalonians 4:2; 2 Timothy 3:16; and so forth).

But does God have an individual will for each believer? That is, does God have a special and unique plan for each believer's personal life, which the individual must somehow discover? If such an individual will doesn't exist, then believers who are looking for it will be frustrated if they don't find that specific will. First Thessalonians 4:3 tells us what God's individual will is (i.e., that we each individually live sanctified lives as holy unto God). He expects us to make wise decisions in the conduct of our lives while operating on information contained in His

Word. By understanding God's will as stated above and individually living His moral will out in our lives, we will automatically be in God's specific will for our lives.

Study Questions on Chapter 8

1. According to verse 1, who is not under condemnation? What is the condemnation in view here? How does this condemnation relate back to the closing verses of chapter 7?

2. What is the "walk after the flesh" of which verse 1 speaks? What is the "walk after the Spirit"?

3. How many laws do you see mentioned in in verses 2 and 3? Name them and explain at what time in Bible history each was instituted.

4. In what sense was the law weak? What did God do to correct the situation of the law being too weak to accomplish what it was ostensibly established to do?

5. What does the believer who walks not after the flesh accomplish?

6. Compare verses 3–4 to Romans 7:18–19 and note the contrast.

7. Who are they who are after the flesh in verse 5, and what do they mind? Who are they who are after the spirit, and what do they mind?

8. What does it mean to be carnally minded? What is it likened to? What is it to be spiritually minded? What is spiritual mindedness likened to?

9. Who are they who are in the flesh? What can't they do? Do they know that?

10. Verse 9 talks about a change of identity (a change of position). What is the believer's spiritual locale? What produced that change of locale?

11. According to verse 10, in what sense is the believer's body dead?

12. In verse 11, why do you think Paul switches from referring to Jesus being raised from the dead to referring to Christ being raised?

13. The "therefore" of verse 12 looks back at verse 11. What does Paul conclude from verse 11?

14. Verse 12 implies that the believer is a debtor but not to the flesh. Why doesn't the believer owe the flesh anything?

15. Verse 13 relates back to verses 2–3, where we saw a connection between walking after the flesh and putting oneself under the law. Is living under the law the same thing as walking after the flesh? In what sense would being under the law cause us to die?

16. Who in verse 14 are the sons of God? Who in verse 16 are the children of God?

17. Can one be a child of God but not a son of God?

18. In verse 17, we are children of God and actually joint heirs with Christ. This verse tells us we share something else with Christ. What is it?

19. Are the sufferings of verse 17 the same as those in verse 18? Are they the same sufferings Paul speaks of in 2 Timothy 2:10–12?

20. The phrases "of this present time" and "the glory that shall be revealed" tell us something about the nature of the sufferings of verses 17–18. What is the nature of the sufferings referred to here?

21. What does the phrase "the creature" refer to? What do we share with the creature today?

22. When will the creature be delivered from its misery?

23. In verse 23, what has God given us to show us He will complete the transaction?

24. In verse 23, the Spirit gives us the hope of adoption as sons. In verse 26, there is something else the Spirit does for us. What is it?

25. What is it in verse 26 that we don't know? What is it in verse 28 that we do know?

26. Who is predestinated, according to verse 29?

27. To be predestinated means to have a preset destiny. At what point in believers' lives were their destinies set to be conformed to the image of Christ?

28. List the sequence of events in the believers' lives, listed in verses 29–30.

29. Who can be against us and prevail?

30. According to verse 27, who intercedes for us? According to verse 30, who intercedes for us?

SUPER ABOUNDING GRACE,
Part 2

Israel's Past Failure, Present Condition, and Future Glory

Romans 9-11

For as ye in times past have not believed God, yet have now obtained mercy through their unbelief: Even so have these also now not believed, that through your mercy they also may obtain mercy. For God hath concluded them all in unbelief, that he might have mercy upon all. O the depth of the riches both of the wisdom and knowledge of God! how unsearchable are his judgments, and his ways past finding out! For who hath known the mind of the Lord? or who hath been his counsellor? Or who hath first given to him, and it shall be recompensed unto him again? For of him, and through him, and to him, are all things: to whom be glory for ever. Amen.

—Romans 11:30–36

Introduction to Romans 9-11

If we were to start in Genesis 1 and study verse by verse through all the books of the Bible, we would certainly (if we have spiritual discernment) find that the first eight chapters of the book of Romans, especially chapter 8, are the greatest message on life, liberty, and soul salvation in the scriptures. There we see Jews and Gentiles can be justified freely be God's grace through the redemption in Christ Jesus. We see He is God not only of the Jews but also of the Gentiles, and either can be justified freely by His grace apart from human merit.

> But now the righteousness of God without the law is manifested, being witnessed by the law and the prophets; Even the righteousness of God which is by faith of Jesus Christ unto all and upon all them that believe: for there is no difference: For all have sinned, and come short of the glory of God; Being justified freely by his grace through the redemption that is in Christ Jesus: Whom God hath set forth to be a propitiation through faith in his blood, to declare his righteousness for the remission of sins that are past, through the forbearance of God; To declare, I say, at this time his righteousness: that he might be just, and the justifier of him which believeth in Jesus. Where is boasting then? It is excluded. By what law? of works? Nay: but by the law of faith. Therefore we conclude that a man is justified by faith without the deeds of the law. Is he the God of the Jews only? is he not also of the Gentiles? Yes, of the Gentiles also: Seeing it is one God, which shall justify the circumcision by faith, and uncircumcision through faith. (Romans 3:21–30)

Further, we see that once a person trusts in the redeeming blood of Christ, he or she is totally secure in Christ.

> For whom he did foreknow, he also did predestinate to be conformed to the image of his Son, that he might be the firstborn among many brethren. Moreover whom he did predestinate, them he also called: and whom he called, them he also justified: and whom he justified, them he also glorified. What shall we then say to these things? If God be for us, who can be against us? He that spared not his own Son, but delivered him up for us all, how shall he not with him also freely give us all things? Who shall lay any thing to the charge of God's elect? It is God that justifieth. Who is he that condemneth? It is Christ that died, yea rather, that is risen again, who is even at the right hand of God, who also maketh intercession for us. Who shall separate us from the love of Christ? shall tribulation, or distress, or persecution, or famine, or nakedness, or peril, or sword? As it is written, For thy sake we are killed all the day long; we are accounted as sheep for the slaughter. Nay, in all these things we are more than conquerors through him that loved us. For I am persuaded, that neither death, nor life, nor angels, nor principalities, nor powers, nor things present, nor things to come, Nor height, nor depth, nor any other creature, shall be able to separate us from the love of God, which is in Christ Jesus our Lord. (Romans 8:29–39)

One can truly rejoice in such blessed truths from the Word of God. But the next logical question that then comes to mind is, What happened to all the promises God made with Israel? The section of the Bible covered in Romans 9–11 answers that question.

CHAPTER 9

ISRAEL'S PAST FAILURE

¹ I say the truth[a] in Christ, I lie not, my conscience also bearing me witness in the Holy Ghost, ² That I have great heaviness and continual sorrow in my heart. ³ For I could wish that myself were accursed from Christ for my brethren, my kinsmen according to the flesh: ⁴ Who are[b] Israelites; to whom pertaineth[c] the adoption, and the glory, and the covenants, and the giving of the law, and the service of God, and the promises; ⁵ Whose are the fathers, and of whom as concerning the flesh Christ came, who is over all, God blessed for ever. Amen. (Romans 9:1–5)

[a] In Romans 9:1–3, Paul expressed great heaviness of heart and deep sorrow for his nation of origin and did so throughout this entire section (chapters 9–11) of Romans. It is much the same sorrow of us believers. We know what has happened to the spiritual, moral, and ethical fabric of our nation; only we would probably not grieve to the extent that an Israelite would over his or her God-ordained nation. While Paul's concern here in 9:1–3 is for the nation at large, in Romans 10:1–3 his concern is for individual members of the nation (i.e., that individual Jews would be saved). At the outset of Paul's ministry, our Lord told him Israel would "not receive thy testimony concerning me" (Acts 22:18–21). In his first epistle (first chronologically), Paul says that the wrath of God had come upon them to the uttermost (1 Thessalonians 2:16). In Romans 11, Paul prays that members of the nation of Israel might now come to the same saving grace being poured out to the equally undeserving Gentiles (Romans 11:13–14).

[b] Here we must stop and talk a bit about what it meant to be an Israelite and understand why Paul picks up this discussion at this point. If one were to go verse by verse through the Bible, beginning in Genesis 1:1, it would be apparent that God's interests primarily focus on one nation: Israel. The first ten chapters of Genesis deal with the Gentiles in general and the nations at large. But with the rebellion against God by the Gentiles at Babel, God set the Gentile nations aside and separated one man (Abraham) unto Himself and made of that one man's descendants His nation. From the call of Abraham to the saving of Saul of Tarsus, God talked through His prophets about a kingdom that would be set up on the earth through Israel, Abraham's multiplied seed. The entire Old Testament speaks of that kingdom in prophecy. The Gospels (Mathew, Mark, Luke, and John) speak of that kingdom as being "at hand." The book of Acts presents the actual offer of that kingdom to Israel (Acts 3:19–26) and Israel's subsequent rejection of that offer (Acts 7:51–53 cf. Luke 19:14; Acts 2:22–38; Psalm 110:1; Hebrews 1:13). From the time God separated Abraham from the Gentiles in Genesis 22:17–18 to the revelation of the mystery through Paul, salvation was "of the Jews" (John 4:22). But when we come to the book of Romans, we find that God hath concluded that they were all in unbelief and that He might have mercy on all (Romans 11:30–31). The question naturally arises then: What happened to the promises God made to Israel? Romans 9–11 is given to us in the scriptures to answer that question.

[c] Israel had special privileges when they were God's special people. The apostle lists seven of them in Romans

9:4–5. To Israel pertains the following:

1. The adoption: In Exodus 4:22–23, God said to Pharaoh, "Israel is my son, even my firstborn: And I say unto thee, let my son go, that he may serve me." Today the adoption belongs to members of the church, Christ's body (Romans 8:14–16). "For as many as are led by the Spirit of God, they are the sons of God. For ye have not received the spirit of bondage again to fear; but ye have received the Spirit of adoption, whereby we cry, Abba, father." But Israel will someday again be the sons of God (Hosea 1:10).

2. The glory: The glory here is the Shechinah glory of the Lord. This glory represents God's presence and power; it belonged to Israel. This glory can be followed throughout Israel's history:

- It was with Israel in the wilderness (Exodus 16:10).

- It was visible to Israel at Sinai (Exodus 24:16).

- Moses was allowed to see only the reflection of that glory lest he die for seeing the full glory of God (Exodus 33:22).

- It filled the tabernacle in the wilderness (Exodus 40:34).

- It is associated with God's miracles (Numbers 14:22).

- It was a visible manifestation that indicated the Lord was present with the nation (Numbers 16:19).

- It was a terrifying thing (Deuteronomy 5:22–27) for the Israelites to see and hear.

- It temporarily departed from Israel with the ark of the covenant (1 Samuel 4:21).

- It filled the temple Solomon had built (1 Kings 8:11).

- That glory departed from Israel during Ezekiel's day:
  - In Ezekiel 9:3 and 10:4, the glory went up from the cherubs to the threshold.
  - In 10:19, it went from the threshold to the door of the east gate.
  - In 11:23, it went to the midst of the city.
  - Then it went to the mount of the east of the city (Mount of Olives [Zechariah 14:4]). Interestingly the Lord took this route when He returned to heaven in Acts.

- This glory will one day return to Israel (Ezekiel 43:2–5), then in the reverse order from that by which it left when it returns in the person of Christ.

- Then the glory of the Lord will go forth to the heathen (i.e., the Gentiles [Ezekiel 39:21]).

- That glory is revealed in Christ.
  - In the star that brought the wise men from the east (Matthew 2:1–29)
  - That glory lit upon Christ.
  - Christ left the temple by the east gate (Matthew 24:1–3).
  - He went up the Mount of Olives and from there to heaven (Acts 1:1–12).
  - He will return a second time to the Mount of Olives (Zechariah 14:4).

    o   Gentiles now rejoice in that glory (Romans 5:2; 8:17), while Israel doesn't have it,

3. The covenants belong to Israel. This would speak of the following:

- Abrahamic covenant of Genesis 12:2–3. This gave Abraham posterity (a nation)

- with Isaac (17:21); and

- with Jacob (Exodus 2:24).

- Mosaic covenant (Exodus 22)

- Palestinian covenant of Genesis 15:18 (Deuteronomy 30:1–5). This assured Abraham's seed of the land of Palestine.

- Davidic covenant (2 Samuel 7:11–16). This assured Israel of the kingdom.

- New covenant (Jeremiah 31:31; Hebrews 8:8–12). This will one day give Israel eternal life.

The Gentiles were strangers from the covenants of promise (Ephesians 2:12) but are now made nigh by the blood of Christ by the mystery revealed through Paul.

4. The giving of the law and temple service

    Israel's temple was "a house of prayer for all nations" (Exodus 25:8–16 cf. Mark 11:17). Today the law has been taken out of the way so we Gentiles can have direct access to God apart from the law (Colossians 2:12–15).

5. The promises are the prophetic promises God made to Israel regarding a kingdom that will be established on the earth through that nation.

- Isaiah 35:1—Desert will blossom as the rose.

- Isaiah 35:5—The eyes of the blind will be opened.

- Isaiah 35:6—The lame man shall leap.

- Isaiah 35:7—The parched ground shall become a pool

- Isaiah 60:3—Gentiles shall come to Israel's light and kings to the brightness of her rising. Today Gentiles are saved by their fall (Romans 11:11).

- Isaiah 61:3—Israel will have received beauty for ashes, joy for mourning, a garment of praise for the spirit of heaviness.

  1. Israel's wasted country shall rebound.

  2. Gentiles will serve Israel.

  3. Israel will be the priests of the Lord.

Today we Gentiles are blessed with all spiritual blessings in heavenly places apart from the promises God made with Israel.

6. Whose are the Fathers (Abraham, Isaac, Jacob, and the Patriarchs)?

7. Christ came through Israel.

Just Being an Israelite Didn't Guarantee Him or Her the Promises

> [6] Not as though the word of God hath taken none effect. For they are not[d] all Israel, which are of Israel: [7] Neither, because they are the seed of Abraham, are they all children: but, In Isaac shall thy seed be[e] called. "[8] That is, They which are[g] the children of the flesh, these are not the children of God: but the children of the promise are counted[h] for the seed. [9] For this is the word of promise, At this time will I come, and Sara shall have[i] a son. [10] And not only this; but when Rebecca also had conceived by one, even by our father Isaac; [11] (For the children being not yet born, neither having done any good or evil, that the purpose of God according to election[j] might stand, not of works, but of him that calleth;) [12] It was said unto her, The elder shall serve the younger. [13] As it is written, Jacob have I loved, but Esau have I hated. (Romans 9:6–13)

[d] The phrase "they are not all Israel, which are of Israel" is explained in the verses that follow. Paul makes the point that, just being a physical descendent of Abraham, Isaac, and Jacob didn't make an Israelite an automatic heir to the promises. Two kinds of Israelites are in view: the natural descendants of Israel (Jacob) for one and the believing remnant of Israel for another. Both are physical descendants of Israel. The promise to Abraham that "thy seed shall possess the gate of his enemies" and "in thy seed shall all the nations of the earth be blessed" (Genesis 22:18; 26:4) was to go to Abraham's seed but only to the seed God chose. The matter between Isaac and Ishmael is a case in point. Paul quotes Genesis 21:12 to make his point. Both Ishmael and Isaac were physically children of Abraham and the physical seed of Abraham. However, Ishmael was the seed Abraham produced in the strength of his flesh. In Genesis 15:1–6, God informed Abraham that he would have seed as numerous as the stars of heaven. He also told him that "he that shall come forth out of thine own bowels shall be thine heir." But as time went on, Sarah didn't bear a son to Abraham. They both then decided that they had to help God out, and Sarah gave Abraham her maid Hagar to bear a child (Genesis 16:2), and Ishmael was the result.

In Genesis 17:7–8, God told Abraham, "I will establish my covenant between me and thee and thy seed after thee in their generations for an everlasting covenant, to be a God unto thee, and to thy seed after thee. And I will give unto thee, and thy seed after thee, the land." God promised Abraham a son by Sarah, who was then past the age of bearing children, and said, "I have blessed [Ishmael] and will make him fruitful, and will multiply him exceedingly; twelve princes shall he beget, and I will make him a great nation. But my covenant will I establish with Isaac, which Sarah shall bear unto thee." There in Genesis 21:12, God reaffirmed to Abraham, "In Isaac shall thy seed be called." This was to the exclusion of Ishmael, who was "born after the flesh" while Isaac was born "of promise." The point is that the promise goes to Abraham's seed but only to the seed God chooses. God chooses to give it to the part of Abraham's seed that finds the fulfillment of the promises of Christ.

[e] The sequence of events and statements to Abraham by God are as follows:

- "My covenant will I establish with Isaac, which Sarah shall bear unto thee at this set time in the next year" (Genesis 17:21).

- "I will certainly return unto thee according the time of life, and, lo, Sarah thy wife shall have a son" (Genesis 18:10). Sarah laughed (Genesis 18:12).

- "Is anything too hard for the Lord? At the time appointed I will return unto thee, according to the time of life, and Sarah shall have a son" (Genesis 18:14).

- "Sarah conceived, and bare Abraham a son in his old age, at the set time of which God had spoken to him" (Genesis 21:2).

[f] The phrase "the children of the flesh" with respect to Abraham's children has two meanings. Here it simply refers to being a physical descendent of Abraham. In Galatians 4:22–31, the phrase refers to the fact that Ishmael was born as a result of Abraham's efforts (i.e., fleshly activity). The point being made in Galatians 4 is that Abraham and Sarah thought they had to help God keep His promise and resorted to their own strength to do for God what God said He would do. Here the point being made was that simply being a physical descendant of Abraham didn't automatically make one a possessor of the promises. The promises would go to those of Abraham's seed, whom God would choose, and God chooses on the basis of faith—those who come to Him by faith receive the promise.

[g] This passage (v. 8) talks about physical descendants of Abraham, who are also the children of promise because they follow in the steps of Abraham in faith. It is interesting to note in Galatians 3:26–29 and 4:28 that we Gentile members of the body of Christ who aren't physical descendants of Abraham are also counted as Abraham's seed. "And if ye be Christ's, then are ye Abraham's seed, and heirs, according to the promise" (Galatians 3:24). "Now we, brethren, as Isaac was, are the children of promise" (Galatians 4:28). We are children of Abraham by being baptized into Christ (Galatians 3:27), who is the physical descendant of Abraham.

[h] God uses these two sets of sons to illustrate the point of verse 1, which is that though the promise goes to the descendants of Abraham, it will be to those of the descendants of Abraham God chooses and not to any and all the descendants of Abraham. The first set of sons (Ishmael and Isaac) were both begotten by Abraham, but they were by different mothers. The second set of sons (Jacob and Esau) not only were by the same father and mother but also were twins. In both cases, God chose one between them to be the possessor of the birthright.

[i] We find a twofold purpose of God in the Bible. There is a purpose for the earth that centers in Israel and is the subject of Old Testament Bible prophecy. There is also a purpose for the heavens that centers in the church, which is Christ's body and is the subject of what Paul calls the mystery. God's purpose is sure as He states in Isaiah 14:24, "The LORD of hosts hath sworn, saying, Surely as I have thought, so shall it come to pass; and as I have purposed, so shall it stand" (cf. vv. 26–27). God's purpose for the earth is to establish a kingdom through His nation Israel and to put down all competing kingdoms. "The LORD of hosts hath purposed it, to stain the pride of all glory, and to bring into contempt all the honourable of the earth" (Isaiah 23:9).

Today, in this dispensation of grace, God's purpose has been expanded from what was stated in the Old Testament. Today He is focused on the heavens as well as the earth. "Having made known unto us the mystery of his will, according to his good pleasure which he hath purposed in himself: That in the dispensation of the fulness of times he might gather together in one all things in Christ, both which are in heaven, and which are on earth; even in him: In whom also we have obtained an inheritance, being predestinated according to the purpose of him who worketh all things after the counsel of his own will" (Ephesians 1:9–11). Paul, the apostle of the Gentiles, speaks of the manifold wisdom of God, which is "according to the eternal purpose which he purposed in Christ Jesus our Lord" (Ephesians 3:11). In 2 Timothy 1:9, Paul speaks of God saving us and calling us "according to his own purpose and grace, which was given us in Christ Jesus before the world began."

[j] Election (v. 11) simply means choosing. God chooses who will be His elect agency, through whom He works to reach lost people. In the Old Testament, He chose to work through a nation and declared that "salvation is of the Jews" (John 4:22). Today God has chosen to work through a new agency, called "the church which is his body" (Ephesians 1:22 and 23; cf. 5:27–30).

Regarding personal salvation, God has again determined who will have eternal life, and He tells us who that is. He chose to give eternal life to everyone who will trust in the atoning work of His Son on Calvary (1 Timothy 1:16; Titus 1:2–4; 3:7). Paul says God the Father chose us in Him (Christ) before the foundation of the world. Note that it doesn't say He chose us "to be in him" but rather that He "chose us in him." A person is in Christ by the baptizing work of the Holy Spirit as a result of personal faith in believing Christ died for our sins and sin's debt paid in full.

[k] God bestows blessings on man based on His mercy and grace. It is an operating principle with God that He won't be beholding to man so as to owe man anything. Salvation is therefore not of works but of grace (Romans 11; Ephesians 2:9; Titus 3:5). God today calls people to salvation by grace through faith apart from works (Ephesians 2:8; cf 1 Thessalonians 2:12; 2 Thessalonians 2:13–14). "But we are bound to give thanks alway to God for you, brethren beloved of the Lord, because God hath from the beginning chosen you to salvation through sanctification of the Spirit and belief of the truth: Whereunto he called you by our gospel, to the obtaining of the glory of our Lord Jesus Christ."

[l] The quote in verse 13 is from Malachi 1:2–3. "Jacob have I loved, but Esau have I hated" is a reference not to God holding Esau in contempt but to God choosing Jacob in favor of Esau. While the quote "the elder [Esau] shall serve the younger [Jacob]" is from Genesis 25:21–23, before either were born, the quote in Malachi is from the last book of our Old Testament—after the seed line of each demonstrated faith or lack thereof. Also, it should be noted that the term hated doesn't necessarily refer to holding one in contempt. We can get a handle on the meaning by examining the following scripture passages.

> And when the LORD saw that Leah was hated, he opened her womb: but Rachel was barren. (Genesis 29:31–33)

> Two wives, one hated. (Deuteronomy 21:15)

> Spareth rod, hateth child. (Proverbs 13:24)

> If one come to me and hate not father, mother. (Luke 14:26)

> He that loveth his life shall lose it; and he that hateth* his life in this world shall keep it unto life eternal. (John 12:25)

> *The term hateth as used in these verses refers to a relative indifference (or lack of special affection) regarding one individual compared to another.

God Is Righteous in All His Doings

¹⁴ What shall we say then? Is there[m] unrighteousness with God? God forbid. ¹⁵ For he saith to Moses, I will

have mercy on whom I will have[n] mercy, and I will have compassion on whom I will have compassion. [16] So then it is not of him that willeth, nor of him that runneth, but of God that sheweth mercy. [17] For the scripture saith[o] unto Pharaoh, Even for this same purpose have I raised[p] thee up, that I might shew[q] my power in thee, and that my name might be declared[r] throughout all the earth. [18] Therefore hath he mercy on whom he will have mercy, and whom he will he hardeneth. [19] Thou wilt say[s] then unto me, Why doth he yet find fault? For who hath resisted his will? [20] Nay but, O man, who art thou that repliest against God? Shall the thing formed say[t] to him that formed it, Why hast thou made me thus? [21] Hath not the potter power over the clay, of the same lump to make[u] one vessel unto honour, and another unto dishonour? [22] What if God, willing to shew his wrath, and to make his power known, endured with much longsuffering the vessels of wrath fitted[v] to destruction: [23] And that he might make[w] known the riches of his glory on the vessels[x] of mercy, which he had afore prepared unto glory, [24] Even us, whom he hath called, not of the Jews only, but also of the Gentiles? (Romans 9:14–24)

[m] Verses 14–21 are historical and dispensational in nature. These verses don't refer to or deal with eternal life per se but rather deal with whom God chooses as His special people (or His elect agency through which He works in this world). In verse 14, Paul raises the rhetorical question "Is there unrighteousness with God?" He then proceeds to answer it simply with "God forbid" and explains the following:

1. God will be under obligation to no one for His mercy and compassion.

2. Receiving God's mercy doesn't depend on

    a. who wants it (i.e., "who willeth"); or

    b. who works for it (i.e., who runneth).

3. God's mercy goes to whomever He wills to give it as a gift of His grace.

[n] In Romans 9:15, Paul quotes God's Word to Moses in Exodus 33:19. God made the statement in response to Moses's intercession on behalf of Israel that God would go with them in their midst. There we find God showing mercy to Israel for the sake of Moses's intercession. In Isaiah 27:11, we read of a time when God will withhold mercy from Israel. Yet again after that we read of a time when God will again show mercy to the remnant of Israel (Micah 7:18). Romans 9–11 is written to explain who is receiving mercy during that time when God isn't showing mercy to Israel. In Romans 9:24, Paul tells us who that is: "Even us whom he hath called, not of the Jews only, but also of the Gentiles."

[o] It is interesting to note in verse 17 that scriptures made this statement to Pharaoh when it was God who spoke to Pharaoh through Moses. No scripture had even been written yet. God is here setting scripture equal to Himself. This is similar to the statement in Galatians 3:8, where scripture is said to have spoken some four hundred years before it was written, and it was again set equal to God and His spoken Word. Some passages in the Exodus account speak of God hardening Pharaoh (Exodus 4:21; 7:3; 9:12; 10:20, 27; 11:10), while others speak of Pharaoh hardening his own heart (Exodus 8:15, 32; 9:34).

[p] This quote in verse 17 is from Exodus 9:16. To get the flow of thought, we need to look at Exodus 9:13–16. "And the LORD said unto Moses, Rise up early in the morning, and stand before Pharaoh, and say unto him, Thus saith the LORD God of the Hebrews, Let my people go, that they may serve me. For I will at this time send all

my plagues upon thine heart, and upon thy servants, and upon thy people; that thou mayest know that there is none like me in all the earth. For now I will stretch out my hand, that I may smite thee and thy people with pestilence; and thou shalt be cut off from the earth. And in very deed for this cause have I raised thee up, for to shew in thee my power; and that my name may be declared throughout all the earth" (emphasis added).

But we ask, How did God raise him up? Did God find a softhearted Pharaoh and harden his heart? In answer to the second question, we simply understand that "God cannot be tempted with evil, neither tempteth he any man: But every man is tempted, when he is drawn away of his own lust, and enticed" (James 1:14). God didn't find a softhearted Pharaoh and harden his heart. Rather, God found an ungodly reprobate, whose heart attitude was in rebellion to God. God then brought out that rebellious heart attitude by simply making a legitimate demand of him. At that point, the natural enmity in Pharaoh's heart (see 1 Corinthians 2:14) manifested itself, and Pharaoh hardened his heart against the Lord. This is yet another application of the principle of Romans 7:8–11. "But sin, taking occasion by the commandment, wrought in me all manner of concupiscence. For without the law sin was dead. For I was alive without the law once: but when the commandment came, sin revived, and I died. And the commandment, which was ordained to life, I found to be unto death. For sin, taking occasion by the commandment, deceived me, and by it slew me."

[q] God is sovereign, but He is not arbitrary in His dealings. This (God simply choosing to do things to accomplish His eternal purposes) is a principle Hannah understood in her prayer of thanksgiving in 1 Samuel 2:7–8. "The LORD maketh poor, and maketh rich: he bringeth low, and lifteth up. He raiseth up the poor out of the dust, and lifteth up the beggar from the dunghill, to set them among princes, and to make them inherit the throne of glory: for the pillars of the earth are the LORD's, and he hath set the world upon them." Mordecai understood this when he told Esther, "Who knoweth whether thou art come to the kingdom for such a time as this?" (Esther 4:14).

This is a lesson Nebuchadnezzar had to learn. Daniel interpreted the tree vision to him to teach the lesson "to the intent that the living may know that the most High ruleth in the kingdom of men, and giveth it to whomsoever he will, and setteth up over it the basest of men" (Daniel 4:17; 5:21, emphasis added). Nebuchadnezzar learned that lesson as he stated,

> I blessed the most High, and I praised and honoured him that liveth for ever, whose dominion is an everlasting dominion, and his kingdom is from generation to generation: And all the inhabitants of the earth are reputed as nothing: and he doeth according to his will in the army of heaven, and among the inhabitants of the earth: and none can stay his hand, or say unto him, What doest thou? At the same time my reason returned unto me; and for the glory of my kingdom, mine honour and brightness returned unto me; and my counsellors and my lords sought unto me; and I was established in my kingdom, and excellent majesty was added unto me. Now I Nebuchadnezzar praise and extol and honour the King of heaven, all whose works are truth, and his ways judgment: and those that walk in pride he is able to abase. (Daniel 4:34–37)

His son Belshazzar, however, didn't learn that lesson. When in his pride Belshazzar profaned the vessels taken from the temple, Daniel instructed him of what had happened to his father.

> When his heart was lifted up, and his mind hardened in pride, he was deposed from his kingly throne,

and they took his glory from him … And thou his son, O Belshazzar, hast not humbled thine heart, though thou knewest all this; But hast lifted up thyself against the Lord of heaven; and they have brought the vessels of his house before thee, and thou, and thy lords, thy wives, and thy concubines, have drunk wine in them; and thou hast praised the gods of silver, and gold, of brass, iron, wood, and stone, which see not, nor hear, nor know: and the God in whose hand thy breath is, and whose are all thy ways, hast thou not glorified. (Daniel 5:20, 22–23)

Jeremiah 27:6–7 states that God gave the kingdoms into the hands of Nebuchadnezzar. In Isaiah 45:1–3, we find God doing the same for Cyrus, king of Persia. In Isaiah 10:5–7, we see that God will use the Assyrian (a reference to the Antichrist) for His own glory to chasten His people, Israel. The Assyrian here doesn't understand that he was set up only to be used (Isaiah 10:7) to bring glory to God. God is just and right in using His rebellious creatures for His own honor and glory because He is in fact the Creator and has creator's rights. This message is stated well in Proverbs 16:4. "The LORD hath made all things for himself: yea, even the wicked for the day of evil."

[r] God makes His sovereignty and power known for many reasons, including the following:

- He might warn others that might take to themselves the glory that belongs only to Him (Exodus 12:12).

- People on earth might know there is no other God but Him (Exodus 14:17–18).

- The enemies of God's people might fear (1 Samuel 4:7 and 8).

- Unsaved people can know God has power to save. Jethro, Moses's father-in-law (Exodus 18:10–11), and Rahab (Joshua 2:9–10) are two cases in point.

- Saved people (God's people) can know they do have a Savior, who can deliver (Isaiah 37:20). Dispensationally, we understand that God's deliverance today is primarily spiritual. We cannot look with certainty today for deliverance from physical enemies and physical ills as Israel did in the Old Testament, because God today is first focused on and interested in the salvation of the inner man (2 Corinthians 4:16). However, our spiritual deliverance is just as sure and is based on the same power God displayed in the physical deliverance of Israel.

It is a principle with both God and man that "a good name is rather to be chosen then great riches, and loving favour rather than silver and gold." (Proverbs 22:1) God is intensely interested in His name for the same reason we are (i.e., that we might have a good testimony to reach others).

[s] Paul anticipates an objection in verse 19. Having stated the conclusion (i.e., God will have mercy on whom He will) of his argument regarding someone considering the possibility that there might be some unrighteousness with God, Paul anticipates the objection: "Why does he yet find fault?" After all, "who hath resisted his will?" This is a logical question because God does find fault with unbelievers, but they sinned by personal choice and, when presented with the truth of redemption, remain in unbelief by personal choice. Job said, "Behold, he taketh away, who can hinder him? who will say unto him, What doest thou? If God will not withdraw his anger, the proud helpers do stoop under him. How much less shall I answer him, and choose out my words to reason with him" (Job 9:12-14).

God will most definitely do according to His will. "Remember the former things of old: for I am God, and there is none else; I am God, and there is none like me, Declaring the end from the beginning, and from ancient times the things that are not yet done, saying, My counsel shall stand, and I will do all my pleasure" (Isaiah 46:9–10). God sovereignly works in the affairs of people but not to overrule their individual free will. Rather, God providentially works in the affairs of people to intervene on behalf of those who will of their own free will submit themselves to the revealed will of God as revealed in the Word of God. Our Lord's sacrificial death on behalf of men is the prime example. "Him, being delivered by the determinate counsel and foreknowledge of God, ye have taken, and by wicked hands have crucified and slain: Whom God hath raised up, having loosed the pains of death: because it was not possible that he should be holden of it" (Acts 2:23–24).

[t] Verse 20 sets the proper perspective that the creature must have for his or her creator. The creature cannot reproach the creator for how man is made. Man does that when man gets "vainly puffed up" with a fleshly mind, though. Job was on the verge of that when "he justified himself rather than God" (Job 32:2). Elihu stated our inability as men to even engage in logical dialogue. "Teach us what we shall say unto him for we cannot order our speech by reason of darkness … Touching the almighty, we cannot find him out: he is excellent in power and in judgement, and in plenty of justice: he will not afflict" (Job 37:19, 23). God's answer to Job was, "Shall he that contendeth with the Almighty instruct him? he that reproveth God, let him answer it" and again, "Wilt thou also disannul my judgment? wilt thou condemn me, that thou mayest be righteous?" (Job 40:2, 8). Read Job 40:8–14. Once God personally confronted him, Job did what every one of us should do; he repented of his self-righteous attitude. "I have heard of thee by the hearing of the ear: but now mine eye seeth thee. Wherefore I abhor myself, and repent in dust and ashes" (Job 42:5–6).

[u] Verse 21 calls to mind many Bible verses that use the illustration of the potter.

- Most notably Isaiah 64:6–8 comes to mind. "But we are all as an unclean thing, and all our righteousnesses are as filthy rags; and we all do fade as a leaf; and our iniquities, like the wind, have taken us away. And there is none that calleth upon thy name, that stirreth up himself to take hold of thee: for thou hast hid thy face from us, and hast consumed us, because of our iniquities. But now, O LORD, thou art our father; we are the clay, and thou our potter; and we all are the work of thy hand."

- God taught Israel by illustration through Jeremiah when God sent Jeremiah to the potter's house in Jeremiah 18:1–6. But the point is that the clay was marred in the hands of the potter—not because of the lack of talent on the part of the potter but because of the resistance of the clay to yield to the hands of the potter. Note from Jeremiah 18:8–9 that the choice was Israel's as to whether they would yield to the shaping hands of God. God would have made a fine vessel of Israel at that time, but instead He had to break the vessel (Jeremiah 22:28) and remake it.

- Paul was a chosen vessel unto the Lord because of his yielded heart (Acts 9:15 cf 9:6).

- God would have each believer today be a vessel unto honor (2 Timothy 2:20–21). But if we do not yield to the working of His hand as He works in us through His Word rightly divided, then we become vessels unto dishonor by default. Note in verse 21 he says, "If a man purge himself of these, he shall be a vessel unto honour, sanctified and meet of the master's use, and prepared unto every good work." The antecedent "these" is the "profane or vain babbling" of verse 16 as opposed to the Word rightly divided of verse 15.

[v] Paul carries on the illustration of the potter here in verse 22 as he speaks of vessels fitted to destruction.

The word fitted is in the middle voice. From this we know that the problem with the vessel wasn't in the potter but in the clay. In Jeremiah's day, God would have made Israel a vessel unto honor, but the nation hardened its heart and wouldn't yield to the work of the Lord to form them into a vessel unto honor. In Paul's day, Israel was again in the same state of hardness. In such a state, Israel wouldn't be the vessel unto honor but rather vessels of wrath. God started out in the epistle, talking about the fact that "the wrath of God is revealed from heaven against all ungodliness and unrighteousness of men, who hold the truth in unrighteousness" (Romans 1:18). In Romans 2:4–5, Paul speaks of wrath people store up against themselves by despising the goodness, forbearance, and long-suffering of God; and by refusing to come to Him in repentance. God's attitude toward the contentious heart that doesn't obey the truth is "indignation and wrath" (2:8). The outworking of that attitude is "tribulation and anguish upon every soul of man that doeth evil, of the Jew first, and also of the Gentile." (Romans 2:9) We find that the wrath God refers to here (Romans 2:8) is what is poured out against the proud and hard heart of man during the tribulation period. There we find men saying to the mountains, "Fall on us, and hide us from the face of him that sitteth on the throne, and from the wrath of the Lamb: For the great day of his wrath is come; and who shall be able to stand" (Revelation 6:16–17). That will be wrath "which is poured out without mixture into the cup of his indignation." (Revelation 14:10)

[w] The long-suffering Paul spoke of here in verse 23 is the long-suffering whereby God withholds His wrath against the world for its rejection of His beloved, only begotten Son—our Lord Jesus Christ. Psalm 2:1–6 speaks of this wrath and the reason for it. "The kings of the earth set themselves, and the rulers take counsel together, against the LORD, and against his anointed, saying, Let us break their bands asunder, and cast away their cords from us. He that sitteth in the heavens shall laugh: the LORD shall have them in derision. Then shall he speak unto them in his wrath, and vex them in his sore displeasure." This is the wrath of the tribulation period. That wrath was due at the time of the stoning of Stephen. But rather than venting that wrath, God is since that day "long suffering to us-ward not willing that any should perish, but that all should come to repentance" (2 Peter 3:9). God interrupted His prophetic program of the seventy weeks of Daniel 9, right after the extra year (Luke 13:8) that had been added between the sixty-ninth week and the seventieth week had expired. God also delayed His wrath so people could get saved under a Gentile dispensation, the dispensation of the grace of God. Just as "the longsuffering of God waited in the days of Noah" (1 Peter 3:20), so too today the long-suffering of the Lord waits while the body of Christ is being formed.

[x] The vessels of wrath who had fitted themselves for destruction were the unbelievers of Israel. By rejecting the risen Lord, Israel had demonstrated that they were on par with the Gentile nations back at Babel. The "vessels of mercy which [God] had afore prepared unto glory" in verse 23 include all believers (Jews and Gentiles) saved during the dispensation of the grace of God. The phrase "afore prepared unto glory" takes us to passages such as the following:

- Ephesians 1:4 says, "According as he hath chosen us in him before the foundation of the world, that we should be holy and without blame before him in love."

- Second Thessalonians 2:13–14 says, "God hath from the beginning chosen you to salvation through sanctification of the Spirit and belief of the truth: Whereunto he called you by our gospel, to the obtaining of the glory of our Lord Jesus Christ."

- Second Timothy 1:9–10 says "Who hath saved us, and called us with an holy calling, not according to our works, but according to his own purpose and grace, which was given us in Christ Jesus before the world began, But is now made manifest by the appearing of our Savior Jesus Christ."

The Doctrine of the Remnant

²⁵ As he saith[y] also in Osee, I will call them my people, which were not my people; and her beloved, which was not beloved. ²⁶ And it shall come to pass, that in the place where it was said unto them, Ye are not my people; there shall they be called the children of the living God. ²⁷ Esaias also crieth concerning Israel, Though the number of the children of Israel be as the sand of the sea, a remnant shall be[z] saved: ²⁸ For he will finish the work, and cut[aa] it short in righteousness: because a short work will the Lord make[ab] upon the earth. ²⁹ And as Esaias said before, Except the Lord of Sabaoth had left us a seed, we had been[ac] as Sodoma, and been made like unto Gomorrha. (Romans 9:25–29)

[y] Small details are important in understanding the Bible. In verse 25 the phrase "as he saith also in Osee" draws a parallel application to what was said. Had the verse read "for he saith in Osee," he would be referring to a fulfillment of Osee. Osee is Hosea, the prophet God asked to take a harlot as a wife that he might be able to communicate to Israel what the nation had done to the Lord. Through Hosea, God told Israel there would be a time when the nation would be loruhamah (not pitied) and loammi (not my people) (Hosea 1:9–10). Then later, the nation would be again ruhama (pitied) and ammi (my people) (Hosea 2:23). Peter identifies the believing remnant as the "chosen generation, a royal priesthood, an holy nation, a peculiar people but are now the people of God: which had not obtained mercy, but now have obtained mercy" (1 Peter 2:9–10).

Peter actually writes this to the circumcision churches of Asia. These are possibly the same seven churches John wrote to in the book of the Revelation (1 Peter 1:1 cf. Revelation 1–3). These were local churches of the circumcision believers, who were scattered from Jerusalem in early Acts. These circumcision epistles instruct future local churches that will proclaim the gospel of the kingdom during the tribulation period. The instruction is in how to get through the tribulation and into the kingdom.

But Israel today is still "loammi" with respect to God. So the question arises: Who are God's people today while Israel is in this "loammi" state?" The answer is in Paul's epistles, in Romans 9:24 and Galatians 3:26–29. "For ye are all the children of God by faith in Christ Jesus. For as many of you as have been baptized into Christ have put on Christ, There is neither Jew nor Greek, there is neither bond nor free, there is neither male nor female: for ye are all one in Christ Jesus" Also, in 2 Corinthians 6:18 we see that God dwells in a temple not of stone in Jerusalem but in the flesh and blood of the body of Christ. "For ye are the temple of the living God; as God hath said [note "as God had said" not "in fulfillment of what God hath said"] I will dwell in them, and walk in them; and I will be their God, and they shall be my people. Wherefore come out from among them, and be ye separate, saith the Lord, and touch not the unclean thing; and I will receive you, And will be a Father unto you, and ye shall be my sons and daughters, said the Lord Almighty" (emphasis added). Paul was using a parallel application of an Old Testament passage. The key to seeing this is again in his use of the phrase "as he saith also in Osee" in Romans 9:25. If this were the fulfillment of Hosea, he would have used terminology as Peter did in Acts 2:16. "This is that which was spoken by the prophet Joel." The verses Romans 9:25–26 cannot refer to a prophesied saving of the Gentiles apart from Israel for two reasons:

- Both Hosea 2:23 (from which verse 25 was quoted) and Hosea 1:9–10 (from which verse 26 is quoted) refer to the believing remnant of Israel after a time when Israel wasn't God's people but are again God's people. That will be the state the believing Jews will be enduring during the tribulation period.

- There was no Old Testament prophecy of Gentiles being saved apart from Israel. The saving of the Gentiles apart from Israel was a mystery "hid in God" (Ephesians 3:9; Colossians 1:26). This mystery was hid not in the Old Testament scriptures but in God.

[z] Romans 9:27–28 quotes Isaiah 10:22–23. "For though thy people Israel be as the sand of the sea, yet a remnant of them shall return: the consumption decreed shall overflow with righteousness. For the Lord GOD of hosts shall make a consumption, even determined, in the midst of all the land."

In Romans 11:4–6, we will see Paul speaking of "a remnant according to the election of grace." That remnant consists of Jews being saved today in the dispensation of grace. However, the remnant in view here in Romans 9:27–28 is the remnant that will be saved of Israel out of the coming tribulation. Isaiah 11:1–11 makes this clear. "And it shall come to pass in that day, that the Lord shall set his hand again the second time to recover the remnant of his people, which shall be left, from Assyria." The glory of that remnant is stated in many Old Testament passages, such as Micah 5:3–8.

[aa] In verse 28, Paul continues the quote from Isaiah 10:22. "He will finish the work, and cut it short in righteousness." Paul calls attention to the fact that, when this remnant will be saved, God will "bring in everlasting righteousness" (Daniel 9:26–27). Paul speaks of this time in Acts 17:31, saying, "[God] hath appointed a day in the which he will judge the world in righteousness by that man whom he hath ordained; whereof he hath given assurance unto all men, in that he hath raised him from the dead."

The short work God will make on the earth speaks of the rapidity of the events when the Lord returns to the earth to put down all rebellion against Him. John describes that time in Revelation 19:11. "And I saw heaven opened, and behold a white horse; and he that set upon him was called Faithful and True, and in righteousness he doth judge and make war."

[ab] Paul points out that God made a promise to preserve the seed of Israel. He alludes to Isaiah 1:9. "Except the LORD of hosts had left unto us a very small remnant, we should have been as Sodom, and we should have been like unto Gomorrah" And he refers to Isaiah 6:13. "But yet in it shall be a tenth, and it [the remnant] shall return." Yet he doesn't quote Isaiah exactly. A seed is different from a remnant. The remnant will be the believing remnant, but a seed is the few from which the believing remnant are called. Jeremiah says in Lamentations 3:22, "It is of the LORD's mercies that we are not consumed, because his compassions fail not." Note that Paul refers to the Lord as the Lord of Sabbath. That is the Lord of "rest." The Sabbath rest of the Lord is the kingdom (Hebrews 3:11; 4:10 cf Psalm 95:11). Sodom and Gomorrah didn't receive such mercy but were totally destroyed (Genesis 19:24–25 cf 2 Peter 2:6; Jude 7).

[ac] Williams in his Student Commentary gives another view of the phrase. "For he will finish the work and cut it short in righteousness; because a short work will the Lord make upon the earth. God will finish the work He started under the prophetic program and will bring to consummation the work He started with Israel. However, "he will cut it short," in that not every one of the descendants of Abraham, Isaac, and Jacob will be saved. He will "cut short in righteousness" because it will be a righteous thing with God not to save a person who will not come to God God's way to find forgiveness of sins. The remnant that will be saved in Israel will be those who

trust in the work of Christ rather than in the works of the law (9:32).

A Stumbling Stone

> ³⁰ What shall we say[ad] then? That the Gentiles, which followed not after righteousness, have attained to righteousness, even the righteousness which[ae] is of faith. ³¹ But Israel, which followed after the law of righteousness[af], hath not attained to the law of righteousness. ³² Wherefore? Because they sought it not by faith, but as it were by the works of the law. For they stumbled at that stumblingstone; ³³ As it is written, Behold, I lay in Sion a stumblingstone and rock of offence: and whosoever believeth on him shall not be ashamed. (Romans 9:30–33)

[ae] Verses 30–33 present to us the logical conclusion that one would come to after having gone through the book of Romans. The Gentiles who weren't even looking for righteousness have attained righteousness by believing the gospel of the grace of God. Upon believing Christ died for their sins, God, through the Holy Spirit's work of baptizing, regenerating, and sealing, imputed the righteousness of Christ to the believer's account. But Israel (as a nation) didn't attain righteousness because they tried to attain it by their own personal worth and merit.

[ad] There is a "righteousness of the law" Romans 8:1–4 talks about. That is the righteous standard the law demanded. There is "the righteousness that is in the law," as Philippians 3:6 talks about. That is the standard of performance God required of Old Testament believers. Paul was blameless in respect to that righteousness. But true righteousness in its purest sense cannot come to human beings by an effort of the body, the soul, or the will of a man. Paul states in Galatians 3:21, "If there had been a law given which could have given life, verily righteousness should have been by the law." True righteousness is always appropriated by faith. Obedience to the Law of Moses was required in the Old Testament. However, apart from faith, that obedience was just an exercise in futility. When Christ came to Israel, He came to a nation under law. The scribes and Pharisees kept the righteousness of the law as well, if not better than, the believing disciples did. However, they didn't keep it as an act of faith. Rather they kept the law as an effort to establish their own righteousness.

God the Father would draw true believers to Christ (John 6:44). Those who were trusting in their own worth and worthiness would naturally not come to Christ. But those who truly understood their righteousness couldn't merit eternal life would come to the salvation God offers. Now that Christ has come, "the righteousness of God without the law is manifested." It is the righteousness of God, "which is by the faith of Jesus Christ unto all and upon all who believe: for there is no difference" (Romans 3:22). The rich young ruler of Matthew 19:16–20 illustrates the difference between "fulfilling the law of righteousness," and "attaining to the law of righteousness." Though he had kept the letter of the law, he didn't truly believe in (in the sense of trusting) the one who had given the law. He therefore didn't have (didn't attain to) the law of righteousness. Israel as a nation was in the same boat. They sought to attain the law of righteousness (i.e., the principle of righteousness) by performing the works of the Law of Moses, but they didn't seek it by faith.

[af] In Romans 9:30 to 10:13, there are several different types of righteousness referred to:

> Romans 9:31 speaks of the law of righteousness. This is the Law of Moses, which contained the righteous standard of God. "And what nation is there so great that hath statutes and judgements so righteous as all this law, which I set before you this day?" (Deuteronomy 4:8).

But Israel didn't attain to this standard of righteousness, because they went about it for the wrong motives. Rather that approaching the law as the standard of conduct of the nation God has blessed as His covenant people, they approached the law as a means of showing God how good they could be. But such motivation didn't move them to true obedience. That is why our Lord tells the disciples (the little flock) "except your righteousness shall exceed the righteousness of the scribes and Pharisees, ye shall in no case enter into the kingdom of heaven" (Matthew 5:20). To enter the kingdom for them was to enter into life (Matthew 18:3, 8). Also, in Matthew 23:3, He tells them of the Pharisees. "All therefore [because they occupy Moses's seat] whatsoever they bid you observe, that observe and do, but do not after their works … for they say, and do not" (emphasis added).

Ezekiel 18:20–32 speaks of this law of righteousness except for the fact that Israel didn't have the ceremonial law or civil law, being captives in foreign lands at the time. An Israelite under captivity was reckoned righteous or wicked based on whether he or she kept the moral law.

Romans 9:32 speaks of "the righteousness of faith" (emphasis added). This is imputed righteousness. God gives this imputed righteousness to the one who comes to Him in faith today during the dispensation of the grace of God. It is the righteousness of Romans 3:21; 4:5; Philippians 3:9; 2 Corinthians 5:21; and so forth.

Romans 10:3 speaks of "their own righteousness." This is the righteousness man can muster up in his or her own strength and ability. This is the righteousness Isaiah describes as "filthy rags" in Isaiah 64:6. This is the best man can do apart from the work of God working in his inner man.

Study Questions on Chapter 9

1. What is the reason for the sadness we see in Paul in verses 1 to 3?

2. List the blessings that pertain to the nation of Israel in verses 4 &5. How many of these apply to us who are members of the church the Body of Christ?

3. What is Paul saying with the words "They are not all Israel that are of Israel?

4. Explain verse 7. Was not Ishmael the seed of Abraham? Also how about the children he had by Keturah?

5. Two sets of sons are discussed in verses 7 thru 13. How were they similar and how were they different?

6. Verse 11 says that God made a choice before the sons were born. Does this mean that He was being arbitrary?

7. Verses 12 and 13 are Old Testament quotes. What Book did each come from? Does this have significance?

8. Why does Paul ask the question of verse 14?

9. What characteristic of God do we see in play in verses 15 &16?

10. In verse 17 we see Pharaoh being hardened. By whom was he hardened and how was he hardened?

11. Who received mercy when Pharaoh was hardened? Who received mercy when Israel was hardened in the Book of Acts?

12. Answer Paul's questions in verses 20 and 21.

13. Who are the vessels unto honor and vessels unto dishonor? Who were the vessels of wrath and vessels of mercy in verses 22 and 23? Who fitted the vessel of wrath for wrath? How about the vessel of mercy?

14. Identify the vessels of mercy prepared unto glory in verses 23 and 24.

15. Does the expression "As he saith in Osee..." in verse 25 mean that what is happening today in the Body of Christ is the fulfilment of prophecy or is it a parallel application of a similar principle?

16. What principle do we see in Paul's quotations of these prophets in verses 27 thru 29 with regard to parallel applications but not fulfillments of the prophecies?

17. What did the Gentiles not follow after but attained to? What did Israel follow after but did not attain to?

18. What did Israel stumble over? What is the rock of offence over which they stumbled?

Chapter 10

ISRAEL'S PRESENT CONDITION

[1] Brethren, my heart's desire and prayer to God for Israel is, that they might be[a] saved. [2] For I bear them record that they have[b] a zeal of God, but not according to knowledge. [3] For they being[d] ignorant of God's[c] righteousness, and going about to establish their own righteousness, have not submitted[e] themselves unto the righteousness[c] of God. [4] For Christ is the end of the law[f] for righteousness to every one that believeth. (Romans 10:1–4)

[a] Paul starts chapter 10 as he did chapter 9, with an expression of his desire for Israel's salvation. He apparently does so to prepare them for the harsh criticism he is about to make of them. Paul's concern for Israel parallels the following:

- Moses's intercession for Israel (Exodus 32:10–13)

- Samuel's intercession for Israel (1 Samuel 12:23)

- Samuel's intercession for Saul (1 Samuel 15:35 cf16:1)

- Jeremiah's intercession for Israel (Jeremiah 17:16 cf. 18:20)

- Our Lord's intercession for Israel (Luke 13:34)

[b] Our Lord foretold of Israel's misguided zeal in John 16:2. "The time cometh, that whosoever killeth you will think that he doeth God service." This zeal was in Saul of Tarsus when he was yet an unbeliever (Acts 22:4). This zeal was in the mob that assaulted Paul in Acts 22:22. Paul was "more exceedingly zealous of the traditions of my fathers" (Galatians 1:14). That zeal led him to persecute the church (Philippians 3:6). But religious zeal is a great detriment if it is and is not according to knowledge. Thus Paul prays for believers "that [their] love may abound yet more and more in knowledge and in all judgment" (Philippians 1:9).

[c] God's righteousness and the righteousness of God are both seen in verse 3. God's righteousness here refers to God's method of justifying sinners. God's righteousness demands that all sin be punished. This is the attribute of God we call "justice." The righteousness of God has to do with His character of absolute holiness. God's holiness demanded that He cannot bring a sin-stained soul into His presence. Anyone who would go into the presence of God must have the righteousness of God. However, no one in his or her own right has it. God's method of saving sinners is revealed in the gospel of Christ. Paul stated this in Romans 1:17. "For therein is the righteousness of God revealed from faith to faith: as it is written, The just [the justified one] shall live by faith." God's method of justifying sinners is by imputing the righteousness of Jesus Christ to the believer's spiritual bank account when the sinner comes in faith to the faithfulness of Christ (i.e., from faith to faith) on the cross. This is "the righteousness of God which is by faith of Jesus Christ unto all and upon all them that believe"

(Romans 3:22). By God having personally paid the debt for our sin in the person of Jesus Christ, He could be both just and the justifier (i.e., the one who reckons sinners as righteous) of those who believe on Jesus (Romans 3:26). By the faithfulness or obedience of Christ, all who were made sinners by the disobedience of Adam can be made righteous by the obedience of Christ (Romans 5:19).

[d] Israel never attained to the law for righteousness (i.e., the righteous Law of Moses) because they did not pursue it by faith but rather did so by their works (Romans 9:31-32). They thus went about to establish their own righteousness. Israel's history is a continuous story of man's departure from God and God's seeking man and bringing him back. In every departure from God, man put his righteousness up before God to declare that he doesn't need God's righteousness. God says to man, "I will declare thy righteousness, and thy works; for they shall not profit thee" (Isaiah 57:12). The true believer will say with Isaiah, "We are all as an unclean thing, and all our righteousnesses are as filthy rags, and we all do fade as a leaf; and our iniquities, like the wind, have taken us away" (Isaiah 64:6). The religious man, however, is as our Lord told the Pharisees. "Ye are they which justify yourselves before men; but God knoweth your hearts: for that which is highly esteemed among men is abomination on the sight of God" (Luke 16:15).

Our Lord communicated the concept of God rejecting man's righteousness in the parable of the Pharisee and the publican in Luke 18:9–12, The faith of Christ (His faithfulness on the cross) is of no avail to the person who would be justified by the law (Galatians 5:3–4). Paul gave up on the "zeal for God" (cf. 10:2), which he once had (Philippians 3:6) as being but dung. He traded that "for the excellency of the knowledge of Christ Jesus my Lord." Paul came to understand that his only hope was to "be found in him, not having mine own righteousness, which is of the law, but that which is of the faith of Christ, the righteousness which is of God by faith" (Philippians 3:9).

[e] The concept of submitting to God is abhorrent to the flesh, as Paul stated in chapter 8:7. "The carnal mind is enmity against God: for it is not subject to the law of God neither indeed can be." The fleshly, carnal mind is especially in opposition to the notion that it cannot produce righteousness God will accept and that righteousness must come from God by faith. Israel had failed under law (Leviticus 26:14 cf. Daniel 9:6–9). Here we see that Israel as a nation also rejected grace.

[f] In verse 4, we see that Christ is the end of the law for righteousness in the sense that Christ is what all the law pointed to. The Old Testament saint was regarded as righteous or wicked (just or unjust), depending on whether he or she walked according to the dictates of the law—including the bringing of the blood sacrifice, which enabled God to remit sin. However, the law of righteousness came short in that it was on a year-by-year basis. Paul stated this to the Jews of the synagogues of Pisidian Antioch: "Be it known unto you therefore, men and brethren, that through this man is preached unto you the forgiveness of sins: And by him all that believe are justified from all things, from which ye could not be justified by the law of Moses" (Acts 13:38–39). Romans 3:21–22 so states, "But now the righteousness of God without the law is manifested, being witnessed by the law and the prophets; Even the righteousness of God which is by faith of Jesus Christ unto all and upon all them that believe: for there is no difference." Paul says in Colossians 2:17 that the law was "a shadow if things to come; but the body [i.e., the body that cast the shadow] is of Christ." The word for "end" is telos—the end purposed or intended. Now that Christ is on the field, the law as a means of righteousness has left the field. Now the righteousness of God is available to every human being in the person and work of Jesus Christ.

The Righteousness of the Law versus the Righteousness of Faith

⁵ For Moses describeth the righteousness which is of the law, That the man which doeth those things shall live[g] by them. ⁶ But the righteousness which is[h] of faith speaketh on this wise, Say[i] not in thine heart, Who shall ascend into heaven? (that is, to bring Christ down from above:) ⁷ Or, Who shall descend into the deep? (that is, to bring up Christ again from the dead.) (Romans 10:5–7)

[g] Verse 5 is a reference to Leviticus 18:4–5. "Ye shall do my judgments, and keep mine ordinances, to walk therein: I am the LORD your God. Ye shall therefore keep my statutes, and my judgments: which if a man do, he shall live in them: I am the LORD." This was a performance-based acceptance system. By faith, the Old Testament saint endeavored to do them. Faith was the real issue, but faith would have done what God required, and when the weak flesh failed, there was the blood-sprinkled mercy seat in the law to cover sin. Nehemiah again quoted Leviticus 18:5 in Nehemiah 9:28–29, speaking of Israel's failure to do so. "But after they had rest, they did evil again before thee: therefore leftest thou them in the land of their enemies, so that they had the dominion over them: yet when they returned … many times didst thou deliver them according to thy mercies; And testifiedst against them, that thou mightest bring them again unto thy law: yet they dealt proudly, and hearkened not unto thy commandments, but sinned against thy judgments, (which if a man do, he shall live in them)."

[h] The "righteousness which is of faith" is here set in contrast with "the righteousness which is of the law." The righteousness which is of faith is imputed righteousness man receives as a gift (i.e., "the gift of righteousness" as Romans 5:17 calls it) from God from the abundance of His grace.

[j] Paul uses a beautiful figure of speech here in making allusion to Deuteronomy but puts it in his own words to communicate a truth about grace that parallels the same truth about law. In speaking of the law, Moses said,

> For this commandment which I command thee this day, it is not hidden from thee, neither is it far off. It is not in heaven, that thou shouldest say, Who shall go up for us to heaven, and bring it unto us, that we may hear it, and do it? Neither is it beyond the sea, that thou shouldest say, Who shall go over the sea for us, and bring it unto us, that we may hear it, and do it? Moses is telling Israel that he holy Law of God has been delivered to them. They do not have to go to heaven to get it, they do not have to go over the seas to get it. It is here to hear and do. (Deuteronomy 30:11–13)

Paul picks up on that and says in verses 6–7 regarding grace,

> Say not in thine heart, Who shall ascend into heaven? (that is, to bring Christ down from above:) Or, Who shall descend into the deep? (that is, to bring up Christ again from the dead.)" Paul is telling us today that we have a revelation from God through him as surely as Israel did through Moses. While Moses refers to the revelation given through him as a law that "if a man do he shall live." Moses added: "But the word is very nigh unto thee, in thy mouth, and in thy heart, that thou mayest do it. See, I have set before thee this day life and good, and death and evil; In that I command thee this day to love the LORD thy God, to walk in his ways, and to keep his commandments and his statutes and his judgments, that thou mayest live and multiply: and the LORD thy God shall bless thee in the land whither thou goest to possess it." (Deuteronomy 30:14–16, emphasis added)

The contrast between the two messages is seen in Romans 10:8: "But what saith it? The word is nigh thee, even in thy mouth, and in thy heart: that is, the word of faith, which we preach" (emphasis added). Just as the "righteousness of the law" comes by doing those things, the "righteousness of faith" comes by believing "the word of faith." The "word of faith" is described in verses 9–11.

The Word of Faith

> [8] But what saith it? The word is nigh thee, even in thy mouth, and in thy heart: that is, the word[j] of faith, which we preach; [9] That if thou shalt confess[k] with thy mouth the Lord Jesus, and shalt believe in thine heart that God hath raised him from the dead, thou shalt be saved. [10] For with the heart man believeth[l] unto righteousness; and with the mouth confession is made[m] unto salvation. [11] For the scripture saith, Whosoever believeth on him shall not be ashamed. [12] For there is no difference between the Jew and the Greek: for the same Lord over all is rich unto all that call upon him. [13] For whosoever shall call upon the name of the Lord shall be saved. (Romans 10:8–13)

[j] The "word of faith" is described here: "That if thou shalt confess with thy mouth the Lord Jesus, and shalt believe in thine heart that God hath raised him from the dead, thou shalt be saved. For ... with the heart man believeth unto righteousness; and with the mouth confession is made unto salvation" (emphasis added). The word of faith involves two concepts: confession and belief. Note the connection of the following passages with confession:

Verse 9 (first point): "that if thou shalt confess with thy mouth the Lord Jesus"

Verse 10 (second point): "with the mouth confessions made unto salvation" and

Verse 13: "Whosoever shall call upon the name of the Lord shall be saved."

Now note the connection of the following passages with belief:

Verse 9 (second point): "That if thou ... shalt believe in the heart that God hath raised him from the dead."

Verse 10 (first point): "For with the heart man believes unto righteousness."

Verse 11: "Whosoever believeth in him shall not be ashamed."

There is a difference between justification and salvation. Also, there is a difference between confession and belief. Belief comes first, then confession. Note that a person is justified based on simple belief. To be justified is to have eternal life. "The righteousness of God which is by faith of Jesus Christ ... upon all them that believe" (Romans 3:22). "Therefore being justified by faith, we have peace with God through our Lord Jesus Christ: By whom also we have access by faith into the grace wherein we stand, and rejoice in the hope of the glory of God" (Romans 5:1–2).

Confession then follows belief. Confession brings suffering. Not every believer will take a stand for the message and will avoid suffering the message 2 Timothy 3:12 speaks of. "All that will live godly in Christ Jesus shall suffer persecution." Therefore, though every believer will live with Christ, not every believer will reign with Christ (2 Timothy 2:9–10). Salvation is a broader term than justification. Salvation is in three parts, and justification is one of those parts. The others are sanctification and glorification. Justification is salvation from the penalty of sin. Sanctification is salvation from sin's power over the believer. Glorification is the eventual salvation from sin's very presence.

[k] To confess with the mouth of the Lord Jesus is to acknowledge our dependence on Him and His ability to

save. As pointed out in our discussion above, not every believer will confess Christ when doing so would result in suffering. Ultimately, every knee shall bow, and every tongue shall confess that Jesus is Lord (Romans 14:11; Philippians 2:11). Today during the present dispensation, faithfulness to suffer will bring rewards. Under the kingdom program, faithfulness to confess Jesus Christ is required to enter the kingdom (Matthew 10:32–33; Luke 12:8). These passages will be applicable in the coming tribulation period. The parents of the man who had been born blind but whose sight was restored by Christ failed to confess the Lord Jesus due to fear. During the tribulation, people will have to endure great persecution to confess that Jesus Christ has come in the flesh—to distinguish Him from the false Christ (1 John 4:2 cf. Matthew 24:24; Mark 13:22; 2 John 1:7).

In 1 Timothy 4:16, Paul tells Timothy, a justified man, that by continuing in reading, exhortation, and doctrine would save him and those who heard him from the apostasy of verses 1–5. Salvation is therefore not always salvation from the penalty of sin. Often in Paul's epistles, salvation is from the power of sin, as in 1 Corinthians 15:2; 2 Corinthians 1:6; 7:10; and Philippians 1:19. Sometimes salvation also has reference to glorification (Romans 13:11; 1 Thessalonians 5:8–9; 2 Thessalonians 2:13). Sometimes all three are in view (e.g., 2 Timothy 3:15; Titus 2:11).

[I] There is a difference between justification and salvation. There is also a difference between confession and belief.

Note from Romans 3–5 that one is justified by simply believing. To be justified is to have eternal life (Romans 3:22; 5:1–2). One has eternal life by simply believing the message of the cross. Confession then has to follow belief and justification. Confession involves opening one's mouth (or making a statement of faith in some other fashion). Such confession involves acknowledging Jesus Christ as Lord. Acknowledging Jesus Christ as Lord involves recognizing (1) our dependence on Him and (2) His ability to deliver us (i.e., to save us). The term salvation as used in scripture has three parts, three tenses:

1. Salvation from the penalty of sin (justification). See 2 Corinthians 2:15; Romans 5:10.

2. Salvation from the power of sin (sanctification). See Romans 6; 1 Timothy 4:16 cf. 1 Corinthians 15:2; 2 Corinthians 1:6; 7:10.

3. Salvation from the very presence of sin (glorification). See Romans 13:11; 1 Thessalonians 5:8–9; 2 Thessalonians 2:13.

Sometimes all three are in view. For example, both one and two are evident in 2 Thessalonians 2:13. "But we are bound to give thanks alway to God for you, brethren beloved of the Lord, because God hath from the beginning chosen you to salvation through sanctification of the Spirit and belief of the truth."

"Confessing" means acknowledging the truth of a body of doctrine, while "believing" means having the certainty that the doctrine is true. The heart belief results in righteousness being imputed to the believer, while the confession (in this case the acknowledging the doctrine that we have a risen Savior who can deliver us) procures a complete salvation for the believer. In 1 Corinthians 15:1–4, we see the same theme of justification and salvation.

First Corinthians 15:1 says, "Moreover, brethren, I declare unto you the gospel which I preached unto you, which also ye have received, [i.e., you believed it] and wherein ye stand [i.e., you are justified]." This is salvation from the penalty of sin. This gives us our standing in grace of being secure in Christ.

First Corinthians 15:2 says, "By which also ye are saved, [this is the present tense and passive voice—i.e., you are in the process of being saved] if ye keep in memory what I preached unto you, unless ye have believed in vain." This is a salvation that depends on keeping in memory what Paul preached. This is salvation from sin's power. This is the doctrine of Romans 6.

Verse 1 involves heart belief to justification, while verse 2 involves acknowledging the saving of the believer from sin's power in his or her life. The rest of 1 Corinthians 15 speaks of the resurrection and rapture in which the believer has the future tense of salvation—salvation from sin's presence.

Israel Did Have Her Preachers

[14] How then shall they call[m] on him in whom they have not believed? and how shall they believe in him of whom they have not heard? and how shall they hear without a preacher? [15] And how shall they preach, except they be sent? as it is[n] written, How beautiful are the feet of them that preach the gospel of peace, and bring glad tidings of good things! [16] But they have not all obeyed the gospel. For Esaias saith, Lord, who hath[o] believed our report? [17] So then faith cometh by hearing, and hearing by the word of God. [18] But I say, Have they not heard? Yes verily, their sound went into all the earth, and their words unto[p] the ends of the world. [19] But I say, Did not Israel know? First Moses saith, I will provoke[q] you to jealousy by them that are no people, and by a foolish nation I will anger you. [20] But Esaias is very bold, and saith, I was found of them that sought me not; I was made manifest unto them that asked not after me. [21] But to Israel he saith, All day long I have stretched forth my hands unto a disobedient and gainsaying people. (Romans 10:14–21)

[m] Romans 10:14–21 contains a logical argument of Israel's guilt in rejecting Jesus Christ as her Messiah. This message starts with a series of questions in verses 14–15 and then answers those questions with quotes of Old Testament scriptures. The argument goes like this:

- First: Calling on the Lord is impossible to one who hasn't believed on the Lord.
- Second: Believing is impossible to one who hasn't heard the message about the Lord.
- Third: Hearing is impossible unless someone comes preaching the message.
- Fourth: Preaching is impossible unless that messenger be sent from God.

Paul presented this argument as a possible defense for Israel's unbelief, and then Paul's quotations from Israel's scriptures answer the objection. The argument is fashioned as a series of questions, which are answered in reverse order.

Fourth: Was a preacher sent?

Yes: Isaiah 53:1; Nahum 1:15

Third: Did they have a preacher?

Yes, they had many: Isaiah 53:1

Second: Have they heard?

Yes. Psalm 19 is cited here to tell us that even creation testifies of God (cf. Romans 1:20). Certainly God's people who have the very oracles of God (Romans 3:20) had to have heard the gospel (John 5:39).

First: Did not Israel know?

They should have but didn't. Paul quotes Deuteronomy 32:21. The "foolish nation" here is not a reference to the Gentiles but to the "little flock" of Matthew 21:43 (cf. Luke 12:32). The believing remnant of Israel is a testimony to Israel that they should have known because some of their brethren did.

[n] Romans 10:15 is a reference taken from Isaiah 52:7. "How beautiful upon the mountains are the feet of him that bringeth good tidings, that publisheth peace; that bringeth good tidings of good, that publisheth salvation; that saith unto Zion, Thy God reigneth!" It is apparent from the context of Isaiah 52 that the feet of him that bringeth good tidings of good things and preach the gospel of peace belong to the Lord Himself and to His disciples as they preached the good news of the kingdom. Isaiah 52:6 says, "They [Israel] shall know in that day that I am he that doth speak: behold, it is I." Jesus Christ is the Lord speaking to Israel, and the "good tidings of good" are the message to Israel that "thy God reigneth" (Isaiah 52:7). Any Jew knowing his or her Old Testament scripture should have known that the Lord Jesus Christ is the one God sent (Nahum 1:15 also quotes Isaiah 52:7).

[o] Paul answers the third question—"How shall they hear without a preacher?"—by referencing Isaiah 53:1. "Who hath believed our report? and to whom is the arm of the LORD revealed?" Israel had many preachers in the past, but they didn't listen to them. This is apparent due to many other Old Testament references, such as Numbers 16:3; Ezekiel 20:49; Amos 7:10–17; Jeremiah 44:16–19, and so forth, to make his point. Just as Israel didn't listen to the preachers sent from God in the Old Testament, so they didn't listen to the Lord either.

[p] Paul answers the second question—"Have they not heard?"—by referencing Psalm 19. (See verse 18.) Psalm 19 speaks of the fact that the creation testifies of a glorious Creator and that the knowledge of God has gone into the entire earth through the testimony of creation (Romans 1:20). But knowing God is possible only through His Word. Thus Psalm 19 also speaks of "the law of the LORD … the testimony of the LORD … the statues of the LORD … the judgements of the LORD" (Psalm 19:7–9). Certainly God's chosen people, to whom were committed the oracles of God (Romans 3:20), had to have heard the gospels. Our Lord said to Israel, "Search the Scriptures for in them ye think you have eternal life: and they are they which testify of me, And ye will not come to me that ye might have life" (John 5:39).

[q] In verse 19, Paul answers the question "Did not Israel know?" by referencing Deuteronomy 32:21. "They have moved me to jealousy with that which is not God; they have provoked me to anger with their vanities: and I will move them to jealousy with those which are not a people; I will provoke them to anger with a foolish nation." This "foolish nation," which God will use to provoke Israel, is the little flock of Luke 12:32. "Fear not, little flock; for it is your Father's good pleasure to give you the kingdom." God told the leaders of Israel, "The kingdom of God shall be taken from you and given to a nation bringing forth the fruits thereof." The term "no people" in verse 19 is not referring to the calling out of the Gentiles today during the dispensation of the grace of God, because the body of Christ was a mystery hid in God (Ephesians 3:3–6) until the Lord revealed the mystery through Paul. Rather, the "no people" is a reference to the believing remnant who will be called out during the tribulation period when Israel will go from being "loammi" (not my people) to being "ammi" (God's people—see Hosea 1:9). If the little flock could figure out Jesus Christ is Israel's Messiah, then the nation should

have been able to do so as well.

Study Questions on Chapter 10

1. Paul says that Israel had a zeal for God but did that get them favor with God? What was lacking in their zeal?

2. In what sense did Israel not submit themselves to the righteousness of God?

3. What does it mean that Christ is the end of the Law for righteousness?

4. What is the righteousness of the Law in verse 5?

5. Paul quotes an Old Testament verse to describe the righteousness of the Law. What is that verse? What is that righteousness?

6. Paul draws a parallel application of an Old Testament passage to describe the righteousness of faith. Show the parallel and the contrasts of Deut. 30:11-17 and Romans 10:9-11.

7. What does it mean to confess with the mouth the Lord Jesus? What does in mean to believe in thine heart that God has raised him form the dead? Is this what people of all ages have done to receive eternal life?

8. Is the reference to the heart and the mouth to be taken literally or figuratively?

9. Does verse 11 connect with the heart's belief or the mouth's confession?

10. The Lord is rich unto who in verse 12?

11. What does it mean to "call upon the name of the Lord" in verse 13?

12. Is there one simple answer to all of the questions that Paul asks in verse 14 and 15? If so, what is it?

13. In verses 16 through 21, Paul actually answers those questions in reverse order of how he presented them in verses 14 and 15. Write out each question and the answer. Does this leave Israel culpable for having rejected her Messiah?

14. Who are the "no people" and who is the "foolish nation" with which God will provoke Israel to jealousy?

CHAPTER 11

ISRAEL'S FUTURE GLORY

¹ I say then, Hath God cast[a] away his[b] people? God forbid[c]. For I also am an Israelite, of the seed of Abraham, of the tribe[d] of Benjamin. ² God hath not cast away his people which[e] he foreknew. Wot ye not what the scripture saith[f] of Elias? how he maketh[g] intercession to God against Israel, saying, ³ Lord, they have killed thy prophets, and digged down thine altars; and I am left alone, and they seek my life. (Romans 11:1–3)

[a] In Romans 9–10, we find that Israel hasn't received the promised blessing God said she would. In Romans 9:30-32, we find that "Israel, which followed after the law of righteousness, hath not attained to the law of righteousness … Because they sought it not by faith, but as it were by the works of the law." In Romans 10:3, the apostle says, "For they being ignorant of God's righteousness, and going about to establish their own righteousness, have not submitted themselves unto the righteousness of God." In Romans 9–10, Paul implies that Israel is in the "loammi" ("not my people") state Hosea spoke of in Hosea 1:9–10. In Romans 9:23–26, Paul draws a parallel between the fulfillments of Hosea 1:10 in Israel and the calling out of the body of Christ today during the dispensation of the grace of God. In Hosea 3:4–5, we find that "the children of Israel shall abide many days without a king, and without a prince, and without a sacrifice, and without an image, and without an ephod, and without teraphim: Afterward shall the children of Israel return, and seek the LORD their God, and David their king; and shall fear the LORD and his goodness in the latter days" (emphasis added). There was to be a future time at the writing of Hosea when Israel would be "not God's people" and then another time "afterward" when the children of Israel shall return and seek the Lord. In Romans 9:24–25, Paul draws a parallel application of this truth in respect to the Gentiles who were "not God's people" being God's people. Note Paul's words: "As he saith in Hosea" (emphasis added). If this were the fulfillment of Hosea's prophecy, Paul would have used terminology as Peter did. "But this is that which was spoken by the prophet Joel" (Acts 2:16, emphasis added). Paul now asks the rhetorical question "Hath God cast away his people?" to press the point that Israel's fall from God's favor is neither permanent nor complete. In this chapter Paul presents three proofs that God has neither completely nor permanently set Israel aside.

1. There is a remnant being saved by grace today, of which Paul is an example; therefore, the blindness is incomplete.

2. Gentiles are being saved today to provoke Israel to jealousy.

3. One day all Israel will be saved; therefore, the blindness isn't permanent.

[b] The question "Hath God cast away his people?" is very relevant considering statements God made to Israel. Consider the following:

- "For the LORD will not forsake his people for his great name's sake: because it hath pleased the LORD to make you his people" (1 Samuel 12:22). This was said in spite of the fact that Israel had sinned against the Lord by asking for a king.

- "Notwithstanding the LORD turned not from the fierceness of his great wrath, wherewith his anger was kindled against Judah, because of all the provocations that Manasseh had provoked him withal" (2 Kings 23:26). This was in spite of all the reforms Josiah instituted, as documented in 2 Kings 23.

- "Thus saith the LORD, which giveth the sun for a light by day, and the ordinances of the moon and of the stars for a light by night, which divideth the sea when the waves thereof roar; The LORD of hosts is his name: If those ordinances depart from before me, saith the LORD, then the seed of Israel also shall cease from being a nation before me for ever. Thus saith the LORD; If heaven above can be measured, and the foundations of the earth searched out beneath, I will also cast off all the seed of Israel for all that they have done, saith the LORD" (Jeremiah 31:35–37). This was stated right after the promise of the new covenant in Jeremiah 31:31. Though the wrath of God would come upon Israel, God would neither permanently nor completely cast away His people Israel. We find in 1 Thessalonians 2:16 that "the wrath is come upon them to the uttermost" because Israel rejected her Messiah and forbade Paul to speak to the Gentiles so they might be saved.

When Israel remembers her sin, this question in Romans 11:1 will be on her heart, as seen in Psalm 77:6–9. "I call to remembrance my song in the night: I commune with mine own heart: and my spirit made diligent search. Will the Lord cast off for ever? and will he be favourable no more? Is his mercy clean gone for ever? doth his promise fail for evermore? Hath God forgotten to be gracious? hath he in anger shut up his tender mercies?"

The Lord's answer to that question in Romans 11:1 is given in Psalm 89:29–37.

"His seed also will I make to endure for ever, and his throne as the days of heaven. If his children forsake my law, and walk not in my judgments; If they break my statutes, and keep not my commandments; Then will I visit their transgression with the rod, and their iniquity with stripes. Nevertheless my lovingkindness will I not utterly take from him, nor suffer my faithfulness to fail. My covenant will I not break, nor alter the thing that is gone out of my lips. Once have I sworn by my holiness that I will not lie unto David. His seed shall endure for ever, and his throne as the sun before me. It shall be established for ever as the moon, and as a faithful witness in heaven. Selah."

Also Psalm 94:14–15 says, "For the LORD will not cast off his people, neither will he forsake his inheritance. But judgment shall return unto righteousness: and all the upright in heart shall follow it."

- Consider Hosea's words regarding Israel being cast off. Hosea 9:1 says, "Rejoice not, O Israel, for joy, as other people: for thou hast gone a whoring from thy God." Hosea 9:17 says, "My God will cast them away, because they did not hearken unto him: and they shall be wanderers among the nations."

- Consider also God's word through Amos. Amos 9:8–9 says, "the eyes of the Lord GOD are upon the sinful kingdom, and I will destroy it from off the face of the earth; saving that I will not utterly destroy the house of Jacob, saith the LORD … I will sift the house of Israel among all nations, like as corn is sifted in a sieve, yet shall not the least grain fall upon the earth."

[c] Paul offers two proofs that God has neither completely nor permanently cast Israel away. The first is that

there is a remnant of Israel being saved by grace today during the dispensation of grace. Paul is part of this remnant. Therefore, God hasn't completely set Israel aside. Second, there is coming a future time when "all Israel shall be saved" (v. 26). Therefore God hasn't permanently cast Israel away.

[d] On several occasions, Paul stressed his pedigree—for example, "an Hebrew of the Hebrews" (Philippians 3:5). One occasion was in Acts 22:3 when he stressed his Jewish background to get the attention of the unbelieving Jews of Jerusalem. Another was in Acts 26:4, when he stood before Agrippa, who knew the customs of the Jews. Here he presses the point so that we might remember that he was physically a Jew, a descendent of Abraham and of the faithful tribe of Benjamin.

[e] Here Paul qualifies the words "his people" from verse 1 by adding the phrase "which he foreknew." This takes us back to Romans 9:6. "They are not all Israel, which are of Israel." Just being a physical descendant of Abraham didn't automatically make one a possessor of the promises made to Abraham. God knew beforehand that He was going to have the nation of Israel as His means of reconciling this earth to Himself. He knew Israel would rebel before He called Abraham and made the promises that his descendants would inhabit the land of Palestine for an everlasting possession (Genesis 17:8; 48:4) and that they would be a blessing to all Gentiles (Genesis 18:18; 22:18; 26:4). Since God knew all this beforehand, He was surely not going to suspend His promises because of the fact that what God knew would happen did happen. Just as in Romans 8:29–30, God chooses and blesses based on His foreknowledge. God foreknew Israel, and He foreknew the church, the body of Christ. God isn't bound and constrained by space, matter, and time as we are. Foreknowledge of God has to do with His determined purpose. Both Israel and the church, the body of Christ, existed in the mind of God from before the foundation of the world. People are members of those two elect agencies based on their choice to believe the gospel. Those who believe are then God's elect, whom He foreknew, because they become members of one or the other of these two groups (i.e., these two elect agencies).

[f] Paul expands on the foreknowledge of God by drawing a parallel to Elijah (see note [g]). As James says in Acts 15:18, "Known unto God are all his works from the beginning of the world." God foreknew what men will do and also what He would do to accommodate what men would do. God foreknew Israel would rebel, yet He testified against them for years before He scattered them among the nations (Nehemiah 9:30). Yet while the nation was in rebellion, God also knew those who remained faithful. To God this remnant was the real Israel.

[g] Elias (Elijah) made intercession against Israel. Moses also did in Numbers 16:15. Jeremiah also did in Jeremiah 18:19–23.

Some Israelites Are Being Saved Today by Grace

⁴ But what saith[h] the answer of God unto him? I have reserved to myself seven thousand men, who have not bowed the knee to the image of Baal. ⁵ Even so then at this present time also there is a remnant according[i] to the election[j] of grace. ⁶ And if by grace, then is it no more of works: otherwise grace is[k] no more grace. But if it be of works, then is it no more grace: otherwise work is no more work. (Romans 11:4–6)

[h] The situation of Israel looked bleak at the time Paul wrote this. Paul quotes from 1 Kings 19 to show the situation looked equally as bleak in Elijah's day. In 1 Kings 18:25–40, we find the account of Elijah going against the 450 prophets of Baal and winning a great victory for the Lord on Mount Carmel. In 1 Kings 19:1–4, we find

Elijah running for his life from Jezebel. In 1 Kings 19:5–13, the Lord gave Elijah a demonstration to show He wasn't using mighty demonstrations of power to persuade people to believe Him. Rather, He uses the still, small voice of His Word working in the hearts of men of faith. In Elijah's day, there were only seven thousand men who remained faithful to the Lord. To God, this was the real Israel.

[i] Paul says in verse 5 that there is, at the writing of Romans, a remnant according to the election of grace. At Pentecost in Acts 2, there was a remnant of Israel that believed the kingdom gospel that Jesus Christ was the Messiah and that the kingdom was "at hand" and in fact was being offered to Israel. However, the remnant Paul speaks of in Romans 11:5 isn't that remnant. Rather, Paul is here speaking of a remnant of Israel that is being saved today under the dispensation of the grace of God. These are being saved by pure grace (i.e., not of works) as the Gentile members of the body of Christ are. These Jews, when they believe Christ died for their sins, become members of "the church which is his [Christ's] body" (Ephesians 1:22; 5:23).

[j] The "election of grace" marks the distinction between a member of the "little flock" (Luke 12:32) and the body of Christ, the elect of the mystery program. Under the kingdom program, the works of the law and water baptism were required manifestations of faith (Matthew 19:21; Mark 10:21; Luke 12:33; Acts 2:44; 4:32). Under the dispensation of the grace of God, the remnant is being saved by the pure, unmerited grace of God (Ephesians 2:8–9).

[k] Romans 11:6 is as clear a statement as the Holy Spirit could make to the effect that works and grace are two mutually exclusive concepts as a means of justification. There is absolutely no mix of the two in Paul's epistles. Justification today in the dispensation of the grace of God is purely on the basis of grace through the means of faith (Romans 4:3–5). Under the kingdom program, works were a factor in justification (James 2:21–22) as an expression of faith.

[l] We might ask here, What was it Israel was seeking? The answer is in Romans 10:3, 6–10; 9:31–32. Israel followed after the law of righteousness but didn't attain to it because they didn't follow after it by faith. Instead they, being ignorant of God's righteousness and going about to establish their own righteousness, hadn't attained the righteousness of God. What Israel was seeking but didn't attain was righteousness. The elect, however, in this passage receive righteousness by faith.

Israel was Blinded by Unbelief

[7] What then? Israel hath not obtained that which he seeketh for; but the election hath obtained it, and the rest were[m] blinded [8] (According as it is[n] written, God hath given them the spirit of slumber, eyes that they should not see, and ears that they should not hear;) unto this day. [9] And David saith[o], Let their table be made a snare, and a trap, and a stumblingblock, and a recompence unto them: [10] Let their eyes be darkened, that they may not see, and bow down their back alway. (Romans 11:7–10)

[m] "The rest" who were blinded here are the unbelievers of Israel at the time when Israel was set aside as a nation. It isn't that they were blind when the gospel of the kingdom was offered to them; that condition would have given them an excuse. Rather, God in a sense blinded them because they refused to see the truth. Let's consider the sequence of events leading up to this blindness:

First, we note that during His earthly ministry to Israel, our Lord began by speaking plainly to Israel. However, in Matthew 12 something started to change. Israel's leaders blasphemed Christ by saying He cast out devils by Beelzebub, the prince of devils. The Lord responded by introducing the unpardonable sin (Matthew 12:28–32).

Then, in Matthew 13, He began to speak in parables so only the disciples could understand what He was saying. He explained His motives by saying,

> Because it is given unto you to know the mysteries of the kingdom of heaven, but to them it is not given. For whosoever hath, to him shall be given, and he shall have more abundance: but whosoever hath not, from him shall be taken away even that he hath. Therefore speak I to them in parables: because they seeing see not; and hearing they hear not, neither do they understand. And in them is fulfilled the prophecy of Esaias, which saith, By hearing ye shall hear, and shall not understand; and seeing ye shall see, and shall not perceive: For this people's heart is waxed gross, and their ears are dull of hearing, and their eyes they have closed; lest at any time they should see with *their* eyes, and hear with *their* ears, and should understand with *their* heart, and should be converted, and I should heal them. (Matthew 13:11–15)

Because they refused to see, He blinded their eyes so they couldn't see. He did this so He could genuinely say on the cross, "Father forgive them for they know not what they do" (emphasis added). However, the blindness lasted only until after His death, burial, and resurrection. That judicial blindness was removed after the cross. For Israel not to believe then would be due solely to the hardness of their hearts by their personal choice.

Israel as a nation finally committed the unpardonable sin when they refused to believe the gospel as the Holy Ghost ministered to the nation through the believing remnant in early Acts. It was at the stoning of Stephen that the nation was set aside and the dispensation of grace began.

[n] In verse 8, Paul cites Isaiah 29:9–10 to explain the nature of the blindness and the reason for it. Going to Isaiah 29, we can see what the nature of the blindness really is.

> Stay yourselves, and wonder; cry ye out, and cry: they are drunken, but not with wine; they stagger, but not with strong drink. For the LORD hath poured out upon you the spirit of deep sleep, and hath closed your eyes: the prophets … the seers hath he covered and your rulers And the vision of all is become unto you as the words of a book that is sealed, which men deliver to one that is learned, saying, Read this, I pray thee: and he saith, I cannot; for it is sealed: And the book is delivered to him that is not learned, saying, Read this, I pray thee: and he saith, I am not learned. (Isaiah 29:9–12)

From Isaiah 29:14 we see that the blindness is that "the wisdom of their [Israel's] wise men shall perish, and the understanding of their prudent men shall be hid" (i.e., God is no longer giving insight to Israel and they therefore no longer have spiritual vision). The result of that spiritual blindness is twofold:

1. Israel's prophets no longer receive instruction from the Holy Spirit (Isaiah 29:11).

2. The people no longer have the discernment to understand what has been written (Isaiah 29:12).

In short, the blindness is the withdrawal of the Holy Spirit from Israel. Israel is then no longer the means whereby God reaches lost men.

Comparing Isaiah 29:9, 13 to 28:1–3, we see the reason for the blindness. Israel became drunk with pride and began to think she was the object of God's blessing and love rather than the channel of blessing to the nations. Israel couldn't see she was in as much need of spiritual redemption as the nations were.

[o] Paul quotes David (Psalm 69:22–23) here in Romans 11:9–10 to further the point that Israel's blindness was prophesied. The table here is a figure of speech to represent the place of spiritual blessing. God spiritually blessed Israel so she would be the channel of blessing to all the families of the earth, as God said to Abraham in Genesis 12:2–3. "And I will make of thee a great nation, and I will bless thee, and make thy name great; and thou shalt be a blessing: And I will bless them that bless thee, and curse him that curseth thee: and in thee shall all families of the earth be blessed."

The figure of speech of the table says a lot about what happened to Israel. Israel's place of spiritual blessing (represented by the table) became a snare and a trap to them in that they took it for granted and began to view themselves as the sole object of the blessing rather than the channel whereby blessing might flow to the Gentiles. It also became a stumbling stone to them, because they started to view themselves as not needing redemption as the Gentiles around them did.

They didn't stumble that they should fall, but they did fall later.

> ¹¹ I say then, Have they stumbled that they should[p] fall? God forbid: but rather through their fall salvation is come unto the Gentiles, for to provoke[q] them to jealousy. (Romans 11:11)

[p] Picking up on his reference to Israel's table being a stumbling block to them, Paul asks, "Did they stumble that they should fall?" The word rendered "fall" here in the original language is a word that means "to fall beyond recovery." Paul answers, "God Forbid." They didn't fall beyond recovery, but they did fall, as Paul continues, "But rather through their fall salvation is come unto the Gentiles, for to provoke them to jealousy." The second word for fall, as used the second time in this verse, is from a different word that carries the idea of deserting one's post. Because Israel deserted her post as the means whereby God reaches lost people, salvation is going to the Gentiles through a new agency, the body of Christ.

[q] Romans 11:11 relates back to Romans 10:19. In Romans 10:19, Paul quotes from Deuteronomy 32:21 to show that God used the believing remnant at Pentecost to provoke the nation of Israel to jealousy. This was the 'little flock" of Luke 12:32 that was going to receive the kingdom of heaven. Here in Romans 11:11; Paul points out that God is now, in the dispensation of grace, using the believing Gentiles to provoke Israel to jealousy. More importantly, we learn from Romans 11:11 that "salvation is come unto the Gentiles." This is in sharp contrast to John 4:22 that, during our Lord's earthly ministry and as long as God reckoned Israel as "His people," "salvation is of the Jews." This provoking is now to individual Jews so they might now come to Christ and find justification by faith. The provoking in Romans 10:19 was to the entire nation so it might trust Jesus Christ as her Messiah.

Today the nation of Israel has been concluded in unbelief and is reckoned by God as being no different from any Gentile nation. The provoking here in Romans 11:11 and that of Romans 10:19 are based on different messages. The message of the little flock to Israel was that Jesus Christ is her Messiah and that by trusting Him, they could enter the kingdom. The message of the body of Christ to Israel is that "Christ died for our sins according the scriptures, and that he was buried and that he rose again on the third day according the scriptures" (1 Corinthians 15:1–4). By believing this message, a Jew could have eternal life as a member of the body of Christ, destined for heaven along with every other member of the body, whether Jew or Gentile.

Paul Magnifies His Gentile Apostleship to Reach Israelites

> 12 Now if the fall of them be[r] the riches of the world, and the diminishing of them the riches of the Gentiles; how much more their[s] fulness? 13 For I speak to you Gentiles, inasmuch as I am[t] the apostle of[u] the Gentiles, I magnify mine[v] office: 14 If by any means I may provoke to emulation them which are my flesh, and might save[w] some of them. (Romans 11:12–14)

[r] The fall of Israel brought riches to the world in the sense that anyone in the whole world (Jew or Gentile) can now come to salvation by personal faith in Christ and can have direct access to God without having to go through Israel. Likewise the diminishing of Israel brought riches to the Gentiles, in that they can come directly to God to be saved by grace without having to embrace Israel's law system. Today the body of Christ is God's agency for reaching the lost rather than Israel.

[s] Israel's fullness in verse 12 is a reference to the future time when Israel will again be God's elect agency for world evangelism. Israel's finest hour for reaching the world and representing God in the world is yet future when prophecies such as Zechariah 8:23 will come true. "In those days it shall come to pass, that ten men shall take hold out of all languages of the nations, even shall take hold of the skirt of him that is a Jew, saying, We will go with you: for we have heard that God is with you." At that time the world will have even greater riches in that not only will people be able to have individual redemption, but the world itself will be a far better place in which to live as prophecies such as Isaiah 35:1 come true. The eyes of the blind will be opened, the ears of the deaf shall be unstopped, the lame man shall leap as the hart (deer), the tongue of the dumb shall sing, the desert shall bloom as the rose, and so forth.

The phrase "their fullness" refers to the coming kingdom of heaven. The phrase "the fall of them" refers to the fact that Israel is no longer God's chosen means of evangelism today. The phrase "the diminishing of them" is a term for the spiritual decline of Israel. Their diminishing spiritually opened the door for the revelation of the mystery; God could now reveal the truth concerning the calling out of the church, the body of Christ, a basically Gentile church. Passages dealing with riches that will come to the world through Israel's fullness include the following:

- Isaiah 11:6–9: The curse is lifted from the animal and vegetative worlds.
- Isaiah 2:4: There will be no more war.
- Jeremiah 23:5: Justice will prevail everywhere, and the Gentiles will be blessed through Israel (Genesis 22:17–18).

[t] Romans 11:13 is one of the most significant verses in the Bible relative to the dispensational layout of the Bible. Here Paul speaks of the Gentiles in the dispensation of grace to specifically instruct them that he is uniquely their apostle. Modern translations miss the point by changing the preposition "of" to "to." Paul isn't simply the apostle "to" the Gentiles. That would imply that he preached the same message as the twelve apostles and carried it "to" the Gentiles. But Paul is uniquely "the" apostle of the Gentiles. He is not "an" apostle of the Gentiles. That would make him one of a number of apostles sent to the Gentiles. By stating unequivocally that he is "the" apostle "of" the Gentiles, he is making the bold statement that the message God is sending to the Gentiles today came through him. The fact that the noun "Gentiles" in the original is in the genitive case dictates that the English should read "of the Gentiles."

Also, it should be apparent to the careful student of scripture as he or she studies Romans 9–11 that God has reckoned Israel today as just one of the nations. In Romans 11:11, we understand that Israel has fallen (i.e., she has abandoned her post as the agency of salvation) and that salvation is now gone to the Gentiles apart from Israel being the instrument whereby God brings it. Today individual Jews and individual Gentiles are saved in one body (Ephesians 2:11–17). The "church which is [Christ's] body" is the subject of a body of doctrine called "the preaching of Jesus Christ according to the revelation of the mystery" (Romans 16:25). Paul is uniquely the apostle our Lord Jesus Christ personally commissioned and sent to be the revealer of this mystery (Ephesians 3:1–6). It was through him that the risen Lord revealed the ministry of reconciliation (2 Corinthians 5:18–21). Since it was Paul's heart desire that Israel be saved (Romans 10:1) and since the only way individual Jews can be saved today is to come to God the same way a Gentile would, Paul would naturally magnify his office as the apostle of the Gentiles. It is only by believing the gospel of the grace of God that anyone (Jew or Gentile) can be saved today.

[u] When Paul says he is the apostle of the Gentiles, he is setting his ministry apart from the ministry of the twelve apostles, whom the Lord called out and appointed during His earthy ministry to Israel. Our Lord told the Twelve, "Ye which have followed me, in the regeneration when the Son of man shall sit in the throne of his glory, ye also shall sit upon twelve thrones, judging the twelve tribes of Israel" (Matthew 19:28). Respecting the Gentiles, our Lord during His earthly ministry to them told them, "Go not into the way of the Gentiles, and into any city of the Samaritans enter ye not: But go rather to the lost sheep of the house of Israel. And as ye go, preach, saying, 'The kingdom of heaven is at hand'" (Matthew 10:5–7). In Acts 11:19, we find that the disciples who went out from the Twelve "traveled as far as Phenice, and Cyprus, and Antioch, preaching the word to none but unto the Jews only." Our Lord had indeed commissioned the Twelve to go to the Gentiles with the gospel of the kingdom.

Go ye into all the world, and preach the gospel to every creature. He that believeth and is baptized shall be saved; but he that believeth not shall be damned. And these signs shall follow them that believe. (Mark 16:15–17)

All power is given unto me in heaven and in earth. Go ye therefore, and teach all nations, baptizing them in the name of the Father, and of the Son, and of the Holy Ghost: Teaching them to observe all things whatsoever I have commanded you. (Matthew 28:18–20)

However, this commission had a specific order to it that must be followed: "But ye shall receive power, after that the Holy Ghost is come upon you: and ye shall be witnesses unto me both in Jerusalem, and in all Judaea, and in Samaria, and unto the uttermost parts of the earth" (Acts 1:8). The Twelve had to see Jerusalem converted before they could go to Judea (the two southern tribes). They then had to see Judea converted before they could to Samaria (the ten northern tribes cf. Ezekiel 37:19; John 10:15–16; Acts 8:14–17). Only after Jerusalem, Judea, and Samaria were saved could they go to the outermost parts of the earth (i.e., to the Gentiles). But in Galatians 2:9, we find Peter and the Twelve loosing themselves from their commission to go to the Gentiles while recognizing that Paul now had a commission from the Lord Jesus Christ to the Gentiles. We must remember that based on Matthew 16:19, Peter had the authority from our Lord to so loose himself from that commission. We understand, therefore, that the commission to evangelize the Gentile masses today rests with Paul (and through the completed Word of God) and with us (2 Corinthians 5:17–21), who are to follow Paul as our pattern (1 Timothy 1:16).

[v] We need to give some attention to the premise some have put forward that Paul was really God's choice to replace Judas Iscariot. In some churches, people who don't see or understand dispensational truth answer the questions "Why Paul? Why another apostle?" by conjecturing that the Twelve were out of the will of God when they chose Matthias to fill Judas's place. But when the facts are examined, it becomes clear that they made the correct decision. Let's consider the facts in the case of their selection of Matthias:

- The replacement for Judas had to have followed the Lord during His earthly ministry (Matthew 19:28). Peter explained that this following started with the baptism of John to the time when our Lord was taken up; the person must have been a witness of His resurrection (Acts 1:22). Paul wasn't even saved yet. In fact, Paul blasphemed the work the Holy Spirit did through the believing remnant at Pentecost (Matthew 12:32 cf. 1 Timothy 1:13).

- The Holy Spirit testified that Matthias was numbered with the eleven (Acts 1:26).

- There was yet a need for another apostle, because there was yet another new program for saving souls God had yet to reveal. That program is what God calls "the mystery," which He revealed through Paul (Ephesians 3:1–4).

- Paul was a logical candidate to be the apostle of the Gentiles, through whom God would reveal the dispensation of grace being both a Jew and a Romans citizen.

[w] In Romans 10:19, we see that God was using the believing remnant of Israel (i.e., the little flock) to provoke the nation to jealousy so that the nation at large might be saved. There, in Romans 10:19, it was the gospel of the kingdom that was being used to provoke Israel. Here, God is using believing Gentiles in the body of Christ to provoke individual Jews to get saved by the gospel of the grace of God. The fact that Paul says, "That I might save some of them" (emphasis added) indicates that national salvation was no longer in view. Romans 11:14 has saving some Israelites in view. Romans 11:11 states that Israel has fallen. Therefore, national salvation won't happen for Israel until the dispensation of grace ends with the rapture. Paul knew that one day "all Israel shall be saved" (Romans 11:26). However, that will be after the close of the dispensation of the grace of God.

He also knew that wouldn't happen until after the church, the body of Christ, was taken out of the earth (1 Thessalonians 5:9). Paul knew that today "some" of them could be saved. The salvation of "all" of Israel would happen only after the tribulation purged the unbelievers out of the nation (Matthew 3:12 cf. 24:40).

Paul's strategy for saving "some of them" was to magnify his Gentile apostleship and get as many Gentiles saved as he could so individual Jews would desire to come to the same salvation. Paul would then tell those who would desire to be saved the same thing he would tell anyone who desired to be saved: "Be ye reconciled to God. For he hath made him to be sin for us, who knew no sin; that we might be made the righteousness of God in him" (2 Corinthians 5:20–21). If they asked how to be saved, he would tell them, "That if thou shalt confess with thy mouth the Lord Jesus, and shalt believe in thine heart that God hath raised him from the dead, thou shalt be saved" (Romans 10:9–10).

The Reconciling of the World and the Future of Israel

15 For if the casting away of them be the reconciling[x] of the world, what shall the receiving[y] of them be, but life[z] from the dead? 16 For if the firstfruit[aa] be holy, the lump is also holy: and if the root[ab] be holy,

so are the branches. (Romans 11:15–16)

[x] Paul speaks of four different reconciliations:

1. The reconciling of Jew and Gentile in one body (Ephesians 2:15)

2. The reconciling of lost sinners to God (2 Corinthians 5:20)

3. The reconciling of all things to God (Colossians 1:20–21)

4. The reconciling of the world unto Himself (2 Corinthians 5:18)

It is the fourth Paul is talking about in Romans 11:15. This reconciliation made the whole world savable apart from Israel. But first the whole world had to be lost. God concluded that the whole world (Jews and Gentiles) was in unbelief when He set Israel aside so He would have mercy on all.

Leviticus 17:8–9 and Isaiah 56:6–7 make it plain that as long as Israel was God's people, the only place where God would accept a sacrifice from anyone, Jew or Gentile, was at the door of the tabernacle of the congregation (Israel's place of worship). Today salvation is offered as a free gift to all who will reach out in faith and receive it anywhere.

[y] The receiving of Israel is a reference to that future time when "all Israel shall be saved." Then Israel's heart will be changed as Zechariah 12:10 says. "And I will pour upon the house of David, and upon the inhabitants of Jerusalem, the spirit of grace and of supplications: and they shall look upon me whom they have pierced, and they shall mourn for him, as one mourneth for his only son, and shall be in bitterness for him, as one that is in bitterness for his firstborn." Zechariah 13:7 is a graphic illustration of Israel's awareness of that time that they had crucified their Messiah.

[z] The phrase "life from the dead" (v. 15) takes us back to Ezekiel 37:1–15, where we see Israel's spiritual deadness portrayed as a valley full of bones. God will give spiritual life to Israel one day when God will put His Spirit within them and cause them to walk in His statutes and keep His judgments.

[aa] The term "first fruits" is a metaphor based on Numbers 15:18–20. The first fruits are the first of the harvest offered to God. They represented the whole harvest. In this context the first fruits are the patriarchs of Israel. The reference to them being holy isn't referring so much to the quality of their lives but rather to the fact that they were set aside as God's chosen people. The point Paul is making is that if God set them apart from the Gentiles as God's chosen people, then the descendants are also set aside as God's chosen people. Just as a portion of a lump of dough was taken to the priest as "the first fruits," which represented the whole lump as being holy, so the nation of Israel is the lump God will one day use as the channel of blessing to the world.

[ab] The term "the root" here introduces the figure of speech of the olive tree. The root here is Abraham. The branches are Israel, the chosen nation that comes from him. This idea takes us back to Genesis 17:7. "And I will establish my covenant between me and thee and thy seed after thee in their generations for an everlasting covenant, to be a God unto thee, and to thy seed after thee." Israel was "planted" as "a noble vine" (Jeremiah 2:21). Our Lord is the vine (stem), while the members of Israel are the branches (John 15:4).

The Olive Tree: Access to God

¹⁷ And if some of the branches be broken off, and thou, being[ac] a wild olive tree, wert grafted in among

them, and with them partakest[ad] of the root and fatness of the olive tree; [18] Boast[ae] not against the branches. But if thou boast, thou bearest not the root, but the root thee. [19] Thou wilt say then, The branches were broken off, that I might be grafted in. [20] Well; because of unbelief they were broken off, and thou standest by faith. Be not[ag] highminded, but[ah] fear: [21] For if God spared[af] not the natural branches, take heed lest he also spare not thee. (Romans 11:17–21)

[ac] The symbolism of trees must be understood here. There are four different trees to represent Israel symbolically in the Bible. We find them in Judges 9:7-15 representing four different aspects of Israel's life as a nation.

1. The olive tree represents spiritual Israel.

2. The fig tree represents religious Israel.

3. The vine represents national Israel.

4. The bramble represents apostate Israel.

Understanding the budding of the fig tree as the reinstituting of the temple service in Israel would enable people to understand the parable of the fig tree in Matthew 24:32 as being the reinstating of the temple service and not the reestablishing of the nation (which would be represented by the vine). The olive represents peace with God (the first reference to the olive was the olive leaf brought back to the ark in Genesis 8:11). Lamps burning with oil of olives were to be outside the tabernacle by night. The cherubim in the temple were made of olive wood (1 Kings 6:23). The doors to the temple were made of olive wood (1 Kings 6:31–33). Therefore, to understand verses 17–18, we must understand that the olive tree here represents the place of spiritual blessing and peace with God. The branches that were broken off are the unbelieving masses of the nation of Israel, who had lost the place of spiritual blessing and access to God. The wild olive tree in this figure of speech represents the Gentile masses. The Gentile masses were grafted into the place where they could receive blessing from God.

[ad] Verses 17–24 can be properly understood only when we realize that the question is not one of individual salvation but rather one of dispensational changes in God's dealings with Israel and the Gentiles. The issue is, Who is God's agency for evangelism? (i.e., Who will be the agency God uses to reach the lost masses of humanity?) The figure of the olive tree (see note [ab]) is understood as we identify the elements.

- The natural olive tree represents Israel as the channel of blessing to the nations according to the Abrahamic covenant (Genesis 12:3).

- The wild olive tree represents the Gentile nations God gave up in Genesis 10 (cf. Romans 1:24, 26, 28).

- Partaking of the root and the fatness of the olive tree is a reference to having access to spiritual blessing from God (i.e., tapping into that channel).

- The branches that were broken off were the unbelieving citizens of Israel (Matthew 21:43; Acts 13:46–47; 26:17–20; 28:26–28; also see Matthew 12:31–32).

- The natural branches left in the olive tree represent the believing remnant of Israel, who had been saved under the gospel of the kingdom.

[ae] The point Paul is making is that Gentiles ought not to get too high minded about their being placed in a

position of having access to God apart from Israel. Paul presses the point that the root (Abraham) is the father of the nation of Israel. The nation that came from him is the rightful possessor of the promises of God. If a Gentile were to boast that Israel, the natural branches, were broken off so that the Gentile might be grafted in, Paul would point out that it was only because of unbelief that the natural branches were broken off. Paul then goes on to tell the Gentiles that they are in the position to receive direct blessing from God only by faith. God took Israel off the field because the nation was unfruitful. The Gentiles were grafted in because they would be fruitful. Note Paul's closing comments to Israel in Acts 28:28. "Be it known therefore unto you, that the salvation of God is sent unto the Gentiles, and that they will hear it."

But Paul would have the Gentiles know that this present Gentile dispensation will continue only as long as the Gentiles are faithful to evangelize (i.e., that they are spiritually fruitful). Unbelief and unfruitfulness go hand in hand (cf. 2 Timothy 2:10–12). Paul's statement "and thou standest by faith" is a reference to faithfulness to accomplish what God would have us accomplish. "Faith" here is used in the same sense in which it was used in 1 Corinthians 16:13. "Watch ye, stand fast in the faith, quit you like men, be strong." Also, as Paul tells the Corinthians again, "Not for that we have dominion over your faith, but are helpers of your joy: for by faith ye stand." (2 Corinthians 1:24) Faithfulness comes from faith in the faith (Colossians 2:7–8).

[af] When Paul says, "If God spared not the natural branches, take heed lest he also spare not thee," he does not pose a threat that an individual Gentile member of the body of Christ would lose his or her salvation. Rather, he continues to address the Gentiles en mass as in verse 13. "For I speak to you Gentiles, inasmuch as I am the apostle of the Gentiles, I magnify mine office." The Gentile masses are in danger of going back to the state they were in before the dispensation of grace started. Ephesians 2:11–12 described that sate.

[ag] It is a principle with God to resist the proud.

- "Though the LORD be high, yet hath he respect unto the lowly: but the proud he knoweth afar off" (Psalm 138:6).

- "Behold, his soul which is lifted up is not upright in him: but the just shall live by his faith" (Habakkuk 2:4).

- "I tell you, this man went down to his house justified rather than the other: for every one that exalteth himself shall be abased; and he that humbleth himself shall be exalted" (Luke 18:14).

- "Casting down imaginations, and every high thing that exalteth itself against the knowledge of God, and bringing into captivity every thought to the obedience of Christ" (2 Corinthians 10:5).

- An elder should not be a novice "lest being lifted up with pride he fall into the condemnation of the devil" (1 Timothy 3:6).

- "God resisteth the proud, but giveth grace unto the humble" (James 4:6).

- A characteristic of men in the last days is that they will be "lovers of their own selves ... boasters, proud ... heady, highminded" (2 Timothy 3:4).

[ah] The fear here is not the fear of punishment from a terrifying God. Such fear is only in unbelievers. Believers "have not received the spirit of bondage again to fear; but ye have received the Spirit of adoption, whereby we cry, Abba, Father" (Romans 8:15). However, there is a sense of fear believers ought to have, and Paul describes it

in Philippians 2:12–13. "Wherefore, my beloved, as ye have always obeyed, not as in my presence only, but now much more in my absence, work out your own salvation with fear and trembling. *For it is God which worketh in you both to will and to do of his good pleasure*" (emphasis added). This kind of fear is a deep reverence for the fact that the believer is engaged in what God is doing and not simply what man is doing. This is the kind of reverential fear that keeps people on their toes. "Wherefore, let him that thinketh he standeth take heed lest he fall" (1 Corinthians 10:12).

Israel, the natural branches of the olive tree, was broken off because they did not bear the fruit of belief. The Gentiles were grafted in and are there only so long as they are fruitful. Once the Gentiles become unfruitful, God will remove them as surely as He did the natural branches, Israel. See the parable of the fig tree in Luke 13:7.

A Warning to Gentiles

> 22 Behold therefore the goodness[ai] and severity of God: on them which fell, severity; but toward thee, goodness, if thou continue in his goodness: otherwise thou also shalt be cut off. 23 And they also, if they abide not still in unbelief, shall be[aj] grafted in: for God is able to graft them in again. 24 For if thou wert cut out of the olive tree which is wild by nature, and wert grafted contrary to nature into a good olive tree: how much more shall these, which be the natural branches, be grafted into their own olive tree? (Romans 11:22–24)

[ai] The goodness and severity of God are set in contract to each other here. The word severity is from the Greek word meaning "to sever from something" (literally to cut off). The Jews were severed from their position of favor. The goodness of God is the opposite of severity. The goodness of God in this context is then to be brought near to God. The Gentiles went from their position of being "without Christ, being aliens from the commonwealth of Israel, and strangers from the covenants of promise, having no hope, and without God in the world" to being "made nigh by the blood of Christ" (Ephesians 2:11–13). Paul says in 2 Corinthians 5:19 "that God was in Christ, reconciling the world unto himself," but that didn't make everyone in the world justified. It simply made everyone in the world savable. Each must respond in faith and "be reconciled to God" personally (2 Corinthians 5:20). When Gentiles cease to be personally reconciled to God by faith in the death, burial, and resurrection of Christ for personal reconciliation, the dispensation of the grace of God will close, the catching away of the body (1 Thessalonians 4:14–16; 1 Corinthians 15:51) will take place, and the seventieth week of Daniel will take place. That event (the catching away we call "the rapture") is the blessed hope of the believer, but it's also the end of the opportunity for Gentiles to come to salvation apart from Israel. The unbelieving Gentiles will then be cut off and will then have to come to God through Israel again as they did before the dispensation of grace started.

[aj] Verse 23 talks about Israel being grafted in again. In 2 Corinthians 3:15–16, Paul says Israel's heart is covered with a veil. That veil will be removed one day when God again works through Israel. That day will come when Israel, as Zechariah says, "shall look upon me [Christ] whom they have pierced, and they shall mourn for him, as one mourneth for his only son" (Zechariah 12:10). In Matthew 23:38, we understand that, when our Lord left Israel's temple, their temple was left desolate. However, in verse Matthew 23:39, we understand that Israel will one day rejoice that Christ will come "in the name of the Lord" to Israel.

A Temporary, Partial Blindness on Israel

> 25 For I would not, brethren, that ye should be ignorant[ak] of this mystery, lest ye should be wise in your

own conceits; that blindness in part is happened to Israel, until the fulness of the Gentiles be come in. ²⁶ And so all Israel shall be[al] saved: as it is[am] written, There shall come out of Sion[an] the Deliverer, and shall turn[ao] away ungodliness from Jacob: ²⁷ For this is my covenant[ap] unto them, when[aq] I shall take away their sins. ²⁸ As concerning the gospel, they are[ar] enemies for your sakes: but as touching the election, they are beloved for the fathers' sakes. ²⁹ For the gifts and calling of God are without repentance. ³⁰ For as ye in times past[as] have not believed God, yet have now obtained mercy through their unbelief: ³¹ Even so have these also now not believed, that through your mercy they also may obtain mercy. ³² For God hath concluded[at] them all in unbelief, that he might have mercy upon all. (Romans 11:25–32)

[ak] Verses 25–27 present one of the seven aspects of the mystery revealed through Paul. This aspect deals with the duration of the present blindness of Israel. The mystery isn't that Israel would be blinded because that was prophesied (Psalm 69 and so forth). The mystery is the duration of the blindness (i.e., "until the fullness of the Gentiles be come in"). The fullness of the Gentiles speaks of the completion of the body of Christ and the rapture of that body to the heavens. Also, the mystery isn't simply that Gentiles would be saved. That too was prophesied (e.g., Isaiah 60:1–3). Prophecy, however, saw Gentiles being saved through the rise of Israel. The mystery is that Gentiles are being saved though the fall of Israel (i.e., "through their fall salvation is come to the Gentiles"). This mystery was "hid in God" (Ephesians 3:9), "hid from ages and generations" (Colossians 1:26). "In other ages [it] was not made known" (Ephesians 3:5). It was "kept secret since the world began" until God revealed it through the apostle Paul (Romans 16:25).

[al] One day "all Israel shall be saved." This doesn't mean every Israelite will automatically believe. Rather, God will purge out the unbelievers from the nation one day so only believers remain to go into the promised kingdom (Zechariah 13:8). We understand this from the words of John the Baptizer in Matthew 3:10–12. We see this prophesied in the Old Testament, in Ezekiel 20:38. "And I will purge out from among you the rebels, and them that transgress against me: I will bring them forth out of the country where they sojourn, and they shall not enter into the land of Israel: and ye shall know that I am the Lord."

[am] There are many prophecies of Israel's future salvation. A few are listed here: Isaiah 11:11–16; 45:17; 54:6–10; Jeremiah 3:17–23; 30:17–22; 32:37–41; 33:24–26; Ezekiel 34:22–31; 37:21–28; 39:25–29; Hosea 3:5; Joel 3:16–21; Amos 9:14–15; Micah 7:15–20; Zephaniah 3:12–20; Zechariah 10:6–12; and so forth.

[an] Verse 26 is a quote from Isaiah 59:20–21. Psalms 14:7 and 106:47 also allude to this future time.

[ao] One day God will remove ungodliness from Jacob by removing the stony heart out of Israel's flesh and giving them a new heart (Ezekiel 11:19; 36:26). In doing so, God will turn away ungodliness from Jacob (Israel).

[ap] The covenant referred to is the promised new covenant of Jeremiah 31:31–34, whereby God will put His law in their inward parts and write them in their hearts; and they will all know the Lord without having to be taught, for they will all know Him from the least of them to the greatest of them.

[aq] The word when in verse 27 is significant here. Israel's sins will be forgiven at a future time when the Lord returns to the nation. For us living under the dispensation of grace, our sins are forgiven the instant we believe the gospel that Christ died for our sins (Colossians 2:13). Peter tells Israel when their sins will be forgiven: "when the times of refreshing shall come from the presence of the Lord" (Acts 3:19). Peter speaks of Israel's salvation in the future tense in Acts 15:11, though he understands the Gentile members of the body of Christ are saved

from sin's penalty the instant they believe. Israel's forgiveness will happen for them as a nation when their real Day of Atonement comes. That will be when Christ comes back to earth to bring salvation to the nation. Israel's Day of Atonement will come when Christ (Israel's high priest) comes back to the nation (Hebrews 9:28). Israelites under law didn't have security as we do. The Lord tells Israel, "If ye forgive men their trespasses, your heavenly Father will also forgive you: But if ye forgive not men their trespasses, neither will your Father forgive your trespasses" (Matthew 6:14–15). Paul, the apostle of the Gentiles, tells us who are living in the dispensation of grace. "And be ye kind one to another, tenderhearted, forgiving one another, even as God for Christ's sake hath forgiven you" (Ephesians 4:32).

[ar] Verse 28 views Israel as an enemy of God. Israel is an enemy of God today for the sake of God, administering the dispensation of grace in which He can have mercy on all. However, this is only a temporary situation. God has chosen (i.e., they are His elect) that nation to be the means whereby He reconciles this earth to Himself (1 Peter 2:9; Isaiah 55:5; 56:6–7; 14:24–27). That is His calling for that nation. God will never change His mind regarding His callings; nor will He ever take back one of His gifts.

[as] Paul makes the same use of tenses here in verse 30 as he did in Ephesians 2:2–7. In times past (i.e., before the mystery of the one body was revealed [Ephesians 3:3–10]), the Gentiles were in unbelief and were "… without Christ, being aliens from the common wealth of Israel and strangers from the covenants of promise, having no hope, and without God in the world" (Ephesians 2:12). Now, though, in the dispensation of grace, the Gentiles have obtained mercy because Israel as a nation hasn't believed.

[at] This (v. 32) is certainly one of the most wonderful passages of the Bible. God concluded that Israel was in unbelief so He could show mercy to the Gentiles, but then He immediately included Israel with the Gentiles so they also could now come to Him in the same way as the Gentiles—by grace through faith apart from any human merit. Israel can now come to the same mercy God has extended to the Gentiles today in the dispensation of grace.

Joyful Exultation

> [33] O the depth of the riches both of the wisdom[au] and knowledge of God! how unsearchable are his judgments, and his ways past finding out! [34] For who hath known the mind of the Lord? or who hath been his counsellor? [35] Or who hath first given to him, and it shall be recompensed unto him again? [36] For of him, and through him, and to him, are all things: to whom be glory for ever. Amen. (Romans 11:33–36)

[au] Verses 33–36 extol the wisdom of God. Ephesians tells us "that now unto the principalities and powers in heavenly places might be known the manifold wisdom of God" (Ephesians 3:10). Let it not be lost on the reader as one reads these closing verses of this section of Romans just how truly deep is the richness of God's grace, mercy, love, patience, justice, holiness, and what glory is in His person. We truly have a wonderful God and Savior.

Study Questions on Chapter 11

1. In what sense are we to take this question in verse 1 "Has God cast away His people?" Is this a permanent or temporary casting away?

2. What proof does Paul offer to show that God has not permanently cast away His people Israel?

3. Why would Paul quote Elijah from 1 Kings 19 in developing his argument regarding the setting aside of Israel?

4. What time period of time is "this present time" in verse 5?

5. Who are the "remnant according to the election of grace?"

6. Are works and grace mutually exclusive?

7. What was it that Israel was seeking after but did not attain to? Who got it if they didn't? Who is "the election" in verse 7?

8. If those in the nation other than the remnant were blinded, why does God hold them accountable? Did He not give them "the spirit of slumber?"

9. Who prophesied that God would give Israel this "spirit of slumber?" Where is it recorded?

10. Who was David prophesying about verses 9 & 10?

11. In verses 11 & 12 we see that Israel stumbled but did not fall but then is is said that they did fall. Explain this. Was this fall temporary or permanent? Was it partial or complete?

12. What did God do through their fall?

13. God provoked Israel to jealousy in 11:11. Is this the same as provoking that we saw in 10:19? How is the message used by God in 11:11 different from that used in 10:19?

14. During what period of time does the statement "the fall of them is the riches of the world and the diminishing of them be the riches of the Gentiles" apply? When will their fullness bring even more blessing for the Gentiles?

15. Taking verses 13 and 14 together, what is it that really motivated Paul to magnify his office as the apostle of the Gentiles?

16. If Paul was the "Apostle of the Gentiles," he is the apostle that is owned by the Gentiles. He is our apostle. Would he then one day be sitting on one of the twelve thrones of Matthew 19:28?

17. What would Paul's plan of attack be to "save some of them"?

18. Verse 2 says that God has not cast away His people but verse 15 implies that He did. Explain the apparent contradiction.

19. In what sense, is the world reconciled to God through Israel's fall?

20. Who is in view in the term "Life form the dead" in verse 15?

21. Identify the firstfruit, the lump, the root, the branches?

22. What does the olive tree represent? Who do the branches that were broken off represent? Who is the wild olive tree? Is this the way grafting is usually done – to graft the wild onto the domestic root?

23. Why were the domestic branches broken off? What attitude should the Gentiles have toward the domestic branches (Israel) be?

24. What is Paul considering in verse 22 in the expression "thou also shalt be cut off?" Is this a good text to show that soul salvation can be lost?

25. What is the mystery or secret that verse 25 is talking about?

26. Verse 26 speaks of all Israel being saved. In light of verse 25, when will this be?

27. Does "all Israel shall be saved" mean that every Jew will one day be saved?

28. Concerning the gospel, the unsaved Israelites are enemies for whose sake? Concerning the election they are beloved for whose sake?

29. What are the gifts referred to in verse 29? What are the callings? Who is it that does not repent?

30. In verse 30, who was it that did not "believe God?" Who has now obtained mercy? The Gentiles have now obtained mercy through whose "unbelief?"

31. What does it mean in verse 31"that through your mercy they also may obtain mercy?"

32. In verse 32, who did God "concluded in unbelief?" When did He do that?

33. Explain verse 33 which speaks of God's ways being past finding out but did you not just find them out?

34. Who is Paul quoting in verses 34-36? Give the reference.

SUPER ABOUNDING GRACE, Part 3

The Believer in Service
A Study of the Book of Romans, Chapters 12-16

I beseech you therefore, brethren, by the mercies of God, that ye present your bodies a living sacrifice, holy, acceptable unto God, which is your reasonable service. And be not conformed to this world: but be ye transformed by the renewing of your mind, that ye may prove what is that good, and acceptable, and perfect, will of God. For I say, through the grace given unto me, to every man that is among you, not to think of himself more highly than he ought to think; but to think soberly, according as God hath dealt to every man the measure of faith.

(Romans 12:1–8)

Romans Chapter 12

A LIVING SACRIFICE

An Overview of the Next Section (Chapters 12– 15)

Seven spheres of Christian service are presented in the last chapters of Romans. These seven spheres are summarized as follows:

1. To God (12:1–2)

This continues the thought of Romans 8:39; 11:30–32.

2. To the Body (12:3–8)

This describes functions that must be served in local assemblies if they are to be viable local churches.

3. To Fellow Believers (12:9–13)

This section describes what should be a believer's attitude and actions toward other believers individually. The previous section looked at the body of believers in the local assembly.

4. To Our Enemies (12:14–21)

The believer, having been forgiven and regenerated, can look at his enemies differently than the unbeliever does.

5. To the State (13:1–4)

This goes back to Genesis 8 and the institution of human government for the protection and provision for order in society.

6. To Society (13:8–14)

The work of believers in society ought always to be positive and for good.

7. To Weaker Brethren (14–15)

Most of this section of Romans is directed to this subject, as is a large part of 1 Corinthians 8–10

Service to God

¹ I[a] beseech[b] you[c] therefore, brethren[d], by[e] the mercies of God, that ye present your bodies[f] a living sacrifice, holy[g], acceptable unto God, which is your reasonable[h] service. ² And be not conformed[i] to

this world: but be ye transformed[j] by the renewing[k] of your mind, that ye may prove what is that good, and acceptable, and perfect, will of God. (Romans 12:1–2)

[a] The "I" here is important. It is Paul, "the apostle of the Gentiles," still talking to the Gentiles. He has been addressing them since Romans 11:13.

[b] The first sphere of Christian service Paul addresses is to God. While the law commands obedience, grace beseeches. Grace beseeches on the basis of what God did for us.

[c] The "you" here in Romans 12:1 is likewise important. They are the Gentiles who, before Israel fell from favor with God, were "in times past Gentiles in the flesh … without Christ, being aliens from the commonwealth of Israel, and strangers from the covenant of promise, having no hope and without God in the world" (Ephesians 2:11–12).

[d] "Brethren" is also significant. The Gentiles who were strangers from the commonwealth of Israel "now in Christ Jesus … are made nigh by the blood of Christ. For he is our peace, who hath made both one, and hath broken down the middle wall of partition between us" (Ephesians 2:13–14).

[e] Paul beseeches "by the mercies of God." These mercies are those listed in Romans 11:30–31. "For as ye in times past have not believed God, yet have now obtained mercy through their unbelief: Even so have these also now not believed, that through your mercy they also may obtain mercy." Having obtained mercy when we did not deserve mercy is pure grace. Therefore it is our reasonable services that we give God our bodies as a living sacrifice."

[f] God didn't want our religion. He doesn't want our lip service. He doesn't want our money. He wants us. The last thing a person gives up is his or her body. Paul says in Ephesians 5:29, "For no man ever yet hated his own flesh; but nourisheth, and cherisheth it." When God has our bodies, He has everything else.

[g] A living sacrifice is in contrast with the dead sacrifices the Old Testament saints brought. Our Lord gave Himself as a sacrifice unto physical death for us. He now asks that we give our bodies as a living sacrifice. The concept of a living sacrifice is evident in Galatians 2:20. "I am crucified with Christ" (i.e., I am a sacrifice). "Never the less I live" (i.e., I am a living sacrifice). "Yet not I but Christ liveth in me" (i.e., He is the source of the life I now live). "And the life that I now live in the flesh I live by the faith of the Son of God who loved me and gave himself for me."

[h] God wants our lives to be separated from the world unto Him.

[i] To be conformed to the world is to take the outward appearance of the world. However, this would be taking the outward form of something we are not. Paul tells believers, "Therefore, if any man be in Christ he is a new creature, old things are passed away, behold all things are become anew." We too no longer walk "according to the course of this world, according to the prince of the power of the air, the spirit that now worketh in the children of disobedience" (Ephesians 2:2).

[j] To be transformed is to be changed from the inside out. This can be done only through regeneration (Titus 3:5).

[k] The renewing of our minds is a daily, moment-by-moment renewing as the Spirit of God works on the inner

man of the believer (that regenerated spirit) through the Word of God. "But though our outward man perish, yet the inward man is renewed day by day" (2 Corinthians 4:16). This renewing is in our minds (note that this renewing doesn't first start in our emotions). It's the mind that has to be renewed for our affections to be touched. We need to think on the things we have in Christ to be renewed. That means we must be reading and studying the Word of God for the continual renewing to occur.

Service to the Body

³ For I say[l], through the grace given[m] unto me, to every man[n] that is among you, not to think[o] of himself more highly than he ought to think; but to think soberly, according as God hath dealt to every man the measure of faith. ⁴ For as we have many members in one[p] body, and all members have not the same office: ⁵ So we, being many, are one body in Christ, and every one members one of another. ⁶Having then gifts differing according to the grace that is given to us, whether prophecy[q], let us prophesy[r] according to the proportion of faith; ⁷ Or ministry[s], let us wait[s] on our ministering: or he that[t] teacheth, on teaching; ⁸ Or he that exhorteth[u], on exhortation: he that giveth, let him do it with simplicity; he that ruleth, with diligence; he that sheweth mercy, with cheerfulness. (Romans 12:3–8)

[l] Paul addresses the second sphere of Christian service in Romans 12:3–8, where he lists a series of gifts of the spirit we might call service gifts because they involve functions rendered in service to the body of Christ. There is a series of gifts listed in 1 Corinthians 12:8–10 that might be regarded as "sign" gifts because God used them as a sign to indicate to Israel when and how He was working. In Ephesians 4:11, a series of gifts are listed that might be called "ministry" gifts, in that they were given to enable men to minister to the body of Christ before the completed revelation of the Word of God was given. In 1 Corinthians 13:13 is a list of what is called the "abiding gifts." The four lists are presented in Table 1.

Service Gifts	Sign Gifts	Ministry Gifts	Abiding Gifts
Romans 12:6–8	1 Corinthians 12:8–10	Ephesians 4:11	1 Corinthians 13:13
1. Prophecy	1. The word of wisdom	1. Apostles	1. Faith
2. Ministry	2. The word of knowledge	2. Prophets	2. Hope
3. Teaching	3. Faith	3. Evangelists	3. Charity
4. Exhortation	4. Healing	4. Pastors and teachers	
5. Giving	5. Working miracles		
6. Ruling	6. Prophecy		
7. Showing mercy	7. Discerning of spirits		
8. Diverse kinds of tongues			
9. Interpretations of tongues			

Table 1

In the first three lists, there is one gift that is common to all: the gift of prophecy. We will consider this one in more detail in note [q]. Of all the gifts, this one cannot be easily feigned.

[m] Paul was constantly aware of the grace that enabled him to be the revealer of the mystery. In 1 Timothy 1:11–14, Paul speaks of "the glorious gospel of the blessed God, which was committed to my trust. And I thank Christ Jesus our Lord, who hath enabled me, for that he counted me faithful, putting me into the ministry; Who was before a blasphemer, and a persecutor, and injurious: but I obtained mercy, because I did it ignorantly in unbelief. And the grace of our Lord was exceeding abundant with faith and love which is in Christ Jesus." Therefore, Paul could tell about grace because he was the foremost recipient of it.

[n] The words "every man" mean every person. The words "think more highly" literally mean to be high minded. The phrase "according as God hath dealt to every man the measure of faith" literally means "to each as God divided a measure of faith" (i.e., God gave to each person an area in which that person was to faithfully serve the body of Christ).

[o] In verse 3, Paul tells each of us not to think of ourselves more highly then we ought to think. The connecting word for at the beginning of the verse indicates he is still carrying over the same thought from verse 2. Being transformed by the renewing of our minds rather than being conformed to this world is therefore related to not thinking of ourselves more highly than we ought to think. In this world, unbelievers love to build themselves up at the expense of others. Paul is saying (and he invokes his apostolic authority in doing so) that we are not to think we are more important before God or men than any other believer. God has given each believer a certain function in the church in which to be faithful. The surrender to God sought in verses 1–2 will produce the humility requested in verses 3–8.

[p] Here in Romans 12:4 is the first place in all the Bible where we find a reference to the body of Christ. The "church which is [Christ's] body" (Ephesians 1:22; Colossians 1:24) is the subject of the mystery that was revealed through Paul (see Colossians 1:25–26; Ephesians 2:13–16:18). This one body is formed by the baptizing work of the Holy Spirit (1 Corinthians 12:12–13).

[q] Of the seven gifts listed in verses 6–8, the first (prophecy) stands out as different in that it defines a function that no longer operates in the world today. The rest of the gifts actually name functions that are still operative in the church today, though they aren't bestowed on the basis of supernatural endowment as they were in the period the book of Acts covered. Let's look at each of these functions:

- Prophecy ceased to function when the canon of scripture was closed. The other six gifts define functions that are still served today. Individual members of the local assembly serve these functions.

- Ministry is from the word from which we get "deacon." This is service to the assemblies of believers expressed in action. This is the work of deacons. It has to do with any activity of a supportive nature to a local assembly. It would include maintenance of the physical facility in which the assembly meets. It would include treasury work, bookkeeping, mailing, waiting on tables, serving food, maintaining order during meetings, visiting and tending to the sick, and so forth.

- Teaching is from the word from which we get "didactic." This is the teaching function in an assembly, whereby a man "labors in the Word and doctrine" (1 Timothy 5:12). During the childhood years (i.e., the Acts period) of the church, which is Christ's body, this was a supernatural gift, as was prophecy. During the Acts period, men were supernaturally endowed with a gift of teaching (Ephesians 4:11). However, today, since the close of that apostolic era, men have to labor in the word to learn it themselves and then labor in the doctrine to teach it. The difference between then and now is that then the Word hadn't been completed during the infancy period of the church. Today the issue is that we have the completed Word of God, and that is the final authority for us today.

- Exhortation is from a word that literally means "to come alongside." It means to come alongside someone who is in need of encouragement. In this competitive world, one must work hard to be successful at one's course of business. Discouragements abound, especially for young people. Such people need to be encouraged. There are many areas of life where people are in need of encouragement. For example:
    o Young married people need encouragement in their efforts to set up godly homes.
    o Duties of home, work, and ministry overwhelm people.
    o Students struggle with getting an education.
    o Parents need encouragement, especially those who have children with special needs.

- Giving is to impart financial support to someone in need. See Philippians 4:15–19 on giving.
    o To financially support those who labor in the word and doctrine (1 Timothy 5:10–18).
    o To give to those who are struggling financially (Ephesians 4:28; 1 Timothy 5:3–6; 6:17–19).
    o The one who gives should do so quietly and with simplicity, not to make a show of it.

- Ruling is from the word from which we get our English "president." This is the function of providing leadership to an assembly of believers. It takes a special talent to do that. It has often been said, "You can't push a rope uphill. You have to pull it." So, too, a leader must lead by example. Therefore, he or she has to be the example of sacrificial giving if others are to follow and give sacrificially. He or she must lead as an example of what a Christian's life should be like if others are to follow. His or her family must be an example of what a Christian's family ought to be like if others are to follow (1 Timothy 3:4–5, 12). The one who rules must be diligent. There is no room for a slacker in leadership. When all others forsake their posts, the leader must still be there. Above all, we must remember that ruling isn't with dictatorial powers (2 Corinthians 1:24) but is by example of the power of a transformed life (1 Corinthians 2:4).

- Showing mercy is to have compassion on those who struggle with handicaps, infirmities, grief, disappointment, and so forth. This is a vitally important function in the local assembly since there are many who need to have a lift in times when they are down. Every believer should cultivate the art of showing mercy. When you are down, go to a believer who is up. When you are up, lift up a believer who is down.

[r] The gift of prophecy is the ability to predict the future. However, the purpose of the gift was to identify for believers what God said and didn't say (i.e., to identify what was to be included in the canon of scripture and what wasn't). They were God's mouthpiece (Acts 3:18, 21, 24; 11:27; 13:1, 40; 15:15, 32; 26:22; Romans 1:2; 16:25).

- First Corinthians 14:29 says, "Let the prophets speak two or three, and let the other judge."
- First Corinthians 14:32 says, "The spirits of the prophets are subject to the prophets."
- Ephesians 3:4–5 says, "My knowledge of the mystery of Christ which in other ages was not made known

unto the sons of man, as it is now revealed unto his holy apostles and prophets by the Spirit; that the Gentiles should be fellowheirs."

The test of a prophet is that he or she can predict the future with 100 percent accuracy. Because the prophet's role was to identify scripture, it was essential that the gift of prophecy be authenticated. A prophet had to be able to predict the short-term future with 100 percent accuracy before that prophet was to be heeded (Deuteronomy 18:22). There was yet another test of a prophet. If a prophet suggested that people were to follow strange gods and violate the written Word of God, that prophet was false and was to die (Deuteronomy 13:1; 18:21), even if he or she could predict future events. The role of the New Testament prophet is identifying what writings were scripture, as seen in Acts 15:23–32 (note especially v. 27). The letter written by the Jerusalem apostles was to be included in the canon of scripture and was so identified by the prophets Judas and Silas (Acts 15:27–32).

In 1 Corinthians 14:37, we see Paul calling on the New Testament prophets to identify his writing as scripture. In Romans 16:25, we see Paul referring to his epistles as having been identified as scripture by the New Testament prophets. All this was necessary while scripture was being revealed progressively. During the time period covered by the book of Acts (AD 34–65), further revelation was being given. During that time, believers could "see through a glass darkly" because only "partial knowledge" of the New Testament was given (1 Corinthians 13:9–10). But when the New Testament was complete, "that which is perfect" (1 Corinthians 13:8–13) would have come. The phrase "that which is perfect" is a reference to the completed Word of God. Until that time came, Paul was continually receiving "visions and revelations" (2 Corinthians 12:1, 17). However, when Paul wrote Ephesians and Colossians, apparently revelation was full and complete. In those books he prays that believers might be "filled with the knowledge of his will in all wisdom and spiritual understanding" (Colossians 1:9). It was the mystery revealed through Paul that completed the Word of God (see Colossians 1:25–26). Once revelation was complete, prophets were no longer needed, and gift of prophecy ceased to function, as did all other supernatural sign gifts. The issue before God today is that we have the completed Word of God as the final authority to govern our lives in all matters of faith and practice.

- Now let's summarize what we have learned so far and know about the gift of prophecy:
- Prophecy was associated with the coming of the Messiah to Israel (Acts 2:17 cf Joel 2:28–37).
- Our Lord was a prophet unto Israel (Deuteronomy 18:15, 18–19).
- False prophets were to die (Deuteronomy 18:20).
- The test of a true prophet was that he or she had to predict the near-term future (Deuteronomy 18:21–22).
- New Testament prophets could do that (Acts 11:27–28).
- Saul (who became Paul) was also a New Testament prophet (Acts 13:1).
- They were God's mouthpiece; they spoke for God (Acts 13:2).
- Their main role was to identify scripture (Acts 15:22–33).
- Paul often called on them to validate his writing as scripture (1 Corinthians 14:37; Romans 16:25; Ephesians 3:4–5).

- The gift of prophecy was temporary in nature (1 Corinthians 13:8). It functioned from AD 33–65. Paul received visions and revelations (2 Corinthians 12:17).
  - Revelation was progressive (Acts 26:16).
  - Now all scripture is complete (Colossians 1:9, 25).

[s] Looking at the function of ministry, we find that it is related to the roles deacons and deaconesses filled in the local assembly. The word defines the work of a deacon. Paul talks about deacons in the local church as an office in 1 Timothy 3:8–16. There in 1 Timothy 3, the office of deacon or deaconess is distinguished from the place of overseer (1 Timothy 3:1–7). It should be noted that a woman can serve as a deaconess. Note the phrase "even so must their wives be grave, not slanderers" (1 Timothy 3:11). The reference there is to women who serve in the capacity of deaconesses. Phoebe is said to be a "servant of the church which is at Cenchrea." The word servant in Romans 16:1 is the word for "deacon" in the feminine gender. New Testament scripture excludes women from filling the office of bishop or overseer (1 Timothy 2:12; 3:2), but they have an important role to fill in the capacity of deaconesses. The qualifications for deacons, in contrast to those of overseers, are listed here for comparison purposes. All items in the table are quotes from the King James Version.

Overseer (1 Timothy 3:1–7)	Deacon (1 Timothy 3:8–16)
Blameless	Grave
The husband of one wife	Not double tongued
Vigilant	Not given to much wine
Sober	Not greedy of filthy lucre
Given to hospitality	Holding the mystery of the faith In a pure conscience
Apt to teach	Let these first be proved Then let them use the office of a deacon, being found blameless
Not given to wine	Even so must their wives be Grave Not slanderous Sober
No striker	Faithful in all things.
Not greedy of filthy lucre	Let the deacons be the husbands of one wife.
Not a brawler	. Ruling their children and their own houses well
Not covetous;	
"One who rules well his own house,	
having his children in subjection with all gravity; (For if a man know not how how to rule his own house, how shall he take care of the church of God?" (KJV)	
Not a novice, lest being lifted up with pride he fall into the condemnation of the devil.	

He must have a good report of them which are with out, lest he fall into reproach and the snare of the devil	

Table 2

[t] We ask now, If prophecy ceased as a gift, then what about the rest of those listed here in Romans 12:6–8? We still have the need for people to function in ministry, teaching, exhortation, giving, ruling, and showing mercy. But do people perform these functions in the body by the Spirit of God giving supernatural gifts or by the Spirit of God working in the lives of believers through His completed Word? Clearly it is God who works in believers to will and do of His good pleasure (Philippians 2:13). But it's the scripture that equips believers today for "every good work" (2 Timothy 3:16 cf. 1 Thessalonians 2:13). Today, it's the Holy Spirit of God working through the completed Word of God as Ephesians 4:15–16 states: "But speaking the truth in love, may grow up into him in all things, which is the head, even Christ: From whom the whole body fitly joined together and compacted by that which every joint supplieth, according to the effectual working in the measure of every part, maketh increase of the body unto the edifying of itself in love."

[u] Lets summarize these gifts:

- The one who prophesies is to do so to the full extent of the revelation revealed thus far.

- The one who ministers (as a deacon or deaconess or any minister of the gospel) is to serve.

- The one who teaches should teach.

- The one who exhorts should exhort.

- The one who gives is to give without complications (e.g., to give without strings attached).

- The one who presides should be diligent to preside well.

- The one who shows mercy should do so cheerfully.

Service to Fellow Believers

> [9] Let love be[v] without dissimulation. Abhor that which is evil; cleave to that which is good. [10] Be kindly affectioned one to another with brotherly love; in honour preferring one another; [11] Not slothful in business; fervent in spirit; serving the Lord; [12] Rejoicing in hope; patient in tribulation; continuing instant in prayer; [13] Distributing to the necessity of saints; given to hospitality. (Romans 12:9–13)

[v] In verses 9–13, Paul addresses the third sphere of Christian service. Service to fellow believers describes services believers render to other believers. A summary of the points are presented here:

1. Let love be unconditional and let it be genuine, unpretentious, and without hypocrisy.

- 2 Corinthians 6:6—"by love unfeigned"

- 2 Corinthians 8:8—"I speak not by commandment, but by occasion of the forwardness of others, and to prove the sincerity of your love."

- Thessalonians 2:3—"For our exhortation was not of deceit, not or uncleanness, nor in guile" (emphasis added).

- 1 Timothy 1:5—"Now the end of the commandment is charity out of a pure *hart* and of a good conscience, and of *faith* unfeigned" (emphasis added).

- John 3:16—"For God so loved the *word* that he gave" (emphasis added).

- Ephesians 4:28—"Let him that stole steal no more: but rather let him labour, working with his hands the thing which is good, that he may have to *give* to him that needeth" (emphasis added).

2. Abhor what is evil. This is connected with the preceding thought of love being genuine and unpretentious.

- Let love be genuine and without hypocrisy, but love still abhors evil. The word evil has to do with the mind or thinking. It is an evil disposition of the mind that hurts and afflicts others.

- "What man is he that desireth life, and loveth many days, that he may see good? Keep thy tongue from evil, and thy lips from speaking guile. Depart from evil and do good; seek peace and pursue it" (Psalm 34:14).

- "The transgression of the wicked saith within his heart, that there is no fear of God before his eyes. For he flattereth himself in his own eyes, until his iniquity be found to be hateful. The words of his mouth are iniquity and deceit: he hath left off to be wise, and to do good. He deviseth mischief upon his bed; he setteth himself in a way that is not good; he abhorreth not evil" (Psalm 36:4).

- "Thou lovest righteousness, and hatest wickedness: therefore God, thy God, hath anointed thee with the oil of gladness above thy fellows" (Psalm 45:7).

- "The fear of the LORD is to hate evil: pride, and arrogancy, and the evil way, and the froward mouth, do I hate" (Proverbs 8:13).

3. Cleave to what is good.

- Cleave is the present passive participle of a verb meaning "to glue or weld together" (J. Vernon McGee). The sense is, "Let brotherly love be without hypocrisy because we have been joined to that which is good." This again is still a continuation of the injunction of verse 9 to let love be without hypocrisy. Genuine, unconditional love is to be maintained while abhorring evil and remembering we have been joined to what is good.

- The concept of cleaving to what is good is illustrated in the following verses:

i. Cleaving to the Lord: "And they sent forth Barnabas, that he should go as far as Antioch. Who, when he came, and had seen the grace of God, was glad, and exhorted them all, that with purpose of heart they would cleave unto the Lord" (Acts 11:23).

ii. The opposite of cleaving is to depart from the Lord. "I will therefore that the younger women marry, bear children, guide the house, give none occasion to the adversary to speak reproachfully. For some are already turned aside after Satan" (1 Timothy 5:14–15).

iii. We are to cleave to fellow believers. "God is faithful, by whom ye were called unto the fellowship of his Son Jesus Christ our Lord. Now I beseech you, brethren, by the name of our Lord Jesus Christ, that ye all speak the same thing, and that there be no divisions among you; but that ye be perfectly joined together in the same mind and in the same judgment" (1 Corinthians 1:9–10).

Our bodies are joined to Christ. "Know ye not that your bodies are the members of Christ? Shall I then take the members of Christ, and make them the members of a harlot? God forbid" (1 Corinthians 6:15).

- Ephesians 4:15–18 tells us what will happen whenever a believer cleaves to what is good. "Christ … From whom the whole body fitly joined together and compacted by that which every joint supplieth, according to the effectual working in the measure of every part, maketh increase of the body unto the edifying of itself in love" (emphasis added).

4. Be kindly affectioned one to another with brotherly love.

In the love believers have for each other as fellow members of Christ, we are to have affections that are deeper than we can have with and for those outside of Christ.

I therefore … beseech you that ye walk worthy of the vocation wherewith ye are called, With all lowliness and meekness, with longsuffering, forbearing one another in love; Endeavouring to keep the unity of the Spirit in the bond of peace. (Ephesians 4:1–3).

Since we heard of your faith in Christ Jesus, and of the love which ye have to all the saints. (Colossians 1:4)

But as touching brotherly love ye need not that I write unto you: for ye yourselves are taught of God to love one another. (1 Thessalonians 4:9)

We are bound to thank God always for you, brethren, as it is meet, because that your faith groweth exceedingly, and the charity of every one of you all toward each other aboundeth. (2 Thessalonians 1:3)

5. Prefer one another in honor. Believers should give honor to one another. This exhortation applies to preferring one another in business, friendship, and all aspects of life.

Ye know that the princes of the Gentiles exercise dominion over them, and they that are great exercise authority upon them. But it shall not be so among you: but whosoever will be great among you, let him be your minister; And whosoever will be chief among you, let him be your servant. (Matthew 20:25–27)

But when thou art bidden, go and sit down in the lowest room; that when he that bade thee cometh, he may say unto thee, Friend, go up higher: then shalt thou have worship in the presence of them that sit at meat with thee. (Luke 14:10)

Let nothing be done through strife or vainglory; but in lowliness of mind let each esteem other better than themselves. Look not every man on his own things, but every man also on the things of others. (Philippians 2:3–4)

6. Do not be slothful in business.

The word for "business" is the word for "diligence." The business here (diligence) isn't the money-making business but that of service to fellow believers. It is the business of brotherly love with fellow believers Paul has in mind here. His instructions are not to be idle in the task of expressing brotherly love.

7. Be fervent in spirit. The word fervent is the word also used for boiling in the present participle. The idea is to be continually boiling in your spirit. To do that, one must be continually in the Spirit (i.e., continually in the Word and in communion with the Holy Spirit).

8. Rejoice in hope and patience in tribulation.

These are two areas of service to fellow believers. We all (i.e., all believers) share the same hope (i.e., the rapture). Paul spoke of that hope to the Roman saints in 5:2–5. "By whom also we have access by faith into this grace wherein we stand, and rejoice in hope of the glory of God. And not only so, but we glory in tribulations also: knowing that tribulation worketh patience; And patience, experience; and experience, hope: And hope maketh not ashamed; because the love of God is shed abroad in our hearts by the Holy Ghost which is given unto us" (emphasis added).

"For we are saved by hope: but hope that is seen is not hope: for what a man seeth, why doth he yet hope for? But if we hope for that we see not, then do we with patience wait for it. Likewise the Spirit also helpeth our infirmities: for we know not what we should pray for as we ought: but the Spirit itself maketh intercession for us with groanings which cannot be uttered" (Romans 8:24–26, emphasis added).

In verses 11–12, five interrelated concepts are joined together.

o   Hope: We will be eventually delivered.

o   Tribulation: We will share tribulation.

o   Patience: We can have patience, knowing deliverance is coming.

o   Prayer: We can be in communication with God in tribulation.

o   The Spirit: The Holy Spirit makes intercessions for us when we pray.

Looking ahead to Romans 15:2–5, we see that Paul again relates patience, hope, and tribulation together "that we through patience and comfort of scripture might have hope. Now the God of patience and consolation grant you to be likeminded one toward another." In 1 Thessalonians 1:3, we see that patience is based on hope (i.e., "patience of hope," the patience that hope produces). In 2 Thessalonians 1:4, Paul adds faith to patience as a means of coping with tribulation and persecutions. All who will live godly shall suffer persecution (2 Timothy 3:12).

Persecution comes when a believer stands for the gospel of the grace of God (Galatians 5:11). "If I yet preach circumcision, why do I yet suffer persecution? Then is the offense of the cross ceased" (emphasis added). Religion is therefore a fleshly activity men devised to avoid persecution. Galatians 6:12 says, "As many as desire to make a fair show in the flesh, they constrain you to be circumcised; only lest they should suffer persecution for the cross of Christ."

9. Continue instantly in prayer.

This is a description of the constant communication with God the believer must maintain to patiently endure tribulation while focusing on the confident assurance of glory (i.e., hope). Paul likens the Christian life to a wrestling match, only the opponent we wrestle with isn't as weak as we are. We wrestle against principalities and powers who are the rulers of the darkness of this world. We wrestle against spiritual wickedness in high places. It takes great desire and motivation to stay in the match as it did for Jacob when he wrestled with the Lord (Genesis 32:24–26). The only way we can stay in the match with supernatural beings is to tap into power outside ourselves. We have to "be strong in the Lord, and in the power of his might" (Ephesians 6:10). Paul refers to the power of God working in the believer as "the power of his resurrection." Unlike Israel of old, who fought physical enemies with physical weapons for a physical inheritance, we fight spiritual enemies with spiritual weapons for a spiritual inheritance.

Prayer is one of these spiritual weapons. "For the weapons of our warfare are not carnal, but mighty through God to the pulling down of strongholds" (2 Corinthians 10:4). Prayer is the constant mental attitude of being in direct and continual communication with God. "Praying always with all prayer and supplication in the Spirit, and watching thereunto with all perseverance and supplication for all saints; And for me, that utterance may be given unto me, that I may open my mouth boldly" (Ephesians 6:18–19). Paul tells the Thessalonians to "pray without ceasing" (1 Thessalonians 5:17). We can continue on in the match with confidence (i.e., being at peace that everything we can do is being done) once we have taken our cares and anxieties to God in prayer (Philippians 4:6–7). We then continue without anxiety, knowing He is at hand.

10. Distribute to the necessity of the saints. We might ask, Which saints? Later in Romans, Paul speaks of a collection for the "poor saints which are in Jerusalem" (Romans 15:25–28 cf. 1 Corinthians 16:1–2).

- Operating on instructions from the Lord to "go and sell that thou hast, and give to the poor, and thou shalt have treasure in heaven: and come and follow me" (Matthew 19:18–21), they did just that. This was said to the rich young ruler (Mark 10:21; Luke 10:22). In Luke 12:32, He tells the little flock the same thing. "Fear not, little flock; for it is your Father's good pleasure to give you the kingdom. Sell that ye have, and give alms; provide yourselves bags which wax not old, a treasure in the heavens that faileth not, where no thief approacheth."

- The messianic church of Pentecost did this very thing, "And all that believed were together, and had all things common; And sold their possessions and goods, and parted them to all men, as every man had need. And they, continuing daily with one accord in the temple, and breaking bread from house to house, did eat their meat with gladness and singleness of heart, Praising God, and having favour with all the people. And the Lord added to the church daily such as should be saved" (Acts 2:44–48).

- They could function successfully in the communal living arrangement because "they were all filled with the Holy Ghost" (Acts 2:4). This was a foretaste of what life in the kingdom of heaven would be like under the new covenant God would make with Israel. "And I will give them one heart, and I will put a new spirit within you; and I will take the stony heart out of their flesh, and will give them an heart of flesh: That they may walk in my statutes, and keep mine ordinances, and do them" (Ezekiel 11:19–20, emphasis added). "And I will ... cause you to walk in my statutes, and ye shall keep my judgments and do them" (Ezekiel 36:27, emphasis added).

- This system worked well so that the little flock could give a powerful witness to the nation as Acts 4:31–35.

- Participation in this communal living wasn't optional as we see in the case of Ananias and Sapphira (Acts

5:2–6).

- But this all changed with Israel's rejection of the offer of the kingdom by the stoning of Stephen (Acts 7 cf. Luke 19:14).

  Today, each believer should provide for his or her own (1 Timothy 5:8) and work so as to have to give to those in need (Ephesians 4:28).

- Paul was an example of distributing to the necessity of the saints. "Yea, ye yourselves know, that these hands have ministered unto my necessities, and to them that were with me. I have shewed you all things, how that so labouring ye ought to support the weak, and to remember the words of the Lord Jesus, how he said, It is more blessed to give than to receive" (Acts 20:34–35).

- Paul presents the Macedonian believers as an example of giving. In 2 Corinthians 8:1–4, he speaks of them. "How that in a great trial of affliction the abundance of their joy and their deep poverty abounded unto the riches of their liberality. For to their power, I bear record, yea, and beyond their power they were willing of themselves; Praying us with much intreaty that we would receive the gift, and take upon us the fellowship of the ministering to the saints."

- There is a simple principle to giving under grace. "For if there be first a willing mind, it is accepted according to that a man hath, and not according to that he hath not" (2 Corinthians 8:12). God doesn't expect anyone to give until God has first blessed him or her with abundance.

- The Philippians (i.e., Macedonian) believers are an example for us. "For even in Thessalonica ye sent once and again unto my necessity. Not because I desire a gift: but I desire fruit that may abound to your account" (Philippians 4:16–17). The security of such giving is seen in Philippians 4:19. "But my God shall supply all your need according to his riches in glory by Christ Jesus."

- There is yet another important principle in the matter of giving, that of reaping a harvest. "But this I say, He which soweth sparingly shall reap also sparingly; and he which soweth bountifully shall reap also bountifully. Every man according as he purposeth in his heart, so let him give; not grudgingly, or of necessity: for God loveth a cheerful giver. And God is able to make all grace abound toward you; that ye, always having all sufficiency in all things, may abound to every good work" (2 Corinthians 9:6–8).

  11. Be given to hospitality.

- Abraham at the plain of Mamre was an example of hospitality when none other than the Lord Himself enjoyed Abraham's hospitality (Genesis 12:2–8).

- Lot's hospitality to the angels who had been sent to Sodom saved his life (Genesis 19:1–3).

- Hospitality is a required characteristic for elders in local churches today (1 Timothy 3:2; Titus 1:8).

- Hospitality on the part of widows qualified them for financial support (1 Timothy 5:10) by the local church.

- Hospitality in Israel's program carried with it the possibility of "entertaining angels unawares" (Hebrews 13:2).

Service to our Enemies

[14] Bless[j] them which persecute you: bless, and curse not. [15] Rejoice[k] with them that do rejoice, and weep with them that weep. [16] Be[l] of the same mind one toward another. Mind not high things, but condescend[m] to men of low estate. Be not wise in your own conceits. [17] Recompense[n] to no man evil for evil. Provide[o] things honest in the sight of all men. [18] If it be possible, as much as lieth in you, live[p] peaceably with all men. [19] Dearly beloved, avenge[q] not yourselves, but rather give place[r] unto wrath: for it is[s] written, Vengeance is mine; I will repay, saith the Lord. [20] Therefore if thine enemy hunger, feed[t] him; if he thirst, give him drink: for in so doing thou shalt heap coals of fire on his head. [21] Be not overcome of evil, but overcome[u] evil with good. (Romans 12:14–21)

[j] In verse 14, Paul begins to address the fourth sphere of Christian service: the subject of the believer's service to his or her enemies. The believer is equipped to deal with persecution differently than the unbeliever. The believer has a regenerated spirit, that being the Spirit of Christ (Romans 8:9). Having the Spirit of Christ within, the believer can deal with the enemies the way our Lord did.

But God commendeth his love toward us in that, while we were yet sinners, Christ died for us. Much more then, being now justified by his blood, we shall be saved from wrath through him. (Romans 5:8–9)

All we like sheep have gone astray; we have turned every one to his own way; and the LORD hath laid on him the iniquity of us all. He was oppressed, and he was afflicted, yet he opened not his mouth: he is brought as a lamb to the slaughter, and as a sheep before her shearers is dumb, so he openeth not his mouth. He was taken from prison. (Isaiah 53:6–8)

Our Lord was the Lord of all His creation (Colossians 1:16 cf. Ephesians 3:10; Revelation 4:11). Yet He entered His creation in the humblest of manner and lived a working class life, and ultimately He willingly submitted to dying a death reserved for only the worst of criminals. This He did not for His friends but for His enemies. His dying words were a prayer, asking the Father's forgiveness of the unjust deed of those who had killed him. (Luke 23:34).

We have many examples of this attitude in the hearts of other believers. Some examples are the following:

- Stephen (Acts 7:60)—"Lay not this sin to their charge."

- Paul—"Being reviled, we bless; being persecuted, we suffer it: Being defamed, we intreat: we are made as the filth of the world, and are the offscouring of all things unto this day" (1 Corinthians 4:12–13).

- Job—"If I rejoice at the destruction of him that hated me, or lifted up myself when evil found him: Neither have I suffered my mouth to sin by wishing a curse to his soul" (Job 31:29–30).

The Bible offers many instructions on dealing with one's enemies in a manner that honors God. Our Lord's instructions to Israel are a case in point.

Ye have heard that it hath been said, Thou shalt love thy neighbour, and hate thine enemy. But I say unto you, Love your enemies, bless them that curse you, do good to them that hate you, and pray for them which despitefully use you, and persecute you; That ye may be the children of your Father which is in heaven: for he maketh his sun to rise on the evil and on the good, and sendeth rain on the just and on the unjust. For if ye love them which love you, what reward have ye? do not even the publicans the same? And if ye salute your brethren only, what do ye more than others? do not even the publicans so? (Matthew 5:43–48)

Luke 6:31 gives us what is called "The Golden Rule."

See that none render evil for evil unto any man; but ever follow that which is good, both among yourselves, and to all men. (1 Thessalonians 5:15)

Or what glory is it, if, when ye be buffeted for your faults, ye shall take it patiently? but if, when ye do well, and suffer for it, ye take it patiently, this is acceptable with God. For even hereunto were ye called: because Christ also suffered for us, leaving us an example, that ye should follow his steps: Who did no sin, neither was guile found in his mouth: Who, when he was reviled, reviled not again; when he suffered, he threatened not; but committed himself to him that judgeth righteously: Who his own self bare our sins in his own body on the tree, that we, being dead to sins, should live unto righteousness: by whose stripes ye were healed. (1 Peter 2:20–24)

Not rendering evil for evil, or railing for railing: but contrariwise blessing; knowing that ye are thereunto called, that ye should inherit a blessing. (1 Peter 3:9)

James points out the inconsistency of cursing in James 3:10. "Out of the same mouth proceedeth blessing and cursing. My brethren, these things ought not so to be."

[k] Joy is one of the fruit of the Spirit (Galatians 5:22). There Paul instructs us to be joyful with them who rejoice so as to share their joy and to weep with those who mourn so as to share their burden (cf. 1 Corinthians 12:26). We ought particularly to rejoice as people get saved. Barnabas's joy at the conversion of Gentiles of Antioch is an example of such rejoicing (Acts 11:22–25).

Though this exhortation here in Romans 12:15 is applied to all men, believers ought to be particularly sure to share the joys and tribulations of fellow believers. Paul tells the Corinthians, "That there should be no schism in the body; but that the members should have the same care one for another. And whether one member suffer, all the members suffer with it; or one member be honoured, all the members rejoice with it" (1 Corinthians 12:25–26). And again: "For if I make you sorry, who is he then that maketh me glad, but the same which is made sorry by me. And I wrote this same unto you, lest, when I came, I should have sorrow from them of whom I ought to rejoice; having confidence in you all, that my joy is the joy of you all" (2 Corinthians 2:2–3).

Paul's joy for fellow believers was so great, it overrode his personal suffering. "Yea, and if I be offered upon the sacrifice and service of your faith, I joy, and rejoice with you all. For the same cause also do ye joy, and rejoice with me" (Philippians 2:17–18).

Epaphroditus understood the joy of sacrificial service to others. "For he longed after you all, and was full of heaviness, because that you had heard that he had been sick." We see Paul's sympathy in the following verse: "For indeed he was sick nigh unto death: but God had mercy on him; and not only, but on me also, lest I should have sorrow upon sorrow" (Philippians 2:26–27).

The apostle Paul is an example of identifying and sympathizing with the saints of God. "Who is weak and I am not weak? Who is offended and I burn not?" (2 Corinthians 11:29).

The Lord through Jeremiah sympathizes with His people. "Oh that my head were waters, and mine eyes a fountain of tears, that I might weep day and night for the slain of the daughter of my people" (Jeremiah 9:1). Our Lord Himself did sympathize with the grief and sorrow of His people (John 11:19, 33–36).

[l] In verse 16. Paul says in effect, "Let love, trust, sympathy, care, and concern be mutual. Reciprocate love for love, concern for concern." Paul instructs the Philippians, "If there be therefore any consolation in Christ, if any comfort of love, if any fellowship of the Spirit, if any bowels and mercies, Fulfill ye my joy, that ye be likeminded, having the same love, being of one accord, of one mind. Let nothing be done through strife or vainglory; but in lowliness of mind let each esteem other better than themselves" (Philippians 2:1–3).

[m] Do not be conceited. Do not seek for an elevated position or title. Rather, condescend to men of low estate. Our Lord gives instruction of this subject in Matthew 18:1–4; 20:21–28. "And said, Verily I say unto you, Except ye be converted, and become as little children, ye shall not enter into the kingdom of heaven. Whosoever therefore shall humble himself as this little child, the same is greatest in the kingdom of heaven" (Matthew 18:3–4).

The greatest in the kingdom will have a humble heart of a servant. "Ye know that the princes of the Gentiles exercise dominion over them, and they that are great exercise authority upon them. But it shall not be so among you: but whosoever will be great among you, let him be your minister; And whosoever will be chief among you, let him be your servant: Even as the Son of man came not to be ministered unto, but to minister, and to give his life a ransom for many" (Matthew 20:25–28).

[n] We see in verse 17 that the believer has an area of service to his or her enemies. "Recompense to no man evil for evil." Our Lord told the believing remnant of Israel, "That ye resist not evil: but whosoever shall smite thee on thy right cheek, turn to him the other also" (Matthew 5:39). That is not to say that a believer is not to defend himself or herself from physical harm. But the believer is not to return evil for evil received. It is a principle with God that He will sustain His people. To take justice on ourselves for ourselves is to say God won't do so. "Say not thou, I will recompense evil; but wait on the LORD, and he shall save thee" (Proverbs 20:22). Paul gives us similar instruction in 1 Thessalonians 5:15. "See that none render evil for evil unto any man; but ever follow that which is good, both among yourselves, and to all men."

[o] God is intensely interested in the testimony of believers. He desires that every believer will conduct business honestly in the sight of all men. Thus, Paul takes the Corinthians to task for accusing one another for wrongdoing and that before unbelievers (1 Corinthians 6:6–7). Paul also was concerned about the possibility of being misunderstood and took action to ensure that not even a false accusation could come up to cause doubts on his honesty. The case of the selection of company in carrying the collection for the saints at Jerusalem is a case in point (2 Corinthians 8:20–21). The believer is to be likewise concerned about his or her testimony and be carefully guarding it.

> Study to be quiet, and to do your own business, and to work with your own hands, as we commanded you; That ye may walk honestly toward them that are without, and that ye may have lack of nothing. (1 Thessalonians 4:11–12)

Walk in wisdom toward them that are without, redeeming the time. (Colossians 4:5)

[p] Verse 18 says, if it's at all possible to do so, to live peaceably with all men. Don't get into a wrangle with men. It will destroy your testimony in the eyes of the person you can't get along with and to others who are watching. But here the apostle adds a qualifying statement: "as much as lieth in you." That is, we should do everything we can to get along well with all men. There are times, however, when it's not possible, but don't let the fault be yours.

[q] Paul presses the point that any bickering over even the slightest issue is counterproductive for the work God is doing in the world today. "For the kingdom of God is not meat and drink [i.e., what believers should or should not eat]; but righteousness, and peace, and joy in the Holy Ghost. For he that in these things serveth Christ is acceptable to God, and approved of men. Let us therefore follow after the things which make for peace, and things wherewith one may edify another" (Romans 14:17–19). To fail to do everything possible to live peaceably with all men is to risk lost souls who might otherwise be won to Christ. To do so would be to "swallow up the inheritance of the LORD" (2 Samuel 20:19). "Deceit is in the heart of them that imagine evil: but to the counselors of peace is joy" (Proverbs 12:20).

Our Lord told Israelites who were looking forward to the kingdom of heaven, "Blessed are the peacemakers: for they shall be called the children of God" (Matthew 5:9). Even when the marriage of a believer to an unbeliever is at stake, God would maintain that marriage (1 Corinthians 7:5).

Paul gives much instruction on living peacefully in the body:

- He closes his epistle to the Corinthians with the admonition "live in peace, and the God of love and peace shall be with you" (2 Corinthians 13:11).

- Peace is love's contentment with life's trials and is the fruit of the Spirit working in the believer (Galatians 5:22).

- God called us in one body so the peace of God might reign in our hearts (Colossians 3:14–15).

- The unity of the Spirit is to be kept in the bond of peace (Ephesians 4:3–4).

- God would have members of the body respect and esteem the leaders of the body so all might live in peace (1 Thessalonians 5:7).

[r] "Give place to wrath" (v. 19) (i.e., back off and give hotheads a chance to cool down).

Rejoice not when thine enemy falleth, and let not thine heart be glad when he stumbleth: Lest the LORD see it, and it displease him, and he turn away his wrath from him. (Proverbs 24:17–18)

Fret not thyself because of evil men, neither be thou envious at the wicked: For there shall be no reward to the evil man; the candle of the wicked shall be put out. (Proverbs 24:19–20)

[s] The quote in Romans 12:19 is from Deuteronomy 32:35. "To me belongeth vengeance and recompence; their foot shall slide in due time: for the day of their calamity is at hand, and the things that shall come upon them make haste." See also Deuteronomy 32:43. "Rejoice, O ye nations, with his people: for he will avenge the blood of his servants, and will render vengeance to his adversaries, and will be merciful unto his land, and to his

people" (cf. Psalm 94:1–3; Hebrews 10:30).

[t] This (v. 20) is repeated from Proverbs 25:21–22. "If thine enemy be hungry, give him bread to eat; and if he be thirsty, give him water to drink: For thou shalt heap coals of fire upon his head, and the LORD shall reward thee."

[u] The coals of fire in verse 21 (and Proverbs 25:22) can be understood from Song of Solomon 8:6–7. "Set me as a seal upon thine heart, as a seal upon thine arm: for love is strong as death; jealousy is cruel as the grave: the coals thereof are coals of fire, which hath a most vehement flame. Many waters cannot quench love, neither can the floods drown it: if a man would give all the substance of his house for love, it would utterly be contemned." The jealousy here is part of one who has wronged a believer who responds in love to the wrong. It is jealousy for the love the believer manifests. Such are the coals of fire of Romans 12:20 and Proverbs 25:22. What an opportunity to turn defeat into victory by simply overcoming evil done to you with the good you do in return.

Study Questions on Chapter 12

1. Verse 1 talks about the mercies of God. Romans 11:30-32 also talked about these mercies. Are these the same mercies? Did we see mercies in Chapter 8? Because of these mercies of God Paul beseeches us to do what?

2. What is a living sacrifice in contrast to?

3. What does it mean to be conformed to the world? What does it mean to be transformed?

4. What do we prove?

5. How might one think of himself more highly than he ought to?

6. What did God deal to every man?

7. What is the measure of faith?

8. What body is verse 4 talking about?

9. What body is verse 5 talking about?

10. In verse 6 we see God distributed gifts base on what principle?

11. Why did the gifts each had differ one from another? What are the gifts ultimately given to edify?

12. What is the gift of prophecy?

13. List the gifts discussed in verses 6 thru 8 and give a brief description of each.

14. What is dissimulation in verse 9?

15. Is the instruction in verse 14 to bless them that persecute you for real? What does it mean to bless? What

does it mean to curse?

16. Why is the qualification "If it be possible…" given in verse 18?

17. What does it mean to "give place to wrath" in verse 19?

18. Who does vengeance belong to?

19. What are the coals of fire in verse 20? What does that have to do with giving food to a hungry enemy or water to him when he is thirsty? Is there an Old Testament passage that might help us here?

20. How can we overcome evil with good?

CHAPTER 13

SERVICE TO THE STATE

Be Subject to the Higher Powers

¹ Let every soul be[a] subject unto the higher powers. For there is[b] no power but of God: the powers that be are[c] ordained of God. ² Whosoever therefore resisteth[d] the power, resisteth the ordinance of God: and they that resist shall receive[e] to themselves damnation. ³ For rulers are not a terror to good works, but to the evil. Wilt thou then not be afraid[f] of the power? do that which is good, and thou shalt have praise of the same: ⁴ For he is the minister of God to thee for good. But if thou do that which is evil, be afraid; for he beareth[g] not the sword in vain: for he is the minister of God, a revenger[h] to execute wrath upon him that doeth evil. ⁵ Wherefore ye must needs be subject, not only for wrath, but also for conscience[i] sake. ⁶ For this cause pay[j] ye tribute also: for they are God's ministers, attending continually upon this very thing. ⁷ Render therefore to all their[k] dues: tribute to whom tribute is due; custom to whom custom; fear to whom fear; honour to whom honour. (Romans 13:1–7)

[a] Here in chapter 13 the apostle moves on to the fifth in addressing seven different areas of Christian service: the believer in relation to government. Paul says that "the powers that be are ordained of God." Before covering this section, we need to understand that God ordained government of man by man. Let's look at God's instructions on government historically and dispensationally.

- The basic principle of human government is found in Genesis 9:5–6, where we find that God, for the first time in human history, gave mankind authority to establish government. "And surely your blood of your lives will I require; at the hand of every beast will I require it, and at the hand of man; at the hand of every man's brother will I require the life of man. Whoso sheddeth man's blood, by man shall his blood be shed: for in the image of God made he man." For the first time in history, man had authority over man. This God-ordained authority went all the way to actually taking the life of another human being (i.e., to inflict capital punishment for the offense of murder).

- This is in contrast to what God required before the flood. Before this, man was actually forbidden to inflict capital punishment. When Cain killed Abel, God not only cursed him but also protected him. We see this in Genesis 4:11–15.

"And now art thou cursed from the earth, which hath opened her mouth to receive thy brother's blood from thy hand; When thou tillest the ground, it shall not henceforth yield unto thee her strength; a fugitive and a vagabond shalt thou be in the earth. And Cain said unto the LORD, My punishment is greater than I can bear. Behold, thou hast driven me out this day from the face of the earth; and from thy face shall I be hid; and I shall be a fugitive and a vagabond in the earth; and it shall come to pass, that every one that findeth me shall slay me. And the LORD said unto him, Therefore whosoever slayeth Cain, vengeance shall be taken on him sevenfold. And the LORD set a mark upon Cain, lest any finding him should kill him."

- Once the principle of human government was implemented in Genesis 9, the human race was to be no longer an amalgamous mass but was to be divided into sovereign nations. Man was to "be fruitful and multiply and bring forth abundantly in the earth and multiply therein." To do that man had to separate from each other while maintaining the covenant God made with Noah (Genesis 9:9) and Adam (Genesis 1:28) to reign on earth and be custodians of it for God.

Given man's fallen state and the fact that the entire race was one language and one speech, the human race organized a one-world government that was designed to be man centered rather than God centered. The tower and city of Babel in Genesis 11 were the result. Their attitude was "Let us build us a city and a tower, whose top may reach unto heaven; and let us make us a name, lest we be scattered abroad upon the face of the whole earth" (Genesis 11:4). What was happening at Babel was the start of the "world" as the Lord saw it in John 15:18 when He said, "If the world hate you, ye know that it hated me before it hated you. If ye were of the world, the world would love his own: but because ye are not of the world, but I have chosen you out of the world, therefore the world hateth you" (John 15:18–19). There was at Babel a one-world government represented by the city, a one-world religious system represented by the tower, and a one-world economic system of Babel represented by Nimrod as the great hunter before the Lord. Had God allowed this to continue, God's purpose for creating man would have been thwarted (Genesis 11:6). Therefore, God confounded the language of the people on earth so they had to separate from each other and establish sovereign nations. However, man was still under the commission whereby man would govern himself in each of these sovereign nations. That would be the case until God finally establishes His kingdom under the reign of Israel's Messiah.

- The end result of the covenant with Noah and the confusion of tongues of Babel was that the family of the sons of Noah established individual sovereign nations "after their generations in their nations: and by these were the nations divided in the earth after the flood" (Genesis 10:32). These nations were established as nations, but because of the rebellious heart demonstrated at Babel, God rejected them and gave them up.

1. They changed the glory of the incorruptible God into an image (Rom.1:23).

   Wherefore God gave them up to uncleanness (Romans 1:24).

2. They changed the truth of God into a lie (Romans 1:25).

   Wherefore God gave them up to vile affections (Romans 1:26).

3. They didn't like to retain God in their knowledge (Romans 1:27).

   Wherefore God gave them over to a reprobate mind (Romans 1:28).

Prophecy goes on to tell us that God has a plan whereby He will one day reconcile the nations to Himself, but for now He lets them continue on in what is essentially a survival-of-the-fittest mode of existence.

- While other nations are established on a survival-of-the-fittest mode, there is one nation God established to be different. Genesis 12:1–3 says, "Now the LORD had said unto Abram, Get thee out of thy country, and from thy kindred, and from thy father's house, unto a land that I will shew thee: And I will make of thee a great nation, and I will bless thee, and make thy name great; and thou shalt be a blessing: And I will bless them that bless thee, and curse him that curseth thee: and in thee shall all families of the earth be blessed." Israel was a nation God personally established. God gave Israel specific instruction in the Law of Moses on how they were to conduct their business so they might flourish as a nation. No other nation was so blessed (Deuteronomy 4:7–9; 2 Samuel 7:23; 1 Chronicles 17:21; Isaiah 14:32).

- Except for Israel, God has for the most part left nations to their own devices. God gave up the Gentile nations at Babel to their own depravity and functioned without God's intervention. The only exceptions were the Gentile nations that had dealings with Israel. Nebuchadnezzar, king of Babylon, learned this lesson (Daniel 4:30–37 cf. verse 17). Government isn't an evil thing man concocted. Government is God ordained and for man's benefit. Corrupt men can run the government, but the institution is still to be respected. God doesn't pick the specific leaders of government in the world today. During the kingdom, He will pick the leaders of government based on demonstrated faithfulness (Luke 19:12–17). The believer should respect the office, even though corrupt people occupy it (Matthew 23:1–3).

- The purpose of government is seen in the violence that existed before the flood (Genesis 6:12–13). Then people were free to do as they pleased. The results were corruption and violence. The purpose then of government was to curb the violence and corruption. This purpose is also seen in God's instruction to Israel (Numbers 35:3–33) and in Paul's instruction to the body of Christ (1 Timothy 2:2).

[b] There is no power but of God (v. 1). God is in control. He doesn't choose leaders today, but He allows them to reign. God, as the supreme authority in the universe, would personally choose our leaders if He were personally reigning. He could take the reins of government on earth at any time, but He chooses to let men reign during man's day (1 Corinthians 4:3). God established the concept and principle of human government (Genesis 9:5–6). God doesn't select individual leaders of government today. He has at times in the past selected specific leaders of governments, but that was always in connection with His dealings with Israel.

- When God called Israel out of Egypt, God selected a specific man to be Pharaoh of Egypt to demonstrate His power in him (Romans 9:17) "Even for this purpose how I raised thee up that I might show my power in thee."

- God raised Nebuchadnezzar to be the instrument of chastisement for Israel (Deuteronomy 4:30–37 cf. 17).

- God gave the kingdom of Babylon to the kings of Media and Persia (Daniel 5:28). Note, though, that through it all, Daniel still was "preferred above the presidents and princes, because an excellent spirit was in him; and the king thought to set him over the whole realm" (Daniel 6:3).

- In the coming future kingdom, God will again select specific leaders of government, but they will be based on demonstrated faithfulness (Luke 19:12–17).

- Daniel's blessing to God in Daniel 2:21 states, "Blessed be the name of God for ever and ever: for wisdom and might are his."

- Our Lord informed Pilate that he (Pilate) would have no power over Him except as God gave it to him.

- It isn't until the Revelation that we find Christ personally taking the reins of power.

   o   Revelation 1:5—"the prince of the kings of the earth"

   o   Revelation 17:4—"These shall make war with the Lamb, and the Lamb shall overcome them: for he is Lord of lords, and King of kings: and they that are with him are called, and chosen, and faithful."

   o   Revelation 19:16—"And he hath on his vesture and on his thigh a name written, KING OF KINGS, AND LORD OF LORDS."

God has at times in the past directly intervened in the affairs of men and government to set up and bring down governments. Tyre is an example (Isaiah 23:8–17).

[c] God ordained the powers that be. The offices are in view here. The authority goes with the office and not that man who fills the office. It's only a rare occasion when God personally chose individual leaders of Gentile nations (e.g., Daniel 4:30–37 cf. v. 17). When He did, it was only for the benefit of His nation of Israel.

[d] To resist the power (exousia, government) is to set oneself against the authority of government. To do so would be to set oneself against what God has established. When government requires believers to violate a clear command of God, the believer must "obey God rather than man" (Acts 5:29). The twelve apostles had to take such a stand in Acts 4:19–20. It must be noted, however, that though they defied the decrees of government, they didn't defy the authority of government. This we see in their willingness to receive the punishment the government saw fit to administer (Acts 5:40–42). Note that they rejoiced that "they were counted worthy to suffer shame for his name." Notice also that they didn't organize a protest march or set out to overthrow the leadership of the government. They didn't make public speeches to denounce the brutality of government or defame those who might abuse their power. They did accept the government's punishment in submission to the government's authority.

Another option would be to escape the hand of government as Paul did (2 Corinthians 11:32–33). The case of Shadrach, Meshach, and Abednego in Daniel 3:14 regarding the furnace and Daniel in Daniel 6:8–16 are Old Testament examples of the believer's proper respect for government in spite of unwise and corrupt leadership in government. The apostle Paul had the same spirit of submission to the authority of government when he appealed to Caesar's judgment seat, saying, "For if I be an offender, or have committed anything worthy of death, I refuse not to die" (Acts 25:10).

[e] To resist the government is to resist the ordinance of God. The result is to receive judgment from the government as a malefactor. This condemnation spoken of in verse 2 is an act of government as is evident from the verses that follow.

[f] Verse 3 indicates that it's appropriate to be afraid of the power. Paul tells Titus, "Put them in mind to be subject to principalities and powers, to obey magistrates, to be ready to every good work" (Titus 3:1). The word exousia is translated "powers or power" three times in Romans 13:1.

Peter tells the circumcision saints, who will be going through the tribulation, "Submit yourselves to every ordinance of man for the Lord's sake: whether it be to the king, as supreme; Or unto governors, as unto them that are sent by him for the punishment of evildoers, and for the praise of them that do well" (1 Peter 2:13–17).

Peter describes the Lord's attitude toward any disrespect on man's part toward the offices of government: "The day of judgment to be punished ... them that ... despise government ... they are not afraid to speak evil of dignities" (1 Peter 2:10–11). Jude likewise expresses such in Jude 8. "Even as Sodom ... these ... despise dominions, and speak evil of dignities" (Jude 8).

[g] The sword here in verse 4 is a symbol of capital punishment. There are three instances in scripture that are recognized as right to kill. They are the following:

1. In battle (Deuteronomy 7:2) for national defense. God wants independent, sovereign nations. Such independent nations provide protection for society. If rules and government become intolerably corrupt in one nation, one can cross the border to another, where one can be free.

2. In personal self-defense (Ecclesiastes 3:1–3). God leaves to a man the right to defend himself and his family.

3. In capital punishment (Genesis 9:5–6). This is necessary for the orderly functioning of society.

Government cannot fulfill its mandate to maintain law and order if it cannot inflict capital punishment. Capital punishment is scriptural.

- It was so before the law (Genesis 9:5–6).
- It was so under the law (Numbers 35:30–33).
- It is so under grace (Romans 13:4).
- It will be so in the kingdom (Isaiah 65:20; 66:24).

There are four institutions of God clearly defined in Genesis and a fifth that is there but not as clearly stated.

1. Volition (i.e., we have free will)

2. Marriage

3. Family

4. Government (sovereign nations were instituted to protect the first three)

5. There might be another institution that was instituted between the institution of volition and marriage—that of the blood atonement. This one is not clearly defined, but certainly the animals sacrificed to give Adam and Eve the skins to replace the fig leaf apparel they had come up with speak of a blood atonement. From that time on, every believer could identify a blood sacrifice that covered his or her sin. Apparently, both Cain and Abel knew what God required. Abel brought a better sacrifice and was accepted. Cain didn't and wasn't.

[h] Verse 4 refers to government as an avenger. In Romans 12:19, we saw that vengeance belongs to God. God reserves to Himself this right to take vengeance. One way God has ordained whereby vengeance can be executed is via magistrates and government. We can be assured that God will execute perfect justice. God will also take vengeance on unbelievers of the great white throne (Revelation 20:11–15). For believers, vengeance can take the form of loss of rewards at the judgment seat of Christ (2 Corinthians 5:9–10). For preachers, God will take vengeance for defiling the body of Christ with bad doctrine by ceasing to use that person in ministry

(1 Corinthians 3:17). However, God provides civil magistrates as a means to take vengeance on all (believers or unbelievers) who would conduct themselves in a manner that would impair the smooth functioning of social order.

[i] Verse 5 speaks of being subject for conscience sake. Respect for God-ordained authority ought to be important to every believer. We can learn a lesson from King David in this respect. Though God had anointed David king to reign instead of Saul (1 Samuel 16:1, 12), David still respected Saul's reign and respected Saul as "the Lord's appointed" (1 Samuel 24:5–6; 26:15–16 cf. 1 Samuel 15:17). Solomon wrote, "Who is as the wise man? and who knoweth the interpretation of a thing? A man's wisdom maketh his face to shine, and the boldness of his face shall be changed. I counsel thee to keep the king's commandment [i.e., of that king], and that in regard of the oath of God. Be not hasty to go out of his sight: stand not in an evil thing; for he doeth whatsoever pleaseth him. Where the word of a king is, there is power: and who may say unto him, What doest thou? Whoso keepeth the commandment shall feel no evil thing: and a wise man's heart discerneth both time and judgment" (Ecclesiastes 8:1–5). Therefore, respect for governing officials as being ordained of God should be based on not only fear of the authority to execute punishment but also on the knowledge (conscience) that such authority is ordained of God. A man must act on the basis of his knowledge. To sin against the knowledge of the truth (i.e., to sin against one's own conscience) is a serious matter. Paul understood this as he stated in Acts 24:16. "And herein do I exercise myself, to have always a conscience void of offense toward God and toward men."

God's instruction is to be subject without regard to the worthiness of the people who fill the position. He instructs the wife to be subject to the husband, the child to the parent, the servant to the master, whether such parties abuse their authority. God would have order in society so His present purpose of reconciling lost sinners to God in one body might have an environment with sufficient structure that it might function. Harmony in society dictates that men be subject to laws for the sake of order. To say that only reasonable laws need to be obeyed opens everything up to man's interpretation of what is reasonable. Peter says, "Submit yourselves to every ordinance of man for the Lord's sake" (1 Peter 2:13, emphasis added).

[j] Verse 6 addresses the issue of taxes. Just as some argue that believers should determine which laws are good laws and thus to be obeyed, so some argue that believers shouldn't pay taxes because taxes are used for immoral purposes. But Paul instructs us to pay taxes that are due. In a free society like ours, it is the responsibility of believers before God to vote for just politicians and laws. But beyond that, it's the responsibility of government to maintain order and the responsibility of the citizen (believer or unbeliever) to be subject, including paying taxes that are due. Our Lord gives similar instructions to His disciples in Matthew 17:24–27. "Notwithstanding, lest we should offend them, go thou to the sea, and cast an hook, and take up the fish that first cometh up; and when thou hast opened his mouth, thou shalt find a piece of money: that take, and give unto them for me and thee." Also in Matthew 22:18–21, we find, "Render therefore unto Caesar the things which are Caesar's; and unto God the things that are God's."

[k] Give to all the due (v. 7) (i.e., give to all what God would have you give).

- Tribute: a tax laid upon subject people
- Custom: a tax as our sales tax. It is a tax on commerce.
- Fear: respect for power

• Honor: respect for authority

Paul's example of showing honor to the high priest in spite of the priest's misuse of power is seen in Acts 23:3–5. There Paul apologizes for having spoken disrespectfully to him and not knowing he was the high priest.

Service to Society

> [8] Owe[m] no man any thing, but to[n] love one another: for he that loveth[o] another hath fulfilled the law. [9] For this, Thou shalt not commit adultery, Thou shalt not kill, Thou shalt not steal, Thou shalt not bear false witness, Thou shalt not covet; and if there be[p] any other commandment, it is briefly comprehended in this saying, namely, Thou shalt love[q] thy neighbour as thyself. [10] Love worketh no ill to his neighbour: therefore love is the fulfilling of the law. (Romans 13:8–10)

Here in Romans 13:8 we start the apostle's instruction on service to society, the sixth sphere of service for the believer. This section ends with verse 14.

[m] God is concerned about His people paying all their just debts. Under law, Israelites were to pay a poor servant a day's wage in the day it was earned (Deuteronomy 24:14–15). Proverbs 3:28 says, "Say not unto thy neighbour, Go, and come again, and tomorrow I will give; when thou hast it by thee." This is not to say believers aren't to borrow money for any purpose. However, when money is borrowed, it must be repaid according to the repayment schedule. That is the key: to pay wages or loan payments when they are due.

[n]. Here in verse 8, love is viewed as something owed to another. But we ask the following:

• To whom do we owe this debt?

• And how did we incur this debt?

• And can we ever fully discharge this debt?

In answer, we consider the following:

1. We owe this debt of love to all men because we are in God's family by regeneration and adoption (Romans 8:14; Galatians 5:4). We are in business with God. God loved the world so much that He gave His only begotten Son to save the world. Being in God's family, we now have a debt of love to the world.

2. We actually incurred this debt when we were born into the human race. We have a responsibility to our fellow man to be concerned for them and to give ourselves to the task of care and concern for them. Abel understood this, but Cain didn't (Genesis 4:9). However, though we were born unto the human race with this responsibility, we didn't have the capacity to fully carry it out. It was only by regeneration that we gained the capacity to do so.

4. Love for fellow man and particularly for fellow believers is a debt we can never fully discharge. It is a responsibility and a privilege we will have for all our lives.

[o] The word for "love" is agape. It is often translated "charity." It's love that is freely given without any anticipation or hope of receiving anything in return. It's an unconditional love, a love with no strings attached. The person who makes every decision in life on this basis will automatically be fulfilling the law. Paul makes the same point in Galatians 5:14. "For all the law is fulfilled in one word, even in this; Thou shalt love thy neighbor

as thyself." Paul tells the Colossians, "And above all these things put on charity, which is a bond of perfectness" (Colossians 3:14). He tells Timothy, "The end of the commandment [i.e., the commandment to teach no other doctrine than grace in verse 3] is charity out of a pure heart, and of a good conscience, and of faith unfeigned" (1 Timothy 1:5). James makes a similar statement in James 2:8: "If ye fulfill the royal law according to the Scripture, Thou shalt love thy neighbour as thyself, ye do well."

[p] The Ten Commandments are listed in Exodus 20:12–17 and again in Deuteronomy 5:6–7. The commandments are divided as follows:

> To God:
>
>> First: Have no other gods.
>>
>> Second: Make no images.
>>
>> Third: Do not take God's name in vain.
>>
>> Fourth: Keep the Sabbath.
>
> To Parents:
>
>> Fifth: Honor your father and mother.
>
> To Society:
>
>> Sixth: Do not kill.
>
> To Neighbors:
>
>> Seventh: Do not commit adultery.
>>
>> Eighth: Do not steal.
>>
>> Ninth: Do not bear false witness.
>>
>> Tenth: Do not covet.

Paul cites the last five here because he is focusing on the believer's service to society. Our Lord cited these same commandments in Matthew 19:18–19, when the rich young ruler asked Him what commandments he was to keep to enter life. Our Lord gave the commandments as the following:

- Thou shalt not commit murder (sixth).
- Thou shalt not commit adultery (seventh).
- Thou shalt not steal (eighth).
- Thou shalt not bear false witness (ninth).
- Do not covet (tenth).

He then added this summary: "Thou shalt love thy neighbor as thy self." He left out the commandments toward God (i.e., the first four) but covered them in the requirement to "go and sell that thou hast and give to the pour and thou shalt have treasure in heaven: and come and follow me." The rich man's reluctance to give his riches to the pour demonstrated that he failed to love his fellow man, so he surely didn't obey the first four (cf. 1 John 4:20) either.

If there be any other commandment for man, it can be summed up and encompassed in the simple command to "love thy neighbor as thyself." This is given as a command in Leviticus 19:18. "Thou shalt not avenge, nor bear any grudge against the children of thy people, but thou shalt love thy neighbour as thyself: I am the LORD."

- In Mark 12:30–31, our Lord gives two commandments to summarize all ten: "And thou shalt love the Lord thy God with all thy heart, and with all thy soul, and with all thy mind, and with all thy strength" and "Thou shalt love thy neighbor as thyself."

- The lawyer in Luke 10:27 knew these two simple commandments as the summary of the ten. However, he needed instruction in application of the commandment. This lawyer knew the commandment but struggled with applying it to life. Therefore, our Lord instructed him with the account of the man robbed on the way to Jericho. Neither the priest nor the Levite, both of whom knew the law, succeeded in applying it to their lives. But the despised Samaritan demonstrated fulfillment of the law, showing love to his neighbor.

- Paul gives us a similar admonition in Galatians 5:13: "For brethren, ye have been called unto liberty; only use not liberty for an occasion to the flesh, but by love serve one another."

- James refers to this as "the royal law" (i.e., "thou shalt love thy neighbor as thyself," James 2:8).

[q] Genuine agape love is defined in 1 Corinthians 11:4–7. Love (charity)

- suffers long;
- is kind;
- envieth not;
- "vaunteth not itself;"
- is not puffed up;
- does not behave itself unseemly;
- seeketh not her own;
- is not easily provoked;
- thinketh no evil;
- rejoiceth not in iniquity but rejoiceth in the truth;
- beareth all things;
- believeth all things;
- hopeth all things; and
- endureth all things.

Charity never fails; it will always work. It is manifestly evident that the person who truly walked in love as defined here would need no law. By walking after the Spirit, the believer produces the fruit of the Spirit (Galatians 5:22–23). Such a believer would produce righteousness independent of the law.

The law covers (forbids) offenses toward God and others. Therefore, true love for God and one's neighbor will automatically encompass everything the law (and scripture) requires (Matthew 22:37–40). Grace accomplishes in a positive way what the law attempted to do in a negative way (1 Timothy 9–10).

Make no Provision for the Flesh

> [11] And that, knowing[r] the time, that now it is high time to[s] awake out of sleep: for now is our salvation[t] nearer than when we believed. [12] The night[u] is far spent, the day is[v] at hand: let us therefore cast[w] off the works[x] of darkness, and let us put on the armour of light. [13] Let us walk[y] honestly, as in the day[z]; not in rioting and drunkenness, not in chambering and wantonness, not in strife and envying. [14] But put[aa] ye on the Lord Jesus Christ, and make not provision[ab] for the flesh, to fulfil the lusts thereof. (Romans 13:11–14)

[r] In scripture, we are often exhorted to know what time it is. Our Lord upbraided His hearers, saying,

- "O ye hypocrites, ye can discern the face of the sky; but can ye not discern the signs of the times?" (Matthew 16:3).

- Our Lord cautions those who will live during the coming tribulation period, saying, "Watch therefore: for ye know not what hour your Lord doth come … Who then is a faithful and wise servant, whom his lord hath made ruler over his household, to give them meat in due season? Blessed is that servant, whom his lord when he cometh shall find so doing. Verily I say unto you, That he shall make him ruler over all his goods. But and if that evil servant shall say in his heart, My lord delayeth his coming" (Matthew 24:42–28).

- "But of the times and the seasons, brethren, ye have no need that I write unto you. For yourselves know perfectly that the day of the Lord so cometh as a thief in the night. For when they shall say, Peace and safety; then sudden destruction cometh upon them, as travail upon a woman with child; and they shall not escape" (1 Thessalonians 5:1–3).

[s] What time is it for the believer? It is high time to awake out of sleep. The sleep here is not physical sleep but spiritual sleep. It is the sleep as in Mark 13:35–37. "Watch ye therefore: for ye know not when the master of the house cometh, at even, or at midnight, or at the cockcrowing, or in the morning: Lest coming suddenly he find you sleeping."

Just as the sleeping is spiritual sleep, the awakening in verse 11 is spiritual awakening. "Awake to righteousness, and sin not; for some have not the knowledge of God: I speak this to your shame" (1 Corinthians 15:34) (i.e., some believers are still asleep to righteousness). Believers were once "dead in trespasses and sins." When they were yet unsaved and "walked according to the course of this world, according to the prince of the power of the air, the spirit that now worketh in the children of disobedience" (Ephesians 2:2). But Paul admonishes such to "awake thou that sleepest and arise from the dead, and Christ shall give thee light" (Ephesians 5:14).

[t] The apostle at various times views salvation in various ways. At times he views salvation as being saved from the penalty of sins (1 Corinthians 1:21; 1 Timothy 1:15; Ephesians 2:8–9). Other times he views it as being saved from the power of the indwelling sin nature (2 Corinthians 7:10; Ephesians 6:17; and so forth) or as deliverance from some peril (1 Timothy 4:16). Here, however, he views salvation as the ultimate deliverance from the effects and presence of sin at the catching away (rapture) of the church. This will also be our salvation from the wrath that will come on the earth (Romans 5:9; 1 Thessalonians 5:9 cf 1 Thessalonians 5:3–8). We look for a salvation

into "a new heaven and a new earth wherein dwelleth righteousness" (2 Peter 3:13–15). We see this new heaven and new earth prophetically in Revelation 21 and 22:12–20.

[u] The "night" here in verse 12 is the darkness of unbelief, in which the believer once found himself or herself. Ephesians 2:1–3 describes our state when we were still in the night. We "were dead in trespasses and sins and walked according to the course of this world, according to the prince of the power of the air, the spirit that now worketh in the children of disobedience ... fulfilling the desires of the flesh and of the mind and were by nature the children of wrath, even as others."

Paul tells the Thessalonians, "We are all the children of light, and the children of the day: we are not of the night, nor of darkness. Therefore let us not sleep, as do others; but let us watch and be sober" (1 Thessalonians 5:5–6).

[v] "The day is at hand." This day in verse 12 is "the day of salvation" (2 Corinthians 6:2). Today, before the rapture, is the day in which God is saving sinners.

[w] God has given us the capacity to put off the old man, the man we were, and the works of darkness the old man did and will yet do. Paul tells us, "That ye put off concerning the former conversation the old man, which is corrupt according to the deceitful lusts" (Ephesians 4:22). "But now ye also put off all these; anger, wrath, malice, blasphemy, filthy communication out of your mouth. Lie not one to another, seeing that ye have put off the old man with his deeds" (Colossians 3:8–9).

[x] Paul was sent to the Gentiles "to open their eyes, and to turn them from the darkness to light and from the power of Satan unto God" (Acts 26:18). The spiritual darkness of unbelief produced works that are to be thrown away. Paul says, "For ye were darkness, but now are ye light in the Lord: walk as children of light" (Ephesians 5:8). "And have no fellowship with the unfruitful works of darkness" (Ephesians 5:11). God delivered us from the power of darkness (Colossians 1:13).

[y] "Let us walk honestly." The believer's life is often referred to as a walk.

- "Zacharias ... and Elizabeth ... were both righteous before God, walking in all the commandments and ordinances of the Lord blameless" (Luke 1:6).

- "This I say then, Walk in the Spirit, and ye shall not fulfil the lusts of the flesh" (Galatians 5:16).

- "If we live in the Spirit, let us also walk in the Spirit" (Galatians 5:2).

- "I ... beseech you that ye walk worthy of the vocation wherewith ye are called" (Ephesians 4:1).

- "Henceforth walk not as other Gentiles walk" (Ephesians 4:17).

- "Walk in love as Christ also loved us" (Ephesians 5:2).

- "Walk as children of light" (Ephesians 5:8).

- "See then that ye walk circumspectly" (Ephesians 5:15).

- "Let us walk by the same rule ... mark them which walk so as ye have us for an ensample. For many walk, of whom I have told you often, and now tell you even weeping, that they are the enemies of the cross of Christ" (Philippians 3:16–18).

- "That ye might walk worthy of the Lord unto all pleasing, being fruitful in every good work, and increasing in the knowledge of God" (Colossians 1:10).

- "As ye know how we exhorted and comforted and charged every one of you, as a father doth his children, That ye would walk worthy of God, who hath called you unto his kingdom and glory" (1 Thessalonians 2:11–12).

- "That ye walk honestly toward them that are without" (1 Thessalonians 4:12).

- The concept of walking is simply to put order to sequential steps with a purpose of arriving at a destination. Spiritually, the believer is to do the same things: put purpose to the sequential steps we take with the purpose of letting our lives be a testimony of what God's grace can do in a believer's life.

[z] The day is for vigilance. "Therefore [because ye are the children of light] let us not sleep as do others; but let us watch and be sober. For they that sleep sleep in the night, and they that be drunken are drunken in the night" (1 Thessalonians 5:7).

[aa] "But put ye on the Lord Jesus Christ" (v. 14, emphasis added). Since this is a command of God, it is evident that the believer can do it. But how do we do it? The Lord Jesus Christ here is the new man. Paul tells us in Ephesians 4:24, "That ye put on the new man, which after God is created in righteousness and true holiness" (emphasis added). So too, the believer is commanded to put off the old man. "That ye put off concerning the former conversation the old man, which is corrupt according to the deceitful lusts; And be renewed in the spirit of your mind" (Ephesians 4:22–23).

[ab] Here are some thoughts on separation. Believers must function in society but must be separate from its attitudes while promoting and manifesting godly character. Our Lord is an example of this. He is "holy, harmless, undefiled, separate from sinners" (Hebrews 7:26). He was in the world (John 1:9) but not of the world (John 8:23cf 17:14). While He was in the world, He was the light of the world (John 9:5). He came to save the world (John 12:47) from Satan, the prince of this world (John 12:31). Though He was a friend of sinners (Matthew 11:19; Luke 7:34), He was also separate from sinners. Today, as we put on the Lord Jesus Christ, we fill the role of being the light of this world. We put on the armor of light when we put on Christ. We then are the means whereby Christ can reach lost people to save them. We are in the world but not of it. This world loves its own (John 15:18), but it hates Jesus Christ and those who are His (John 15:19; 17:14–17). The world is what it is because of the spiritual darkness of the masses of humanity. Apart from having the indwelling Spirit of God, men are incapable of spiritual understanding and discernment. The light that illuminates the mind's eye is the light of scripture. We function in society to be that light of Christ.

For Israel, physical salvation would come first and then spiritual. Israel was born physically as a nation at the crossing of the Red Sea. That was a water birth (i.e., the physical birth of the nation). Israel looks forward to a spiritual birth (being reborn as a nation as John 3:3ff says). It is apparent from passages as Acts 2:38; 3:19 and Romans 11:26–27 that Israel's Day of Atonement is still future. We members of the body of Christ have a spiritual salvation the instant we believe. "And not only so, but we also joy in God through our Lord Jesus Christ, by whom we have now received the atonement" (Romans 5:11). It is our physical salvation that is yet future for us. That physical salvation is at the rapture (1 Corinthians 15:51; 1 Thessalonians 4:15–17).

Study Questions on Chapter 13

1. What does the term higher powers in verse 1 mean?

2. Is this unlimited subjection to the higher powers or is there some limits to the degree to which one is to be subject?

3. The powers that be are ordained of God but how? What does the term "ordained" mean? Does he select who occupies the positions of power?

4. What kind of resistance is verse 2 talking about? In what sense do those who resist receive damnation?

5. What are rulers supposed to do according to verse 3? What actions should the believers take so as not to have to be afraid of the power?

6. In what sense are the powers that be a minister of God to the believer?

7. What does the sword in verse 4 refer to?

8. Romans 12:19 told us that vengeance belong to God. How might we expect God to take vengeance according to 13:4?

9. What are the two reasons for being subject to the powers in verse 5?

10. Why are we to pay taxes according to verse 6?

11. Define tribute, custom, fear, and honor as we find them in verse 7.

12. What is the debt in verses 8 and 9 that can never be entirely satisfied?

13. What is the fulfilling of the law in verse 10?

14. What salvation is verse 11 talking about?

15. Verses 12 and 13 speak of the day and the night. What day is in view here?

16. How would one make provision for the flesh?

Chapter 14

SERVICE TO WEAKER BRETHREN

Consider him that is weak inn the faith

> [1] Him that is weak[a] in the faith[b] receive[c] ye, but not to doubtful[d] disputations. [2] For one believeth that he may eat all[e] things: another, who is[f] weak, eateth herbs. [3] Let not him that eateth despise him that eateth not; and let not him which eateth not[h] judge him that eateth: for God hath received[i] him. (Romans 14:1–3)

[a] God is interested in the weak. He upbraids the shepherds of Israel, saying, "The diseased have ye not strengthened, neither have ye healed that which was sick, neither have ye bound up that which was broken, neither have ye brought again that which was driven away, neither have ye sought that which was lost; but with force and with cruelty have ye ruled them ... I will seek that which was lost, and bring again that which was driven away, and will bind up that which was broken, and will strengthen that which was sick" (Ezekiel 34:4, 16). We find the Lord fulfilling Ezekiel 34:16 in the case of Zacchaeus (Luke 19:8–10). "For the son of Man is come to seek and save that which is lost."

During His earthly ministry, our Lord was gentle to the weak. "A bruised reed shall he not break" (Matthew 12:20). He warns of offending those who are weak. "But whoso shall offend one of these little ones which believe in me, it were better for him that a millstone were hanged about his neck, and that he were drowned in the depth of the sea" (Matthew 18:6, 10). The first words of Eliphaz to Job were words of praise to Job regarding Job upholding the weak (Job 4:3–4). Doubtless this is what prompted our Lord to direct Satan's attention to Job, saying, "Hast thou considered my servant Job, that there is none like him in the earth, a perfect and an upright man, one that feareth God, and escheweth evil?" (Job 1:8).

[b] Let's consider what it means to be "weak in the faith." Note: it's not "weak in faith" but "weak in the faith" (emphasis added). The person in view here isn't necessarily weak in faith in God. Every believer came to the same faith Abraham did (i.e., "And being not weak in faith, he considered not his own body now dead, when he was an hundred years old, neither yet the deadness of Sarah's womb" [Romans 4:19]). Being weak in the faith isn't being carnal either as the Corinthians were (1 Corinthians 3:1). Being carnal is to focus on the flesh rather than on the Spirit. Being weak in the faith is to simply lack understanding in the doctrines of grace. The one who is weak in the faith has a desire to please God but doesn't entirely know how to do so. Being weak in the faith doesn't necessarily lead one to carnality but probably does tend toward leading one to legalism. Understanding the doctrines of grace is important. "We that are strong ought to bear the infirmities of the weak, and not to please ourselves." (Romans 15:1)

[c] "Receive" here means to receive them to oneself in full fellowship. Paul says, "Receive ye one another, as Christ also received us to the glory of God" (Romans 15:7). Our Lord said, "Whoso shall receive one such little child in my name receiveth me" (Matthew 18:5). The young man Timothy understood such reception of the saints, since Paul said, "For I have no man likeminded who will naturally care for your state" (Philippians 2:20). There are some we aren't to receive into fellowship. "If there come any unto you, and bring not this doctrine [of Christ], receive him not into your house, neither bid him God speed" (2 John 1:10). Fellowship is a precious thing in the family of God. It must not be withheld for any reason other than doctrinal error. Diotrephes (3 John 1:8–10) is an example of one who used fellowship and the withholding of fellowship as a means to control people. Fellowship among sincere believers is too precious to have it broken because of ignorance on the part of believers. Even Peter had to be withstood when he broke free fellowship with Gentiles by not eating with them when "certain came from James" (Galatians 2:12).

[d] "But not to doubtful disputations" is a reference to disputings believers involve themselves in with each other, but this involves a matter in which the scripture doesn't give a clear direction. Paul says here that variations in opinions in those things for which scripture is silent shouldn't be a factor in fellowship among believers.

[e] The particular "doubtful disputations" Paul focuses on here is that of eating meats versus eating only herbs. The one who eats only herbs is said here to be the one who is weak in the faith. The apparent issue at the time of the writing of Romans 14 is that there was a pagan practice of offering meat to idols before it was sold in the market. Paul spent three chapters addressing this basic issue with the Corinthians (1 Corinthians 8–10). There he sums up his instruction with the words "Whatsoever is sold in the shambles, that eat, asking no question for conscience sake: For the earth is the Lord's, and the fulness thereof" (1 Corinthians 10:25).

[f] Here in verse 2, as in 1 Corinthians 8–10, the person who believes he or she may eat all things is the one who is stronger in the faith. He or she is stronger because he or she has a better understanding of spiritual reality (i.e., "We know that an idol is nothing in the world, and that there is none other God but one" [1 Corinthians 8:4]). Likewise "every creature of God is good, and nothing to be refused, if it be received with thanksgiving: For it is sanctified by the word of God and prayer" (1 Timothy 4:4–5). Paul says in Romans 15:1, "We then that are strong ought to bear the infirmities of the weak, and not to please ourselves. Let every one of us please his neighbour for his good to edification." Paul would have the one who has spiritual understanding match such knowledge with charity extended toward the one who doesn't yet have that knowledge. "But if thy brother be grieved with thy meat, now walkest thou not charitably. Destroy not him with thy meat, for whom Christ died" (Romans 14:15).

[g] The believer who is weak in the faith is simply lacking in some basic understanding. We have all been there. All of us were once "babes in Christ." In 1 Corinthians 8–10, the issue was clearly the eating of things offered to idols. Here, it is apparently a matter of whether meat should be eaten (i.e., "Another who is weak eateth herbs"). The confusion could come from not understanding the Bible dispensationally. Note the shift of God's dietary considerations:

- Genesis 1:29 says, "And God said, Behold, I have given you every herb bearing seed, which is upon the face of all the earth, and every tree, in the which is the fruit of a tree yielding seed; to you it shall be for meat." Man was to eat only the seeds and fruit of herbs and trees.

- Genesis 9:3 says, "Every moving thing that liveth shall be meat for you; even as the green herb have I given you all things." After the flood, God expanded man's diet to include meat.

- Yet there was a restriction. Genesis 9:4 says, "But flesh with the life thereof, which is the blood thereof, shall ye not eat."

- When God gave the law to Moses, certain meats weren't to be eaten. See Leviticus 11:41–47; 20:25 (cf. Daniel 1:12–16 on Daniel and company).

- Today under the dispensation of the grace of God, all things are allowed for food (1 Timothy 4:3).

[h] The tendencies of the two sides of this potential disputation are here presented. The believer who understands that all food is to be eaten has a tendency to look down on (i.e., despise) him or her who doesn't eat. This believer sees weaker believers as not standing in the liberty they have in Christ and regards them as ignorant. Those who don't eat operate in what they consider to be superior scruples and (in their mind at least) judge the one who freely partakes as being unscrupulous. Both attitudes are harmful to spiritual vitality of an assembly of believers. Paul tells the Corinthians, "But when ye sin so against the brethren, and wound their weak conscience, ye sin against Christ" (1 Corinthians 8:12).

[i] The weaker brother is to understand that God has received the brother who eats. Therefore, he is not to judge the strong. Peter learned that from the sheet vision of Acts 10, saying, "I perceive that God is no respecter of persons" (Acts 10: 24). Peter applied this knowledge wisely in Acts 15:8–10. "Now therefore why tempt ye God, to put a yoke upon the neck of the disciples, which neither our fathers nor we were able to bear?" The word received is the same word as verse 1, and it means "to receive unto oneself." God has received believers who understands their liberty in Christ. In verse 4, Paul says it is to Christ that they stand or fall, and under grace God is able to make them stand; they will stand because they are standing in the liberty wherewith Christ has made them free (Galatians 2:5; 5:1). Grace enables believers to do what any demand for or appeal to the flesh the law ever required but couldn't produce.

Use Great Wisdom, Care, and Charity in the Matter of Judging Your Brothers

> [4] Who art thou that judgest[j] another man's servant? to his own master he standeth[k] or falleth. Yea, he shall be holden up: for God is able to make him stand. [5] One man esteemeth one day above another: another esteemeth every day alike. Let every man be fully persuaded in his own mind. [6] He that regardeth[l] the day, regardeth it unto the Lord; and he that regardeth not the day, to the Lord he doth not regard it. He that eateth, eateth to the Lord, for he giveth[m] God thanks; and he that eateth not, to the Lord he eateth not, and giveth God thanks. [7] For none of us liveth to himself, and no man dieth to himself. [8] For whether we live, we live[n] unto the Lord; and whether we die, we die[o] unto the Lord: whether we live therefore, or die, we are[p] the Lord's. (Romans 14:4–8)

[j] Regarding the matter of judging others, there is much that could be said. In 1 Corinthians 4–5, we find injunctions in one place not to judge, and then in another place Christians are enjoined to judge fellow believers. In 1 Corinthians 4:3–5, Paul says, "It is a very small thing that I should be judged of you, or of man's judgment: yea, I judge not mine own self. For I know nothing by myself; yet am I not hereby justified: but he that judgeth me is the Lord. Therefore judge nothing before the time, until the Lord come, who both will bring to light the

hidden things of darkness, and will make manifest the counsels of the hearts: and then shall every man have praise of God." But in 1 Corinthians 5:9–12, Paul enjoins believers to judge between two believers who are living in sin and to separate from them. Paul says in 1 Corinthians 6:5, "I speak to your shame. Is it so, that there is not a wise man among you? no, not one that shall be able to judge between his brethren?" In 1 Corinthians 11:31, Paul instructs us to judge ourselves so we aren't judged. In Romans 16:17, he instructs believers to "mark [i.e., judge and identify] them which cause divisions and offenses contrary to the doctrine which ye have learned; and avoid them. For they that are such serve not our Lord Jesus Christ, but their own belly."

So how do we assess this situation? The key to understanding in the matter of judgment is in "what saith the scripture?" It is in the areas where scripture is silent that we aren't to judge one another or to set one another aside (i.e., "at naught").

[k] It is Jesus Christ alone who has the right to judge a believer's service because He paid sin's debt and accomplished redemption. What a rebuke to a believer who judges and sets up an arbitrary standard to then judge a fellow believer.

[l] The day "regarded" here in verse 6 isn't one of the feast days or holy days of the Law of Moses. Paul tells the Galatians who were keeping such days, "But now, after that ye have known God, or rather are known of God, how turn ye again to the weak and beggarly elements, whereunto ye desire again to be in bondage? Ye observe days, and months, and times, and years. I am afraid of you, lest I have bestowed upon you labour in vain" (Galatians 4:9–11). The "day" here is probably Sunday, and many perceive it as the Christian Sabbath. It is a great strength for a society that has a day when believers get together to fellowship and study the scripture. But it's not the Christian Sabbath; the Sabbath is a sign of the Mosaic covenant. But here again the weaker brother who doesn't understand that yet would be offended to see a brother not hold Sunday as holy. But the point Paul makes is that both the one who regards it as holy and the one who regards it not as holy (understanding that all days are alike) regard it unto the Lord, rejoicing in God's grace.

[m] The point of this verse is that the one who eats does so in thanks to God, and the one who doesn't eat does so as well. We are dealing with good intentions and godly sincerity on the part of each.

[n] We belong to the Lord, whether we live or die (v. 8). This is a continuation of the thought of verse 4. "Who art thou that judgest another man's servant?" Our Lord Jesus Christ earned to Himself the right to judge both the living and the dead (v. 9).

> Our Saviour Jesus Christ; Who gave himself for us, that he might redeem us from all iniquity, and purify unto himself a peculiar people, zealous of good works. (Titus 2:14)

> Who died for us, that, whether we wake or sleep, we should live together with him. (1 Thessalonians 5:10)

> For ye are bought with a price: therefore glorify God in your body, and in your spirit, which are God's. (1 Corinthians 6:20)

> And that he died for all, that they which live should not henceforth live unto themselves, but unto him which died for them, and rose again. (2 Corinthians 5:15)

For I through the law am dead to the law, that I might live unto God. I am crucified with Christ. (Galatians 2:19–20)

So now also Christ shall be magnified in my body, whether it be by life, or by death … For to me to live is Christ, and to die is gain … For I … desire to depart … Nevertheless to abide in the flesh is more needful for you. (Philippians 1:20–24)

Yea, and if I be offered upon the sacrifice and service of your faith, I joy, and rejoice with you all. (Philippians 2:17)

[o] "We die unto the Lord" (i.e., we die in service unto the Lord). Peter knew this (John 21:19). Paul understood this, too.

Neither count I my life dear unto myself, so that I might finish my course with joy, and the ministry, which I have received of the Lord Jesus. (Acts 20:24)

I am ready not to be bound only, but also to die at Jerusalem for the name of the Lord Jesus. (Acts 21:13)

If I be offered upon the sacrifice and service of your faith, I joy, and rejoice with you all. (Philippians 12:17)

David served and died (Acts 13:36), yet those who died in service to the Lord weren't truly dead. "God is not the God of the dead but the living" (Luke 20:37–38).

[p] Whether we live therefore or die, we are the Lord's. Because Jesus Christ conquered death, all things are ours to use to the glory of God. Even our deaths can be used to bring glory to Him.

For all things are yours; whether … the world, or life, or death or things present. (1 Corinthians 15:23)

Even so then also which sleep in Jesus will God bring with him. (1 Thessalonians 4:14)

We Shall All Stand before the Judgment Seat of Christ

9 For to this end Christ both[q]died, and rose, and revived, that he might be Lord both[r] of the dead and living. 10 But why dost thou judge[s] thy brother? or why dost thou set at nought thy brother? for we shall all stand before the judgment seat of Christ. 11 For it is written, As I live, saith the Lord, every knee shall bow[t] to me, and every tongue shall confess to God. 12 So then every one of us shall give[u] account of himself to God. 13 Let us not therefore judge one another any more: but judge this rather, that no man put[v] a stumblingblock or an occasion to fall in his brother's way. (Romans 14:9–13)

[q] Our Lord's death for sin was stated in Isaiah 53:10–12 but was described in such a fashion that no one beforehand could understand what was meant, and yet, once accomplished, no one could miss seeing that God had planned it beforehand. Note how our Lord after the resurrection points the disciples' minds back to this passage, saying, "Ought not Christ to have suffered these things, and to enter into his glory? And beginning at Moses and all the prophets, he expounded unto them in all the scriptures the things concerning himself" (Luke 24:26–27). Christ had to die for all because all were dead (2 Corinthians 5:14). He "for the joy that was set before him endured the cross, despising the shame, and is set down at the right hand of the throne of God" (Hebrews 12:2).

[r] Believers belong to the Lord, whether they be dead (physically) or alive. Jesus Christ has authority to execute judgment because He has been in our shoes (John 5:27–29; Acts 10:36, 42). He was tempted in all points as we are (Hebrews 4:15 cf 1 John 2:16; Matthew 4:1–10; Luke 4:1–12; Genesis 3:6) yet without sin. God the Father raised Christ from the dead so He could put all things under Christ's feet (Ephesians 1:2–23; Philippians 2:9–10). Jesus Christ alone will therefore be the one who will judge the living and the dead (2 Timothy 4:1).

[s] Here in verse 10, it is the weaker brother doing the judging of the stronger, while the stronger sets "at naught" the weaker. The stronger ought to remember that King Herod and his men did the same to Christ (Luke 23:11) as did also the leaders of Israel (Acts 4:11).

[t] The judgment seat of Christ is mentioned in 2 Corinthians 5:10. Only believers will stand before that judgment seat. All unbelievers will stand before the great white throne of Revelation 20:11–15. But every human being will one day stand before God in judgment. "For God shall bring every work into judgment, with every secret thing, whether it be good, or whether it be evil" (Ecclesiastes 12:14). This passage (Romans 14:11) is a quote from Isaiah 45:22–25, where the Lord (Jehovah, see Isaiah 45:19) speaks, saying that unto Him will every knee bow and ever tongue confess. In Philippians 2:11, we find out that ever tongue shall confess that "Jesus Christ is Lord." From this we understand that Jesus Christ is Jehovah.

[u] This is an awesome fact to realize. This realization alone would be enough to persuade us to set aside any pride toward others or any belittling of others. "For if any man think himself to be something, when he is nothing, he deceiveth himself. But let every man prove his own work, and then shall he have rejoicing in himself alone, and not in another" (Galatians 6:3–4).

[v] A stumbling block is something placed in the path of someone, which might cause him or her to trip. Our Lord is a stumbling block for the person walking according to the course of this world (Romans 9:31–32). But what to the unbelieving man of this world is a stumbling block is to the believer "a foundation stone, a tried stone, a precious corner stone, a sure foundation (Isaiah 26:16) and "a living stone, disallowed indeed of men, but chosen of God, and precious" (1 Peter 2:4). But the stumbling stone here in Romans 14:13 is an occasion to fall that is thrown in the path of a believer. Our Lord's instruction is, "Take up the stumbling block out of the way of my people" (Isaiah 57:14). In the law God said, "Thou shalt not curse the deaf nor put a stumbling block before the blind" (Leviticus 19:14). Peter threw a stumbling block (translated "offence" in Matthew 16:23) in our Lord's way on His way to the cross when Peter said to Him, "Be it far from thee, Lord: this shall not be unto thee" (v. 22). "Woe unto the world because of offences [stumbling blocks] for it must needs be that offences come; but woe to that man by whom the offence cometh" (Matthew 18:7). Paul picks up the discussion of the stumbling blocks here to warn the one who is stronger in the faith that his or her liberty can actually be a stumbling block to one who is weak (1 Corinthians 8:7–13).

Take heed lest by any means this liberty of yours become a stumbling block to them that are weak. (v. 9)

Whether therefore ye eat, or drink, or whatsoever ye do, do all to the glory of God. Give none offence, neither to the Jews, nor to the Gentiles, nor to the church of God. (1 Corinthians 10:31–32)

Giving no offence in any thing, that the ministry be not blamed: But in all things approving ourselves as the ministers of God, in much patience, in afflictions, in necessities, in distresses. (2 Corinthians 3:4)

Follow after things that make for peace and things whereby one may edify another.

¹⁴ I know, and am persuaded by the Lord Jesus, that there is nothing unclean[w] of itself: but to him that esteemeth[x] any thing to be unclean, to him it is unclean. ¹⁵ But if thy brother be grieved[y] with thy meat, now walkest thou not charitably. Destroy not him with thy meat, for whom Christ died. ¹⁶ Let not then your good be evil[z] spoken of: ¹⁷ For the kingdom[aa] of God is not meat[ab] and drink; but righteousness, and peace, and joy in the Holy Ghost. ¹⁸ For he that in these things serveth[ac] Christ is acceptable to God, and approved of men. ¹⁹ Let us therefore follow after the things which make[ad] for peace, and things wherewith one may edify another. ²⁰ For meat destroy not the work[ae] of God. All things indeed are[af] pure; but it is evil[af] for that man who eateth with offence. (Romans 14:14–20)

[w] This point about something being unclean is a dispensational statement. Prior to Paul and the revelation of the mystery, there was much declared to be "unclean" in the Word of God. The Gentiles as a group were regarded as "unclean" (Acts 10:28). The law declares many "things" unclean (Leviticus 5:3; 7:21; and so forth). Israel was to "put difference between holy and unholy and between unclean and clean" (Leviticus 10:10). But here Paul says, "I know and am persuaded by the Lord Jesus: that there is nothing unclean of itself" (Romans 14:14). Therefore, he instructs us, "Whatsoever is sold in the shambles, that eat, asking no question for conscience sake" (1 Corinthians 10:25). Also, he says, "Every creature of God is good and nothing is to be refused, if it be received with thanksgiving" (1 Timothy 4:4).

[x]. Here in verse 14, the matter of the believer's perception versus reality enters into his or her sense of propriety. Paul states in verse 23, "He that doubteth is damned if he eat, because he eateth not of faith: for whatsoever is not of faith is sin." The word damned is used in the same sense as condemnation in Romans 8:1 (i.e., the self-condemnation people bring on themselves when they suppose they have sinned against God). In 1 Corinthians 8:7 we see that "some with conscience of the idol unto this hour eat it as a thing offered unto an idol; and their conscience being weak is defiled."

[y] Verse 15 speaks of a brother being grieved. A brother is grieved in emotional turmoil when he perceives that he has sinned against God. In this case, it is perceived that he sinned by partaking of the meat that one stronger in the faith would partake of freely. Paul says that such flaunting of one's liberty is not charity (love).

Love worketh no ill to his neighbour. (Romans 13:10)

Let every one of us please his neighbour for his good to edification. (Romans 15:2)

But when ye sin so against the brethren, and wound their weak conscience, ye sin against Christ. (1 Corinthians 8:12)

[z] "Let not the good be evil spoken of" (v. 17). It has been well said that we don't have the right to give up our blood-bought liberty, but we do have the liberty to yield our rights for the good of our neighbor. Paul cites himself as an example of this in 1 Corinthians 9:19. "For though I be free from all men, yet have I made myself servant unto all, that I might gain the more … To the weak became I as weak, that I might gain the weak: I am made all things to all men, that I might by all means save some" (v. 22).

[aa] There is a difference here between "the Kingdom of Heaven" and "the Kingdom of God." The kingdom of God is the realm in which God is king. The kingdom of God encompasses only saved people and the elect

angels. It involves all believers and excludes unbelievers. It transcends all dispensations. David described the kingdom in 1 Chronicles 29. "Thine, O LORD is the greatness, and the power, and the glory, and the victory, and the majesty: for all that is in the heaven and in the earth is thine; thine is the kingdom, O LORD, and thou art exalted as head above all." Paul refers to the kingdom of God (1 Corinthians 4:20; 6:9; 15:50; Galatians 5:21; Ephesians 5:5; Colossians 4:11; 1 Thessalonians 2:12; 2 Thessalonians 1:5; 2 Timothy 4:1; and so forth) as the eternal realm of glory, of which believers in the dispensation of grace are already a part. The term "Kingdom of Heaven" is defined in Daniel 2:44 and Matthew 6:10 as the time when God's will is done in the earth as it is in heaven under the reign of Jesus Christ as Israel's Messiah. The kingdom of heaven encompasses both believers and unbelievers (Matthew 13:25–27). The term "Kingdom of Heaven" is used only in Matthew's gospel (Matthew 3:2; 4:17; 5:3, 10, 19, 20; 6:10; 7:21; 8:11; 10:7; 11:11; 13:11; 16:19; 18:3, 23: 19:23; 20:1;; 23:13; 25:1, 14; 33:2).

[ab] Life in the kingdom of God isn't carnal observances, such as refraining from eating meat or not refraining from it.

> But meat commendeth us not to God: for neither, if we eat, are we the better; neither, if we eat not, are we the worse. (1 Corinthians 8:8)

> Let no man therefore judge you in meat, or in drink, or in respect of an holyday, or of the new moon, or of the Sabbath days: Which are a shadow of things to come; but the body is of Christ. (Colossians 2:16–17)

Rather, life in the kingdom of God is righteousness, peace, and joy in the Holy Ghost.

The righteousness of the kingdom of God is not one of human origin, however. Paul's desire was that "I may win Christ, And be found in him, not having mine own righteousness, which is of the law, but that which is through the faith of Christ, the righteousness which is of God by faith" (Philippians 3:8–9). The believer is made "the righteousness of God in [Christ]" (2 Corinthians 5:21). "But of him are ye in Christ Jesus, who of God is made unto us wisdom, and righteousness, and sanctification, and redemption: That, according as it is written, He that glorieth, let him glory in the Lord" (1 Corinthians 1:3–31). This imputed righteousness is lived out as practical righteousness in the believer who "walks not after the flesh but after the spirit" (Romans 8:11) because "it is God which worketh in you both to will and to do if his good pleasure" (Philippians 2:13). Though the mode by which God does this work varies with dispensations, the basic operating principles remain the same. God does the work in believers.

> Surely, shall one say, in the LORD have I righteousness and strength: even to him shall men come; and all that are incensed against him shall be ashamed. In the LORD shall all the seed of Israel be justified, and shall glory. (Isaiah 45:24–25)

> He shall be called, THE LORD OUR RIGHTEOUSNESS. (Jeremiah 23:6)

God first gives the peace of the kingdom of God. "Therefore being justified by faith, we have peace with God through our Lord Jesus Christ" (Romans 5:1). That peace is readily available to the believer and is appropriated to the same degree that the believer is spiritually minded. "For to be carnally minded is death; but to be spiritually minded is life and peace" (Romans 8:6). Such peace comes from the knowledge that we are the children of God (8:5, 16). It is the fruit the Spirit bears as it works in the believer (Galatians 5:22).

The joy in the Holy Ghost, which characterizes life in the kingdom of God, is the confidence that the believer has the working of God within him or her.

> For we are the circumcision, which worship God in the spirit, and rejoice in Christ Jesus, and have no confidence in the flesh. (Philippians 3:3)

> Strengthened with all might, according to his glorious power, unto all patience and longsuffering with joyfulness; Giving thanks unto the Father, which hath made us meet to be partakers of the inheritance of the saints in light. (Colossians 1:11–12)

[ac] He that "in these things (i.e., righteousness, peace and joy, emphasis added) serveth Christ" in verse 18 is a reference to believers who live out their imputed righteousness as practical righteousness and their intrinsic peace by being at peace with their fellow men and manifesting the joy that comes from the confidence in the working of God. "For in Christ Jesus neither circumcision availeth any thing, nor uncircumcision, but a new creature. And as many as walk according to this rule [i.e., of the new creation], peace be on them, and mercy, and upon the Israel of God" (Galatians 6:15–16). Such a one is (1) acceptable to God and (2) approved of men.

God has "made us accepted in the beloved" (Ephesians 1:4). This has reference to the believer's reasonable service of "presenting our bodies a living sacrifice" (Romans 12:1–2). Our service to God, when done out of a heart of gratitude, is "acceptable, well pleasing to God" (Philippians 4:18). The believer who manifests righteousness, peace, and joy is also approved of men.

> In all things approving ourselves as the ministers of God. (2 Corinthians 6:4)

> Providing for honest things, not only in the sight of the Lord, but also in the sight of men. (2 Corinthians 8:21)

Remember, both God and men are watching.

[ad] If the kingdom of God is, in essence, righteousness, peace, and joy, then we should pursue such actions and activities that make for peace. Also, since the kingdom of God consists of people, then we should pursue activities whereby we can build each other up. In Romans 12:8, the apostle considered the believer dealing with hostile activity others directed at the saints. Here the focus is on activity of the believer that could disrupt peace and harmony. Peace is a fruit of the Spirit and is a key ingredient in the vitality of an assembly of believers. The apostle closes 2 Corinthians with the exhortation "Be perfect, be of good comfort, be of one mind, live in peace; and the God of love and peace shall be with you" (2 Corinthians 13:11). The sevenfold unity of the Spirit (Ephesians 4:3–7) is to be kept "in the bond of peace." The apostle's desire for peace among the brethren is seen in Philippians 2:1–4. "If there be therefore any consolation in Christ, if any comfort of love, if any fellowship of the Spirit, if any bowels and mercies, Fulfil ye my joy, that ye be likeminded, having the same love, being of one accord, of one mind. Let nothing be done through strife or vainglory; but in lowliness of mind let each esteem other better than themselves" (Philippians 2:1–3). Also: "Let the peace of God rule in your hearts, to the which also ye are called in one body; and be ye thankful" (Colossians 3:15).

Regarding the matter of building one another up, the apostle is again our example: "Even as I please all men in all things, not seeking mine own profit, but the profit of many, that they may be saved" (1 Corinthians 10:33). It is charity (agape love) that edifies; knowledge in and of itself serves only to puff up (1 Corinthians 8:1 cf 14:12–17). God designed the body of Christ to "edify itself in love" (Ephesians 4:29).

[ae] The work of God referred to here is His work in each believer. Paul says in Ephesians 2:10, "We are his workmanship, created in Christ Jesus unto good works, which God hath before ordained that we should walk in them." He further describes this work as the building of a body that edifies itself in Ephesians 4:15–16. "But speaking the truth in love, may grow up into him in all things, which is the head, even Christ: From whom the whole body fitly joined together and compacted by that which every joint supplieth, according to the effectual working in the measure of every part, maketh increase of the body unto the edifying of itself in love" (emphasis added). This is the "good work" God began in us and will "perform ... until the day of Jesus Christ" (Philippians 1:6).

Meats are temporal, but the work of God is eternal (1 Corinthians 6:12–13).

> But meat commendeth us not to God: for neither, if we eat, are we the better; neither, if we eat not, are we the worse. (1 Corinthians 8:8)

> Wherefore, if meat make my brother to offend, I will eat no flesh while the world standeth, lest I make my brother to offend. (1 Corinthians 8:13)

[af] All things are pure (v. 20) today with respect to dietary requirements of God (1 Timothy 4:3; Acts 10:15). However, there are some things that aren't pure (Philippians 4:8). Paul, addressing the freedom and the believer's liberty from the law, says, "All things are lawful unto me, but all things are not expedient: all things are lawful for me, but I will not be brought under the power of any" (1 Corinthians 6:12). But the apostle tells us in 1 Corinthians 8:9, "Take heed lest by any means this liberty of yours become a stumbling block to them that are weak." It has been well said that we don't have the right to give up our liberty (Galatians 15:1), but we do have the liberty to yield our rights for the sake of our brothers and sisters in Christ.

It's a Happy Man Who Tolerates a Weaker Brother's Proclivities

> [21] 't is good neither to eat flesh, nor to drink wine, nor any thing whereby thy brother stumbleth, or is offended, or is made weak. [22] Hast thou[ag] faith? have it to thyself before God. Happy is he that condemneth not himself in that thing which he alloweth. [23] And he that doubteth[ah] is damned if he eat, because he eateth not of faith: for whatsoever is not of faith is sin. (Romans 14:21–23 KJV)

[ag] The faith in question here in verse 22 is the faith of the stronger believer that an idol is nothing in the world. In essence Paul says here, "Enjoy that confidence but do not foist it on a brother who is not ready for it." The believer who doesn't have to lay judgment on himself (i.e., "condemneth not himself") because of some unloving use of his liberties is spiritually prosperous.

[ah] "He that doubteth is condemned of himself" (not of God or anyone else). The word for "damned" here in verse 22 is the same work rendered "condemnation" in Romans 8:1 except this is the verb form. Both here and in Romans 8:1, a self-condemnation is in view. When weaker brothers eat something they regard as being somehow unclean (as having been offered by idols), they condemn themselves, thinking they have sinned against God. Any action taken that is contrary to the will of God is understood by all to be sin. Thus Paul reminds us that "whatsoever is not of faith is sin." To eat of faith is to eat believing that all things are pure. The one who eats without having that understanding eats not of faith.

I list below some area of doubtful disputations people use to judge each other today. These are areas in which there is no clear statement made in scripture; therefore, Christian charity should be the guide in regard to fellowship with fellow believers. Each will have his or her own convictions in these areas, but such convictions are one's own and should not be forced on others.

- Having wine with dinner
- Men deciding to wear beards
- Women deciding to wear pants
- Participating in mixed swimming
- Going to the beach
- Going to movies
- Participating in dating
- Wives working outside the home
- Working on Sundays (Galatians 4:9–11)
- Participating in dancing
- Women deciding whether to use a head covering

The seven spheres of Christian service we have been studying lay out seven principles, which, if obeyed universally, would produce an ideal social order during "this present evil world." Some years ago, I came across the following layout of these seven principles. I don't recall the source, but the list summarizes the seven spheres of service well. The spheres of service are:

To God: (12:1–2)

To the Body of Christ: (12:3–8)

To Fellow Believers: (12:9–13)

To All Men (including enemies): (12:14–21)

To the State: 13:1–7)

To Society: (13:1–7)

To Weaker Brethren: (14:1–15:11)

Study Questions on Chapter 14

1. Who is a person that is weak in the faith?

2. What does it mean to receive such a one? Should we receive anyone and everyone who claims to be a believer?

3. What are the doubtful disputations that we are to avoid?

4. One who is strong in the faith believes that he can eat all things but another who is weak eats herbs. What does this have to do with being strong or weak in the faith?

5. There are times when the scripture tells us to judge others (e.g. in 1Cor.verses 5:3 – 8) but here in 12 & 13 those who ate are admonished not to judge those who did not and those who did not are admonished not to despise those who did eat. What is the difference in the situations?

6. There is an important principle being taught in verse 4. What is it? Does it apply today?

7. Are the issues in verses 4 through 6 sin questions or matters of personal opinions? Should we hold personal opinions and set our personal standards? Should we then impose them on others?

8. What does the last part of verse 8 say about the matter of personal opinions?

9. According to verse 9, what did Christ do that he might be the one to judge the living and the dead?

10. In consideration of verse 12 is it important that we set high standards for ourselves? Is it also important that we walk in love toward our brothers in regard to whether we judge them or despise them?

11. In verse 13 there is something that we are not to judge and something that we are to judge. What are they?

12. Do you agree with Paul that there is nothing unclean of itself? Is there an issue of how things are perceived by others that needs to be respected?

13. If your brother is grieved because of his perception of an action you took freely would it be loving toward him for you to flaunt that freedom? In what sense can a believer destroy a brother by his meat?

14. According to verse 17 what should be the main focus for the believer in the kingdom of God enjoying your liberties or righteousness, peace and joy? According to verse 18, what two benefits does such a focus bring? Is the term "the kingdom of God" in verse 17 in a general sense or dispensational sense?

15. If there be anything that summarizes the chapter it would be verse 19. Commit it to memory. If you keep that as the guiding principle on which all of your actions are taken the righteousness, peace and joy in the Holy Ghost (verse 17) will also be in your life.

16. Is the faith of verse 22 on the part of the one who is strong or the one who is weak in the faith? Tell me how it is that a man condemns not himself in the thing that he allows. "Whatsoever is not of faith is sin" Please explain that in the context of this chapter.

Chapter 15

LET'S PLEASE OUR NEIGHBOR FOR GOOD

Bearing the infirmities of the weak

¹ We then that are strong ought to bear the infirmities of the[a] weak, and not to please[b] ourselves. ²Let every one of us please[c] his neighbour for his good to edification. ³ For even Christ pleased[d] not himself; but, as it is[e] written, The reproaches of them that reproached thee fell on me. ⁴ For whatsoever things were written[f] aforetime were written for our learning, that we through patience and comfort of the scriptures might have[g] hope. (Romans 15:1–4)

[a] Paul in Romans 15:1 isn't talking about the weakness of 1 Corinthians 4:10 ("We are weak but ye are strong") or 2 Corinthians 12:10 ("When I am weak then I am strong"). Rather, he is yet talking about "him that is weak in the faith" (Romans 14:1). This is the weak person Paul referred to in 1 Corinthians 9:22 ("To the weak I became weak that I might gain the weak") and 1 Thessalonians 5:14. Paul is simply continuing his thought of chapter 14.

[b] The verb please is used three ways in the first three verses. It refers to meeting someone's expectations so as to satisfy that person's desire. In verse 1, the ones who are strong (note: Paul includes himself in the number) ought to seek to satisfy not their own desires but the desires of their neighbor. In verse 2, we see that we ought rather to seek to meet the desires and expectations of our neighbors for the purpose of building them up. In verse 3, we find that Christ is the prime example of one who didn't please Himself; rather, He sought to please His Father.

[c] Paul lived this exhortation to please his neighbor for his good to edification.

- Corinthians 9:10–22—"For though I be free from all men, yet have I made myself servant."

- 10:24—"Let no man seek his own, but every man another's wealth."

- 13:5—"Charity ... seeketh not her own."

- Also, Philippians 2:4–5 says, "And being found in fashion as a man, he humbled himself, and became obedient unto death, even the death of the cross."

[d] Christ pleased not Himself. Jesus is fully God and fully man. The humanity of our Lord is seen in His desire to escape the cross. Both His desire to avoid it and His yieldedness to the Father's will are expressed in the gospels.

O my Father, if it be possible, let this cup pass from me: nevertheless not as I will, but as thou wilt.

(Matthew 26:39)

My meat is to do the will of him that sent me, and to finish his work. (John 4:34)

I seek not mine own will, but the will of the Father which hath sent me. (John 5:30 cf. 6:38; 8:29)

Now is my soul troubled; and what shall I say? Father, save me from this hour: but for this cause came I unto this hour. (John 12:27–28)

As the Father gave me commandment, even so I do. (John 14:31)

If ye keep my commandments, ye shall abide in my love; even as I have kept my Father's commandments, and abide in his love. (John 15:10)

And being found in fashion as a man, he humbled himself, and became obedient unto death, even the death of the cross. (Philippians 2:8)

[e] This is a quote (v. 3) from Psalm 69:7–9. "Because for thy sake I have borne reproach; shame hath covered my face. I am become a stranger unto my brethren, and an alien unto my mother's children [Isaiah 53:3; John 1:11; 7:5]. For the zeal of thine house hath eaten me up [John 2:17]; and the reproaches of them that reproached thee are fallen upon me." The unregenerate heart of man has the attitude of Psalm 2:2–3. "The kings of the earth set themselves, and the rulers take counsel together, against the LORD, and against his anointed, saying, Let us break their bands asunder, and cast away their cords from us." The natural animosity the unregenerate heart had for God couldn't be vented for some four thousand-plus years of human history because people couldn't get their hands on God. But when God entered humanity in the person of Jesus Christ, all that changed, and man could finally express his contempt for his Creator. Jesus Christ bore that contempt in His body on the cross as He gave Himself to redeem His fallen creature—man. John 15:23 says, "He that hateth me, hateth my Father also."

[f] The things written "aforetime" are things written in the Old Testament scriptures.

Now it was not written for his sake alone ... but for us also. (Romans 4:23–24)

For it is written in the law of Moses ... for our sakes ... this is written. (1 Corinthians 9:9–10)

Now all these things happened unto them for examples: and they are written for our admonition, upon whom the ends of the world are come. (1 Corinthians 10:11)

[g] The things written in the Old Testament scripture are written that we living during the dispensation of grace might, through patience and comfort of scripture, have hope. Note, in Paul's quoting of the Old Testament, he uses the phrase "as it is written" (emphasis added). This is a term referring to a parallel application of an event or prophecy. Compare this to the definite expression "This is that which was spoken by the prophet Joel" of Acts 2:16. Paul's message was that "which in other ages was not made known unto the sons of men, as it is now revealed unto his holy apostles and prophets by the Spirit; that the Gentiles should be fellowheirs" (Ephesians 3:5–6; Romans 16:25). Paul often quotes the Old Testament to make a parallel application of the quoted passage, not to make a note of the fulfillment of an Old Testament prophecy.

Let's Receive One Another as Christ Received Us

⁵ Now the God of patience[h] and consolation grant you to be likeminded[i] one toward another according to Christ Jesus: ⁶ That ye may with one mind and one mouth glorify God, even the Father of our Lord Jesus Christ. ⁷ Wherefore receive[j] ye one another, as Christ also received us to the glory of God. (Romans 15:5–7)

[h] Patience is an attribute of the saint that comes from enduring tribulation (Romans 5:3–5; 8:24–25; 12:12). It's the testimony of scripture regarding saints who have come before us that enables us to patiently endure tribulation. The end result of patience and comfort of the scriptures is hope, the confident assuring of a future blessing. Patience is also an intrinsic attribute of God. Because God is intrinsically patient, He can comfort and console us. The end result of His work of comfort and consolation is that we can "be like minded one toward another" according to the example of Christ.

[i] In verse 5, Paul wanted them to be likeminded to God. He addresses this same thing in 1 Corinthians 1:10. "Now I beseech you, brethren, by the name of our Lord Jesus Christ, that ye all speak the same thing, and that there be no divisions among you; but that ye be perfectly joined together in the same mind and in the same judgment."

[j] The conclusion of the matter of chapters 14:1–15:7 is here given. "Receive ye one another as Christ received us to the glory of God." Receiving one another brings glory to God.

Jesus Christ <u>Was</u> a Minister of the Circumcision

⁸ Now[k] I say that Jesus Christ was[l] a minister of the circumcision for the truth of God, to confirm the promises made unto the fathers: ⁹ And that the Gentiles might glorify God for his mercy; as[m] it is written, For this cause I will confess to thee among the Gentiles, and sing unto thy name. ¹⁰ And again he saith, Rejoice, ye Gentiles, with his people. ¹¹ And again, Praise the Lord, all ye Gentiles; and laud him, all ye people. ¹² And again, Esaias saith, There shall be a root of Jesse, and he that shall rise to reign over the Gentiles; in him shall the Gentiles trust. (Romans 15:8–12)

[k] The "Now" of verse 8 is a dispensational term. Paul says "now" during the dispensation of the grace of God that Jesus Christ was (during His earthly ministry) a minister of the circumcision. That fact is obvious from passages such as Matthew 10:6–7; 15:24. "I am not sent but to the lost sheep of the house of Israel." Verse 8 brings several questions to our minds:

1. Who are the circumcision?

2. When was Jesus a minister of the circumcision?

Obviously the term "the circumcision" refers to the rite we know of as the sign of the Abrahamic covenant. In fact, that covenant is called the "covenant of circumcision" (Acts 7:8). In Acts 11:2, we see they of the "circumcision" contended with Peter because he "wentest in unto men uncircumcised." In Romans 2:29, we see the true circumcision is not just outward but "of the heart, in the Spirit." In Romans 3:30, we see God "shall justify the circumcision by faith, and the uncircumcision through faith." There is therefore an uncircumcision that is being justified through faith as certainly as there is a circumcision that will be justified by faith. Abraham was "in uncircumcision" before he was "in circumcision" (Romans 4:10) and was justified while he was yet in uncircumcision; at which time "he received the sign of circumcision, a seal of the righteousness of the faith which he had yet being uncircumcised." In Romans 4:12, Abraham is "the father of the circumcision to them who are not of the circumcision only, but who also walk in the steps of that faith of our father Abraham." In Galatians 2:7–8, we see there is a gospel of the circumcision and a gospel of the uncircumcision. There is also an apostleship of the circumcision (that of Peter and the Twelve) and an apostleship of the uncircumcision (that of Paul and company). In Galatians 2:9, we find Peter (and those with him) make an agreement with Paul (and associated with him ministering to the uncircumcision) that they (Peter and those with him who were ministering to the circumcision) would confine their ministry to the circumcision. At that point in the Acts period, the circumcision included just the believers of Israel who believed the gospel of the circumcision. In that agreement, Paul and those associated with him would minister to the heathen (the Gentiles), which now at that time included the unbelievers of Israel.

In Philippians 3:3, we see there is a spiritual sense in which all members of the body of Christ are regarded as the spiritual circumcision, but that is "the circumcision made without hands" of Colossians 2:11. However, we are not the circumcision Jesus Christ came to minister to. When He came to Israel, we were still those "who are called Uncircumcision by that which is called the Circumcision in the flesh made by hands; That at that time ye were without Christ, being aliens from the commonwealth of Israel, and strangers from the covenants of promise, having no hope, and without God in the world" (Ephesians 2:11–12). Toward the end of Paul's ministry, the term "the circumcision" referred to believers of the nation of Israel who had trusted in Jesus Christ as the Messiah of Israel, though it's apparent from Titus 1:10 that the term was also used in reference to some of the circumcision who were opposing Paul. The term "the circumcision" is a reference to the nation of Israel in respect to God's purpose for the nation.

Regarding the second question, it is apparent from verse 8 that Jesus isn't today a minister of the circumcision, but He once was. During our Lord's earthy ministry, He said, "I am not sent but unto the lost sheep of the house of Israel" (Matthew 15:24).

The Gospels record only two Gentiles who received anything from Jesus Christ, and each of them came to Him, acknowledging that they had no call or claim to be able to come to Him. The centurion of Luke 7:7ff said, "Lord, trouble not thyself: for I am not worthy that thou shouldest enter under my roof: Wherefore neither thought I myself worthy to come unto thee: but say in a word, and my servant shall be healed." The woman of Canaan, after our Lord informed her that "it is not meet to take the children's bread, and to cast it to dogs, said, "Truth, Lord: yet the dogs eat of the crumbs which fall from their masters' table" (Matthew 12:24–28). In doing so, she acknowledged she was outside the commonwealth of Israel and had no direct claim on Israel's Messiah. During the period covered by the four Gospels, the Lord was a minister of only the circumcision.

[I] Jesus Christ was a minister of the circumcision to accomplish two things according to this verse. They are (1) to confirm the promises made unto the fathers and (2) to ensure that the Gentiles might glorify God for His mercy, as it is written. That is, (1) Israel must first be saved, and (2) Israel would then reach the Gentiles with the gospel of the kingdom.

Both of these were to be carried out under God's prophesied program with the circumcision. The promises made to the fathers include all the things Paul lists in Romans 9:4–5.

My kinsmen, according to the flesh:

Who are Israelites;

to whom pertaineth the *adoption*,

and the *glory*,

and the *covenants*,

and the *giving of the law*,

and the *service of God*,

and the *promises*;

Whose are the fathers,

and of whom as concerning the flesh *Christ came*.

(emphasis added)

The word fathers here in Romans 15:8 is a reference to Abraham, Isaac, and Jacob. The most basic form of these promises is found in Genesis 12:2–4. "And I will make of thee a great nation, and I will bless thee, and make thy name great; and thou shalt be a blessing: And I will bless them that bless thee, and curse him that curseth thee: and in thee shall all families of the earth be blessed." The ultimate expression of these promises is in the kingdom promised to Israel in Daniel 2:44. "And in the days of these kings shall the God of heaven set up a kingdom, which shall never be destroyed: and the kingdom shall not be left to other people, but it shall break in pieces and consume all these kingdoms, and it shall stand for ever." This kingdom is "the kingdom of heaven" preached by John the Baptist and our Lord as being "at hand" (Matthew 3:2; 4:7; 10:7). It is "the kingdom of Heaven" because "the God of Heaven" sets it up and because, in it God's will shall be done in the earth as it is in heaven (Matthew 6:9 cf. Daniel 4:34).

The blessings that will go to Israel in that kingdom will overflow to all the Gentile nations. God told Abraham after He had tested Abraham to offer Isaac, "That in blessing I will bless thee, and in multiplying I will multiply thy seed as the stars of the heaven, and as the sand which is upon the sea shore; and thy seed shall possess the gate of his enemies; And in thy seed shall all the nations of the earth be blessed; because thou hast obeyed my voice" (Genesis 22:17–18, emphasis added).

The kingdom of heaven will be set upon earth. "Behold, the days come, saith the LORD, that I will raise unto David a righteous Branch, and a King shall reign and prosper, and shall execute judgment and justice in the earth. In his days Judah shall be saved, and Israel shall dwell safely" (Jeremiah 23:5–6).

Let's now consider the chronology of the New Testament scriptures relative to God's dealings with Israel (the circumcision) and the Gentiles.

First, our Lord appears in Israel, saying, "I am not sent but to the lost sheep of the house of Israel" (Matthew 15:24).

Second, our Lord said to Israel, "And other sheep I have, which are not of this fold: them also I must bring, and they shall hear my voice; and there shall be one fold, and one shepherd" (John 10:16). These other sheep are not the Gentiles but the ten northern tribes of Israel, which rebelled under Jeroboam (1 Kings 11:30–33). God prophesied the reuniting of the ten northern tribes with the two southern tribes in

Ezekiel 37:16–22. In Acts 8:14–17, we see a foretaste of this as the ten northern tribes had to recognize Judah and Jerusalem to receive the Holy Ghost.

Third, our Lord told Israel He came "to give his life a ransom for many" (Matthew 20:28). The many here were Israelites. In John 1:12, we see "many" used in the same sense. "But as many as received him, to them gave he power to become the sons of God." The "many" here are those "of his own"—Israel. Note, however, that Paul in 1 Timothy 2:6 says Christ "gave himself a ransom for all, to be testified in due time."

Fourth, the twelve apostles (to the twelve tribes, Matthew 19:28) remind Israel at Pentecost, "Ye are the children of the prophets, and of the covenant which God made with our fathers" (Acts 3:25–26), and in addressing Israelites in the coming tribulation, "ye are a chosen generation, a royal priesthood, an holy nation, a peculiar people; that ye should shew forth the praises of him who hath called you out of darkness into his marvelous light; Which in time past were not a people, but are now the people of God: which had not obtained mercy, but now have obtained mercy" (1 Peter 2:9–11). This is the fulfillment of the prophecies of Hosea 2:23 as Paul refers to the event, which is yet future from where we are (dispensationally) today (see Romans 9:25–26). What the Lord was doing through Peter and the Twelve at Pentecost was to actually offer the kingdom to Israel. In fact, that offer made at Pentecost (Acts 3:13–26) was the real official offer of the kingdom to Israel. Israel's stoning of Stephen was Israel's official rejection of that offer of the kingdom.

Fifth, Paul came on the scene at the stoning of Stephen and was saved by God's grace. Our Lord then sent him to the Gentiles (Acts 22:17–21) as the apostle of the Gentiles.

Sixth, the Gentiles gladly received Paul's testimony concerning Christ (Acts 13:42–46). Paul turned his ministry to the Gentiles (Acts 26:17, 20; 28:20).

Seventh, God is today making "known the riches of his glory on the vessels of mercy, which he had afore prepared unto glory, Even us … but also of the Gentiles" (Romans 9:22–30). "But now, in Christ Jesus, Ye who sometimes were far off are made nigh by the blood of Christ" (Ephesians 2:12–22).

Eighth, one day the dispensation of grace will close, and the fullness of the Gentiles will have come in. At that time, the rapture (i.e., the catching away) of the body of Christ will take place, and then God will turn again to the nation of Israel to bring about the fulfillment of their Old Testament promises.

Ninth, God made a dispensational change in His dealings with man. Today in the dispensation of grace (Ephesians 3:1–8), God is dealing with the entire human race on the basis of grace.

Tenth, one day "all Israel shall be saved" (Romans 11:26). This will happen when God "will thoroughly purge his floor, and gather his wheat into the garner and burn up the chaff with unquenchable fire" (Matthew 3:12). This is God's purpose for the coming tribulation period (i.e., to get Israel saved).

[m] The passages from 15:9–12 are all quotes from the Old Testament concerning God's prophesied program of teaching the Gentiles through Israel. That term Gentile is used ten times in verse 9 through the end of chapter 15. The passages point out God's intention to reach the Gentiles through the gospel of the circumcision. In verse 9, Paul quotes Psalm 18:49. In verse 10, he quotes Deuteronomy 32:43. In verse 11, he quotes Psalm 117:1; and in verse 12, he quotes Isaiah 11:1–10. There is a progression of thought here:

1. The Gentiles will be reached through the prophetic program.

2. The Gentiles will rejoice with His people (Israel) in verse 10.

3. The Gentiles praise the Lord with His people.

All these passages look forward to the millennium (i.e., to the kingdom of heaven). The quotes come from the law, the prophets, and the Psalms to indicate that the entire Old Testament foresaw the Gentiles being reached through God's prophetic program with Israel. Note the constant repetition to press the point:

"I will confess to thee among the Gentiles."

And again: "Rejoice ye Gentiles with his people" (emphasis added).

And again: "Praise the Lord all ye Gentiles."

And again: "There shall be a root of Jesse, and he shall rise to reign over the Gentiles, in him shall the Gentiles trust."

Paul Puts Us in Mind of His Ministry of the Gospel of God to the Gentiles

13 Now the God of hope fill[n] you with all joy[o] and peace in[p] believing, that ye may abound in hope, through the power of the Holy Ghost. 14 And I myself also am persuaded of you, my brethren, that ye also are[q] full of goodness, filled with all knowledge, able also to admonish one another. 15 evertheless, brethren, I have written the more boldly unto you in some sort, as putting you in mind, because of the grace[r] that is given to me of God, 16 That I should be the minister of Jesus Christ to the Gentiles, ministering the gospel[s] of God, that the offering[t] up of the Gentiles might be[u] acceptable, being[v] sanctified by the Holy Ghost. (Romans 15:13–16)

[n] Verse 5 presents God as the God of patience and consolation. These are intrinsic qualities of God. Verse 13 has a similar structure. Note:

- God is the God of hope (i.e., the God who instills hope in His children).
- God (and Him alone) fills us with joy and peace as we believe.
- We can abound in hope as we tap into the power of the Holy Ghost.
- These blessings come only to the believing heart.
- It is the will of God that all believers be filled with joy and peace.

[o] Verse 13 relates back to verse 10. In verse 10, the Gentiles will rejoice with His people (Israel). This is not being fulfilled today in that Israel isn't rejoicing today. Also, though Jesus Christ "confirmed" the promises to Israel, they aren't fulfilled with Israel today. However, the God of hope is filling Gentiles with joy and peace today.

[p] Gentiles are filled with joy and peace in believing, but we ask, Believing what? The promises of verses 9–12? No, these promises cannot be realized until Israel is saved. Rather, we go back to Romans 3:22–26 to find the object of our faith (i.e., redemption through faith in His blood). Today Gentiles have the forgiveness of sins but not on the basis of any promises or covenants God made with anyone. Rather, we have "redemption

through his blood, the forgiveness of sins according to the riches of his grace" (Ephesians 1:7). Today God offers reconciliation to His enemies (2 Corinthians 5:14–21).

[q] Paul prefaces his statement of verses 15–16 with his words in verse 14. He assures them that he is persuaded that they are full of goodness, filled with all knowledge, and able also to admonish one another.

[r] Paul informs us in verse 8 that Jesus Christ was personally a minister of the circumcision for the truth of God to confirm the promises made unto the fathers. Here in verse 16, Paul informs us that he was given the grace to be the minister of Jesus Christ to the Gentiles. Paul talks about that grace often. In 1 Corinthians 3:10, he says, "According to the grace of God which is given unto me, as a wise masterbuilder, I have laid the foundation, and another buildeth thereon." Note his emphasis on grace in the following verses

> *But by the grace of God I am what I am*: and his grace which was bestowed upon me was not in vain; but I laboured more abundantly than they all: yet not I, *but the grace of God which was with me.* (1 Corinthians 15:10, emphasis added)

> But when it pleased God, who separated me from my mother's womb, and *called me by his grace,* To reveal his Son in me, that I might preach him among the heathen; immediately I conferred not with flesh and blood. (Galatians 1:15–16, emphasis added)

> And when James, Cephas, and John, who seemed to be pillars, *perceived the grace that was given unto me,* they gave to me and Barnabas the right hands of fellowship; that we should go unto the heathen, and they unto the circumcision. (Galatians 2:9, emphasis added)

> Whereof I was made a minister, according *to the gift of the grace of God given unto me* by the effectual working of his power. (Ephesians 3:7, emphasis added)

> And I thank Christ Jesus our Lord, who hath enabled me, for that he counted me faithful, putting me into the ministry; Who was before a blasphemer, and a persecutor, and injurious: but I obtained mercy, because I did it ignorantly in unbelief. And the grace of our Lord was exceeding abundant with faith and love which is in Christ Jesus. (1 Timothy 1:12-14)

> And account *that* the longsuffering of our Lord is salvation; even as our beloved brother Paul also according to the wisdom given unto him hath written unto you... (2 Peter 3:15)

[s] Paul's use of the phrase "the gospel of God" is significant. The following sketch was taken from the book *Things That Differ* by C. R. Stam. The narrative explains the significance.

Illustration

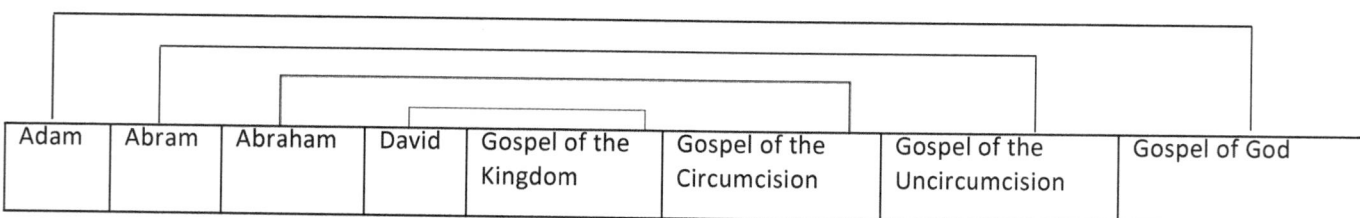

While the gospel of the kingdom goes back to David and the gospel of the circumcision goes back to the circumcised Abraham, and the gospel of the uncircumcision has roots in the uncircumcised Abram, the gospel of

God is a term Paul used first (Peter also used the term in 1 Peter 4:17). The gospel of God is the good news God first spoke in Genesis 3:15, but it had a hidden element Jesus Christ finally revealed through Paul. The gospel of God is the good news regarding the seed of woman (Genesis 3:15), destroying the seed of the serpent and redeeming man in the process. The element of that gospel that wouldn't be revealed until it was accomplished was the work of redemption accomplished on the cross of Calvary. This is what Paul refers to as "the mystery of the gospel for which I am an ambassador in bonds" (Ephesians 6:19). Paul calls this "my gospel" (Romans 16:25; 2:16; 2 Timothy 2:8). In this context, God has good news that involves Jesus Christ being ministered to the Gentiles. Paul's single purpose in life was "to testify the gospel of the grace of God" (Acts 20:24). "We were bold in our God to speak unto you the gospel of God with much contention" (1 Thessalonians 2:2), "laboring night and day, because we would not be chargeable unto any of you, we preached unto you the gospel of God" (2 Thessalonians 2:9).

[t] The offering up of the Gentiles here in verse 16 isn't something Paul did. Rather, it is the Gentiles offering up of themselves in the context of Romans 12:1–2. Paul's ministry was, as he stated in verse 18, "to make the Gentiles obedient, by word and deed." Paul speaks of the churches of Macedonia, who "gave themselves to the Lord" (2 Corinthians 8:5). They did so by joining in "the fellowship of the ministering to the saints." The Philippians' financial support of Paul was "an odour of a sweet smell, a sacrifice acceptable, well pleasing to God" (Philippians 4:18). The Gentiles have the Lord's example in sacrifice (Philippians 2:7–8).

There is an interesting comparison of this passage to Isaiah 66:19–20, where we see that the children of Israel will bring the Gentiles as "an offering in a clean vessel into the house of the LORD" in the kingdom. The significance of Paul's statement in Romans 15:16 is that positionally Paul's ministry through the mystery program (Ephesians 3:1–10) is doing today among the Gentiles what Israel was supposed to be doing through the prophetic program.

[u] Paul is concerned here that the offering up of the Gentiles (i.e., the Gentiles' service to God) "might be acceptable" (i.e., acceptable to God). An acceptable sacrifice is a sacrifice given in the proper manner. Under the law, a sacrifice had to be made in the prescribed manner (Leviticus 6–7), and so it is today. But today the acceptable sacrifice is a living sacrifice. Here, though, we must understand that positionally God "hath made us accepted in the beloved" (Ephesians 1:6). Our standing is that we are accepted of God in Christ, yet our state is dependent on our obedience to His Word. "Wherefore we labour, that, whether present or absent, we may be accepted of him" (2 Corinthians 5:9). Paul therefore defines acceptable service as follows:

- Romans 14:17—"Righteousness, and peace, and joy in the Holy Ghost."
- Ephesians 5:98–10—"Walk as children of the light … proving what is acceptable unto the Lord"
- Philippians 4:18—"Yet ye sent to my necessity … a sacrifice acceptable … to God."
- Timothy 2:1–3—"Prayers, intercession, and giving thanks … for all men … is good and acceptable" (emphasis added).
- Timothy 5:4—"To requite their parents … is good and acceptable before God."

[v] The opportunity for the Gentiles to "present [their] bodies a living sacrifice, holy, acceptable unto God" (Romans 12:1) is a God-ordained opportunity (i.e., it is sanctified by the Holy Ghost). The Holy Ghost is given to each believer for the following reasons:

- Through the Holy Ghost, the love of God is spread abroad in our hearts (Romans 5:5).

- He makes intercession for believers in that we, walking by faith and not by sight, do not know (today) what to pray for as we ought (Romans 8:26–28).

- Believers are washed, sanctified, and justified by the Spirit of our God (1 Corinthians 6:11).

- The believer's body is the temple of the Holy Ghost (1 Corinthians 6:19; Ephesians 2:22).

- The Holy Spirit gives the believer access to the Father (Ephesians 2:18).

Paul Didn't Build on Another Man's Foundation

[17] I have therefore whereof I may glory[w] through Jesus Christ in those things which pertain to God. [18] For I will not dare to speak[x] of any of those things which Christ hath not wrought by me, to make[y] the Gentiles obedient, by word and deed, [19] Through[z] mighty signs and wonders, by the power of the Spirit of God; so that from[aa] Jerusalem, and round about unto Illyricum, I have fully preached the gospel of Christ. [20] Yea, so have I strived[ab] to preach the gospel, not where[ac] Christ was named, lest I should build upon another[ad] man's foundation: [21] But as it is[ae] written, To whom he was not spoken of, they shall see: and they that have not heard shall understand. (Romans 15:17–21)

[w] Paul appears to be boasting here in verse 17, yet we know from other scripture that he wouldn't do that. "Not that we are sufficient of ourselves to think any thing as of ourselves; but our sufficiency is of God" (2 Corinthians 3:5). In 2 Corinthians 11:16–30, we find Paul boasting, but he did so to shame the Corinthians for their foolish boasting. Paul learned a lesson about boasting when God allowed a messenger of Satan to buffet him lest he be "exalted above measure through the abundance of the revelations" (2 Corinthians 12:7). What some might regard as boasting on Paul's part is simply his statement of the truth regarding his God-given ministry. "For though I would desire to glory, I shall not be a fool; for I will say the truth: but now I forbear, lest any man should think of me above that which he seeth me to be, or that he heareth of me" (2 Corinthians 12:6). Proverbs 25:14 says it all: "Whoso boasteth himself of a false gift is like clouds and wind without rain."

[x] Paul's statement in verse 18 is similar to his statement in 2 Corinthians 10:12–18. "For we dare not make ourselves of the number, or compare ourselves with some that commend themselves: but they measuring themselves by themselves, and comparing themselves among themselves, are not wise. But we will not boast of things without our measure, but according to the measure of the rule which God hath distributed to us, a measure to reach even unto you" (vv. 12–13). The only thing Paul would boast in is the work God had wrought through him. When Paul went to Antioch. he "rehearsed all that God had done with them [Paul and Barnabas], and how he had opened the door of faith unto the Gentiles" (Acts 14:27). At Jerusalem he did the same (Acts 15:4, 12; 21:19). Paul understood that "he that wrought effectually in Peter to the apostleship of the circumcision, the same was mighty in me toward the Gentiles" (Galatians 2:8). Paul lived daily with the realization that "our sufficiency is of God" (2 Corinthians 3:5).

[y] The goal of Paul's ministry is stated here: "to make the Gentiles obedient by word and deed." The purpose of Paul's apostleship, as stated in Romans 1:5, was "for obedience to the faith among all nations." It is the doctrine of grace given to us in Paul's epistles that produces such obedience. "But God be thanked, that ye were the servants of sin, but ye have obeyed from the heart that form of doctrine which was delivered you" (Romans 6:17). Paul describes the spiritual warfare we are involved in today as "casting down imaginations, and

every high thing that exalteth itself against the knowledge of God, and bringing into captivity every thought to the obedience of Christ; And having in a readiness to revenge all disobedience" (2 Corinthians 10:4–6). This obedience of the Gentiles is to be both in what they say and in what they do (cf. Colossians 3:17; 2 Thessalonians 2:17).

[z] God wrought the work of making the Gentiles obedient by word and deed through the means of mighty signs and wonders, by means of the powers of the Spirit of God. The mighty signs and wonders were necessary because, and only because, a dispensational change was in progress. God temporarily interrupted His prophetic program. To give creditability to this change, to validate it, God wrought special signs and wonders through Paul such that no one could logically deny such works were of God. However, the normal course of God's dealing with man is on the principle of Hebrews 11:6. "But without faith it is impossible to please him: for he that cometh to God must believe that he is, and that he is a rewarder of them that diligently seek him." Therefore, God used the mighty signs and wonders only to validate that Paul's ministry was the work of God. Thus, these signs and wonders were operative only during the periods covered in the book of Acts. The end result of the mighty signs and wonders was the implanting in planet earth of the church, which is Christ's body, and the completed Word of God. The church has, from that day until now, been functioning (or is supposed to function) on the basis of the Word of God as its final authority. Let's now consider how God used these signs and wonders to validate Paul's ministry:

- Acts 14:3—At Iconium God granted signs and wonders to be done by their hands.

- Acts 14:10—At Lystra and Derbe, the man crippled from his mother's womb leaped and walked.

- Acts 15:12—Paul and Barnabas told the disciples of Jerusalem what miracles God had wrought among the Gentiles by them.

- Acts 16:18—At Philippi, Paul cast a spirit of divination out of a child.

- Acts 19:11–12—While at the school of Tyrannus at Ephesus, people could touch Paul's body with a handkerchief and then touch a sick person so the sick person recovered.

- In 2 Corinthians 12:12, Paul refers to these signs and wonders as the signs of an apostle (cf. Galatians 3:5).

[aa] We can trace Paul's journey from Jerusalem and around about unto Illyricum in the book of Acts.

- Acts   9: 28–29 In Jerusalem, Paul meets Barnabas.

- 11:25   In Antioch, Barnabas sees Grecians getting saved and seeks Saul.

- 13:4   The Holy Ghost sends Saul and Barnabas out.

- 13:5   In Solimas, they are in the synagogue.

- 13:6–10   In Paphos, Sergious Paulus, the Gentile, is saved; Elymus, the Jew. is blinded.

- 13:14, 42   In Pisidian, Antioch, Gentiles gladly receive the gospel.

- 13:51   In Pisidia, Jews stir up trouble for Paul.

- 14: 6   In Iconium, unbelieving Jews stir up trouble.

- 14:25   Paul travels to Pamphylia, Perga, Attalia, and back to Antioch.

- 15:1–35   The Jerusalem conference resolves the circumcision issue.

- 15:35–41   Paul and Barnabas split. Paul and Silas go on.

- 16:1–5   Timothy joins Paul in travels.

- 16: 6–12   They visit Phrygia, Galatia, and Troas.

- 16:10–40   In Macedonia, they visit the Philippian jailor.

- 16:15   They visit Lydia.

- 17:1–10 In Thessalonica, Jews recruit certain lewd men, who beat Paul.

- 17:12–14   In Berea, Jews come from Thessalonica to cause trouble.

- 17:15   In Athens, Paul gives his sermon on Mars Hill.

- 18:1–6   In Corinth, Paul meets Pricilla and Aquila. Jews oppose them.

- Chrispus, leader of the synagogue, is saved.

- They stay in Corinth for eighteen months.

- They experience Jewish opposition.

- 18:19   In Ephesus, Paul is with Pricilla and Aquila.

- 18:22–28   Appollus learns the way more perfectly.

- 19:1–9   Twelve disciples of John learn the way more perfectly.

- 19:9   Paul is at the school of Tyrannus for two years.

- 19:24–41   In Ephesus, there is uproar over Diana.

- 20:1–2 In Greece (at Corinth for three months), Paul travels with Sopater of Berea, Aristarchus and secundus of Thessalonica, Gaias and Timotheus of Derbe, and Tychicus and Trophimus of Asia.

- 20:6   Paul is in Troas for five days.

[ab] Paul preached the gospel as one who was under special obligation to do so. In Romans 1:14–16, he says, "I am debtor both to the Greeks, and to the Barbarians; both to the wise, and to the unwise. So, as much as in me is, I am ready to preach the gospel to you that are at Rome also." We ask, How is it that Paul pictured himself as a debtor to the Gentiles so that he felt obliged to preach the gospel to them? The answer is in this passage of Romans 15. Israel was to be the channel of blessing to the Gentiles in the gospel of the kingdom. However, the unbelieving nation, largely under the leadership of Paul, stopped up that channel of blessing so that the program was interrupted. Now the gospel of the grace of God was to go to the Gentiles, and Paul was to be the one to "fully preach it." Thus Paul had motivation as none other did. Paul preached the gospel "publicly and from house to house" (Acts 20:20). But he "fully preached the gospel" in the sense that he "kept back nothing that was profitable." He tells the Ephesian elders, "I have not shunned to declare unto you all the counsel of God" (Acts 20:27). It was Paul's ministry to complete the Bible as he states "for his body's sake, which is the

church: Whereof I am made a minister, according to the dispensation of God which is given to me for you, to fulfil the word of God; Even the mystery which hath been hid from ages and from generations, but now is made manifest to his saints" (Colossians 1:24–26). Paul was God's chosen vessel (Acts 9:15) to be the one to reveal this message. "The Lord stood with me, and strengthened me; that by me the preaching might be fully known, and that all the Gentiles might hear" (2 Timothy 4:17).

[ac] Paul strived to preach the gospel elsewhere from where Christ was named. This wasn't for the purpose of moving into new territory with the same message as was preached where Christ was named. Rather, it was to go to those who hadn't heard the gospel of Christ with a new message.

> If ye have heard of the dispensation of the grace of God which is given me to you-ward: How that by revelation he made known unto me the mystery; (as I wrote afore in few words, Whereby, when ye read, ye may understand my knowledge in the mystery of Christ) Which in other ages was not made known unto the sons of men, as it is now revealed unto his holy apostles and prophets by the Spirit; That the Gentiles should be fellowheirs, and of the same body, and partakers of his promise in Christ by the gospel: Whereof I was made a minister. (Ephesians 3:2–7)

[ad] "Another man's foundation" is a significant statement here in verse 20. In 1 Corinthians 3:9–15, Paul describes the foundation he laid. "We [Paul and Apollos] are labourers together with God: ye are God's husbandry, ye are God's building. According to the grace of God which is given unto me, as a wise masterbuilder, I have laid the foundation, and another buildeth thereon. But let every man take heed how he buildeth thereupon. For other foundation can no man lay than that is laid, which is Jesus Christ" (vv. 9–11). The foundation Paul laid is said here to be Jesus Christ. This is talking about a body of believers, which is associated with Jesus Christ as "the preaching of Jesus Christ according to the revelation of the mystery" (Romans 16:25). This is Jesus Christ personally as the head of the body together with the church, which is his body (Ephesians 1:22; 5:23, 30; Colossians 1:18, 24) to form "one news man" (Ephesians 2:15).

Paul used this term foundation in 1 Corinthians 3:9–15 to refer to the Bible blueprint for the body of Christ. Paul as an architect acted as a draftsman who drew up the blueprints for the building God is building for Himself to dwell in. God designed the building, but Paul is the one chosen to put the plan down on paper. But this building isn't of brick and mortar. This is a building of flesh and blood. The tools used in building the Word of God are rightly divided (2 Timothy 2:15; 3:16). The workmen are believers as they carry on the work of the ministry (Ephesians 4:12) in edifying the body of Christ. The end product will be "an habitation of God through the Spirit" (Ephesians 2:20–22). Paul wouldn't build on the foundation of the Twelve (2 Corinthians 10:13–16) because he was given a different message than they (Galatians 2:6–9).

[ae] Romans 15:21 is a quote from the second half of Isaiah 52:15. This is prophecy that was fulfilled in spite of the fact that the prophesied program (i.e., the kingdom of heaven) hadn't been fulfilled. This is a prophecy of the Gentiles hearing the gospel of Christ and responding. But the Gentiles didn't hear the gospel of Christ through Israel because Israel herself remained in unbelief. However, the gospel of Christ went to the Gentiles through the mystery program in spite of this fact that Israel refused to be the channel of blessing to them. The first part of Isaiah 52:15 couldn't be applied here because that wasn't fulfilled of yet. "So shall he sprinkle many nations; the kings shall shut their mouths at him: for that which had not been told them shall they see; and that which they had not heard shall they consider."

Paul's Plans to Go through Rome to Spain

²² For which cause also I have been much hindered[af] from coming to you. ²³ But now having no more place in these parts, and having a great desire these many years to come unto you; ²⁴ Whensoever I take my journey into Spain, I will come to you: for I trust to see you in my journey, and to be brought on my way thitherward by you, if first I be somewhat filled with your company. ²⁵ But now I go[ag] unto Jerusalem to minister[ah] unto the saints. ²⁶ For it hath pleased them of Macedonia and Achaia to make a certain contribution for the poor[ai] saints which are at Jerusalem. ²⁷ It hath pleased them verily; and their debtors[aj] they are. For if the Gentiles have been made partakers of their spiritual things, their duty[ak] is also to minister unto them in carnal things. ²⁸ When therefore I have performed this, and have sealed to them this[al] fruit, I will come by you into Spain. ²⁹ And I am sure that, when I come unto you, I shall come[am] in the fulness of the blessing of the gospel of Christ. (Romans 15:22–29)

[af] Paul was hindered in coming to the Romans because he was occupied with the task of taking the gospel of Christ to the Gentiles to "make the Gentiles obedient by word and deed" (v. 18) and to "make all men see what is the fellowship of the mystery, which from the beginning of the world hath been hid in God, who created all things by Jesus Christ" (Ephesians 3:9). Paul's ministry was to do what Israel was supposed to do but didn't.

[ag] Here in verse 25 we see grace in action. Paul, who was once the persecutor of these saints (Acts 22:4; 26:11; 1 Corinthians 15:9; Galatians 1:13, 23), now ministers to them. It is the grace of God that made the change (1 Corinthians 15:10). We see this purpose of Paul in Acts 19:21. "Paul purposed in the spirit, when he had passed through Macedonia and Achaia, to go to Jerusalem, saying, 'After I have been there, I must also see Rome.'" We find Paul's steadfast determination in action to go to Jerusalem in Acts 20:16, 22 (cf. Acts 18:21). His main purpose in doing so was to bring alms and offerings to his nation. This was the desire of the Jerusalem saints at the Jerusalem council of Acts 15:4–29, as stated in Galatians 2:10. "Only they [Jerusalem elders] would that we should remember the poor; the same which I also was forward to do." We see from 1 Corinthians 16:1–3 how systematically Paul went about the task of taking such a collection.

[ah] The saints here in verse 25, whom Paul went to minister to, were "the poor saints which are at Jerusalem." Going back to Acts, we find that these saints "were together, and had all things common; and sold their possessions and goods, and parted them to all men, as every man had need" (Acts 2:44). "And the multitude of them that believed were of one heart and of one soul: neither said any of them that ought of the things which he possessed was his own; but they had all things common ... Neither was there any among them that lacked: for as many as were possessors of lands or houses sold them, and brought the prices of the things that were sold, And laid them down at the apostles' feet: and distribution was made unto every man according as he had need." (Acts 4:32–35). All this was done in accordance with our Lord's instructions to the rich young ruler. "If thou wilt be perfect, go and sell that thou hast, and give to the poor, and thou shalt have treasure in heaven: and come and follow me" (Matthew 19:21; Mark 10:24).

This then was a requirement for entrance into the kingdom of heaven. They were to sell their possessions and give the income to the poor. This couldn't be done successfully today. It did work (for a time) back then at Pentecost because God was giving Israel a picture of what life would be like in the kingdom of heaven under the new covenant. God supernaturally filled them with the Holy Ghost (Acts 4:31–32). In the kingdom, under the new covenant, God could "remove ungodliness from Jacob." He would do that by removing the sin nature from them and replacing it with His Holy Spirit. "A new heart also will I give you, and a new spirit will I put within you: and I will take away the stony heart out of your flesh, and I will give you an heart of flesh. And I will put my Spirit within you, and cause you to walk in my statutes, and ye shall keep my judgments, and do them" (Ezekiel 36:26–27).

[ai] The reference to the poor saints in verse 26 is striking. If the saints at Jerusalem once had no lack ("Neither was there any among them that lacked"), how is it that they became poor? The answer is simply that Israel as a nation today is fallen from their position of being God's people, and the prophetic program has been interrupted. Paul states in Romans 11:11 that "through their fall salvation is come unto the Gentiles, for to provoke them to jealousy." Also in Romans 11:25, he says, "That blindness in part is happened to Israel until the fullness of the Gentiles be come in." One day after the fullness of the Gentiles (i.e., the catching away of the body), "all Israel shall be saved … For this is my [God's] covenant with them, when I shall take away their sins … For the gifts and calling of God are without repentance. For as ye in times past have not believed God, yet have now obtained mercy through their unbelief: Even so have these also now not believed, that through your mercy they also may obtain mercy. For God hath concluded them all in unbelief, that he might have mercy upon all" (Romans 11:25–32).

It was at Pentecost, in Acts 2–4, that the kingdom of heaven was offered to Israel. The stoning of Stephen in Acts 7 marks the point of the withdrawal of that offer. Stephen was the messenger Israel sent to Christ to tell Him they wouldn't have Him (Christ) as their Messiah (cf. Luke 19:14). Matthew 19:21 isn't our instruction for financial management today. So, too, Mark 6:8 isn't the proper missionary method for today. Communal living could work only if people didn't have a sin nature as will be the case in the kingdom.

Proper financial management for us today in the dispensation of grace is laid out for us in the Pauline epistles:

1. Providing for your own (1 Timothy 5:8)
2. Working so to have excess to give (Ephesians 4:26)
3. Not supporting those who won't work (1 Thessalonians 3:10)
4. Giving as God prospers you (1 Corinthians 16:2)
5. Realizing that God doesn't expect you to give what He hasn't first given (1 Corinthians 8:12)
6. Following God's instructions on giving won't put you in financial jeopardy (Philippians 4:19).
7. Giving abounds to the believer's account (Philippians 4:17).

[aj Here in verse 27, Paul pictures the Gentiles to whom he ministered as debtors to the poor saints of Jerusalem. As noted above, in note 36, these saints were poor because God had interrupted their program to bring on the dispensation of the grace of God, a basically Gentile program. This takes us back to Romans 11:17. "And if some of the branches be broken off, and thou, being a wild olive tree, wert grafted in among them, and with them partakest of the root and fatness of the olive tree; Boast not against the branches. But if thou boast, thou bearest not the root, but the root thee." The olive tree represents the place of spiritual blessing and access to God. However, when Israel, as a nation, refused to trust Jesus Christ as her Messiah, God temporarily suspended His dealings with the nation. When He set the nation and the prophetic program aside, the unbelievers of the nation were broken off that place of spiritual blessing. The believers of the "little flock" then wouldn't see their hopes of entering the promised kingdom of heaven realized in their lifetimes. Therefore, the financial sacrifices the believing remnant of Israel made for the sake of entering the kingdom were for naught. Those among whom none lacked were now "the poor saints which were at Jerusalem."

At the Jerusalem conference of Acts 15, we see Paul and Barnabas declaring what miracles and wonders God had wrought among the Gentiles. It was there that these circumcision believers learned of the work God was now doing among the Gentiles. One outcome of that meeting was that Paul took up a collection for these poor saints (see Galatians 2:10—"Only they would that we should remember the poor, the same which also was forward to do"). We see Paul doing this very thing in 1 Corinthians 16:1–3 and 2 Corinthians 8:1–4.

[ak] Paul presents a duty of ministering carnal things (things necessary to maintaining one's physical existence) to those who sacrifice for the sake of the spiritual welfare of others. Here the circumcision believers at Jerusalem suffered deprivation because their program was interrupted. But God supplied their need by means of collections from among the Gentile churches. Paul conveys the same argument of duty regarding teachers who sacrifice to teach spiritual things (Galatians 6:6).

[al] The Gentile concern for the circumcision believers' plight, demonstrated by the Gentiles' monetary support, is here seen as "fruit." It is indeed the fruit of the Spirit, the outworking of the doctrines of grace on the heart of yielded saints. Paul tells the Philippians, "But I desire fruit that may abound to your account" (Philippians 4:17, emphasis added). Paul tells the Colossians, "The word of the truth of the gospel; bringeth forth fruit, as it doth also in you, since the day ye heard of it, and knew the grace of God in truth" (Colossians 1:5–6).

[am] This (v. 29) is a significant statement. Paul had confidence that when he did get to Rome, he would "come in the fulness of the blessing of the gospel of Christ." Paul received the revelation of the mystery in a series of revelations (2 Corinthians 12:1). In 1 Corinthians 13:8–13, written in AD 59, Paul spoke of a time coming when complete knowledge and complete prophecy would come. That would be when the New Testament scriptures were completed with the full revelation of the mystery. That hadn't come yet with the writing of Romans. However, Paul anticipated that it would have come when he reached Rome.

Study Questions on Chapter 15

1. Here as in the previous chapter we again must define who is weak and who is strong. Which are you?

2. If we are not to please ourselves, who are we to please? For what purpose?

3. Did Christ please Himself? Who did He seek to please?

4. Verse 4 talks about things written aforetime. What time was that? Were Old Testament scriptures written for our learning or for our instructions? Where in the Bible do we find that which was written for our instruction?

5. The "like-mindedness" of verse 5 goes back to which verse? How can a fellowship of believers be of one

heart and one mind?

6. According to verse 7, did we receive Christ or did He receive us?

7. Verses 8 & 9 go together and list two aspects of our Lord's earthly ministry. What are they?

8. Verses 9 thru 12 quote five Old Testament passages that prophesy of the Gentiles being blessed with Israel. However, as we recall from chapters 9 thru 11, are the Gentiles being blessed through Israel's rise or through her fall? Find the source of Paul's quotations.

9. According to verse 8, who was God's minister to Israel? According to Romans 11:13 and verse 16 of this chapter, who is God's minister to the nations today?

10. What is the gospel of God? What is "the offering up of the Gentiles"? Would that be an unclean offering? Explain.

11. Taking verses 17 through 20 together, in what was Paul glorying in things that pertain to God? Hint: It has something to do with Gentile obedience.

12. Looking back in the Book of Acts, what journey covered the territory of verse 19?

13. If indeed Paul preached Christ where he was not named, where did he preach, where did he not preach?

14. In verse 19 he talks about mighty signs and wonders done through him by the power of the Spirit of God. Why does he cite these? What do they prove regarding Paul's ministry? Why do you suppose Paul references Isa. 52:15 in verse 21? Is his ministry fulfilling prophecy? What would be the difference in our understanding if Paul said "for it is written..." instead of "as it is written..."?

15. What is Paul hoping for in verse 24 in saying "and to be brought on my way thitherward by you..."?

16. In what way is Paul intending to minister to the saints in Jerusalem? Who are the poor saints in Jerusalem and why were they poor?

17. Why in verse 27 does Paul say that the saints in Macedonia and Achia are debtors to the poor saints in Jerusalem?

18. What do you think the fullness of the blessing of the gospel of Christ is in verse 29?

19. Paul wants the Romans to strive together with him in prayer. What is he asking them to pray for?

20. Paul seemed apprehensive about how the offering for the saints in Jerusalem might be received. Why do you suppose that could be? How was it receive? Go to Acts chapter 15 to see.

CHAPTER 16

STABILITY IN THE CHRISTIAN LIFE

Here is an overview of the closing chapter of Romans. The body of the epistle to the Romans closes with Romans 15:33. "Now the God of peace be with you all. Amen." In chapter 16, we find three separate postscripts and a word of caution.

First postscript: Paul greets his fellow saints of Rome (Romans 16:1–20).

Second postscript: Those with Paul at Corinth send their greetings (Romans 16:21–24).

Third postscript: Paul emphasized the importance of the stabilizing impact of his gospel and the preaching of Jesus Christ according to the revelation of the mystery (Romans 16:25–27).

Paul had never been to Rome yet, but still he knew many of the saints of Rome personally. He named twenty-seven persons in his salutations, nine of whom are women. It appears there were three different local churches at Rome when Paul wrote to them.

1. The church at Priscilla and Aquila's home (16:3–5)

2. The church mentioned in 16:14: "Salute Asyncritus, Phlegon, Hermas, Patrobas, Hermes, and the brethren which are with them."

3. The church mentioned in 16:15: "Salute Philologus, and Julia, Nereus, and his sister, and Olympas, and all the saints which are with them."

It appears that at least six of those mentioned in the chapter are Paul's relatives (vv. 7, 11, 21) or perhaps Israelites.

- "Salute Andronicus and Junia, my kinsmen, and my fellow-prisoners, who are of note among the apostles, who also were in Christ before me" (16:7).

- "Salute Herodion my kinsman" (16:11).

- "Lucius, and Jason, and Sosipater, my kinsmen, salute you" (16:21).

Rufus, mentioned in verse 13, might well have been the son of the Simon who carried our Lord's cross (cf. Mark 15:21). In the first postscript, Paul cautions the Romans to be wary of those in the assemblies who would "cause divisions and offenses contrary to the doctrine which ye have learned and avoid them" (Romans 16:16–20).

The Apostle's Circle of Fellowship

[1] I commend unto you Phebe[a] our sister, which is a servant of the church which is at Cenchrea: [2] That ye receive[b] her in the Lord, as becometh saints, and that ye assist her in whatsoever business she hath

need of you: for she hath been a succourer of many, and of myself also. ³ Greet Priscilla[c] and Aquila my helpers in Christ Jesus: ⁴ Who have for my life laid down their own necks: unto whom not only I give thanks, but also all the churches of the Gentiles. ⁵ Likewise greet the church[d] that is in their house. Salute my wellbeloved Epaenetus, who is the firstfruits[e] of Achaia unto Christ. ⁶ Greet Mary[f], who bestowed much labour on us. ⁷ Salute Andronicus[g] and Junia, my kinsmen, and my fellowprisoners, who are of note among the apostles, who also were in Christ before me. ⁸ Greet Amplias[h] my beloved in the Lord. ⁹ Salute Urbane[i], our helper in Christ, and Stachys my beloved. ¹⁰Salute Apelles approved[j] in Christ. Salute them which are of Aristobulus' household. ¹¹ Salute Herodion my kinsman. Greet them that be of the household of Narcissus, which are in the Lord. ¹²Salute Tryphena[k] and Tryphosa, who labour in the Lord. Salute the beloved Persis, which laboured much in the Lord. ¹³ Salute Rufus[l] chosen in the Lord, and his mother and mine. ¹⁴ Salute Asyncritus, Phlegon, Hermas, Patrobas, Hermes, and the brethren which are with them. ¹⁵ Salute Philologus, and Julia, Nereus, and his sister, and Olympas, and all the saints which are with them. ¹⁶ Salute one another with an holy kiss. The churches of Christ salute you. (Romans 16:1–16)

[a] Phebe is a sister "in Christ" in the sense of Matthew 12:50 and 1 Timothy 5:2. "The younger [women] as sisters." Phebe was a servant (deaconess) of the local church, which was at Cenchrea. As a deaconess, she would have involved herself with the activities listed in 1 Timothy 5:9–10. "Well reported of for good works … lodged strangers … washed the saints' feet … relieved the afflicted … diligently followed every good work." The footnote to Romans indicates Phebe carried the epistle to Rome. Paul apparently met Phebe (who apparently is a merchant) while traveling from Corinth to Syria with Priscilla and Aquila in Acts 18:18. Priscilla and Aquila were apparently at Rome at the time of the writing of Romans (vv. 3–4).

[b] The saints at Rome where to "receive" Phebe when she arrived with the epistle. Beyond that, they were to assist her in her business. In doing so, the saints could reward her for her service to the saints. Paul says in effect, "Bring her instantly into fellowship with the believers there at Rome."

[c] Priscilla and Aquila were Jews who were expelled from Rome when Claudius reined there (Acts 18:1–2). They were tentmakers and went into business as such with Paul for a time in Corinth (Acts 18:3). They traveled with Paul from Corinth and stayed at Ephesus for a time (Acts 18:19–20). We find them again with Paul at Philippi (1 Corinthians 16:19) when Paul writes to the Corinthians. When Paul writes his last epistle (2 Timothy), they are again at Ephesus (2 Timothy 4:19). It is therefore apparent that they made another trip to Rome and were there in Rome during Paul's second residence at Corinth. It was this couple who presented the Word rightly divided to Apollos, "an eloquent man, and mighty in the scriptures" (Acts 18:24). Priscilla and Aquila were courageous people who truly lived what they professed. They literally risked their lives by associating with Paul and helping him. Their courageous act earned not only Paul's gratitude but also that of all the churches of the Gentiles.

[d] There are five local churches referred to in this chapter. There is the church at Cenchrea (16:1) and three churches of Rome. Here we see that one of them was meeting at Priscilla and Aquila's home. The other two are mentioned in Romans 16:14–15. The church at Corinth is indirectly referred to in verses 22–23 by reference to some of the members.

[e] Epaenetus is apparently Paul's first convert from Achaia. Comparing this verse to 1 Corinthians 15:16, we conclude that Epaenetus was of the household of Stephanas, a family that had "addicted themselves to the

ministry of the saints." Achaia is the area around Philippi. The saints of Achaia were ready to contribute to the "poor saints of Jerusalem" long before any others joined the cause (2 Corinthians 9:2).

[f] Here is another of the different Marys listed in the New Testament. Whoever she was, she expended much effort to help Paul somewhere along his journeys. There appear to be six women named Mary in the New Testament:

- Mary, the mother of Jesus (Matthew 1:16)

- Mary Magdalene (Luke 8:2)

- Mary, the mother of James (the less) and Joses (also called Barnabas, Mark 15:40), the wife of Alphaeus (John 19:25). Alphaeus is also called Cleopas (Matthew 10:13).

- Mary of Bethany, the sister of Lazarus and Martha (Luke 10:39, 42; John 11:1, 2, 19, 20; etc)

- Mary, the mother of John Mark (the sister of Barnabas, Acts 12:12)

- This Mary in verse 6

[g] Andronicus and Junia are said here to be Paul's kinsmen. This could mean they were either his close relatives (Acts 10:24) or his fellow Jews (Romans 9:3). Paul also refers to Herodion, Timotheous, Lucious, Jason, and Socipater (vv. 11, 21) as kinsmen. Both Andronicus and Junia had also been in prison with the apostle. In 2 Corinthians 11:23, Paul speaks of himself as being "in prisons more frequent." It could also be that they were in different prisons but were "fellow prisoners" in that they were imprisoned for the sake of the gospel as was Epaphras (Philemon 23). It could well be that John was exiled to the isle of Patmos as a prisoner "for the word of God, and for the testimony of Jesus Christ" (Revelation 1:9). Paul says of these two (Andronicus and Junia) that they "are of note among the apostles." There were men who had the supernatural gift of being apostles during the period of time covered by the Acts of the Apostles. Barnabas is an example of such. In Acts 14:4, we find Barnabas referred to as an apostle as he is again in Acts 14:14. In 1 Corinthians 4:9, Paul associates others with himself as apostles to the body. These are the apostles our Lord gave after His ascension (1 Corinthians 12:28–29; Ephesians 4:11 cf. Ephesians 2:20; 3:5). Paul's statement in 1 Thessalonians 2:6 associates Silvanus and Timothy with him as apostles. Here it appears that Junia and Andronicus are apostles as well.

[h] Amplias was possibly in need of reassurance that he was "Beloved" by Paul, as was Stachys in verse 9.

[i] Urbane was one who helped Paul elsewhere.

[j] Apelles in verse 10 is said to be approved. There are several ways to be approved. Notably, one must rightly divide the Word of truth (2 Timothy 2:15). Also, he or she must stand against what would destroy the unity of the Spirit (1 Corinthians 11:19). Third, he or she must follow Pauline instruction (2 Corinthians 2:9). Fourth, he or she must be reliable (2 Corinthians 8:22; Philippians 2:22).

[k] Tryphena and Tryphosa, who are sisters, not only are "in the Lord" as believers but also "labor in the Lord." Persis is one who personally labored with Paul.

[l] This Rufus could be the son of Simon of Cyrene, who was compelled to help our Lord carry His cross (Mark 15:21). Rufus's mother apparently acted as a mother to Paul as well.

A Word of Caution

> [17] Now I beseech you, brethren, mark[m] them which cause divisions and offences contrary to the doctrine[n] which ye have learned; and avoid them. *18* For they that are such serve not our Lord Jesus Christ, but their own belly; and by good words and fair speeches deceive the hearts of the simple. *19* For your obedience is come abroad unto all men. I am glad therefore on your behalf: but yet I would have you wise unto that which is good, and simple concerning evil. *20* And the God of peace shall[o] bruise Satan under your feet shortly. The grace of our Lord Jesus Christ be with you. Amen. (Romans 16:17–20)

[m] There are two kinds of people Paul says to "mark." The term mark means to take special note of them for a purpose. In Philippians 3:17, Paul instructs believers to "mark them which walk so as ye have us for an ensample." Paul says to take note of such and follow them. Paul is the "pattern" we today are to follow (1 Timothy 1:16). Believers are perpetuate that pattern (Titus 2:7). Paul also says to "mark them which cause divisions and offenses contrary to the doctrine which ye have learned; and avoid them" (Romans 16:17). Such people don't serve the Lord Jesus Christ but their own belly (i.e., their interest is in what promotes their personal gain). Paul uses the same terminology in Philippians 3:18–19 regarding those believers who walk as enemies of the cross of Christ.

[n] Those who are to be marked are those who cause division and offenses contrary to the doctrine Paul taught. Any such activity is to be dealt with immediately as Paul dealt with the Judaizers in Acts 15:1–5 when they tried to impose circumcisions on believing Gentiles. The dogged determination of the Judaizers to cause trouble for Paul is seen in their constant attacks in the book of Acts (note Acts 24:1–9). The most damaging divisions, however, are often those that come from within the assembly. The Corinthian church is a case in point (1 Corinthians 1:10–13; 8:8; 11:18). As is often the case, those who cause division use scripture to do so. Unless believers are well grounded in the Word, they can be "removed … unto another gospel" (Galatians 1:7–9). The divisions and offenses often come out of jealousy over the liberty believers have in Christ. It is often "false brethren unawares brought in, who came in privily to spy out our liberty which we have in Christ Jesus, that they might bring us into bondage" (Galatians 2:4). Paul refers to such as "dogs" and "evil workers" (Philippians 3:2). Their goal was to "spoil" the believers by taking a treasure from them. The treasure is the liberty the believer has in Christ (Colossians 2:8; Galatians 5:1).

The division they cause has purposes—that of setting forth doctrines contrary to the truth. Note in verse 18 that their interest isn't in advancing the Lord's work but in making personal gain. These people are good with words. The "good words" are smooth words. They have cultivated the art of deception by use of words. The words "fair speeches" comes from the Greek word transliterated "eulogize." They speak flattering words to people for the purpose of deception. The "simple" in verse 18 are people who are innocent or harmless. They are people who aren't used to these tricksters and easily fall prey to them. Paul would have us put a mark on these people so they are called out as people to be guarded against.

[o] Paul tells them that the God of peace will shortly bruise Satan's head under their feet. The position of the believers when this happens is interesting. They will be over Satan when Satan is bruised. This is describing the events that conclude the dispensation of grace with the catching away of the church, the body of Christ, to the heavens (2 Thessalonians 4:17). The church, which is Christ's body, will be in heaven (2 Corinthians 5:1) to reign there (2 Timothy 2:12) while the great tribulation is going on here on earth. Satan, however, will have been cast out of heaven into the earth (Revelation 12:7). It will be at the conclusion of the great tribulation that the Lord

will bruise Satan's head in fulfillment of Genesis 3:15.

Second Postscript

> [21] Timotheus my workfellow, and Lucius, and Jason, and Sosipater, my kinsmen, salute you. [22] I Tertius, who wrote this epistle, salute you in the Lord. [23] Gaius mine host, and of the whole church, saluteth you. Erastus the chamberlain of the city saluteth you, and Quartus a brother. [24] The grace of our Lord Jesus Christ be with you all. Amen. (Romans 16:21–24)

The book itself ends with chapter 15, verse 33. Verse 20 concludes the first postscript of the book. Verses 21–24 comprise the second postscript. It tells us who took the dictation of the book and put it on paper as Paul dictated it. It tells us also that Paul was a guest at the home of Gaius. It also tells us that Timothy, Luke, Jason, and Sosipater were with him. Paul was at Corinth at the writing of the epistle. The church here is apparently the church at Corinth that originally met in Justus's house (Acts 18:7).

Two Things That Give Stability in the Christian Life

> [25] Now to him that is of power to stablish you according to my gospel, and the preaching of Jesus Christ, according to the revelation of the mystery, which was kept secret since the world began, [26] But now is made manifest, and by the scriptures of the prophets, according to the commandment of the everlasting God, made known to all nations for the obedience of faith: [27] To God only wise, be glory through Jesus Christ for ever. Amen. (Romans 16:25–27)

This passage is the final postscript. It contains very valuable information for our learning about Paul and his ministry. Paul concludes this great epistle of Roman with two things that will "stablish believers." The translators used the word stablish for a good reason. To establish is to set up. The word stablish means "to make something stable." There are two things that give believers stability in their Christian lives. One is what Paul calls here "my gospel," and the other is what he calls "the preaching of Jesus Christ according to the revelation of the mystery." What Paul calls "My Gospel" is the full meaning of what really happened on Calvary. Paul described this for us in chapter 3. In Romans 1:1–2, Paul says he was "separated unto the gospel of God (which he had promised afore by his prophets in the Holy Scriptures)." That gospel of God he promised afore was in Genesis 3:15 concerning the seed of the woman crushing the serpent's head. This was accomplished on Calvary, but the full meaning of it was finally revealed to the world through the apostle Paul.

What Paul calls "the preaching of Jesus Christ according to the revelation of the mystery" is the revelation of the truth concerning the dispensation of grace and the calling out from the lost masses of humanity (now including Israel—see notes on chapter 11) for an eternal home in the heavens. This body of doctrine (i.e., the mystery) actually comprises Paul's epistles. It stands in contradistinction to what the prophets had been saying since the world began. The prophets talked about a kingdom vested in the nation of Israel. That kingdom will one day be set upon the earth under the reign of Jesus Christ as Israel's Messiah. However, until then, God is calling out the church, Christ's body. The subject of the preaching of Jesus Christ according to the revelation of the mystery is a full book in itself. However, Appendix 1 presents a brief summary of this subject for your enjoyment and contemplation.

One needs to do some carful thinking to understand the meaning of the phrase "the scriptures of the prophets."

I direct the reader's attention to notes [q] and [r] in chapter 12. Also see Appendix 3 for an interesting comparison between the first few verses of Romans 1 and the closing verses of chapter 16.

Study Questions on Chapter 16

1. Based on 16:1, 2, what was the occasion for the Apostle Paul's writing the this Epistle to the Romans?

2. In what sense is Phebe a servant of the church of Cenchrea?.

3. Where was Priscilla and Aquila living at the time Paul wrote Romans? What did they have in their house? Where did Paul first meet them?

4. What does the term "Firstfruits of Achaia" mean? Compare verse 5 with 1 Corinthians 16:15, and tell me who is the firstfruits of the Achaia.

5. Paul mentions two believers as being "in Christ before me." What does it mean to be "In Christ?" How can one be in Christ and not be a member of the Body of Christ? Is it a term exclusive to this dispensation?

6. What relationship does verse 13 seem to indicate between Paul and Rufus? Where they brothers?

7. Does verse 16 tell us how our greetings should be done today?

8. Who is to be avoided in verses 17 and 18?

9. What does verse 19 mean when it says to be "wise unto that which is good, and simple concerning evil?"

10. Who will God bruise according to verse 20? Where and when will that happen?

11. List the names of all of the believers who were with Paul when he wrote this letter. Make note of any who helped him write this letter and state what part they had in it.

12. List those mentioned in this chapter who appear to be relatives of Paul.

13. What is meant by "my gospel" in 16:25?

14. What is the "preaching of Jesus Christ according to the revelation of the mystery?" What other word could be used for mystery?

15. How long was the preaching of Jesus Christ accordingtothe revelation of the mystery kept secret? When was the first time God made this preaching known? Through whom?

16. What scriptures are the "scriptures of the prophets?" Who are these prophets?

17. What is the stated purpose for the revelation of the mystery?

18. What is meant by "the obedience of faith?" Have you been obedient to God in this regard?

APPENDICES

APPENDIX 1

Rightly Dividing the Word of Truth

In Romans 16:25, Paul speaks of "my gospel and the preaching of Jesus Christ according to the revelation of the mystery." There is a body of doctrine in the Bible called "the mystery." The apostle talks about it in association with the dispensation of the grace of God in Ephesians 3:1–13.

> ¹ For this cause I Paul, the prisoner of Jesus Christ for you Gentiles, ² If ye have heard of the dispensation of the grace of God which is given me to you-ward: ³ How that by revelation he made known unto me the mystery; (as I wrote afore in few words, ⁴ Whereby, when ye read, ye may understand my knowledge in the mystery of Christ) ⁵ Which in other ages was not made known unto the sons of men, as it is now revealed unto his holy apostles and prophets by the Spirit; ⁶ That the Gentiles should be fellow-heirs, and of the same body, and partakers of his promise in Christ by the gospel: ⁷ Whereof I was made a minister, according to the gift of the grace of God given unto me by the effectual working of his power. ⁸ Unto me, who am less than the least of all saints, is this grace given, that I should preach among the Gentiles the unsearchable riches of Christ; ⁹ And to make all men see what is the fellowship of the mystery, which from the beginning of the world hath been hid in God, who created all things by Jesus Christ: ¹⁰ To the intent that now unto the principalities and powers in heavenly places might be known by the church the manifold wisdom of God, ¹¹ According to the eternal purpose which he purposed in Christ Jesus our Lord: ¹² In whom we have boldness and access with confidence by the faith of him. ¹³ Wherefore I desire that ye faint not at my tribulations for you, which is your glory. (Ephesians 3:1–13)

Actually that body of doctrine encompasses the entirety of Paul's epistles. It is the doctrine that governs life for us members of the body of Christ in this present dispensation of grace. The mystery stands in contrast to the rest of the Bible outside the Pauline epistles, in that the non-Pauline portions of the Bible present what we call "prophecy." The two bodies of doctrine are clearly different. Prophecy involves "all things which God hath spoken by the mouth of all his holy prophets since the world began" (Acts 3:21). In Colossians 1:25, the apostle states that his ministry was to complete the Word of God and then goes on to tell us what it was that still had to be added to the Word to make it complete. "Even the mystery which hath been hid from ages and from generations, but now is made manifest to his saints: To whom God would make known what is the riches of the glory of this mystery among the Gentiles; which is Christ in you, the hope of glory: Whom we preach, warning every man, and teaching every man in all wisdom; that we may present every man perfect in Christ Jesus: Whereunto I also labour, striving according to his working, which worketh in me mightily" (Colossians 1:26–29).

The apostle instructs us to study to show ourselves approved unto God as workmen who need not to be ashamed by rightly dividing the Word of truth. Rightly dividing the Word of truth is simply a matter of making a distinction between prophecy and the mystery. The following page presents the New Testament divided between prophecy and the mystery. These two terms define two programs in the Bible. One program (prophecy) is Israel's program, which focuses on Jesus Christ as the Messiah who will reign over Israel one day in an earthly kingdom. The other program (the mystery) is the program that involves us who live in the dispensation of grace and focuses on Jesus Christ as the head of the church, which is His body, and looks forward to that church being raptured (caught up) to its eternal home in the heavens. Note that point by point the two programs are different.

The New Testament Scripture—Rightly Divided

The New Testament is very structured. In fact it is symmetrical. Half of the New Testament scriptures is about Israel and God's plan for that nation while the other half is about the Church which is Christ's Body – a Gentile church. The body of doctrine that pertains to Israel is called Prophecy. It is called prophecy because it is what "…God hath spoken by the mouth of all His Holy Prophets since the world began" (Acts 3:21). The other half of the New Testament scriptures (the portion written by Paul the apostle of the Gentiles) is called the Mystery because it is the body of doctrine that our Lord kept secret until He revealed it to us who live in this present Dispensation of Grace. Paul refers to it as "…The mystery which from the beginning of the world hath been hid in God who created all things by Jesus Christ" (Eph. 3:9). When Paul, the apostle of the Gentiles tells us to study to show ourselves approved unto God and be workmen who need not to be ashamed, he is talking about rightly dividing the word of truth between Prophecy and the Mystery.

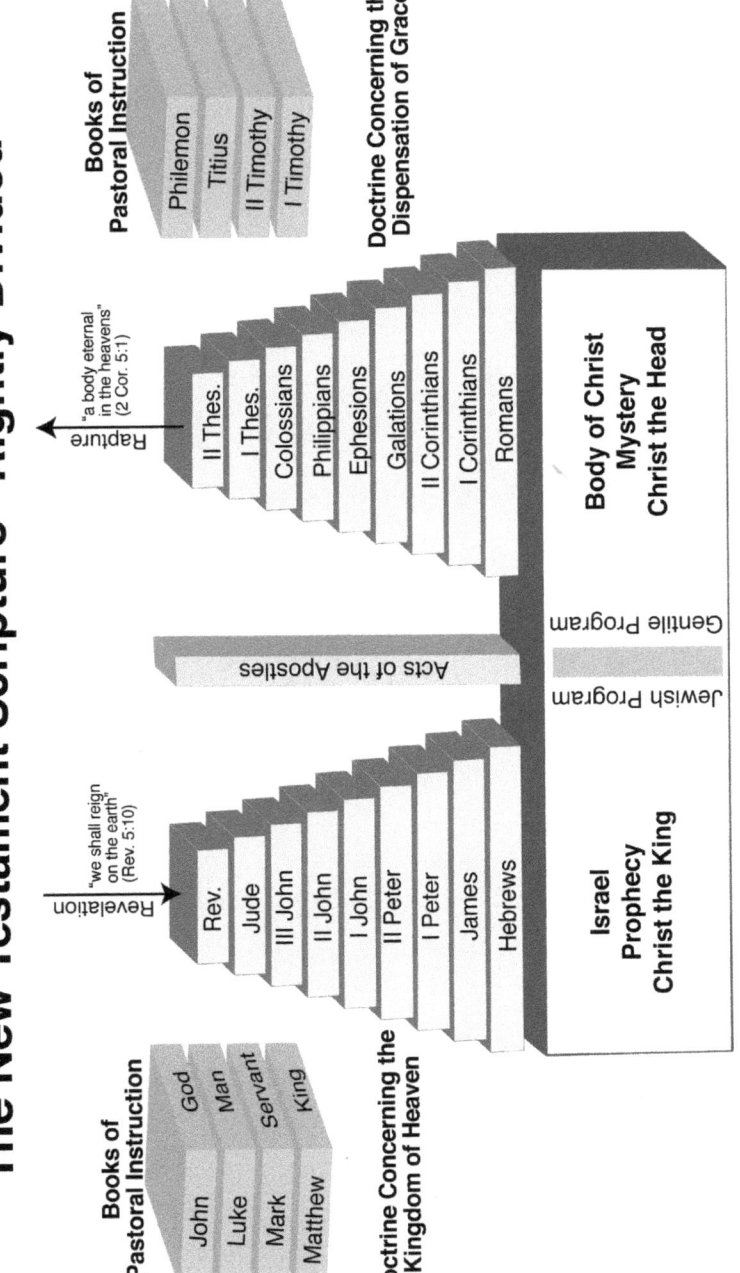

The New Testament Scripture–Rightly Divided

	Prophecy	Mystery
Purpose	That Christ reign on earth (Zech. 9:9-11)	That Christ preeminent in all things (Col. 1:18)
Goal	A Kingdom on Earth Jer. 23:5)	A Body reigning in heaven (2Cor. 5:1; 2Tim. 2:10-12; Eph. 1:23)
Elect Agency	Redeemed Israel (Ex. 19:5 & 6; 1Pet. 2:9)	The Body of Christ (Col. 1:18, 24)
Relationship to Christ	Christ the King (Isa. 9: 6 & 7)	Christ its the Head of the Body (Eph. 1:21-23; 5:23)
Blessings to the Gentiles	Through Israel's rise (Gen. 22:18; 26:3 &4)	Through Israel's fall (Acts 28: 27-28; Rom. 11:11-15)
Relationship of Jew and Gentile	Israel Supreme (Isa. 60:1 – 3)	Jew and Gentile on the same level (Rom. 3:9; 10:12;\ cf. 11:30-32; Eph. 2:16-17)
View of Nations	Mainly concerns nation (Isa. 2:4. Ezek. 37:21 – 22)	Concerned with individuals (Rom. 10:12 – 13; 2Cor. 5:14 – 17)
The nature of Blessings to Men	Blessings both Physical and Spiritual on earth (Isa. 2:3; 11:1-9)	All Spiritual Blessings in Heavenly Places in Christ (Eph. 1:3-13; Col. 3:1-3)
View of the Lord's presence on earth	Concern's Christ's presence on earth (Isa. 59:20; Zech. 14:4)	Explains His present absence from the earth (Eph. 1:18-23)
Means of Salvation	Faith demonstrated by works (James 2:14-22)	Through Faith alone (Rom. 3:21 – 26; 4:4 & 5; Eph. 2: 8 & 9)
Relation to the Law of Moses	The Law remains in effect (Mat. 28:20 cf. 23:2; Acts 21:20)	The Law taken out of the way (Eph. 2:14-16; Col. 2:14)
Structure	Concerns God's Nation in the earth (Dan. 2:44; Mat. 6:10)	Concerns a body – a living organism (1Cor. 12:12 & 13; Eph. 4:12 – 16)
Miraculous signs and wonders	Required as evidence of faith (Mark 16:10)	Done away to be replaced with unfeigned love (1Cor. 13:8)
Apostleship	Twelve apostles, twelve thrones, twelve tribes of Israel Mat. 19:28)	One apostle to the one body (Rom. 11:13; Gal. 2: 8 & 9; Eph. 3:1-13)
Commission	Preach and baptize (Mat. 28:19; Mark 16:16)	Preach without Water baptism (1Cor. 1:17; 2Cor. 5:19 – 21; 1Cor. 12:13 cf. Eph. 4:5)
View of the Lord's Return	His return to the earth to Reign (Acts 1:11 cf. 2:36)	Return to the air to catch the Body of Christ away (1Thess. 4:17)

APPENDIX 2

History to Prophecy: It Is All His Story

The chart on page 265 presents the interesting layout of the Bible events as they unfold for us in the pages of the scriptures. Going down the left-hand side, we see Bible history as it happened in the past. Across the bottom we see the present dispensation of grace as it has been for the past two thousand years of human history. We notice we are at the balancing point in the Bible. Going up the right-hand side of the chart, we see the prophetic future as it is laid out in the Bible. Note the symmetry of the prophetic future after the close of the dispensation of grace, with the historical past leading up to the dispensation of grace. The present dispensation of grace was revealed to the world through Paul, the apostle of the Gentiles. In Colossians he tells us his ministry was to complete the Word of God by adding to it a body of doctrine called the mystery. That body of doctrine defines a relationship that exists between God and believers of this present dispensation of grace. That unique relationship can exist because of four reconciliations God brings about during the course of this dispensation of grace.

Do spend some time studying the chart. It is certainly fascinating to see God's design in His creation and the plan He has for man in His eternal purposes. As we study the Bible, we see how ordered and structured this book is and how purposeful our God is in all His actions. What a wonderful God we have. What a magnificent book He has left us to follow. What joy should fill our hearts as we read and study God's plan for the ages and realize we are part of that plan.

The Pauline Doctrine of Reconciliation

Certainly one of the most blessed and glorious of the Pauline doctrines, connected with the gospel of the grace of God and the revelation of the mystery, is the doctrine of reconciliation. For sure it is interesting to study the Word about God's work of reconciliation as we find it in Paul's epistles. The doctrine of reconciliation is, in fact, central to the revelation the apostle received from the Lord Jesus Christ. The believer will never fully understand what the apostle calls "the preaching of Jesus Christ according to the revelation of the mystery" (Romans 16:25; Ephesians 3:1–3; Colossians 1:26; and so forth) until he or she understands the doctrine of reconciliation. This study explores four passages that address this basic Pauline doctrine involving reconciling antagonistic parties in which God does the reconciling work. All four of these reconciliations have to do with the work of redemption the Lord accomplished on Calvary.

Let's consider what it means to be reconciled. To be reconciled to someone is to have the status you have with that particular person changed in a positive way. It might be a change from alienation to friendship or simply from hostility to peaceful coexistence. If you were angry with someone because of some bad thing that person intentionally did to you, you would have a sense of being alienated from that person. But if that person then came to you and sincerely apologized and you gladly accepted that apology, you and that person would be reconciled. That person's status with you would be changed from alienation to friendship. The term reconcile refers to our relationship with someone and presupposes alienation over something that has to be addressed before a change of status can be effected. It's an important Bible term that deals with God's relationship to us and our relationship to Him.

There are four different reconciliations that can be identified in Paul's epistles. Two of them are in 2 Corinthians 5:18–21, another is referenced in Colossians 1:20–21, and yet another is referenced in Ephesians 2:14–15. Let's consider the four different reconciliations Paul talks about in more detail:

The Reconciling of the World

"To wit that God was in Christ, reconciling the world unto himself, not imputing their trespasses unto them, and hath committed unto us the word of reconciliation." (2 Corinthians 5:19).

In 2 Corinthians 5:18–21, there are two different relationships in view. In both cases, the relationship affected is with God. In verse 19, the relationship is between God and the world. Today, in the dispensation of grace, God has changed the relationship He has with the world from being ready for God's wrath to pour out on the world for its rejection of His Son to offering terms of peace to every man, woman, and child in the world. This is a reconciliation that puts the whole world in a position where anyone the world over can come to salvation by God's grace through faith in the shed blood of Christ apart from works or human merit and apart from Israel and Israel's Law of Moses. In short, this reconciliation made the salvation of lost souls as we find it in Paul's epistles possible. Romans 11:25–36 also talks about this reconciliation.

This work of reconciliation God performed involves the changing of the status of the entire world (saved and lost alike). This raises some important questions relative to exactly what the status of the world was before God before this reconciliation took place and what the status of the world is before God now. One important question is, Is this a once-for-all-time act by God of reconciling the world to Himself, or is this a continuing action by God that is ongoing? Another important question in regard to this reconciliation is, In what sense did God reconcile the entire world to himself? To get the sense of this passage, we need to go to another Pauline passage that also talks about the reconciling of the world to get the background of this status change. That would be Romans 11:15, where Paul talks about the casting aside of Israel being the reconciling of the world. "For if the casting away of them be the reconciling of the world, what shall the receiving of them be, but life from the dead?" (Romans 11:15).

We need an understanding of the Romans 11:15 passage and the context of Romans 11 to get a clear understanding of this passage in 2 Corinthians 5:19. In fact, it's the understanding of the dispensational significance of what Paul is saying in all Romans 9–11 that gives us the background for understanding our passage here or any passage in that portion of the Bible we call the Pauline epistles. The casting away of Israel as Paul presents it in Romans 11 is what enables God to reconcile the World to Himself. Until the Lord sent the apostle Paul to the world with information concerning the dispensation of grace, salvation was of the Jews (John 4:22). When God set Israel aside temporarily and started the dispensation of grace, He reconciled the world to Himself in the sense that He concluded all (both Jews and Gentiles) in unbelief so He could have mercy on all (Romans 11:32). That is to say, He made the whole world savable without having to come through Israel and Israel's law.

What was due and on the schedule when God saved Saul of Tarsus was the tribulation period (the seventieth week of Daniel 9:25–27). Daniel 9 is one of the most fascinating passages of scripture because of the significance of the prophecy regarding a kingdom set up on the earth under the reign of Israel's Messiah and the present dispensation of the grace of God in which we live today.

24 Seventy weeks are determined upon thy people and upon thy holy city, to finish the transgression, and to make an end of sins, and to make reconciliation for iniquity, and to bring in everlasting righteousness, and to seal up the vision and prophecy, and to anoint the most Holy. 25 Know therefore and understand, that from the going forth of the commandment to restore and to build Jerusalem unto the Messiah the Prince shall be seven weeks, and threescore and two weeks: the street shall be built again, and the wall, even in troublous times. 26 And after threescore and two weeks shall Messiah be cut off, but not for himself: and the people of the prince that shall come shall destroy the city and the sanctuary; and the end thereof shall be with a flood, and unto the end of the war desolations are determined. 27 And he shall confirm the covenant with many for one week: and in the midst of the week he shall cause the sacrifice and the oblation to cease, and for the overspreading of abominations he shall make it desolate, even until the consummation, and that determined shall be poured upon the desolate. (Daniel 9:24–29)

1. In this amazing passage of scripture, God defined a measurable period of time until the establishing of a kingdom on this earth that starts with the going forth of a commandment to restore and build (actually rebuild) Jerusalem. It culminates in the arrival of Israel's Messiah in a period of sixty-nine weeks. We understand from passages such as Genesis 29:27 that a week in scripture is (or can be) seven years long. We understand further then that there will be a period of 483 years from the issue of that commandment until Messiah, the prince. Then after an undefined period of time there will be a seventieth week or another seven years. We can also see from the passage in Daniel 9 that there will be a break in the action between the end of the sixty-ninth week and the beginning of the seventieth week, during which Messiah will be cut off. We understand now that this is a reference to His death for the sins of the world. We see too in Daniel 9:26 that there will be a destruction of the city between the end of the sixty-ninth week and the beginning of the seventieth week. Then at the end of the seventieth week, a number of things will occur that bring the promises God made to Israel to fruition. Note what they are:

2. "To finish the transgression" (this is the transgression of the old covenant [Hebrews 9:15])

3. "And to make an end of sins" (that is the bringing of Israel's sins to an end [i.e., the new covenant of Jeremiah 31:31 and Ezekiel 36: 24–28])

4. "And to make reconciliation for iniquity" (this we understand to be the cross and the redemption through the blood of Christ [Isaiah 53:5])

5. "And to bring in everlasting righteousness" (this is the eternal kingdom in which Messiah reigns in righteousness [Isaiah 32:1])

6. "And to seal up the vision" (this is the vision of Daniel 8 concerning the four coming kingdoms and the last days)

7. "And prophecy" (all the Old Testament prophecy focused on a kingdom prepared from the foundation of the world for those who will inherit it [Matthew 25:34])

"And to anoint the most holy" (i.e., to have Israel's Messiah sit on the throne of David on earth in an eternal kingdom [Daniel 2:44])

In Daniel 9:27, we see that the prince who shall come (see v. 26) will make a covenant with many for one week, and then in the midst of that week, he shall break that covenant. That coming prince is the one whom John calls the Antichrist (1 John 2:18; 2:22; 4:3; 2 John 1:7). Gabriel describes the seventieth week spoken of in Daniel 9:27 to Daniel in Daniel 12:1, saying it will be "a time of trouble such as never was since there was a nation even to that same time: and at that time thy people [Israel] shall be delivered, every one that shall be found written in the book." The sixty-ninth week ended with the Lord riding into Jerusalem on a donkey. For those who would like to check out the mathematics of the chronology, I refer you to an excellent study on the subject by Sir Robert Anderson, titled The Coming Prince (Kregel).

What would have followed the sixty-ninth week would have been the seventieth week, though we can see in the narrative from Gabriel that there was a break in the action at the end of the sixty-ninth week foreseen. However, the Lord personally defined the duration of that break as being another year in Luke 13:8, in the parable of the fig tree. In that parable, a certain nobleman (Christ) had a fig tree (a type of religion in scripture) in his vineyard (a type of Israel as a nation) for three years (the duration of the Lord's public ministry to Israel). He came looking for fruit on that fig tree but found none. The fruit He was looking for is repentance in the nation (Luke 13:3–6). The vinedresser (in this case, the Holy Spirit) said He would hoe around it and dung it (a type of the Holy Spirit's ministry to Israel at Pentecost through the believing remnant) for one year. One year later, after the Lord presented Himself to Israel as her king, takes us to the stoning of Stephen.

Stephen is a significant character in the events surrounding the official offer of the kingdom of heaven to Israel. There is a misconception among Christians that God set aside the nation of Israel at the cross. While it is true that Israel's guilt was real in the crucifixion of her Messiah, the Father nonetheless forgave the nation of that deed in response to the Lord's plea from the cross. "Father forgive them for they know not what they do" (Luke 23:34).

God then made the official offer of the kingdom to Israel through Peter at Pentecost (Acts 3:19–26) as the Holy Ghost ministered the Word to Israel through the believing remnant of Israel. Remember that the Lord said to the then leaders of Israel (i.e., the scribes, Pharisees, and ruling class of Israelite) that "the kingdom of God was going to be taken from them and given to a nation bringing forth the fruits of thereof" (Matthew 21:33–43). The nation the Lord had in view was the little flock of believing Israelites (Luke 12:32), who were to receive the kingdom. It was the rejection by Israel as a nation of the testimony of the Holy Spirit as He testified through the "little flock" at Pentecost that God regarded as the unpardonable sin of Matthew 12:31; Mark 3:29; and Luke 12:10. The nation of Israel under the leadership of the scribes and Pharisees blasphemed the Father by rejecting the ministry of John the Baptist (Matthew 21:25). They then blasphemed the Lord (i.e., the Son) by attributing the work He did to devils (Matthew 12:22–32).

Finally, they blasphemed the Holy Ghost by rejecting the testimony the Holy Ghost made when they stoned Stephen. Stephen is the messenger the nation sent to Christ after His death, burial, resurrection, and ascension back to heaven. The message Israel intended to convey to God with the stoning of Stephen was simply, "We [Israel] will not have this man [Christ] reign over us" (Luke 19:14).

The posture our Lord had when Stephen saw Him is also significant. David spoke of the Messiah, saying, "The LORD said unto my Lord, Sit thou at my right hand, until I make thine enemies thy footstool" (Psalm 110:1). We understand this to be the Father's words to the Son. Peter at Pentecost set the time frame for this as at the Lord's ascension back in heaven after His resurrection. "This Jesus hath God raised up, whereof we all are witnesses. Therefore being by the right hand of God exalted, and having received of the Father the promise of the Holy Ghost, he hath shed forth this, which ye now see and hear. For David is not ascended into the heavens: but he saith himself, The LORD said unto my Lord, Sit thou on my right hand, Until I make thy foes thy footstool. Therefore let all the house of Israel know assuredly, that God hath made that same Jesus, whom ye have crucified, both Lord and Christ" (Acts 2:32–36).

We understand from Luke 13:6–9 that the duration of the Lord's sitting at the Father's right hand was for one year. One year takes us to the stoning of Stephen. Stephen, as he was being stoned, saw "the glory of God, and Jesus standing on the right hand of God" (Acts 7:55). The Lord was standing because it was time for His enemies to be made His footstool.

This is what would happen in the seventieth week of Daniel. That is when it will be said, "The kingdoms of this world are become the kingdoms of our Lord, and of his Christ; and he shall reign for ever and ever" (Revelation 13:15). The process of the Lord taking what is rightly His by right of creation wasn't going to be pretty. Isaiah said of that day, "Behold, the day of the LORD cometh, cruel both with wrath and fierce anger, to lay the land desolate: and he shall destroy the sinners thereof out of it. For the stars of heaven and the constellations thereof shall not give their light: the sun shall be darkened in his going forth, and the moon shall not cause her light to shine. And I will punish the world for their evil, and the wicked for their iniquity; and I will cause the arrogancy of the proud to cease, and will lay low the haughtiness of the terrible" (Isaiah 13:9–11). The world was in for the wrath of God to be poured out and for the Lord's coming to take what is rightly His. The world's status before God wasn't good.

The Lord did come right on schedule. However, instead of bringing the day of the Lord, He saved the leader of His enemies. He saved Saul of Tarsus on the road to Damascus and revealed the mystery concerning the dispensation of the grace of God and the calling out of the church, His Body, through him.

Israel had finally after so many years joined the Gentiles in rejecting the Lord and His Christ as stated in Psalm 2. Historically the Gentiles rebelled against God and rejected His reign over them at Babel; God set them aside in Genesis 11. The Gentiles' rejection of God's reign over them was followed by God's calling Abraham and making him and his seed a nation (Israel), through which He would eventually reconcile the world to Himself. Now, with the stoning of Stephen, Israel did as the Gentiles did in Genesis 11. God would now have to return to establish His kingdom by force if His purpose in creation was to be realized. Psalm 2 tells the story of the state of the world at that time and of what would have come on this world as a result of the world's rejection of Christ.

Psalm 2:1–6 (KJV)

"Why do the heathen rage, and the people imagine a vain thing? The kings of the earth set themselves, and the rulers take counsel together, against the LORD, and against his anointed, saying, Let us break their bands asunder, and cast away their cords from us." This passage (vv. 1–3) is a prophecy of what happened with the stoning of Stephen. The heathen had been raging since God gave up on them at Babel. Now, with the stoning of Stephen, the people (of Israel, God's people) now took counsel together with the heathen to reject God and take action to exclude Him from His right to enjoy His creation.

"4 He that sitteth in the heavens shall laugh: the Lord shall have them in derision. Then shall he speak unto them in his wrath, and vex them in his sore displeasure. Yet have I set my king upon my holy hill of Zion." This is prophecy of what should have happened when Israel joined the heathen in rejection of Christ. God was to pour out His wrath on the world for its rejection of Christ and the kingdom. That is not, however, what happened. Instead of bringing in the seventieth week of Daniel and the tribulation period, God chose to instead reveal the dispensation of grace, in which He deals with the whole world on the basis of grace. God has in doing so changed the status of the world before Him. Instead of the world population being vessels of wrath for rejection of His Son, the world is in a position to receive grace, mercy, and peace from God. In doing so, God reconciled the world onto Himself so as to make the whole world savable by grace through faith apart from works. God demonstrated the greatness of this by saving the leader of Israel's rejection and using him as the revealer of grace. Today, therefore, any one (Jew or Gentile) could come to Him by faith and be saved (Romans 11:15). Today and as long as the dispensation of grace continues (and it has for almost two thousand years so far), God has resolved that He would postpone the pouring out of His wrath on this world for its rejection of Christ but that He would save anyone who would come to Him in faith and simply trust in the finished work of redemption Christ accomplished on Calvary.

If the casting away of Israel was the reconciling of the world (Romans 11:15), the receiving of them will mean the end of reconciling the world by means of the dispensation of grace in the sense that the seventieth week of Daniel will then come on the world. Then the Lord will speak to the world in His wrath for the world's rejection of Christ and His grace.

> Paul speaks of the casting away of Israel and then again of the receiving of them being life from the dead. We understand from Paul that the setting aside of Israel and Israel's program is only temporary. Paul addresses this matter in Romans 11 in his discussion of the olive tree (which in Bible typology represents access to God). Note his warning to the Gentiles in this passage as he warns them that the dispensation of the grace of God can and will end, and then the tribulation period will come.

> For if thou wert cut out of the olive tree which is wild by nature, and wert graffed contrary to nature into a good olive tree: how much more shall these, which be the natural branches, be graffed into their own olive tree? For I would not, brethren, that ye should be ignorant of this mystery, lest ye should be wise in your own conceits; that blindness in part is happened to Israel, until the fulness of the Gentiles be come in. And so all Israel shall be saved: as it is written, There shall come out of Sion the Deliverer, and shall turn away ungodliness from Jacob: For this is my covenant unto them, when I shall take away their sins. As concerning the gospel, they are enemies for your sakes: but as touching the election, they are beloved for the fathers' sakes. For the gifts and calling of God are without repentance. For as ye in times past have not believed God, yet have now obtained mercy through their unbelief: Even so have these also now not believed, that through your mercy they also may obtain mercy. For God hath concluded them all in unbelief, that he might have mercy upon all.

> O the depth of the riches both of the wisdom and knowledge of God! how unsearchable are his judgments, and his ways past finding out! For who hath known the mind of the Lord? or who hath been his counsellor?

Or who hath first given to him, and it shall be recompensed unto him again?

For of him, and through him, and to him, are all things: to whom be glory for ever. Amen. (Romans 11:24–36)

The significance of the olive tree needs to be addressed here. The olive tree in scripture represents access to God. The door to the temple was made of olive wood (1 Kings 6:32–33). The two cherubim around the mercy seat were made of olive wood (1 King 6:23). Here in Romans 11 the olive tree again represents access to God. Israel is the natural olive tree. However, some of the branches were broken off—those being the unbelievers of the nation. The Gentiles were then grafted in. The Gentiles (which now include unbelieving Israelites) are now grafted into the olive tree and have access to God. That does not mean all the branches represent believers. It means everyone the world over can now come to God to be saved by grace through faith in the shed blood of Jesus Christ as the full payment of their sin's debt. One day the dispensation of grace will end, and the Gentiles will again be broken off. Then salvation will again be of the Jews.

There is an important note to make at this point regarding trespasses that won't be imputed to the men who comprise "the world" as a result of the reconciliation of 2 Corinthians 5:19. We understand what the transgression is from Romans 11:17–20, as we understand what it was that resulted in Israel being cast away to bring in the reconciling of the world. Israel was set aside because of their unbelief (Romans 11:20). Israel was set aside due to her rejection of God's reign over her. This was her transgression. The Gentiles had committed a similar transgression back in Genesis 11 when they rebelled against God in an effort to keep God from enjoying His creation. These are serious transgressions that will one day bring the tribulation period on the world. However, today during the dispensation of grace, God isn't imputing these trespasses to the men of this world. Today God is holding back His wrath and postponing His judgment of the world for its rejection of His Son and is instead calling out and building a body of believers He will use to bring honor and glory to His name both now and in eternity future by showing forth His wisdom to men and angels. This body of believers is called the church, which is Christ's body. That is the only church God is forming today, and what a wonderful work of grace it is. That is the theme of the second reconciliation we find in Paul's epistles.

The Reconciling of Jew and Gentile in One Body

"For he is our peace, who hath made both one, and hath broken down the middle wall of partition between us; Having abolished in his flesh the enmity, even the law of commandments contained in ordinances; for to make in himself of twain one new man, so making peace; And that he might reconcile both unto God in one body by the cross, having slain the enmity thereby" (Ephesians 2:14–16). This reconciliation made the forming of the church, Christ's body, possible. God has only one elect agency, through which He works in the world at one time. Prior to the saving of Saul of Tarsus, the Lord worked though Israel as His elect agency through which He would accomplish salvation of souls. Salvation then was of the Jews (John 4:22). Today, however, He has concluded Israel in unbelief so He can have mercy on all (Romans 11:32).

- The term church needs to be defined and understood here. It literally means "the called out ones" or "the called out assembly." The term implies that the group referred to has been called out from a larger group for a defined purpose. The term therefore needs a qualifier to clarify which or what called-out assembly is being referred to. To identify the particular church then, one must understand what the assembly is called out from and what the assembly is called out to. Three different churches can be identified in the New Testament scriptures.

- The church in the wilderness as Stephen referred to it in Acts 7:38 was a nation God called out from Egypt to be in the land promised to Abraham.

- There is the church the Lord referred to in Matthew 16:18, which is going to be built on the confession Peter had just made that Jesus is the Christ, the Son of the living God. That church was called out from among the unbelieving nation of Israel and called to be the "little flock" of believers to whom God was going to give the kingdom (Luke 12:32).

There is the church, Christ's body, which Paul refers to as the one new man of Ephesians 2:15. (See also Ephesians 5:23; Colossians 1:18, 24.) This is a body of believers called out from the lost masses of humanity during the dispensation of grace and called to live and reign for the honor and glory of Jesus Christ in the heavenly places in eternity future.

There is only one church God is forming today, a body of believers composed of Jews and Gentiles both saved by grace through faith in Christ's work of redemption on Calvary. This church (which is Christ's body) together with Jesus Christ, the head forming the one new man, is what the apostle refers to as the preaching of Jesus Christ according to the revelation of the mystery. The term "the mystery," as we find it in Paul's epistles, refers to a body of doctrine that tells us how the one new man is formed, how he is designed by God to live and function in the world today, and what God has for him to do in the ages to come. In the above passage (Ephesians 2:15), this union of believer with Jesus Christ today in the dispensation of grace is referred to as "one new man." This one new man is what 2 Corinthians 5:17 refers to as a new creature. This new creature is Jesus Christ according to the revelation of the mystery. The Lord Jesus Christ, together with the church, which is His body composed of Jews and Gentiles in one body, saved by grace through faith apart from works and apart from the law, is a new creature. He is "New" in the sense that he didn't exist until Christ started forming him by saving Saul of Tarsus on the road to Damascus in Acts 9. Every believer since the saving of Saul of Tarsus, who responded in faith to believe the gospel of the grace of God, is a member of this one new man. This one new man is God's elect agency for doing the work of evangelism in the world today and will in eternity come to be the means by which God in Christ will one day reconcile the heavenly places to Himself (as will be discussed below).

This one new man is formed by the Holy Ghost as He baptizes believers into Jesus Christ and into His death, burial, and resurrection. Paul explains this in 1 Corinthians 12:12–13. "For as the body is one, and hath many members, and all the members of that one body, being many, are one body: so also is Christ. For by one Spirit are we all baptized into one body, whether we be Jews or Gentiles, whether we be bond or free; and have been all made to drink into one Spirit."

Note the words "so also is Christ" in reference to this body of believers referred to as the body of Christ. The body is so totally identified with Christ as to be called Christ. This total identification of each believer (each member of Christ) with Christ enables Christ to take our sin and guilt on Himself (Romans 6:1–4). Not only that, but he takes our old sin nature upon Himself so as to crucify the old man (Romans 6:6).

The apostle states that there is a seven-fold unity for this body of believers, according to Ephesians 4:4–6. "There is one body [only one body of believers during the dispensation of grace], and one Spirit [that being the

Holy Spirit, who forms the one body], even as ye are called in one hope of your calling [the hope of believers today is the rapture in which we will be given celestial bodies in which to live and reign for the honor and glory of Christ in heaven], One Lord [the Lord Jesus Christ], one faith [the Pauline epistles as the one body of doctrine for the one body], one baptism [the baptizing work of the Holy Spirit to form the one body], One God and Father of all, who is above all, and through all, and in you all [One Father under whose authority all of this happens]." Paul also states in Ephesians 1:10 that God will use this one new man "to gather together in one all things in Christ, both which are in heaven and which are on earth even in him" in the dispensation of the fullness of times.

The Personal Reconciling of Sinners to God

"And all things are of God, who hath reconciled us to himself by Jesus Christ, and hath given to us the ministry of reconciliation" (2 Corinthians 5:18). This reconciliation is what changed our status (individually) as believers from being under God's wrath for sin to being in God's family as children. This reconciliation is what makes personal soul salvation possible today in the dispensation of grace. This personal reconciliation takes place in the life of a believer only when (and not until) the believer makes a heart decision to trust Jesus Christ as Savior. It becomes operative by the Holy Ghost baptizing the individual into an eternal spiritual union with Jesus Christ so as to make the believer spiritually one with Jesus Christ. The Holy Spirit does this operation of God in response to the believer's heart decision to trust Jesus Christ as Savior.

- "And you, that were sometime alienated and enemies in your mind by wicked works, yet now hath he reconciled In the body of his flesh through death, to present you holy and unblameable and unreproveable in his sight" (Colossians 1:21–22). God does this reconciling work as the Holy Spirit baptizes the believer into the death, burial, and resurrection of Jesus Christ (Roman 6:1–4). The baptism of Romans 6 has nothing to do with water. It is a spiritual baptism, but it is a very real work wherein the believer is totally identified with the Lord Jesus Christ; and in fact the Lord becomes the owner of the believer—body, soul, and spirit (1 Corinthians 6:20). When the Lord received the believer to Himself (Romans 15:7), He received to Himself our sin and guilt as well so He could legitimately pay the debt for our sins. Jesus Christ died for the sins of everyone, but the transfer of sin and guilt isn't made until the believer comes to Him in faith and decides to trust in the death, burial, and resurrection of Christ for his or her sins. Not only did Christ take our sins on Himself, but He went further in taking the old sin nature that produced the sin on Himself so as to crucify the old man so He could set the believer free from sin's power. (He was truly "made to be sin for us … that we might be made the righteousness of God in Him" [2 Corinthians 5:21].) This reconciling work is all God's work and none of ours. We are but the receivers of the action. This personal reconciliation involves at least eight things God does the instant one first trusts Jesus Christ as Savior. They include the following:

- Being baptized into a living and eternal, spiritual union with Jesus Christ (Romans 6:1–4; 1 Corinthians 12:12–13; Galatians 3:27; and so forth)

- Being forgiven of all our sins (Colossians 2:13) through the redemption that is ours in Christ because of the cross (Ephesians 1:7).

- Being circumcised with a spiritual circumcision (Colossians 2:10) that makes us complete in Christ and frees us from having to perform anything in the flesh to make ourselves acceptable to God (Philippians

3:3)

- Being regenerated so as to have genuine vital spiritual life within our previously dead human spirits (Titus 3:5; Ephesians 2:2)

- Indwelt by the Holy Spirit of God (1 Corinthians 6:19; Romans 8:9) so as to have the Holy Spirit give personal testimony to our human spirits that we are the children of God through Christ (Romans 8:14–15) and to enable us to live the life of Christ in our mortal bodies (Romans 8:11).

- Being sealed with the Holy Spirit to be absolutely secure in Christ (Ephesians 1:13–13; 4:30; 2 Corinthians 1:22; 2 Timothy 2:19)

- Being set apart from the rest of unsaved masses to be God's possession (1 Corinthians 6:11; 2 Thessalonians 2:13)

- Being justified (1 Corinthians 6:11; Romans 3:24–26) by faith (Romans 3:28; 5:1) without the Law of Moses (Romans 4:5) so as to be reckoned as having the righteousness of Jesus Christ imputed to our spiritual bank account (2 Corinthians 5:21).

Being spiritually washed of the stain of our sin so as to be clean in God's sight (1 Corinthians 6:11)

The Reconciling of All Things to God

For by him were all things created, that are in heaven, and that are in earth, visible and invisible, whether they be thrones, or dominions, or principalities, or powers: all things were created by him, and for him: And he is before all things, and by him all things consist. And he is the head of the body, the church: who is the beginning, the firstborn from the dead; that in all things he might have the preeminence. For it pleased the Father that in him should all fulness dwell; And, having made peace through the blood of his cross, by him to reconcile all things unto himself; by him, I say, whether they be things in earth, or things in heaven. (Colossians 1:16–20)

- This passage starts out with a presentation of Jesus Christ as the Creator of all things in heaven and earth. Other similar passages include the following:

- John 1:1–3 says, "In the beginning was the Word, and the Word was with God, and the Word was God. The same was in the beginning with God. All things were made by him; and without him was not any thing made that was made."

- Hebrews 1:1–3 says, "God, who at sundry times and in divers manners spake in time past unto the fathers by the prophets, Hath in these last days spoken unto us by his Son, whom he hath appointed heir of all things, by whom also he made the worlds; Who being the brightness of his glory, and the express image of his person, and upholding all things by the word of his power, when he had by himself purged our sins, sat down on the right hand of the Majesty on high;."

Revelation 4:11 says, "Thou art worthy, O Lord, to receive glory and honour and power: for thou hast created all things, and for thy pleasure they are and were created."

All things in heaven and earth. whether they be the visible things in the earth or the invisible things in heaven, belong to the Lord Jesus Christ by right of the fact that He created all things. We note, however, that the focus in the passage in Colossians 1 isn't on the created elements themselves but on the thrones and dominions, principalities, and powers (i.e., on the governing structure of all things in earth and in heaven). The passage addresses the issue of who is in charge of all things Christ created for Christ.

Though all things are created by and for Christ, not all things are under His direct control today. There has been a usurper who has taken control of what is rightfully Christ's by right of creation. We understand this from passages that speak of the forty days of fasting by which the Lord started His public ministry. In Matthew 4, the Lord, after He had fasted for forty days and nights, was tempted of the devil. In the third of the threefold temptation, "the devil took Him to an exceeding high mountain, and sheweth him all the kingdoms of the world, and the glory of them; And saith unto him, All these things will I give thee, if thou wilt fall down and worship me" (Matthew 4:8–9). It is interesting to note that the Lord did not refute the devil or deny that the kingdoms of this world had indeed fallen into the hands of Satan. It is truly as the apostle Paul says in 2 Corinthians 4:3–4. "But if our gospel be hid, it is hid to them that are lost: In whom the god of this world hath blinded the minds of them which believe not, lest the light of the glorious gospel of Christ, who is the image of God, should shine unto them."

It's also interesting to note that Satan was willing to offer the kingdoms of this world to Christ. We might ask why. The answer is that he still had the rulership of the kingdoms of heaven in his hip pocket. The apostle writes in Ephesians 2:1–2, "And you hath he quickened, who were dead in trespasses and sins; Wherein in time past ye walked according to the course of this world, according to the prince of the power of the air, the spirit that now worketh in the children of disobedience."

> We need to understand that for all the Old Testament prophets said in scripture, there was no indication that the heavens were at risk of being reconciled back to God. The prophets wrote of a kingdom in which Israel's Messiah would have the government on His shoulder, and of the increase of His government and peace there would be no end (Isaiah 9:6–7).
>
> The earth shall be full of the knowledge of the LORD, as the waters cover the sea. (Isaiah 11:9)

Behold, the days come, saith the LORD, that I will raise unto David a righteous Branch, and a King shall reign and prosper, and shall execute judgment and justice in the earth. (Jeremiah 23:5)

This reconciling involves God removing the rebellious occupants from the positions of responsibility in both heaven and earth and replacing them with genuine believers, whom He had personally reconciled to Himself by means of the cross. This reconciling will enable Jesus Christ to be preeminent in all things.

- With an understanding of the reconciling of all things back to God, let's look at the prophetic future with this in mind. The benchmark events in the prophetic future as we see them laid out in the Word of God are the following;

- The rapture of the church, which is Christ's body (1 Corinthians 15:51; 2 Thessalonians 4:15–18). This event will take the one new man to heaven, where we will spend eternity in resurrection bodies (2 Corinthians 5:2) designed to live there (Philippians 3:21; 1 Corinthians 15:40).

- Judgment seat of Christ (2 Corinthians 5:9–10; 1 Corinthians 3:12–17), in which the fitness of each believer for positions of responsibility in heaven will be determined (2 Timothy 2:10–12).

- War in heaven, in which Satan and his angels were expelled from heaven so the one new man could assume his place in God's plan for the ages (Revelation 12:8–9; Isaiah 34:5)

- Armageddon (Revelation 16:16), in which the armies of this world unite in a futile attempt to keep the Lord Jesus Christ from taking possession of what is His by right of creation.

- Kingdoms of this world are become the kingdoms of our Lord and of His Christ (Revelation 11:15).

All things will be made new so as to remove the stain and damage sin has wreaked on God's creation (Revelation 21:5). This will be the culmination of God's work of reconciling all things back to God. There will be a new heaven, new earth, and New Jerusalem. This will be the beginning of God's eternal kingdom, in which righteousness reigns from shore to shore.

Conclusion

- There are four reconciliations presented in Paul's epistles. Understanding them will enable the believer to see God's purpose for the mystery hid in God from before the foundation of the world but was revealed through Paul for our understanding. Understanding these four reconciliations also enables us to learn where we fit into God's program for the ages and how it is through the church, the body of Christ, that Christ will be preeminent in all things. To summarize then, let's consider the following:

- The reconciliation of the world in 2 Corinthians 5:19 postponed the seventieth week of Daniel 9 to make the present dispensation of grace possible.

- The reconciling of Jew and Gentile in one body (Ephesians 2:11–18) made the formation of the church, Christ's body (the one new man of Ephesians 2:15), possible.

- The reconciling of sinners to God as we see the message in Paul's epistles (Colossians 1:21–22; 2 Corinthians 5:21) made the salvation of souls apart from Israel, apart from the law, and apart from any human merit possible.

The reconciling of all things to God (Colossians 1:16–20) enables Christ to have the preeminence in all things—not only the things in the earth as the Old Testament prophets stated would happen through Israel but also all things in heaven as we learn from Paul's epistles through the church, Christ's body.

From History to Prophecy it is all His Story

For by him were all things created (Col. 1:16)

He is before all things, and by Him all things consist

All things reconciled unto Him (Col. 1:20; I Cor. 15:27)

All things gathered together in Christ (Eph. 1:10)

History – God's record of the past | | Declaring the end from ancient times (Isaiah 46:20) / I have declared the former things from the beginning (Isaiah 48:3) / In the latter days ye shall consider it perfectly (Jer. 23:20) | | Prophecy – God's story of the future

History – God's record of the past	Declaring the end from ancient times (Isaiah 46:20) / I have declared the former things from the beginning (Isaiah 48:3) / In the latter days ye shall consider it perfectly (Jer. 23:20)	Prophecy – God's story of the future
The Creation of Heaven and Earth (Gen 1:1)		The New Heaven and New Earth (Rev 21:1)
The first rebellion – Satan and angels Isa. 14:28; Ezek. 28: The first judgment – chaos (Gen 1:2)		The final rebellion – Satan and men The final judgment – fire (Rev 21:8)
The Earth made ready for man (Gen 1:3-31)		The Earth a perfect habitat for man (Rev 22:1-7)
The first man and his bride (Gen 2:18-25)		The last Man and His Bride (Rev 21:9-21)
The subjection to Satan (Gen 3:1-19)		The subjecting of Satan (Rev 20:10)
The earliest gospel (Gen 3:15) Universal rebellion (Gen 6:1-7) Judgment by water (Noah –Gen 6:8-22) The earth purged by water (Gen 7:17-24) Governments setup (Gen 9:5-7)		Gospel of the Kingdom (Mat. 24:14) Universal rebellion Judgment by fire (2Pet. 3:10) The floor purged (Mat. 3:12) Kingdom setup Perfect Government
Institution of Babylon (Gen. 10:10) Idolatry invented (Gen 11:1-4) Nations scattered (Gen 11:5-9)		Destruction of Babylon (Rev. 18:2) Idolatry ended (Isa. 2:18-21) Nations gathered (Rev 16:4; 20:8)
Call of Israel (Gen 12:1 thru Duet.) Blessing on Israel (1Sam. and 2Sam.) Declension in Israel (I & II Kings) Judgment on Israel (Isaiah, Jer. Ezek.)		Restoration of Israel (Rev 5:10) Judgment of tribulation (Mat. 24:21) Repentance of the nation (Rev, 7:4) Blessing of the nation (Rev. 21)
The times of the Gentiles begins (Dan, Ezra, Neh.)		The times of the Gentiles ends (Lk. 21:24; Rev. 11:5)
The first advent of Christ to the manger		The second advent of Christ to the throne
Ministry of Christ The Truth His rejection and death His resurrection and ascension		Ministry of Anti-Christ The Lie His reception and reign His destruction and doom
The Spirit poured out (Acts 2:17) Second coming in view The fall of Israel (Rom. 11:11)		The Spirit again poured out (Rev 19:10; 22:17) Second coming in view Rise of Israel (Isa. 60:3)
The Mystery revealed (Eph. 3:1-3) The Body called out (Eph. 2:11-18) Gentiles brought in (Rom. 11:16-25)		The Mystery ended with the rapture (2Thes 2:7) The Body caught up (1Thess. 4:15-17) Gentiles cut off (Rom. 11:26)

APPENDIX 3

An Overview of Romans 1 Compared to Romans 16:25

Paul was "separated unto the gospel of God, which He had promised afore by his prophets in the holy scripture." This is the first verse of Romans. This message is set in sharp contrast to the closing verses of Romans. Note Romans 16:25–26. "Now to him that is of power to stablish you according to my gospel, And the preaching of Jesus Christ, according to the mystery, which was kept secret since the world began. But now is made manifest, and by the scriptures of the prophets, according to the commandment of the everlasting God, made known to all nations for the obedience of faith."

Paul starts the epistle with reference to the gospel of God, which He had promised before, in the holy scriptures, and then closes the book with a reference to mystery, which was kept secret since the world began. Paul talks about this mystery in Ephesians 3:2–6. "If ye [Gentiles] have heard of the dispensation of the grace of God which is given me to youward; How that by revelation he made known unto me the mystery: which in other ages was not made known unto the sons of men, as it is now revealed unto his holy apostles and prophets by the spirit."

- The subject of this mystery is the one body (Ephesians 3:6).

- The ministry of this mystery is given to Paul (Ephesians 3:7–8).

- The operations of this mystery is fellowship (Ephesians 3:9).

- The divine purpose for it is to show the wisdom of God (Ephesians 3:10).

Back now to Romans 1:1, we look at what appears to be a contradiction when compared to 16:25. Realizing that there are no contradictions in the Bible, we look for the solution to this dilemma whereby Paul says he is "separated unto the gospel of God which he [God] had promised afore by his prophets" in Romans 1:1 and talks about the mystery, which was kept secret and "in other ages not made known." The solution is to recognize Paul is talking about two different things in Romans 16:25, when he speaks of "my gospel" and "the preaching of Jesus Christ according to the revelation of the mystery." What Paul calls "my gospel" in 16:25 is what he calls "the gospel of God" in Romans 1:1. This is the gospel God spoke of in Genesis 3:15 regarding the "seed of the woman," which would one day crush Satan's head. The means by which the seed of the woman would do that wasn't revealed until after it was accomplished. It was the work of the Lord Jesus Christ on the cross, which totally defeated Satan. This fact was first made known through Paul as "the mystery of the Gospel" (Ephesians 6:19). Paul therefore calls it "the gospel of Christ" (Romans 1:1) and "my gospel" (Romans 2:16).

What our Savior accomplished on the cross had to be kept a secret, or it wouldn't have been accomplished (1 Corinthians 2:6–10). What was accomplished on the cross is actually presented for the first time in the Bible in Romans 3:21–28. The gospel is stated in plain and simple terms in 1 Corinthians 15:3–4. "How that Christ died for our sins according to the scripture: and that he was buried, and that he rose again the third day according to the scriptures." What Paul calls "the mystery" involves God calling out from the Gentiles a body of believers called "the church which is his body" (Colossians 1:24). Since God has temporarily set Israel aside during the course of the present dispensation of the grace of God, God regards the nation of today as just another Gentile nation (Romans 11:32). No Old Testament prophet spoke anything about this mystery because it was "hid in God" (Ephesians 3:9) from the beginning of the world until it was revealed through Paul.

The gospel "promised" by the prophets wasn't made known to the prophets (compare Isaiah 64:4 to 1 Corinthians 2:6–10). "For since the beginning of the world men have not heard, nor perceived by the ear, neither hath the eye seen, O God, beside thee, what he hath prepared for him that waiteth for him" (Isaiah 64:4). What eye had not seen, nor ear heard, nor entered onto the heart of men in Isaiah 64:4 is now made known to us in Paul's epistles (1 Corinthians 2:6–10). If you asked Paul what the gospel is, he would give you 1 Corinthians 15:3–4. But the Twelve during our Lord's earthly ministry and at Pentecost couldn't tell anyone that because they didn't know it yet. Note carefully that the Twelve preached what was called "gospel" (Luke 9:6). But the truth about the cross was hid from them (Luke 9:45; 18:34). Note also that their message at Pentecost didn't include the cross (Acts 2:38). It's not until you come to Romans 3:25–26 in the Bible that you find out how God could remit sins of believers of the past dispensations and how God can "be just and the justifier of him which believeth in Jesus."

Note that in Romans 1:3–4 the Jesus Christ, our Lord, was made of the seed of David according to the flesh. This refers to His earthly ministry to Israel under the gospel of the kingdom, which the Twelve preached. This gospel included the following:

1. A king (Jeremiah 23:5). "Behold the days come saith the Lord that I will raise up unto David a righteous Branch, and a king shall reign and prosper and execute judgment and justice on the earth."

2. A kingdom

   - Daniel 2:44 says, "The God of heaven will set up a kingdom."

   - Our Lord ministered this gospel to Israel. Matthew 4:23 says, "And Jesus went about all Galilee teaching in their synagogues, and preaching the gospel of the kingdom."

   - This will be the tribulation message. Matthew 24:14 says, "And this gospel of the kingdom shall be preached in all the world for a witness unto all nations."

   - This promise of a kingdom will ultimately be fulfilled when Jesus Christ returns after the tribulation period. Revelation 11:15 says, "The seventh angel sounded … The kingdoms of this world are become the kingdoms of our Lord and of his Christ."

3. The kingdom, however, has been temporarily postponed until the dispensation of the grace of God runs its course and the church, the body of Christ, is raptured to heaven. One day God's promises to Israel will be fulfilled (Romans 11:25–26).

Note in Romans 1:4 that Jesus Christ is "declared to be the Son of God with power … by the resurrection from the dead." Though our Lord did many miracles and demonstrated His power during His ministry here on earth, His power was fully demonstrated by the resurrection from the dead. Ephesians 1:19–23 says,

And what is the exceeding greatness of his power to usward who believe, according to the working of his mighty power, which he wrought in Christ when he raised him from the dead and set him at his own right hand in the heavenly places, far above all principality and power, and might, and dominion, and every name that is named, not only in this world, but also in that which is to come: and put all things under his feet and gave him to be the head over all things to the church which is his body, the fullness of him that filleth all in all. (Ephesians 1:19–23)

Hebrews 5:5–6 refers to our Lord's resurrection as the day He was begotten as the Son (cf. Psalm 2:7; Acts 13:33; Hebrews 1:5). Though He was begotten of God when He was conceived in Mary's womb, (Luke 1:35), He is declared to be the Son of God with power by His resurrection. As a result, He will be preeminent from eternity past to eternity future (2 Timothy 1:9; Ephesians 1:10) and from things under the earth to things far above all heavens (Philippians 2:20). As a result of His resurrection, He could say "all power is given unto me in heaven and in earth."

Who are the "we" of Romans 1: 5 and the "ye" of Romans 1:6? Verse 5 speaks of Paul and his companions Timothy, Luke, Jason, Sosipater (Romans 16:21), and Tertius, the gramateus—the one who took the dictation of the book of Romans from Paul (16:22). The apostleship spoken of is that of Paul and Timothy (Paul's workfellow). This is the apostleship of the uncircumcision. If you read Galatians 2:7–8, you will find that there is a gospel of the circumcision and a gospel of the uncircumcision; the former was committed to Peter and the latter to Paul. There are also two apostleships: one to the circumcision committed to Peter and the Twelve, and the apostleship of the uncircumcision to Paul. The "ye" of verse 6 speaks of the saints at Rome who received salvation and were called to be saints because of their "obedience of faith.""

The phrase "for the obedience of faith among all nations" (emphasis added) is significant here because our Lord's earthly ministry was only "to the lost sheep of house of Israel" (Matthew 10:6; 14:24; Romans 15:8). However, with Israel temporarily set aside and the mystery concerning the body of Christ and the dispensation of grace revealed, the gospel of the grace of God is to be preached to all nations for the obedience of faith.

SUPER-ABOUNDING GRACE

The Book of Romans is the foundational book for the Christian life. The title of the book "Super-Abounding Grace is taken from Romans 5:19-21 "For as by one man's disobedience many were made sinners, so by the obedience of one shall many be made righteous. Moreover the law entered, that the offence might abound. But where sin abounded, grace did much more abound: That as sin hath reigned unto death, even so might grace reign through righteousness unto eternal life by Jesus Christ our Lord." Where sin abounded, grace literally, according to this verse, did super-abound.

The greatest problem that has plagued humanity through all of history has been sin. Sin (the act) is the fruit of the sin nature which entered the human race by the disobedient act of Adam the seminal head of our race. As a result, everyone who entered humanity having been begotten by a human father was born with the same sin nature. We sin because we are the offspring of a fallen begetter. The message of Romans is that there is only one thing that can defeat sin in humanity. This is the case either with sin personally in our individual lives or with sin that is corporate in nature as it affects society at large. It is the grace of God that can deliver victory over sin. The ability of the grace of God to defeat sin is laid out in its full power and glory in the Book of Romans.

Paul tells the Romans: "But God be thanked, that ye were the servants of sin, but ye have obeyed from the heart that form of doctrine which was delivered you." (Romans 6: 17) What delivers people from slavery to sin is a form of doctrine. That special form of doctrine that delivers from sin is revealed to us by our Savior though Paul the apostle of grace in the book of Romans. This study is a tour through the Book of Romans to gain an understanding of the life changing effect of the gospel of grace.

About the Author

Michael J. Tiry came to know the Lord Jesus Christ as his personal Savior at the age of twenty nine while in the midst of a successful career as an engineer. His deep appreciation for having the assurance of eternal life, his passion for study, and his quest for truth compelled him to search deeply into the Bible with a desire to learn its truth that he might present the riches of God's grace to others. Over the last forty five plus years Michael has been involved in itinerat preaching, a church planting ministry, and a teaching and preaching ministry at Berean Bible Church in Chippewa Falls, Wisconsin. Michael also serves Berean Bible Church as director of the Timothy Institute, designed to prepare men for leadership in local churches. Additionally, Mike has been active over a span of twenty three years in a prison ministry. Michael and his wife of forty five years (Linda) have raised five daughters.

Other Books by the same author

Michael has written over sixteen books which are used as study guides in the Timothy Institute. This book is one of the two that has been published. Another is "You and Your Creator." Both are available through Barnes and Noble and other book distributors. .